Church Disputes Mediation

To Deborah, Emma-Jane and Henry

Church Disputes Mediation

by

James Behrens

MA (Cantab), LLM (Canon Law), PhD
Barrister of Lincoln's Inn and the Middle Temple
Mediator and Chartered Arbitrator
Chancellor of the Diocese of Leicester

GRACEWING

First published in 2003

Gracewing
2 Southern Avenue,
Leominster
Herefordshire HR6 0QF

ISBN 0 85244 578 4

Typesetting by James Behrens

Printed in England by
Antony Rowe Ltd
Eastbourne BN23 6QT

Contents – Summary

APPENDICES

Contents

CONTENTS

APPENDICES

CONTENTS

Illustrations

PREFACE

How churches resolve their disputes is important, both to the parties involved and to the Christian gospel. The world ridicules the Church when disputes get out of hand, and lawyers get involved. My experience of mediation convinces me that it provides a better way of resolving most church disputes than using some formal legal process.

But how can one convince the Church that this is the case? What evidence is there that mediation actually works for church disputes? What sort of cases are suitable for mediation? What sort of cases are not? These, and other, questions led to my researching the subject for my PhD thesis at Cardiff University. The result, I believe, is a resounding endorsement for the use of mediation for church disputes.

What is needed now is for those who are involved in church disputes to have the confidence to use mediation whenever it is appropriate. My hope, indeed my prayer, is that the Church will see the vision of how mediation can transform dispute resolution, and that this, in turn, will be a witness to the world of the transforming power of Christ.

I have been extremely fortunate to have had as my supervisor at Cardiff the Revd Professor Thomas Watkin, who suggested to me many of the areas of research. I am grateful too for the training and encouragement I received from CEDR, the London Mennonites, and Camden Mediation Service. The law is stated as at 1 January 2003, though a few later developments have been incorporated where possible.

JB

August 2003

FOREWORD

The Archbishop of York
The Most Reverend and Right Honourable
Dr David Hope

Each of us is uniquely created by God. At its best this means that we each have fresh perspectives which can be shared thus deepening our understanding both of each other and of God's creation. Yet so often, difference in perception leads not to mutual enrichment but rather to disagreement and even worse, conflict. This general human experience is also part of the fabric of church life. It can find expressions in a variety of ways – clashing between members of a congregation who do not easily mesh with each other, arguments over the right hymn book to choose, even whether the Sunday sermon was a help or a hindrance. In many such cases people talk the issues out in a way which benefits all concerned, as relationships are deepened and understanding enriched. Sadly, though, there are occasions when disagreements do not seem to go away; rather they threaten the well-being of the church community. In the face of the beginnings of such escalation many church leaders can feel powerless, which can lead them either to ignore the warning signs or simply impose authoritarian decisions as a means of seeming to solve the problem. Both approaches may make the minister feel better in the short term and stave off imminent conflict, but in the longer term the lack of resolution means that problems return with even greater intensity.

In this book by James Behrens we are given a framework within which to understand conflict in the form of the 'conflict triangle of problem, people and process' which can give a more rounded perspective on difficult situations; he also provides us with the means of addressing such conflict which seeks to build bridges, rather than create adversaries. He sets such models of mediation in a thoroughly biblical and theological context, drawing on Old Testament figures such as Moses, the teachings and life of Jesus, and going on to explore understandings of mediation in the Patristic period and in formulations of Canon Law. Within this framework he explores the application of the mediation process to church disputes using a variety of examples. By painting the big picture he provides us with the opportunity to reflect on the differing situations we meet in the context where we are and serve.

James Behrens himself recognizes that theory is no substitute for practice, and part of the call of his book is to encourage mediation training within the Christian denominations. I very much hope that in reflecting on his findings many people, both ordained and lay, will feel challenged to develop their mediation skills as a response to God's initiative of love as revealed in Jesus Christ – Jesus Christ who illustrates so profoundly that even in the darkest and most broken of situations there can still be the hope of renewal and of new beginnings.

✠David Ebor:

FOREWORD

The Lord Chief Justice of England and Wales
The Right Honourable the Lord Woolf

Mediation is a well-established process for resolving disagreements in which an impartial third party (the mediator) helps those in dispute to find a solution to the dispute that is mutually acceptable. The key advantage of mediation, which has long been recognised, is that time and expense are saved and the tension that will often be created by an adversarial trial is avoided.

This valuable book examines whether mediation is both a suitable and an effective means for the resolution of church disputes. James Behrens, in the course of *Church Disputes Mediation*, considers a broad range of issues which include the theological and scriptural understanding of conflict resolution, the use of mediation by the Church from New Testament times to date, the current use of mediation in the Roman Catholic Church and the financial cost of resolving disputes by mediation as compared with a court process.

He has also compiled extensive empirical evidence of current mediation practice from both the Church of England and Anglican dioceses in Australia, Canada, Hong Kong, New Zealand, South Africa and the USA.

Mr Behrens's admirable conclusions endorse the use of mediation in the context of church mediation and note its compatibility with the tradition of the Church for almost the whole of its history.

This book is a unique contribution to the jurisprudence on church mediation. The author is to be warmly commended. This book will provide a valuable resource for practitioners and academics and everyone in the wider constituency that is interested in the role that mediation can play in resolving disputes.

Harry Woolf
The Right Honourable the Lord Woolf of Barnes

Chapter 1

INTRODUCTION

But nathelees, this meditacioun
I putte it ay under correccioun
Of clerkes, for I am nat textueel;
I take but the sentence, trusteth weel.
Therfore I make protestacioun
That I wol stonde to correccioun.[1]

---

[1] Geoffrey Chaucer, *The Canterbury Tales*, 'The Parson's Prologue'
lines 55–60 (London, Penguin Books, 1996). In David Wright's translation:
> But all the same I place this homily
> Under correction of the learned; I am
> Unversed in texts, and so I'll give you nothing,
> Trust me, beyond the bare essential meaning.
> Therefore I make this solemn protestation,
> That what I say is subject to correction.

Geoffrey Chaucer, *The Canterbury Tales*, translated by David Wright
(Oxford University Press, 1985).

1. PURPOSE OF THIS BOOK

This book examines whether mediation is both a suitable and an effective means for the resolution of church disputes. Both suitability and effectiveness are important. Suitability, because the Church[2] is more than just an institution: it is a living body, seeking to follow its living Lord. The Church's actions need therefore to be consistent with Christian theology, and with the Church's ecclesiology.[3] The need for effectiveness is ob-

---

[2] The author will adopt the following practice regarding capitalisation of the word 'church'. Lower case 'c' is used whenever possible, but upper case 'C' is used for names – St Peter's Church, Ropley – and where it is necessary to show that the Church is being referred to as an institution – e.g. the view of the Church, the Anglican Church in Australia, and the Roman Catholic Church. Thus, the expressions 'church dispute' and 'a church matter' are written in lower case. It has not been possible to be wholly consistent.

[3] Ecclesiology is concerned with the nature of the Church, and derives from the Greek word ἐκκλεσία, meaning 'a church'. There is no agreed definition of the word, but the definition adopted in the first report of the Archbishops' Review Group on bishops' needs and resources, *Resourcing Bishops* (London, Church House Publishing, 2001) is: 'The principles which underlie the structure and organization of the Church of England and the roles of its office holders, both ordained and lay, in-

2

vious: if mediation is ineffective at resolving disputes, it is unlikely to be a process to be recommended for this task.

2. SOME TERMS

Two terms need some explanation, if not a precise definition, at
the outset. The first is what is meant by a conflict or dispute; the
second is what is meant by mediation.

i Conflict

One church lawyer has referred to conflict as 'the more serious
types of dispute'. Conflict, for him, was 'such impasse whereby
neither protagonist will alter his position, the disagreement having crossed the rubicon (*sic*) from a difference of opinion to an irreconcilable mutual intransigence'. He considered that conflict
was more than minor differences of opinion, honestly held, and
had become 'diametrically opposed views in relation to which
there is little, or no, common ground'.[4]

In this book both the 'more serious' and the 'less serious' types
of dispute are included. While agreeing that a conflict or dispute
is more than just a difference of opinion, many of the cases which
it is argued are suitable for mediation are of the 'more serious'
type of dispute.

ii Mediation

Mediation is a voluntary and confidential process in which an
independent third party, the mediator, assists the parties to

---

cluding their respective rights, duties and obligations.' (*Resourcing Bishops*, par. 2.5.1.)

[4] Mark Hill, *The Resolution of Conflict in English Canon Law* (University of
Wales unpublished LLM Dissertation, Cardiff Law School, 1994), pg. 4.

3

achieve their own settlement to the dispute.[5] There are several elements in this definition.

The process is *voluntary*, because the parties cannot be compelled to take part for longer than they wish, or even at all.

The process is *confidential*. Anything which is said during the mediation will not be disclosed outside the confines of the mediation room.[6] It is also confidential as between the parties. If one party discloses anything to the mediator privately, the mediator will not disclose that information to the other party without the first party's consent.[7]

The mediator is *independent*: he has no financial or other interest in the dispute. In some cases he may be known by one or more of the parties, but any such connection must always be disclosed to all the parties, and all parties need to agree on the choice of the mediator.

---

[5] This definition is the author's, and combines elements from many others. CEDR, the Centre for Effective Dispute Resolution, is one of the leading providers of commercial mediation services in the UK. CEDR defines mediation as follows: 'Mediation is a voluntary, non-binding, private dispute resolution process in which a neutral person helps the parties try to reach a negotiated settlement', *Mediator Training Course Handbook* (London, CEDR, 1997), pg. 30. Brown and Marriott, *ADR Principles and Practice*, 2nd edn. (London, Sweet & Maxwell, 1999), pg. 127 give the following definition: 'Mediation is a facilitative process in which disputing parties engage the assistance of an impartial third party, the mediator, who helps them to try to arrive at an agreed resolution of their dispute'.

[6] There are a few exceptions to the duty of confidentiality: for example, where a party discloses information relating to child abuse, money laundering or tax evasion: see Brown and Marriott, *ADR Principles and Practice*, 2nd edn., pg. 473–476.

[7] On confidentiality, see pg. 241 and pg. 170, fn. 62.

Any settlement reached by the parties is *their own settlement to the dispute*. A common misconception is that the mediator is some kind of judge. He or she is not. The mediator is not there to express views as to the rightness or wrongness of anything done by either party, or as to the strengths of either party's case. He is there to help the parties explore options for settlement. He may suggest possible solutions, but he does not and can not impose them on the parties.

The forms the process may take, and how the mediator sets about assisting the parties to reach a settlement, are described in detail in later chapters.[8]

3. SCRIPTURAL FOUNDATIONS FOR DISPUTE RESOLUTION

i The reality of conflict

Conflict is not necessarily destructive. The Bible is full of conflict, between Israel and its neighbours,[9] between Jesus and demonic powers,[10] between Jesus and the religious leaders of his day,[11] between the early Church and the world,[12] between Paul and Barnabas,[13] and between the forces of good and the forces of evil in the end times.[14] God uses conflict as part of his plan of salvation: it was conflict which led Israel out of Egypt, and conflict which took Jesus to the cross.

It is clear that Christians are bound to have conflicts, notwithstanding Paul's advice to the Romans about living in peace with

---

[8] In particular, chapter 4, 'Commercial mediation'; chapter 5, 'Community mediation'; and chapter 6, 'Consensus-building mediation'.

[9] e.g. Joshua 6–12.

[10] Matthew 17:18.

[11] Matthew 23:27–35.

[12] Acts 6:8–15.

[13] Acts 15:39.

[14] Revelation 12:7.

one another.[15] There is conflict between man's sinful nature and the life in the Spirit,[16] and conflict as Christians struggle to live as Christ's new creation.[17] Indeed, many Christians believe that Christians are called to use conflict to bring about change in society: to attack oppression, injustice, and discrimination where they see it.[18]

ii The response to conflict

Generally, we should try to resolve conflicts, unless there is some particular reason not to do so. We should go and speak to someone with whom we have a dispute; and if they will not listen at first, take one or two others with us; and then finally bring it to the Church.[19] Because God has forgiven us, we must forgive.[20] The responsibility to take the initiative to solve a dispute is always with a Christian person. Jesus tells us to go to our brother with whom we have a grievance and to settle it before coming to offer a gift to God.[21]

---

[15] Romans 12:18.

[16] Galatians 5:16–17; Romans 7:21–25.

[17] 2 Corinthians 5:17.

[18] In the 20th century, for example, 'liberation theology' encouraged the Church in South America to confront social structures which were seen as oppressive. This teaching has led on occasions to church communities endorsing particular political parties, and, for example, becoming involved in the support of the Sandenista guerrillas in Nicaragua. See the entry 'liberation theology' in the *Oxford Dictionary of the Christian Church*, 3rd. edn. (Oxford University Press, 1997).

[19] Matthew 18:15–17.

[20] Matthew 6:12–15.

[21] Matthew 5:21–26.

God is the 'author of peace and lover of concord'.[22] Dishar-
mony in the Christian community is a serious matter. Christians
must be active to promote peace,[23] not merely as the elimination
of discord, but as the harmony and true functioning of the body of
Christ.[24] In particular, bringing lawsuits 'before the ungodly for
judgment instead of before the saints' is to be discouraged.[25]

In the sphere of human relations, there are only a few examples of mediation in the Bible. Moses sought to reconcile two
fighting Israelites, but they would not accept his mediation.[26] Joab
acted the part of mediator between David and Absalom.[27] In the
New Testament Euodia and Syntyche are urged to agree with
each other, and one particular Christian is urged to help them to
resolve their dispute.[28]

---

[22] The second collect, for peace, in the Order for Morning Prayer according to the Book of Common Prayer: for 'author of peace', see 1 Corinthians 14:33 (Authorised Version); for 'lover of concord', see Psalm 133
and 1 Peter 3:8.

[23] Ephesians 4:3.

[24] Romans 14:1–19.

[25] 1 Corinthians 6:1. By implication, bringing a dispute to 'the saints' for
resolution is acceptable; though in verse 8 St Paul goes on to criticise the
Corinthian Christians for cheating and wronging each other, thus creating the disputes which needed to be resolved.

[26] Exodus 2:14 as explained in Acts 7:26.

[27] 2 Samuel 14:1-23.

[28] Philippians 4: 2–3. The identity of the mediator is not clear. Matthew
Henry's *Commentary* (Grand Rapids, MI, USA, Zondervan, 1999) gives
two possibilities: Epaphroditus, who is supposed to have been one of the
pastors of the church of the Philippians; and 'some eminently good
woman, perhaps Paul's wife'. Another possibility is the individual
Syzygus, mentioned in the New International Version fn. for verse 3, as
the word translated 'yokefellow' in that verse is also a proper name: see
Vine's *Expository Dictionary of Biblical Words* (Nashville, TN, Thomas
Nelson Publishers, 1985). The *New Bible Dictionary* (London, Inter-

7

But at the more profound, theological, level, 'the idea of mediation and therefore of persons acting in the capacity of mediator permeates the Bible'.[29] Moses was the mediator of the old covenant, because it was through him that the covenant at Sinai was effected.[30] He mediated between God and the Israelites when they sinned against God.[31] Similarly, Jesus is the mediator of the new covenant,[32] the 'one mediator between God and men'.[33] Jesus' death on the cross resulted in 'peace with God',[34] and his continued intervention as mediator[35] brings to us the fruits of our redemption.[36] Christ's mediation enables the Father to see men in a new light;[37] and enables men to see their need of salvation.

> The work of Christ, as indicated by the word mesites,[38] is twofold. ...He propitiates the just displeasure of God by expiating the guilt of sin, making intercession for those whom the Father has given Him, and actually makes their persons and services acceptable to God. ... He reveals to men the truth concerning God and their relation to Him with the conditions of acceptable service, persuades and enables them to receive the truth, and directs and sustains

---

Varsity Press, 1962) entry for Synzygus (an alternative spelling for Syzygus) suggests that the mediator is Luke.

[29] The *New Bible Dictionary* entry for mediation.

[30] Exodus 19:3–8; Exodus 24:3–8; Acts 7:37–39; Galatians 3:19–20.

[31] Exodus 32:30-32; Numbers 12 .

[32] Hebrews 9:15; Hebrews 12:24.

[33] 1 Timothy 2:5.

[34] Romans 5:1; Ephesians 2:13–18.

[35] John 14:6; 1 John 2:1.

[36] See generally, the *New Bible Dictionary* entry for mediation.

[37] Colossians 1:12.

[38] The Greek word μεσίτης (*mesites*) means 'mediator', and is used in 1 Timothy 2:5, Galatians 3:19–20; and Hebrews 8:6, 9:15 and 12:24.

them in all circumstances of life, so as to perfect their deliverance.[39]

This theme of enabling each party to recognise the other party's position is a key concept in mediation. It will be considered in detail in chapter 5.[40]

iii The final reconciliation of conflict

The Old Testament prophets looked forward to a time when there will be no conflict. 'The wolf and the lamb shall feed together';[41] 'nation shall not lift up sword against nation'.[42] Until that time we must learn to handle conflict properly.

iv Application

Two conclusions follow. First, a method that assists and encourages Christians to resolve disputes, especially disputes which may involve lawsuits, is to be welcomed. Second, mediation is not only consistent with Scripture; it is the word used to describe some of the most important doctrines in Scripture. It is indeed the work of Christ. It is no surprise therefore that in the Sermon on the Mount, Christ described peacemakers as sons (and daughters) of God.[43]

---

[39] Louis Berkhof, *Systematic Theology* (Edinburgh, Banner of Truth Trust, 1958), pg. 283.

[40] See the section 'The object of mediation: resolution or transformation?', pg. 223.

[41] Isaiah 65:25.

[42] Micah 4:3.

[43] Matthew 5:9.

4. MEDIATION IN CHURCH HISTORY

a) The early Church

Moving on from the New Testament to the early Church, we see a pattern emerging of the Church encouraging reconciliation of church disputes Thus in the *Didache*, Christians are urged to 'pacify contending parties', though the context is in relation to possible schism rather than disputes in general.[44] The same text appears in the *Epistle of Barnabas*.[45]

In the early Church, bishops were not only judges, but arbitrators and mediators as well. The bishop had a traditional role as a mediator and a reconciler of disputes between members of his congregation. In the third century *Didascalia Apostolorum*, there were set out rules about how bishops should behave when trying to handle disputes between the Christian faithful.[46]

> The language employed is that of healing, not judgement. The bishop is the physician of his flock and, if disputes arise, the bishop's first task is to act as mediator or go-between, and seek to reconcile the conflicting parties. Only if his negotiations ... had no effect was the bishop to allow the case to go to him as judge.[47]

---

[44] The *Didache* 4:3. The *Didache* (New York, Paulist Press, 1948). The date of the *Didache* is a matter of debate. Some scholars date it in the first century, others as late as the third. The *Oxford Bible Commentary* (Oxford University Press, 2001) dates it in the first half of the second century.

[45] The *Epistle of Barnabas* 19:12. The Epistle of Barnabas is published in the same volume as *The Didache* (New York, Paulist Press, 1948). The *Oxford Bible Commentary* dates the Epistle of Barnabas between 117 and 132.

[46] *Didascalia Apostolorum*, 2.41.3–9; 46;53–4, cited by Jill Harries, *Law and Empire in Late Antiquity* (Cambridge University Press, 1998), pg. 192.

[47] Jill Harries, *Law and Empire in Late Antiquity*, pg. 192.

The bishop was not strictly a judge in the formal sense of someone appointed to apply Roman or any other system of law. His judgments were not enforceable by the state authority, and he had limited formal sanctions available to him. Nor was he an arbitrator in the strict Roman law sense of a person appointed by formal agreement (a *compromissum*)[48] to determine a dispute. His jurisdiction was of his own initiative, rather than that of the parties. Nor, for the same reason, was he strictly a mediator: the source of the final decision was the bishop, not the parties, whereas in a mediation, it is the parties who ultimately determine the matter. But 'these problems of definition were irrelevant. The system worked in practice'.[49]

In the fourth century, Constantine extended the bishops' jurisdiction by instructing the provincial *iudex* to allow anyone wishing to appeal a civil suit to the episcopal court for judgment on Christian principles to do so.[50] In practice, Constantine's *episcopalis audientia* was very much a continuation of what the bishops were already doing: seeking to resolve a dispute by reconciliation of the parties rather than acting as decision makers.[51]

The personal authority of bishops enabled them to offer solutions, rather than conducting themselves strictly as mediators by allowing the parties concerned to come up with solutions them-

---

[48] The word *compromissum* means not to compromise in the modern sense, but an agreement to submit to arbitration: see W.W. Buckland, *A Text-Book of Roman Law from Augustus to Justinian*, 3rd edn. revised by Peter Stein (Cambridge University Press 1968) pg. 532. An informal arbitration award was not generally binding, so it was usual to embody in the arbitration agreement a penalty if the decision was not obeyed; and this penalty was enforceable: *ibid.*

[49] Jill Harries, *Law and Empire in Late Antiquity*, pg. 195.

[50] i.e. according to the *Lex Christiana*: see H.F. Jolowicz and Barry Nicholas, *Historical Introduction to the study of Roman Law*, 3rd edn. (Cambridge University Press 1972), pg. 448–9.

[51] Jill Harries, *Law and Empire in Late Antiquity*, pg. 197.

11

selves. But in some cases even the most highly respected bishops acted as pure mediators: Harris cites as an example one dispute where Ambrose[52] urged a settlement without suggesting what it should be, even though the law clearly favoured one party.[53]

Augustine[54] wrote that his job was to make his disputants live in earthly harmony with each other; not just to resolve their disputes about gold, silver, farms, and herds.[55] He saw that transformed relationships were more important than resolving disputes, but that one can lead to the other.[56]

b) The early medieval period (c. 400 to 1100)

There are two features of the early medieval period which are relevant to this study. The first is the great political and legal changes which took place over this period, the second is the great increase in the power and authority of the Church. The western Roman empire came to an end during the fifth century, with the invasion of tribes from the north and the east. In western Europe, following the fall of the Roman Empire, the new kingdoms used indigenous systems of law, which bore no comparison to the sophistication of Roman law.[57] However the eastern empire continued, with its capital at Constantinople. It was thus from Con-

---

[52] St Ambrose (born c. 339, died 397) became bishop of Milan in 374. He baptised St Augustine of Hippo, the great Christian theologian, in 387.

[53] Jill Harries, *Law and Empire in Late Antiquity*, pg. 205.

[54] St Augustine of Hippo (born 354, died 430).

[55] A letter of St Augustine, cited in Jill Harries, *Law and Empire in Late Antiquity*, pg. 204.

[56] The link between transformed relationships and dispute resolution is discussed below, pg. 223.

[57] See Thomas Watkin, *A Historical Introduction to Modern Civil Law* (Aldershot, Ashgate, 1999), chapter 4; Peter Stein, *Roman Law in European History* (Cambridge University Press, 1999), pg. 29-32.

stantinople that the emperor Justinian's compilation of the Roman law, known as the Digest, became law in 533.

In 773–774 the Frank Charlemagne reconquered Italy, and in 800 he was crowned Holy Roman Emperor at Rome by the Pope. The Carolingian reforms followed: an ambitious effort to reform ecclesiastical institutions and discipline.[58]

Despite these momentous changes, the quiet reconciling role of bishops continued unabated.

> From the seventh to the twelfth centuries, the procedural activity of the church provided not so much a judicial decision as a reconciliation of the parties.[59]

c) The later medieval period (1100 to 1450)

In the later medieval period, again two developments stand out. The first is the systematisation of Church law, the second is the adoption of the inquisitorial procedure for Church courts.

The first major systematisation of Church law was the *Decretum* of Gratian, completed about 1140. With the publication of the *Decretum*, 'decretists' commented on Gratian's work, and new

---

[58] On Charlemagne's church reforms, see James Brundage, *Medieval Canon Law* (London, Longman, 1995), pg. 28. For example, they included the *Capitulary of Herstal* (779), which called upon imperial officials to enforce payment of the tithe, a reform which provided the basis for church finance for more than 1000 years.

[59] James Coriden, 'Alternative dispute resolution in the church', Canon Law Society of America Proceedings 48 (1986), pg. 64–77 at pg. 68, citing J. Calvo, *Codigo de Derecho Canonico* (Pamplona: EUNSA, 1983) 870. In very similar words, Caparros, Thériault and Thorn, *Code of Canon Law Annotated* (Montreal, Wilson & Lafleur Limitée, 1993), at pg. 902, commenting on canon 1446 state:

> From the 7th to the 12th Centuries, the focus of ecclesiastical procedure was towards conciliation and mediation rather than solving a problem through a judicial sentence.

collections followed: the *Liber extra*[60] of 1234, the *Liber sextus*[61] of 1298, the *Constitutiones Clementinae* of 1317, the *Extravagantes* of 1327, and what became known as the *Corpus Iuris Canonici* of 1582, which remained the foundational body of canon law until the promulgation of the 1917 Code.[62]

The explanation for the adoption of inquisitorial procedure for Church courts is two-fold: the need to delegate, and the means of study of canon law. Bishops, busy with other administrative and political concerns, no longer had the time to sit in judgment hour after hour, day after day, on routine disputes among members of their flock. A range of courts developed, from the *Papal Curia* in Rome, down to diocesan consistory courts and the archdeacons' courts.[63] Disputes were delegated to legal specialists to resolve, a

---

[60] i.e. the book 'outside of' Gratian's *Decretum*.

[61] i.e. 'the sixth book' after Gratian's five part *Decretum*.

[62] There was also a collection called the *Extravagantes communes* published in 1500 and 1503, which were reprinted in all subsequent editions of the *Corpus Iuris Canonici*. See James Brundage, *Medieval Canon Law*, pg. 196 to 200.

[63] The opening lines of the Friar's Tale in Chaucer's *Canterbury Tales* (London, Penguin Books, 1996) gives a good picture of the jurisdiction of the archdeacon's court in 1180.

> Whilom ther was dwellynge in my contree
> And erchedeken, a man of heigh degree,
> That boldely dide execucioun
> In punysshynge of fornicacioun,
> Of wicchecraft, and eek of bawderye,
> Of difamacioun, and avowtrye,
> Of chirche reves, and of testamentz,
> Of contractes and of lakke of sacramentz,
> Of usure, and of symonye also.
> But certes, lecchours dide he grettest wo;
> They sholde syngen if that they were hent;
> And smale tytheres weren foule yshent,
> If any persoun wolde upon hem pleyne.
> Ther myghte asterte hym no pecunyal peyne.
> For smale tithes and for smal offrynge

growing body of professionals who had been trained in Roman law. It was therefore understandable that Church courts adopted procedure based on Roman law.

It is this which provided the key to the continuation of mediation. Church courts adopted the Roman law *cognitio* procedure.[64]

He made the peple pitously to synge.
For er the bisshop caughte hem with his hook,
They weren in the erchedeknes book.

For those who prefer the modern translation by David Wright (Oxford University Press, 1985).

In my part of the world lived an archdeacon
Once on a time; a man of high position,
A stern executant of the retribution
The law imposes upon fornication,
Slander, and witchcraft, and church-robbery,
On procuration and adultery,
Forging of wills and breaches of contract,
Usury and simony and neglect
Of sacraments, and other kinds of crime
We need not enter into at this time.
He'd castigate whoremongers most of all;
If he caught them at it, how he'd make them squall!
And as for those who hadn't paid their tithes,
He came down on them like a sack of bricks
If any parish priest reported them;
He never missed a chance to take a fine.
For a skimped tithe, or scanty offering,
How piteously he'd make people sing!
Before the bishop caught them with his crook,
They'd be put down in the archdeacon's book.

[64] See James Brundage, *Medieval Canon Law*, chapter 6. Roman law terms were used for numerous stages of the procedure: examples include the *libellus* (the statement of case), *litis contestatio* (the trial of the case), and *interrogatio* (interrogatories – i.e. written questions). For their use in Roman law procedure, see H.F. Jolowicz and Barry Nicholas, *Historical Introduction to the study of Roman Law*, 3rd edn., pg. 442, and W.W. Buckland, *A Text-Book of Roman Law from Augustus to Justinian*, 3rd edn., pg. 666.

A principal feature of the *cognitio* procedure was its inquisitorial or investigative[65] nature, in contrast to the common law adversarial trial. Questions to witnesses are not put by the parties, but by the judge, though probably counsel could suggest questions for the judge to ask.

There is a strong parallel here with mediation, because one of the many skills of a mediator is his or her ability to ask questions to bring out the real issues in the dispute, and to see where there is common ground between the parties. The mediator's inquisitorial role thus resembles that of the judge in early Church courts. Many Church cases ended with a compromise, and there is evidence from the fifteenth century record books in England that Church judges understood their role as mediators as well as judges. Thus, a judge adopting an inquisitorial role could suggest ways in which a dispute might be compromised; and in many such cases the suggestion was acted on by the parties.

Helmholz lists examples ranging from quarrels between neighbours where criminal accusations were made,[66] affiliation proceedings,[67] and usury cases.[68] In an article about papal judges delegate, Helmholz writes:

> No one could safely assert that smoothing the way to compromise was the primary thought of the canonists, but it does seem fair to say that such was among their aims.[69]

In this, the later-Medieval period, the jurisdictional divide between Church courts and the common law courts was not clear

---

[65] Investigative is a less tendentious word than inquisitorial, and is the word used by Bishop Kemp: see Eric Kemp, 'The spirit of the canon law and its application in England' (1987–1988) 1 Ecc LJ (1,2) 5 at pg. 6.

[66] R. H. Helmholz, Canon Law and the Law of England, (Hambledon Press, 1987), pg. 141–2.

[67] R. H. Helmholz, Canon Law and the Law of England, pg. 180, 183–4.

[68] R. H. Helmholz, Canon Law and the Law of England, pg. 336.

[69] R. H. Helmholz, Canon Law and the Law of England, pg. 36–37.

cut. Glanvill's treatise on the law and current practice and usage at the king's court at the Exchequer was written between 1187 and 1189.[70] Book VIII of this treatise gives precedents for concords or agreements reached to compromise an action in the king's court. It is speculative whether the precedent for a settlement of a dispute concerning an advowson[71] indicates that mediation of church disputes took place in the king's court also.[72] All Glanvill says is that 'it often happens that cases begun in the lord king's court are ended by amicable composition'.

d) The Reformation (1450-1600)

Other legal historians have reached the same conclusions from the records for their own periods of research. Houlbrooke carried out research on the court records in the dioceses of Norwich and Winchester. He found that matrimonial, testamentary, tithe and defamation cases accounted between them for over nine-tenths of the identifiable court business over the period 1520–1570.[73] Houlbrooke says

> It was the duty of the ecclesiastical judge to encourage the peaceful settlement of most types of dispute by compromise or arbitration. In the consistory courts of both dioceses far fewer cases were pushed as far as the expensive

---

[70] *Tractatus de legibus et consuetudinibus regni Anglie qui Glanvilla vocatur,* *(The treatise on the laws and customs of the realm of England commonly called Glanvill)* (Oxford, Clarendon Press, 1993).

[71] An advowson is a right to present to an ecclesiastical living. The right is now very much restricted by the Patronage (Benefices) Measure 1986. For the history of the right, see P. Smith, 'The Advowson: The history and development of a most peculiar property' (2000) 5 Ecc LJ 320.

[72] Glanvill, VIII, 3.

[73] Ralph Houlbrooke, *Church Courts and the People during the English Reformation* (Oxford University Press, 1979) pg. 39.

17

formality of final sentence than were settled by peaceful agreement.[74]

Houlbrooke refers to and agrees with Helmholz' comment:

> Lawyers today almost always try to settle without going into court at all. Medieval litigants and their lawyers began lawsuits with less hesitation. They went to law more quickly. But they were no less ready to compromise in the end. Agreement of the parties was the most satisfactory way of ending a dispute.[75]

He cites examples of the court's role in helping settlement of both testamentary cases,[76] and tithe disputes.[77]

Wunderli,[78] describes the mediation efforts of London Church courts in the 1500s as follows:[79]

> Not all suits in London church courts were prosecuted to the bitter end. Canonists had long taught that the preferable ends of justice are peace and concord between litigants: this could be reached, they said, through outside arbitration and concord as well as through court trial. Henry of Susa, the great Hostiensis,[80] for example, taught that a judge ought to induce litigants to concord and to reconcile them when possible: otherwise he risks giving an

---

[74] R.H. Helmholz, *Marriage Litigation in Medieval England* (Cambridge University Press, 1974), pg. 43–44.

[75] R.H. Helmholz, *Marriage Litigation in Medieval England*, pg. 137.

[76] Ralph Houlbrooke, *Church Courts and the People during the English Reformation*, pg. 112.

[77] Ralph Houlbrooke, *Church Courts and the People during the English Reformation*, pg. 138–139.

[78] Richard M. Wunderli, *London Church Courts and Society on the Eve of the Reformation* (Cambridge, MA, The Medieval Academy of America, 1981), pg. 42–3.

[79] Footnote references in the quotation added by the present author.

[80] Hostiensis was born just before 1200, and died in 1271.

unjust decision.[81] This was a common theme of canonists and was repeated by the fifteenth-century English legist, William Lyndwood.[82] ... Lyndwood echoed Hostiensis by repeating the familiar tagline that a judge first and foremost ought to lead contending parties to an amicable peace: 'Judex primo et ante omnia debet partes inducere ad concordiam si possit.' [83]

e) The seventeenth to the nineteenth centuries

There is no published research as to the use of mediation in church disputes over this period. So far as the Roman Catholic Church is concerned, the 1917 Code of Canon Law[84] was a codification of the existing canon law dating back to the 1500s. This

---

[81] Hostiensis, *Lectura in quinque libros Decretalium* (Venice, 1581), 2.4.1, #19, fol. 20v: 'Primo debet iudex partes inducere ad concordiam et componere inter ipsas si potest. Alioquin iniuste pronunciabit.' (The judge must first of all if possible lead the parties to an agreement and a resolution of the dispute. Otherwise he will pronounce injustice.)

[82] Lyndwood was born in 1375, and died in 1446. Lyndwood's *Provinciale* cites a canon of Stephen Langton which encouraged out-of-court settlement (title 16). Lyndwood added the gloss set out in the main quotation.

> that no Archdeacons and their officials or other judges for the prosperity or good continuance of peace, if they that were at variance will agree together, may ask or require anything; but that it shall be lawful, for the parties asking licence, to depart by composition from the law when they will, so that the matter be such as may admit composition.

Lyndwood's *Provinciale*, the text of the canons therein contained, reprinted from the translation made in 1534, edited by J.V. Bullard and H. Chalmer Bell (London, Faith Press, 1929) (copy in the Inner Temple library).

[83] 'The judge must first and above all lead the parties to a settlement if he can.'

[84] *Corpus Iuris Canonici* (1917 Code of Canon Law) (Vatican, 1917).

code contains provisions encouraging mediation;[85] and it may be inferred that there was no change, at least in theory, in the importance of mediation between the seventeenth and the nineteenth centuries.

It was in this period that the Church of England courts changed from using the civilian inquisitorial procedure to the common law adversarial procedure. Until the 1850s the lawyers who fought in the Church courts were all trained in civilian procedures.[86] Following legislation of the 1850s,[87] the procedure in

---

[85] See pg. 22.

[86] See R.H. Helmholz, *Roman Canon Law in Reformation England* (Cambridge University Press, 1990).

[87] The short statute which led the way was the Ecclesiastical Courts (England and Wales) Act 1854 (17 & 18 Vict. c. 47). The long title of the Act describes it as 'An Act to alter and improve the mode of taking Evidence in the Ecclesiastical Courts of England and Wales'. The full text is as follows:

> Be it enacted by the Queen's most Excellent Majesty, by and with the Advice and Consent of the Lords Spiritual and Temporal, and Commons, in this present Parliament assembled, and by the Authority of the same, That in any Suit or Proceeding depending in any Ecclesiastical Court in England or Wales the court (if it shall think fit) may summon before it and examine or cause to be examined Witnesses by Word of Mouth, and either before or after Examination by Deposition or Affidavit; and Notes of such Evidence shall be taken down in Writing by the Judge or Registrar, or by such other person or Persons, and in such Manner, as the Judge of the Court shall direct.

See Holdsworth, *A History of English Law* (London, Sweet & Maxwell, 1922-66) volume XII, pg. 683-4. Prior to this change, the witnesses were examined secretly by an examiner, and their answers taken down in writing: Holdsworth, *A history of English law*, volume XII, pg. 679-680. The text of the statute does not make it clear that the new procedure included cross-examination and re-examination. In contrast, when jurisdiction for probate and administration of estates was transferred from the ecclesiastical courts to the new Court of Probate, it was expressly

Church Courts became adversarial, and no longer the exclusive province of civil lawyers.[88] The London base of the civil lawyers who practised ecclesiastical law, Doctors' Commons, was sold in 1865.[89]

This procedural change affected the ability of the judge to act as mediator in a dispute; though judges could and did still encourage compromise.[90] That said, the extent to which mediation of church disputes took place over this period is not known.

f) A continuum of reconciliation

From the early Church fathers up to the Reformation and afterwards, there is thus clear evidence that bishops and, later, ecclesiastical judges saw their duty first and foremost as being to reconcile the parties; and they fulfilled this duty. In the early Church, the informal procedure adopted by bishops enabled them both to offer solutions, and to let the parties reach their own solutions. The bishops only acted as judge where that became necessary. In the later Middle Ages, and at the time of the Reformation, the Church courts' procedure became standardised, based on the Roman *cognitio* procedure. This investigative, as opposed to adversarial, procedure enabled the judges to help the parties to reach a settlement in many cases.

---

provided that there was to be oral cross-examination and re-examination of witnesses, and the common law rules of evidence were to be observed: Court of Probate Act 1857 (20 & 21 Vict. c. 77) sections 31 and 33.

[88] On the rights of audience of barristers in the ecclesiastical courts, see J.H. Baker, *Monuments of Endlesse Labours* (London, Hambledon Press, 1998), pg. 130, 144 and 162.

[89] J.H. Baker, *Monuments of Endlesse Labours*, pg. 144; and Paul Barber, 'The Fall and Rise of Doctors' Commons?', 4 Ecc LJ 462.

[90] 'They [judges] tried to effect a compromise if they could see that the result of going on would swallow up the property in costs.' Holdsworth, *A history of English law*, volume XII, pg. 682.

Whether the same efforts were made to mediate disputes in the seventeenth to nineteenth centuries as had been made previously is not known; but it is clear that there has been a continuum and tradition of mediation within the Church for almost the whole of its history. For the Church once again to espouse mediation would thus be a return to Church tradition.

5. MEDIATION IN THE ROMAN CATHOLIC CHURCH

This book is primarily about mediation within the Church of England and the Anglican Communion. But the legal structures and recent experience of other Churches may be of assistance. In particular, as the Roman Catholic Church is the largest Christian denomination in the world, with a fully developed legal system of its own,[91] it is useful to see the extent to which the legal structures of the Roman Catholic Church provide for mediation.[92]

a) The 1917 Code of canon law

The 1917 Code of Canon Law[93] was the first proper systematised codification of Roman Catholic canon law. It replaced the *Corpus Iuris Canonici* published in 1582 following the Council of Trent of 1545–1563.[94] In Book IV (De Processibus) of the 1917 Code there was a title on 'Ways To Avoid Contentious Trials'. It contained two short chapters, one on *De Transactione* or negotiated

---

[91] For the text and a commentary on the Roman Catholic Code of Canon Law, see Caparros, Thériault and Thorn, *Code of Canon Law Annotated*.

[92] For the extent to which the Roman Catholic Church makes use of these provisions in practice, see pg. 481.

[93] *Corpus Iuris Canonici* (1917 Code of Canon Law) (Vatican, 1917)

[94] For the history, see Peter Huizing, 'Canon Law', in Jordan Hite and Daniel Ward, *Readings, cases, materials in Canon Law* (Collegeville, Minnesota, Liturgical Press, 1990), pg. 62, and Coriden, Green and Heintschel, *The Code of Canon Law, a text and commentary* (New York, Paulist Press, 1985), pg. 3–4.

settlement,[95] and the other on *De Compromisso in arbitros* or arbitrated agreements.[96] The canons on negotiated settlement called for the judge to take the initiative, at any time before or during the trial, to urge the parties to work out an agreement, but stated that usually someone other than the judge should assist them in doing so.

These two provisions of the 1917 Code were rarely used but they stood as official reminders of the Church's desire that disputes be settled in modes that were simpler and more reconciliatory than a contentious trial.[97]

b) The 1983 Code of canon law

i Diocesan courts

The 1917 Code was itself revised following the Second Vatican Council.[98] The revised Code of 1983 gives warm encouragement to the use of mediation. In Book VII (processes), the very first canon (c. 1446) under the rubric 'The Discipline To Be Observed in Trials' urges the Christian faithful to avoid lawsuits as much as possible, and to resolve their conflicts quickly. The canon calls upon the judge to encourage the parties to work out a fair solution to their dispute; he should suggest ways of doing so, and he may employ the services of mediators.

> Can. 1446 §1. All Christ's faithful, and especially Bishops, are to strive earnestly, with due regard for justice, to ensure that lawsuits among the people of God are as far as possible avoided, and are settled promptly and without rancour.

---

[95] *Corpus Iuris Canonici* (1917 Code) Canons 1925–28.

[96] *Corpus Iuris Canonici* (1917 Code) Canons 1929–32.

[97] James Coriden, 'Alternative dispute resolution in the church', Canon Law Society of America Proceedings 48 (1986), pg. 64–77.

[98] The task of revising the 1917 code was formally inaugurated on 20 November 1965. The new code was promulgated on 25 January 1983, and came into effect on 27 November 1983.

§2. In the early stages of litigation, and indeed at any other time as often as he discerns any hope of a successful outcome, the judge is not to fail to exhort and assist the parties to seek an equitable solution to their controversy in discussions with one another. He is to indicate to them suitable means to this end and avail himself of serious-minded persons to mediate.

§3. If the issue is about the private good of the parties, the judge should find out whether it can be resolved through a negotiated settlement, or through arbitration in accordance with the norms of canons 1713–1716.

One commentary describes this obligation as follows

This is an obligation which weighs heavily upon the judge, not only at the beginning of the lawsuit but at any moment of the trial prior to the judgement, if there appears to be some hope of success. He must try to avail himself of every opportunity to encourage and assist the litigants to reach an agreement that will avoid a lawsuit and resolve the controversy.[99]

ii Administrative recourse

Diocesan courts, in actual practice, are almost exclusively occupied with matrimonial cases, i.e. adjudicating the validity or nullity of marriages.[100] More important for everyday disputes in Church life is the Roman Catholic system of administrative recourse.

Probably the largest amount of ecclesial decision-making is administrative in character rather than legislative or judicial. While only a certain percentage of believers are involved in marriage nullity procedures, all believers are affected in one way or another by decisions of church administrators, especially at the diocesan or parish levels. The

---

[99] Caparros, Thériault and Thorn, *Code of Canon Law Annotated*, pg. 902 (commentary on canon 1446).

[100] James Coriden, *An Introduction to Canon Law* (New York, Paulist Press, 1991), pg. 184.

potential for conflict is extensive in the administrative arena, e.g. the removal or perhaps the failure to remove a pastor, the suppression of a parish, the imposition of a diocesan tax on parishes, the removal of a university professor, etc.[101]

Ombres lists the following examples of administrative acts:

> One can soon see their importance. They include loss of the clerical state, nomination of the parish priest, admission to the novitiate, the dismissal of religious, the application of ecclesiastical penalties, and the removal of parish priests.[102]

Administrative acts include a wide range of decisions, orders, policies and decrees which are issued by those with executive (rather than judicial or legislative) authority. They include the administrative acts of a bishop,[103] a chancellor,[104] a superintendent of schools, a diocesan director of an agency, a clerical provincial superior, or a pastor, and cover such matters as church govern-

---

[101] Thomas Green, 'Rights and duties of diocesan bishops', Canon Law Society of America Proceedings 45 (1983), pg. 18–36, cited in Jordan Hite and Daniel Ward, *Readings, cases, materials in Canon Law*, pg. 229 at pg. 245.

[102] Robert Ombres OP, 'Justice and Equity in the 1983 Code', (1987) *Priests & People* 143 at pg. 147.

[103] No administrative recourse is available against acts of the pope or an ecumenical council: canon 1732.

[104] A chancellor in the Roman Catholic Church is very different from a Church of England Chancellor. In the Church of England, a chancellor acts as legal advisor to the bishop, as a judge in faculty cases, and very occasionally a judge also in discipline cases. In the Roman Catholic Church, his function under canon 482 is to collect, arrange and keep the documents of the diocesan curia. In practice, in many dioceses (especially in the USA), the chancellor is much more than that of archivist and notary: he is the 'executive officer' or 'general manager' of the diocesan administration: see James Coriden, *An Introduction to Canon Law*, pg. 87. He combines many of the functions of both diocesan registrar and diocesan secretary in the Church of England.

ance, the alteration of church buildings,[105] church discipline,[106] property and financial matters.

This system is a process of appealing to the one who has taken administrative action, or to his or her hierarchical superior. Administrative acts cannot be challenged in church courts,[107] so the code sets out the procedure for this administrative recourse.[108]

The canons on administrative recourse at the end of book VII (Canons 1732–1739) make the bishop the key figure in resolving any controversies surfacing in the diocese as a result of allegedly arbitrary administrative discretion. Canon 1733 indicates that the conference of bishops may require each bishop to set up an office or board to deal with conflict-resolution issues, in effect, a diocesan conciliation service. Even if the conference does not do this, the bishop may initiate such conflict-resolution mechanisms on his own.

> Can. 1733 §2. The Bishops' Conference can prescribe that in each diocese there be established a permanent office or council which would have the duty, in accordance with norms laid down by the Conference, of seeking and suggesting equitable solutions. Even if the Conference has not demanded this, the Bishop may establish such an office or council.[109]
> §3. The office or council ... is to be diligent in its work principally when the revocation of a decree is sought in accordance with canon 1734 and the time-limit for recourse has not elapsed. If recourse is proposed against a decree, the superior who would have to decide the recourse is to encourage both the person having recourse and the author

---

[105] Book V of the Code (Canons 1254–1310) deals with the administration of the Church's temporal goods.

[106] Book VI of the Code (Canons 1311–1399) deals with sanctions.

[107] Canon 1400 §2.

[108] Canons 1732–1739

[109] Canon 1733 §2.

of the decree to seek this type of solution, whenever the prospect of a satisfactory outcome is discerned.[110]

One commentary suggests how this may apply in practice:

> Through appropriate conciliation efforts, conflicts may be avoided or resolved in some suitable way. Perhaps the superior may voluntarily modify the decree, e.g. changing of (*sic*) a bishop's decision to deny excardination.[111] Perhaps the aggrieved parties may be appropriately compensated, e.g. a more satisfactory arrangement worked out for parishioners whose parish is being suppressed. Perhaps the administrator will be vindicated against an unwarranted charge or arbitrariness in alienating property.[112]

The bishop is not the only figure charged to resolve disputes by alternative dispute resolution. The canon requires the parties to the dispute – the person who feels aggrieved by the administrative action and the person who took the action – and also the superior to whom recourse is made to seek a peaceful solution before using the administrative recourse procedures set out in the Code.

> Can. 1733 §1. When a person believes that he or she has been injured by a decree, it is greatly to be desired that contention between that person and the author of the decree be avoided, and that care be taken to reach an equitable solution by mutual consultation, possibly using the assistance of serious-minded persons to mediate and study

---

[110] Canon 1733 §3.

[111] Every cleric must be incardinated in a particular Church, and under the authority of a particular bishop. Acephalous or 'wandering' clergy are not allowed. Excardination is a document signed by the diocesan bishop which releases a cleric from that bishop's diocese so that he can be incardinated into another diocese: Canon 267 §2.

[112] Coriden, Green and Heintschel, *The Code of Canon Law, a text and commentary*, pg. 1031.

the matter. In this way, the controversy may by some suitable method be avoided or brought to an end. [113]

Coriden gives examples of a broad range of disputes which arise within the everyday life of a church, and which could be settled by alternative dispute resolution procedures.

> Employment problems, pastoral decisions which are perceived to be arbitrary or injurious, conflicts within parish communities – all could be submitted to ADR. Flagrant criminal activity or doctrinal interpretation may not be suitable subject matter.[114]

c) The 1990 code of canons of the Eastern Churches

In the 1990 Code for the Eastern Churches there are two provisions which mirror the provisions in the 1983 Code for the Western Church: the first, for trials; the second, for administrative recourse.

Dealing first with trials, Title XXIV (Trials in general), Chapter III (The obligations of judges and other tribunal officers) commences with canon 1103, which reads almost identical to canon 1446 of the Western church:

> Can. 1103 §1. With due regard for justice, all the Christian faithful especially bishops are to strive earnestly to avoid lawsuits among the people of God as much as possible or to resolve them peacefully as soon as possible.
> §2. At the very start or even at any point during the litigation, whenever some hope of a happy outcome is perceived, the judge is not to neglect to encourage and assist the parties to collaborate in working out an equitable solution to the controversy as well as indicating suitable ways of reaching such a solution, perhaps even employing the services of reputable persons for mediation.

---

[113] Canon 1733.

[114] James Coriden, 'Alternative dispute resolution in the church', Canon Law Society of America Proceedings 48 (1986), pg. 73.

§3. If, however, the case concerns the private good of the parties, the judge should find out whether it can profitably be resolved through a negotiated settlement or through an arbitrated compromise.

Administrative recourse is dealt with in Title XXII of the Code.

Can. 996 – What is determined concerning decrees in the canons of this title is also to be applied to all particular administrative acts which are placed by any legitimate power in the Church in the external forum outside of a trial with the exception of those issued by the Roman Pontiff or an ecumenical council

Can. 997 – §1. One who considers himself to be injured by a decree can make recourse to the superior authority of the one who gave the decree according to the norm of law.

§2. The first recourse against decrees of the protosyncel-lus[115] or the syncelli is made to the eparchial[116] bishop; against those who act by delegated power, recourse is made to the one who gave the delegation.

Can. 998 – §1. It is very desirable that whenever someone feels injured by a decree, there not be a dispute between this person and the author of the decree but that they seek to find an equitable solution between them, perhaps through the use of wise persons in mediation or study so

---

[115] The protosyncellus is the equivalent office under the Code of Canons of the Eastern Churches to the office of vicar general under Canon 475 of the Western Code. The syncellus is equivalent to an episcopal vicar under Canon 476 of the Western Code. The vicar general is the main executive officer for the bishop in his diocese. An episcopal vicar's authority is similar to that of a vicar general, but is limited to a particular territory of the diocese, a specific type of activity, such as education, clergy, or health care, of a specific category of persons designated by rite or by some other characteristic such as language or culture: Beal, Coriden, and Green, *New Commentary on the Code of Canon Law* (New York, Paulist Press, 2000), pg. 628–630.

[116] In the Eastern Church, an eparchy is the name for an ecclesiastical province. See the *Oxford Dictionary of the Christian Church*, 3rd. edn.

that through a voluntary emendation of the decree or through just compensation or by some other suitable means the controversy may be avoided.

§2. The superior authority should encourage the parties to do this before he receives the appeal.[117]

There is no provision in the Eastern Code equivalent to Canon 1733 §2 and §3 of the Western Code, which deals with diocesan mediation offices or councils to handle administrative disputes. But, this apart, the texts of the two Codes are almost identical.[118]

---

[117] *Code of Canons of the Eastern Churches* (Washington, Canon Law Society of America, 1990).

[118] There are slight differences in the Latin text for the Western and Eastern churches.

Western Code

1446 §1. Christifideles omnes, in primis autem Episcopi, sedulo annitantur ut, salva iustitia, lites in populo Dei, *quantum fieri possit,* vitentur *et pacifice* quam primum componantur
1446 §2 Iudex in limine litis, et etiam quolibet alio momento, *quotiescumque spem aliquam* boni exitus perspicit, partes hortari et adiuvare ne omittat, ut de aequa controversiae solutione quaerenda communi consilio curent, viasque ad hoc propositum idoneas ipsis indicet, gravibus quoque hominibus ad mediationem adhibitis.
1733 §1. Valde optandum est ut, *quoties* quis gravatum se decreto *putet, vitetur inter ipsum et decreti auctorem contentio atque* inter eos de aequa solutione quaerenda *communi consilio curretur*, gravibus quoque *personis* ad mediationem *et* studium forte adhibitis, ita ut *per idoneam vel* dirimatur.

Eastern Code

1103 §1. Christifideles omnes, in primis autem Episcopi, sedulo annitantur ut, salva iustitia, lites in populo Dei, *quatenus fieri potest,* vitentur *vel pacifice* quam primum componantur
1103 §2. Iudex in limine litis, et etiam quolibet alio momento, *quoties spem* boni exitus perspicit, partes hortari et adiuvare ne omittat, ut de aequa controversiae solutione quaerenda communi consilio curent, viasque ad hoc propositum *assequendum* idoneas ipsis indicet, gravibus quoque hominibus ad mediationem adhibitis.

In summary, the Canon law codes for both the Western and the Eastern Roman Catholic Church provide expressly for mediation as a means for resolving church disputes.

6. FORMAL DISPUTE RESOLUTION WITHIN THE CHURCH OF ENGLAND

Against this background of scriptural, historical, and comparative support for the use of mediation, how does the Church of England resolve its disputes? The answer is, by both formal and informal means. The extent to which the Church of England uses informal means such as mediation will form the subject of chapter 3. At this stage it is appropriate to look at the formal means.

A number of courts and tribunals are available to deal with church disputes within the Church of England. Some are specifically Church courts and tribunals, established by Measure.[119] Others are secular courts and tribunals, which have jurisdiction over church matters as well as secular matters. As will be shown,[120] many church disputes are not specifically related to Church law. For such disputes, the ordinary secular courts and tribunals are the forum where they may be resolved. There is also an important administrative jurisdiction exercised by bishops and others.

---

998 §1. Valde optandum est, ut, *si* quis gravatum se decreto *putat, non fiat inter ipsum et decreti auctorem contentio, sed* inter eos de aequa solutione quaerenda *tractetur*, gravibus quoque *hominibus* ad mediationem *vel* studium forte adhibitis ita, ut *per voluntariam decreti emendationem vel per iustam compensationem vel per aliam idoneam viam controversia* dirimatur.

[119] The General Synod of the Church of England has the power to legislate by Measure: Synodical Government Measure 1969, section 2(1). Measures have the full force and effect of Acts of Parliament: Church of England Assembly (Powers) Act 1919, section 4.

[120] See figure 2 on pg. 90; and chapter 3 generally.

a) Church courts and tribunals

Church courts and tribunals exist to deal with disciplinary matters arising from the conduct of deacons, priests, bishops and archbishops, issues concerning church buildings and their contents, and matters of doctrine. There are also tribunals to deal with proceedings under the Incumbents (Vacation of Benefices) Measure 1977.[121]

i Consistory court

The Ecclesiastical Jurisdiction Measure 1963 provides that for each diocese there is to be a court known as the consistory court, presided over by a judge known as a chancellor.[122] By far the majority of the work of the consistory court is dealing with matters relating to church buildings and property through the exercise of the faculty jurisdiction. It also deals with proceedings in relation to offences under the Ecclesiastical Jurisdiction Measure 1963 by priests or deacons in the diocese, but not if the offence is one concerning doctrine, ritual or ceremonial.[123] Those matters are heard in a separate court known as the Court of Ecclesiastical Causes Reserved.

---

[121] See generally, Mark Hill, *Ecclesiastical Law*, 2nd edn. (Oxford University Press, 2001), chapter 6.

[122] Ecclesiastical Jurisdiction Measure 1963, s 1(1). In Canterbury, the court is known as the commissary court. Chancellors must be at least 30 years old, and have held a 7 year qualification within the meaning of the Courts and Legal Services Act 1990, or a person who has held high judicial office. If the chancellor is a layman, the bishop shall satisfy himself that the person to be appointed is a communicant: Ecclesiastical Jurisdiction Measure 1963, s. 2(2).

[123] Ecclesiastical Jurisdiction Measure 1963, s. 6.

ii Jurisdiction over offences against church law

The criminal jurisdiction applies to all in holy orders.[124] There are two types of proceedings, doctrine cases, and 'conduct' cases.[125] Proceedings concerning a matter of doctrine, ritual or ceremonial are heard by the Court of Ecclesiastical Causes Reserved; proceedings in respect of all other ecclesiastical offences, including conduct unbecoming the office and work of a clerk in holy orders, and serious, persistent or continuous neglect of duty, are heard in the consistory court.

Proceedings are commenced by way of a written complaint in the prescribed form. Whenever a priest or deacon is accused of an offence under the Ecclesiastical Jurisdiction Measure 1963 or in a secular court of a criminal offence the bishop may order him not to perform any services in the diocese pending the resolution of the proceedings, if the bishop considers it desirable in the interests of the Church.[126]

Where the complaint in a conduct case is laid against a priest or deacon,[127] the accused person is first interviewed privately by

---

[124] Ecclesiastical Jurisdiction Measure 1963, s. 17.

[125] Ecclesiastical Jurisdiction Measure 1963, s. 14.

[126] Ecclesiastical Jurisdiction Measure 1963, s 77. Although the section refers to cases where a charge is pending, there may be occasions where action is necessary even earlier. Thus, in May 2001, the Bishop of Blackburn suspended one of his archdeacons, the Ven. Dr John Marsh, after police investigation into visits to child-pornography sites on the Internet, before any formal charges were brought: *Church Times*, 25 May 2001, News, pg. 3. (Dr Marsh later resigned as archdeacon, even though police cleared him of having committed any offence: *Yorkshire Post*, 29 October 2001.)

[127] The procedure is different where the accused person is a bishop or archbishop: see Ecclesiastical Jurisdiction Measure 1963, s. 32–37. The complaint is referred to a committee rather than an examiner to decide whether there is a case to answer. If there is a case to answer, it is heard not in the consistory court, but by a Commission of Convocation.

33

the bishop. The bishop may decide to take no further action. If the bishop considers the matter should go further, he refers the complaint to an examiner for inquiry. The examiner examines affidavit evidence in support of the complaint, and decides whether there is a case to answer.[128] Both the accused and the complainant are entitled to be represented before the examiner. If there is no case to answer, that is an end of the matter. If there is, the bishop nominates a person to prosecute the case in the consistory court. A system of legal aid is available for the proceedings in the consistory court, based on merit and financial need.[129] The procedure at the hearing is broadly similar to a criminal trial in the Crown Court.[130] The penalties which the court may impose range from a public reprimand[131] to removing the priest from any preferment[132] which he or she holds and disqualification from

---

[128] This is similar to the criminal process known as committal procedure in the magistrates' court under the Magistrates' Court Act 1980, s. 6. The magistrates' court will commit the accused for trial if it is of opinion that there is sufficient evidence to put him on trial by jury for any indictable offence.

[129] See the Church of England (Legal Aid) Measure 1994 and the Church of England (Legal Aid) Rules 1995, SI 1995/2034.

[130] Ecclesiastical Jurisdiction Measure 1963, s. 28.

[131] This censure is called a rebuke: Ecclesiastical Jurisdiction Measure 1963, s. 49(1)(e).

[132] 'Preferment' includes an archbishopric, a bishopric, archdeaconry, dignity or office in a cathedral or collegiate church, and a benefice, and every curacy, lectureship, readership, chaplaincy, office or place which requires the discharge of any spiritual duty: Ecclesiastical Jurisdiction Measure 1963, s. 66(1).

holding any future preferment,[133] together with deposing the priest from holy orders.[134]

There have been only three contested proceedings under the Ecclesiastical Jurisdiction Measure 1963, and these three have cost the Church of England £425,000. Such expense, and the difficulty of establishing the criminal standard of proof have led to proposals for reform,[135] and to the Clergy Discipline Measure 2003, which was approved by Synod in November 2000 but only received the Royal Assent in July 2003.[136]

---

[133] This censure is called 'deprivation': Ecclesiastical Jurisdiction Measure 1963, s. 49(1)(a).

[134] Ecclesiastical Jurisdiction Measure 1963, s. 50. Deposing the priest from holy orders is commonly called 'unfrocking'. The other censures are (a) monition (an order to do, or not to do, a specific act), (b) suspension, a disqualification for a specified time from exercising any functions relating to his preferment, and (c) inhibition, a disqualification for a specified time from exercising any of the functions of his or her order. See the Ecclesiastical Jurisdiction Measure 1963 s. 49(1)(a)–(e).

[135] See *Under Authority, Report on Clergy Discipline* (London, Church House Publishing, 1996). For a critique of one case, see Stephen Pix, 'Archdeacon of Cheltenham v Bland: A sledgehammer to crack a nut', 6 Ecc LJ 135.

[136] For the procedure for parliamentary approval, and how this can lead to legislation which has been approved by Synod needing to be amended, see James Behrens, 'The Churchwardens Measure 2001', 6 Ecc LJ 97. The procedure under the Clergy Discipline Measure 2003 is summarised in Mark Hill, *Ecclesiastical Law*, 2nd edn., pg. 163. The implementation of the Clergy Discipline Measure 2003 will be a very substantial process, and the advice of the chief legal advisor to General Synod is that the measure is unlikely to be brought into force before the end of 2005.

iii Faculty jurisdiction

A faculty is a permission to effect some alteration to a church building, its contents or to its churchyard.[137] The principal Measure dealing with the faculty jurisdiction is the Care of Churches and Ecclesiastical Jurisdiction Measure 1991, and the procedure for applying for a faculty is set out in the Faculty Jurisdiction Rules 2000. Most cases are resolved without the need for a court hearing. Even where there is opposition to the proposed work, the chancellor can sometimes determine the application on the basis of written representations instead of a hearing in open court.[138] But where a court hearing is necessary, it usually takes place in the church where the works are to be carried out.

A description of one such hearing may give a feel for the procedure.[139] Counsel for the vicar and churchwardens arrived at about 9 a.m., was shown round the church, saw the areas in dispute, and discussed various points about the case with the vicar. Shortly afterwards the barrister for the party opposing the grant of a faculty arrived, and he too was shown round the church by his client. The chancel area of the church had three tables set up, making three sides of a square. One table was for the chancellor, and one table for each of the parties. A chair for witnesses made up the fourth side of the square. Microphones were set up on each table, but the acoustics were sufficient to proceed without them. At about 10 a.m. the chancellor and registrar arrived, and they and the lawyers all went to robe.

---

[137] For a general survey, see Mark Hill, *Ecclesiastical Law*, 2nd edn., chapter 7, and James Behrens, *Practical Church Management* (Leominster, Gracewing, 1998),chapter 20.

[138] Faculty Jurisdiction Rules 2000, rule 26.

[139] This is the author's impression of the hearing in *Re St Nicholas, Arundel* (2002) 6 Ecc LJ 290 (Chichester Consistory Court, 26 June 2001, Hill Ch). It should be noted that the hearing is the culmination of the faculty process. The chancellor had made various procedural directions before the author's involvement in the case.

At 10.30 the formal hearing started. In addition to the parties and witnesses, there were between 10 and 20 people sitting in the congregation pews observing the proceedings. The chancellor and registrar processed into the church, and bowed to the cross. The chancellor opened with a prayer asking for 'righteous judgment', and led the people present in the Lord's prayer. The hearing then proceeded in the normal way for a civil trial. The judge had read the trial bundle and the skeleton argument which had been prepared, so the opening lasted a matter of a couple of minutes before the first witness gave evidence. The chancellor is addressed the first time as 'Worshipful Sir', thereafter simply as 'Sir'. The chancellor indicated that he did not require evidence to be given on oath, so the witnesses simply came and sat in the witness chair, confirmed that their witness statements were accurate, explained any parts which needed further comment, and were then cross-examined. The chancellor had asked the bishop to attend as a judge's witness, to give evidence of theology and liturgical practice where that was in issue, so both sides had the privilege of cross-examining a bishop. The court adjourned for lunch at about 1 p.m., and resumed hearing evidence at 2 p.m. There were then submissions by each barrister to close the case. The proceedings were finished by 4 p.m. At the end, the chancellor indicated that he would reserve his judgment, and asked the congregation to stand again for prayer. The proceedings closed with the Grace. The chancellor then looked round the church by himself before leaving. His typed judgment was sent to the parties within a fortnight.

Impressions of the hearing included: the formality of the process; a comment by the vicar that he felt the whole procedure was an intrusion into his church, although he welcomed the fact that the chancellor opened the proceedings with prayer; and a clear sense of Christ's presence during the hearing. The procedure was, in name, adversarial, but all parties were trying to discern God's will, and that was uplifting. While cross-examining the party opposing the faculty, to show that his arguments were mistaken, the atmosphere changed. Did Christ leave at that point? I do not know.[140]

iv Cathedrals

As with the faculty jurisdiction, there is a general prohibition against carrying on any works to cathedrals without specific approval.[141] Applications for such approval are made to a body called the Cathedrals Fabric Commission.[142] If the Cathedrals Fabric Commission refuses to give approval to any proposed works, the administrative body of the cathedral may appeal to a Commission of Review, whose decision is final.[143]

v Appellate courts

Appeals from the consistory court exercising its criminal jurisdiction lie to the Court of the Arches for cases in the province of Canterbury, or to the Chancery Court of York for cases in the province of York. Appeals from faculty cases are heard by the Court of Arches, unless they concern doctrine, ritual or ceremonial.[144] If they concern these 'reserved matters', the appeal lies to

---

[140] This adversarial nature is perhaps the worst feature of a consistory court trial, and can significantly increase the costs of a hearing. In a letter to the author dated 10/12/1998 the rector emeritus of St Helen's, Bishopsgate commented that he considered that the adversarial spirit from the Guildhall planners cost the church £150,000. For the issues in the case, see *Re St Helen's, Bishopsgate* (1993) 3 Ecc LJ 256; (1993) 12 Consistory and Commissary Court Cases, Case 23.

[141] Care of Cathedrals Measure 1990, s. 2.

[142] Care of Cathedrals Measure 1990, s. 6.

[143] Care of Cathedrals Measure 1990, s. 10.

[144] For the procedure for faculty appeals, see the Faculty Jurisdiction (Appeals) Rules 1998.

the Court of Ecclesiastical Causes Reserved.[145] This esteemed court[146] has only sat twice since it was created in 1963.[147]

vi Vacation of benefices

In cases of serious breakdown in the pastoral relationship between the incumbent and the parishioners, a formal procedure exists to bring matters to a resolution: the Incumbents (Vacation of Benefices) Measure 1977. The Measure allows for an inquiry to be made at the request of the incumbent, the archdeacon or two-thirds of the lay members of the PCC. Notice of intention to request an inquiry is given to the bishop. There is then an obligatory delay of between six and twelve months to enable the parties to see if they can resolve the breakdown.

If matters are not resolved, the bishop directs the archdeacon to make a report. If the archdeacon considers that an inquiry would be in the best interest of the incumbent and the parishioners, then the bishop may direct the secretary of the diocesan

---

[145] Ecclesiastical Jurisdiction Measure 1963 s.10. The Court of Ecclesiastical Causes Reserved in theory also sits as a court of first instance in cases of ecclesiastical offences involving a matter of doctrine, ritual or ceremonial: Ecclesiastical Jurisdiction Measure 1963 s. 14(1)(a), 10(1). In practice it has never done so, and if the current proposals to amend clergy discipline are passed by parliament, it never will.

[146] The composition of the Court of Ecclesiastical Causes Reserved is two persons holding or formerly holding high judicial office and three current or former diocesan bishops: Ecclesiastical Jurisdiction Measure 1963 s. 5. In *In re St. Michael and All Angels, Great Torrington* [1985] Fam. 81 the court comprised Sir Hugh Forbes, Sir Anthony Lloyd, the Bishop of Rochester, the Bishop of Chichester and the Rt Revd Kenneth Woollcombe, former bishop of Oxford. In *In re St. Stephen's, Walbrook* [1987] Fam. 146 the court comprised Sir Anthony Lloyd, the Bishop of Rochester, the Bishop of Chichester, the Rt Revd Kenneth Woollcombe and Sir Ralph Gibson.

[147] *In re St. Michael and All Angels, Great Torrington* [1985] Fam. 81, and *In re St. Stephen's, Walbrook* [1987] Fam. 146.

synod to institute an inquiry. This inquiry is conducted by a provincial tribunal consisting of five persons appointed by the vicar-general of the province.[148] The tribunal may order the incumbent to undergo a medical examination, and may draw inferences from his failure to co-operate. The tribunal reports to the bishop whether in its opinion there has been a serious breakdown in the pastoral relationship, and it must recommend the action to be taken by the bishop.

On the basis of the tribunal's recommendation the bishop may (a) make a declaration of avoidance, declaring the benefice vacant, (b) rebuke the incumbent, (c) rebuke the parishioners, and (d) disqualify them from holding office. Where an incumbent resigns his benefice or is removed from office under this procedure, he is entitled to very significant financial compensation.[149] The procedure has been described as 'pretty unworkable in practice'.[150] The size of this potential financial compensation must also be a significant disincentive to many dioceses bringing proceedings under this Measure.

---

[148] For the procedure, see the Incumbents (Vacation of Benefices) Rules 1994.

[149] Incumbents (Vacation of Benefices) Rules 1994, s. 13 and Schedule 2. A person under 50 is entitled to monthly payments for a minimum of 3 years. In the first year, he or she gets the national minimum stipend (slightly in excess of £16,000 in 2001), in the second year 3/4 of the stipend, and thereafter 2/3 of the stipend. A person over 50 is entitled to monthly payments until five years before retirement age. This is 65 in the case of men, and 60 for women: see the Church of England Pensions Regulations 1988, SI 1988/2256 regulation 2(1), as applied by the Incumbents (Vacation of Benefices) Rules 1994, SI 1994/703, Schedule 2, section 8(1) and (2). The person also gets a housing allowance for the whole of this period, and a resettlement allowance of 3/10 of the national stipend for one year.

[150] Archdeacon of Basingstoke (Diocese of Winchester).

b) Secular courts

i Judicial review

The courts of the Church of England are subject to judicial review if they act *ultra vires* or in breach of natural justice.[151] Bishops exercising administrative functions are also subject to judicial review over such areas as suspension of presentation,[152] women priests,[153] disciplinary proceedings,[154] and the failure to renew the licence of a team rector.[155]

ii Employment tribunals (for non-clergy)

Ordained clergy are not employees, and so have no right to compensation for unfair dismissal.[156] The failure to renew the licence of a team rector is however an administrative act which is subject to judicial review.[157] Section 23 of the Employment Relations Act 1999 empowers the Secretary of State to make provision that certain persons be treated as employees for the purpose of employment legislation,[158] and the Department of Trade and Industry is currently (2001) considering making an order under sec-

---

[151] See Mark Hill, *Ecclesiastical Law*, 2nd edn., pg. 166.

[152] See pg. 98.

[153] *R v Dean and Chapter of St Paul's Cathedral and another ex parte Williamson*, Queen's Bench Division (Crown Office List), CO/992/97, (hearing date 22 August 1997), reported at (1997) 5 Ecc LJ 129 and [1998] COD 130.

[154] See *R v Provincial Court of the Church in Wales ex parte Williams*, 23 October 1998, *Lexis* report, and (1999) 5 Ecc LJ 217.

[155] *R v Bishop of Stafford ex parte Owen* (2000) 6 Ecc LJ 83. The judgment is set out in Mark Hill, *Ecclesiastical Law*, 2nd edn., pg. 723.

[156] *Diocese of Southwark v Coker* [1998] ICR 140.

[157] *R v Bishop of Stafford ex parte Owen* (2000) 6 Ecc LJ 83; Mark Hill, *Ecclesiastical Law*, 2nd edn., pg. 723.

[158] Including specifically the Trade Union and Labour Relations (Consolidation) Act 1992 and the Employment Rights Act 1996.

tion 23 relating to clergy and ministers of religion.[159] Employment legislation does however apply to non-clergy, and cases of unfair dismissal have arisen.[160]

iii Privy Council

Before the Reformation, parties could appeal to Rome from the provincial court of appeal (the Court of the Arches or the Chancery Court of York). At the Reformation, appeals to Rome were abolished,[161] and in their place a final appeal lay to the King in Council, the jurisdiction being exercised by a tribunal known as the Court of Delegates.[162] In the nineteenth century, this appellate jurisdiction was transferred to the Judicial Committee of the Privy Council.[163] Under the Ecclesiastical Jurisdiction Measure 1963 there is now a final appeal to the Privy Council only for faculty cases not involving matters of doctrine, ritual or ceremonial.[164]

The Privy Council does however exercise an important jurisdiction concerning draft schemes under the Pastoral Measure 1983.[165]

---

[159] See Stephen Trott, 'Dignity at Work', 6 Ecc LJ 51.

[160] See 'Employment disputes', pg. 107.

[161] Ecclesiastical Appeals Act 1532.

[162] Submission of the Clergy Act 1533.

[163] Privy Council Appeals Act 1832. For this history, see Timothy Briden and Brian Hanson's *Moore's Introduction to English Canon Law*, 3rd edn. (London, Mowbray, 1992), pg. 112.

[164] Ecclesiastical Jurisdiction Measure 1963 section 8. For the procedure, see the Faculty Jurisdiction (Appeals) Rules 1998, rules 25 and 26.

[165] Pastoral Measure 1983, s. 9(1). *Cheesman v Church Commissioners* [2000] 1 AC 19; (1999) 5 Ecc LJ 305, concerning the Gaulby Group Benefice, was an appeal under this jurisdiction. The case is discussed at pg. 102.

iv High Court and County Court

Church disputes involving title to property, defamation, personal injury, and commercial contracts[166] are all determined in the High Court or the County Court as appropriate.[167] Recent High Court cases with an ecclesiastical element have included such varied issues as the liability for chancel repairs,[168] an injunction to prevent the ordination of a curate,[169] a defamation action,[170] the legislative powers of Synod,[171] the investment policy of the Church Commissioners,[172] and allegedly negligent tax advice.[173]

---

[166] For examples of each of these categories, see chapter 3.

[167] CPR Part 7 Practice Direction sets out the rules to determine which claims should be brought in the High Court and which in the County Court. For example, in general proceedings may not be brought in the High Court unless the value of the claim is over £15,000. In the case of personal injury claims, proceedings may not be brought in the High Court unless the value of the claim is over £50,000. Tax disputes are usually determined by a tribunal, with an appeal to the High Court on a point of law. Thus, for example, *St Dunstan's Roman Catholic Church, Southborough v Customs and Excise Commissioners* [1998] V & DR 264 is a decision of the VAT and Duties Tribunal.

[168] *Aston Cantlow PCC v Wallbank* [2003] UKHL 37, [2003] 3 WLR 283.

[169] *Gill v Davies* (1997) 5 Ecc LJ 131. The full judgment is printed in Mark Hill, *Ecclesiastical Law*, 2nd edn., pg. 707.

[170] *St James, Hockwold, near Thetford, Norfolk* (Mr and Mrs Dallimore), see 'Defamation', pg. 114.

[171] *Brown v Runcie, Times,* 20 February 1991. The full judgment is printed in Mark Hill, *Ecclesiastical Law*, 2nd edn., pg. 649.

[172] *Harries v Church Commissioners* [1992 1 WLR 1241.

[173] *Liverpool RC Diocese v Goldberg* [2001] 1 All ER 172. The claim was settled after the draft judgment was circulated to the parties: *Liverpool RC Trustees Inc v Goldberg (No. 3) (Practice Note)* [2001] 1 WLR 2337.

c) Administrative oversight

i Visitation

'Visitation, the policing of administrative activities, is treated as a pastoral exercise; its purposes are investigation, prevention and cure.'[174] The purpose of a visitation is that the bishop may 'get some good knowledge of the state, sufficiency, and ability of the clergy and other person whom he is to visit'.[175] Archbishops, bishops and archdeacons have the right to visit their province, diocese or archdeaconry to perform acts for 'the edifying and well-governing of Christ's flock, that means may be taken thereby for the supply of such things as are lacking and the correction of such things as are amiss'.[176] The procedure begins with the bishop[177] delivering to the minister of the parishes concerned 'such articles of inquiry' as the bishop shall require, containing questions relating to the administration of the parish and the life and health of the parish generally. The minister and churchwardens answer these articles, and the bishop then takes matters on from there, as necessary.

Diocesan bishops act as visitor for the cathedral of the diocese.[178] As visitor, the bishop must hear and determine questions as to the construction of the cathedral constitution and statutes. He may hold a visitation when he considers it desirable, or on request. In the course of a visitation, he may give directions to the cathedral Chapter or to any office holder or employee, and these

---

[174] Norman Doe, *Legal Framework of the Church of England* (Oxford, Clarendon Press, 1996), pg. 122.

[175] Canon C 18 par. 4.

[176] Canon G 5 par. 1.

[177] Or archbishop or archdeacon, as appropriate.

[178] Cathedrals Measure 1999, s. 6(3). Section 38(2) of the measure sets out transitional provisions for the application of the measure to particular cathedrals. See Mark Hill, *Ecclesiastical Law*, 2nd edn., pg. 225 for some of the transitional dates.

persons must observe any such determinations or directions.[179] The bishop also has powers as visitor to deal with any failure by the cathedral Chapter to carry out its duties of care and maintenance.[180]

Royal peculiars[181] have their own statutes, and their own provisions for visitation. Under the Royal Charter of 21st May 1560 the reigning monarch is the visitor for Westminster Abbey. It was therefore to the Queen that Dr Neary appealed his suspension as organist of Westminster Abbey.[182]

ii Revocation of licences

Parochial clergy fall into two categories: beneficed and unbeneficed. A beneficed cleric holds a freehold office, if he so wishes, until retirement, subject to being removed following proceedings under the Incumbents (Vacation of Benefices) Measure 1977 or the Ecclesiastical Jurisdiction Measure 1963. An unbeneficed cleric holds no freehold office. Unbeneficed clergy include priests-in-charge, those appointed to team ministries, curates, chaplains, lecturers and preachers, ministers of chapels, and retired clergy.[183] Unbeneficed clergy require the bishop's licence to officiate within the bishop's diocese. Team vicars hold office for a term of years, and during that term can only be removed by proceedings under the Incumbents (Vacation of Benefices) Meas-

---

[179] Cathedrals Measure 1999 s. 6(4)–(7).

[180] For these duties, see the Care of Cathedrals Measure 1990; for their enforcement, see the Care of Cathedrals (Supplementary Provisions) Measure 1994.

[181] A peculiar is a place which, although surrounded by a diocese, is not under the control of the bishop, nor is it visitable by him. They include the Temple, the Universities of Oxford and Cambridge, and certain Oxbridge colleges. Royal peculiars have the Crown as visitor.

[182] *Neary v Dean of Westminster* [1999] IRLR 288, (1998) 5 Ecc LJ 303. This case is fully considered in chapter 2.

[183] See Mark Hill, *Ecclesiastical Law*, 2nd edn., pg. 100.

ure 1977 or the Ecclesiastical Jurisdiction Measure 1963.[184] All
other licences may be revoked summarily at any time 'for any
cause which appears to the bishop to be good and reasonable'.[185]
Similar provisions apply for readers,[186] lay workers,[187] and dea-
conesses.[188]

This power to revoke a licence is a very wide power, considerably easier to invoke than the cumbersome procedure under the
Incumbents (Vacation of Benefices) Measure 1977 or the Ecclesiastical Jurisdiction Measure 1963. This ease has given cause for
concern.[189] Even easier is a bishop's decision not to renew a licence. Against this no appeal lies to the archbishop, and the only
route which appears to be open to a priest who wishes to challenge such a decision is to seek judicial review.[190]

---

[184] Pastoral Measure 1983 s. 20(3). See *Calvert v Gardiner* [2002] EWHC
1394, [2003] 7 Ecc LJ 99.

[185] Canon C 12, par. 5. The bishop must first serve a notice giving the
minister sufficient opportunity of showing reason to the contrary, and
there is a right of appeal to the archbishop of the province.

[186] Canon E 6 par. 3.

[187] Canon E 8 par. 5.

[188] Canon D 3 par. 3A.

[189] G. R. Evans, *Discipline & Justice in the Church of England* (Leominster,
Gracewing, 1998), chapters 3 and 6.

[190] Judicial review is only available where the decision is procedurally
unfair or manifestly unreasonable. *R v Bishop of Stafford ex parte Owen*
(2000) 6 Ecc LJ 83 is one case where this was alleged, but the bishop's
decision was upheld. The judgment is set out in Mark Hill, *Ecclesiastical
Law*, 2nd edn., pg. 723. Strictly the case was not one of dismissal, but of
refusal to renew a licence. The practical effect is the same, and the court
was prepared to assume that it had jurisdiction. However Schiemann LJ
sounded a note of caution against pressing the analogy with summary
dismissal too far.

iii Church services

Lastly, the bishop has a number of powers to determine liturgical disputes within his diocese. Before a parish priest changes the type of robes he wears he should consult the PCC. If they do not agree, the bishop decides the point.[191] Similarly, if the minister cannot agree with the parties which form of service to use for one of the services known as occasional offices,[192] the matter may be referred to the bishop for his decision.[193] If any question arises as to whether a particular form of service is lawful, this too may be referred to the bishop for his decision.[194] A similar provision concerns refusal of admission to communion.[195]

It will be seen that disputes over forms of worship cover a much broader spectrum than those to which these express powers apply.[196] These powers are not therefore sufficient to resolve all types of worship and doctrine disputes.

---

[191] Canon B 8, par. 2.

[192] It is not entirely clear what services are known as the 'occasional offices': Rupert Bursell, *Liturgy, Order and the Law* (Oxford, Clarendon Press, 1996), pg. 61. The *Oxford Dictionary of the Christian Church*, 3rd. edn. distinguishes the occasional offices (offices used only as occasion may demand) from the 'constant offices' of the Church (Mattins, Evensong and the Holy Communion). Thus the occasional offices include Baptism, Confirmation, Matrimony, Visitation of the Sick, Communion of the Sick, and Burial of the Dead.

[193] Canon B 3, par. 4.

[194] Canon B 5, par. 4. The Canon provides that such a reference is without prejudice to the matter in question being made the subject matter of proceedings under the Ecclesiastical Jurisdiction Measure 1963.

[195] Canon B 16.f.

[196] See pg. 103.

7. SCHEME OF RESEARCH

i *The adversarial system*

Mention has been made of the fact that the procedure in Church courts is now adversarial. The examination begins with a detailed analysis of one recent and much publicised dispute: the Westminster Abbey dispute of 1998 (chapter 2). The adversarial way this dispute was handled shows what can happen under the present dispute resolution system used in the Church of England.

ii *The types of Church dispute*

Chapter 3 seeks to do two things: first, to categorise the types of dispute which occur, and second, to analyse how they are currently handled within the Church of England. A combination of methods was used to identify the types of disputes which occur. These included computer searches using *Lexis/Nexis* into newspaper reports over a seven-year period (1993–1999). Reference was made to the law reports, legal textbooks, and the extensive Christian literature on the subject of church disputes. Use was also made of the author's personal experience of church disputes both professionally as a barrister involved in this work,[197] and as a former church warden. Personal experience of being involved in the planning of an interdenominational conference on the subject of church conflict held in October 1989[198] provided useful contact

---

[197] The author is recommended by *Chambers & Partners Guide to the Legal Profession 2002–2003* (London, Chambers & Partners Publishing, 2002) as a barrister specialising in church law. He is the author of two books on church law: *Confirmation, Sacrament of Grace* (Leominster, Gracewing, 1995), and *Practical Church Management* (Leominster, Gracewing, 1998). He holds the degree of Master of Laws (Canon Law), is a member of the executive committee of the Ecclesiastical Law Society, and is Chancellor of the Diocese of Leicester.

[198] The conference was organised by CEDR (pronounced as in the cedar tree). The letters CEDR stand for the Centre for Effective Dispute Resolution.

with members of the Scottish Episcopal Church, the United Reformed Church, the Roman Catholic Church, Lutherans, Methodists, Baptists, Mennonites, Pentecostals, and the Church in Wales, as well as Church of England members. In particular the conference indicated that there was much common ground between the different denominations present at the conference concerning the types of church disputes.

Ecclesiastically, England is divided into 43 dioceses, each under the charge of a bishop. Each diocese is divided into a number of archdeaconries, with each archdeaconry under the charge of an archdeacon. A survey was conducted of all 112 archdeacons and 43 diocesan secretaries in England, to build up a picture of how each diocese handles conflict.[199] From previous work,[200] the author had found that archdeacons are often the first people in authority in the Church of England to whom congregations turn when conflicts arise. The diocesan secretary is the point of contact for any inquiries about administrative arrangements in the diocese.

iii The three main models of mediation

The three main models of mediation – commercial mediation, community mediation, and consensus-building mediation – are next examined to assess their suitability for church disputes (Chapters 4, 5 and 6).

Use was made of the author's previous experience of commercial mediation,[201] of his current involvement with community

---

[199] See appendix 2 for the text of the letters sent to archdeacons and diocesan secretaries.

[200] James Behrens, *Practical Church Management*, chapter 15, 'Resolving Conflicts'.

[201] The author became a CEDR registered mediator in 1998, and has had practical experience of commercial mediation since this date as part of his work as a barrister.

mediation,[202] of two Christian-based mediation training courses,[203] and of the training course organised by a local community mediation service.[204]

iv Mediation in the Anglican Communion

It will be seen in chapter 4 that a number of other countries have wide experience of mediation. During 2000 an extensive survey of the Anglican Churches in Australia, Canada, Hong Kong, New Zealand, South Africa and the USA was therefore conducted to see, in particular, how helpful they find mediation for each type of dispute identified in chapter 3, and what model or format of mediation they use. The results of this survey are contained in chapter 7.

8. SUMMARY

We have seen that there are good Scriptural foundations for the use of informal dispute resolution processes; that from the early Church almost to the present day mediation has been used by bishops and judges of Church courts to reconcile disputing parties; and that mediation is expressly provided for as part of the dispute resolution processes of the Roman Catholic Church. We have seen that Church courts in England adopted an inquisitorial

---

[202] The author does voluntary work as a community mediator for Camden Mediation Service. In November 2000 the author became a director of Mediation UK, a registered charity which acts as an umbrella organisation, providing support for local community mediation services. His work with Mediation UK has enabled him to compare the work of Camden Mediation Services with other services elsewhere in the country.

[203] The author attended four courses run by the London Mennonite Centre, including a five-day training course in 2000, which covered both community and consensus-building mediation. He also took part in a two-day mediation training course run by the United Reformed Church.

[204] A six-day training course run by one local community mediation service in London (Camden Mediation Service).

procedure until about 1850, and that this inquisitorial procedure has parallels with the investigative skills used in mediation. There is thus good reason to believe that mediation might have a role, or more of a role, in dispute resolution within the Church of England. There is also reason to suspect that the modern adversarial procedure used by Church courts in England may make settlement of these disputes more difficult, and for this reason may not be in the Church's best interests.

As an example of the modern adversarial approach, and to show clearly, first, what can happen when the Scriptural principles set out above[205] are not followed, and second, that the present system needs to be amended, the Westminster Abbey dispute is now examined in detail.

---

[205] See pg. 6.

Chapter 2

THE WESTMINSTER ABBEY DISPUTE

The proceedings of the appeal heard by Lord Jauncey have not been made public. In writing about this dispute the author has had recourse to press reports of the case and the reasons Lord Jauncey published for his finding.

The dispute between the Dean and Chapter of Westminster Abbey and the organist Dr Martin Neary in 1998 created considerable adverse publicity for the Church of England. The lessons to be learned from the dispute are not limited to cathedrals and royal peculiars, but embrace all lay employment within the Church. Two principal lessons will be shown to emerge from this dispute. First, it is clear that modern management methods suitable for a commercial organisation are not always appropriate for the resolution of conflict in a Christian organisation. Second, it is clear that the Church needs a better way of resolving disputes than the formal procedures used in this case.

From the very start, the reporting of the dispute by some of the press was very prejudiced against the Dean. In particular, the *Sunday Times'* reporting was described subsequently as 'unremitting propaganda against the Dean'.[1] Significantly, the *Sunday Times* was silent when the Dean ultimately emerged the victor. In relying on press reports there is clearly a possibility that some of the facts stated may be erroneous and that some of this may have affected the author's analysis.

1. THE BACKGROUND

Dr Neary's appointment as Organist and Master of the Choristers at Westminster Abbey took effect from 1st January 1988.[2] On 20th March 1998 Dr Neary was suspended on full pay. On 9th April 1998 a disciplinary hearing took place before the Dean, and on 22nd April 1998 Dr Neary was dismissed with immediate effect.

On 6th December 1988 Mrs Neary was appointed as temporary part-time secretary to Dr Neary, working a two-and-a-half day week. This appointment was confirmed in April 1989. In December 1991 she was appointed as concert secretary which increased her part-time work to three days a week. She also was suspended on 20th March and dismissed on 22nd April 1998.

Dr Neary's musical ability was not in issue. Like one of his predecessors, Henry Purcell, he began his career as a chorister at the Chapel Royal. He was an organ scholar at Gonville and Caius College, Cambridge. Prior to moving to Westminster Abbey he

---

[1] *Church Times,* 18 December 1998, pg. 15.

[2] Dr Neary's predecessor, the internationally distinguished organist Simon Preston, left Westminster Abbey in 1987.

had been the organist of Winchester Cathedral. He was also president of the Royal College of Organists.

From 1974 to 1987 Dr Carr was chaplain and then canon residentiary of Chelmsford Cathedral, where he overlapped with the Very Revd John Moses, its provost and now Dean of St Paul's Cathedral. In 1987 he moved from Chelmsford to Bristol Cathedral, where he was known as an imaginative and efficient moderniser.

Shortly after his appointment to Westminster Abbey, the Abbey was used for the funeral of Diana, Princess of Wales on 6 September 1997. The Dean had overall command of the organisation, and the music was organised by Dr Neary. The service was widely praised. Dr Neary was appointed Lieutenant of the Royal Victorian Order in the New Year honours 1998, in recognition of his musical direction at the funeral.[3]

Amongst the changes that occurred during Dr Carr's first year of office at Westminster Abbey was a programme called 'recovering the calm'. This was a crowd control operation, to restore peace in an environment which had become noisy and crowded. It was a success. He also introduced entry charges of £5 to the royal chapels, and installed security cameras. More controversial was the decision to dismiss volunteers aged over 70, and the manner in which this was accomplished.[4] After the dismissal of Dr Neary, the Dean found himself in further controversy in October 1998 when an attempt was made to ban the Christmas tree from the Abbey. This was changed when it was found that

---

[3] He was also praised for his musical direction of the service for the golden wedding celebration of the Queen and the Duke of Edinburgh in 1997.

[4] A matter which was the subject of adverse comment in the programme *The Abbey Story* (part 1), broadcast on BBC Radio 4 on 10 June 1999.

the tree was an annual gift from the Queen.[5] He was also criticised for the decision to sell several hundred wooden chairs from the Abbey.[6]

2. THE INITIAL SUSPENSION

The first press report of Dr Neary's suspension appeared on 30 March 1998. Initial reports in the newspapers were vague as to the reason why Dr Neary had been suspended. On 31 March 1998, *The Times* reported

> Although the details have not been disclosed, the allegations concerned the administration of the abbey's music department, and centred on a number of foreign concerts performed by the choir, including a recent trip to Oslo.

Likewise, the *Guardian* of 31 March reported that Dr Neary

> has been suspended pending a disciplinary hearing over alleged 'financial irregularities' concerning overseas trips by the choir. His letter of suspension warned that the hearing could lead to him being sacked.

Christopher Compston, a circuit judge whose son Rupert was at the time an Abbey chorister, wrote to the Dean, offering to meet him, but the Dean refused to discuss the matter.[7] *The Times* quotes Judge Compston as saying

> This is all extremely sad. Dr Neary is a talented musician who has done the abbey considerable service for ten years, as has his wife, in a quiet and kindly way. Although I make no judgment on the actual facts, if true at all they do seem to be very minor. It seems to me that this affair has been blown out of all proportion.

---

[5] *The Times*, 10 October 1998; *Independent*, 9 November 1998, comment, pg. 3.

[6] *Church Times*, 23 October 1998, pg. 3.

[7] The author has seen a copy of the letter sent by Judge Compston to the Dean.

56

He said the charges against Dr Neary were 'extremely small fry', adding 'In my view, there is no fault at all'.

Judge Compston pleaded for Christian spirit to prevail at the Abbey.

> I have offered to try to resolve things. I would like people to shake hands, solve some minor points, and have a good Easter.

On 1 April, in a letter to *The Times,* Judge Compston called for an independent tribunal.

The *Guardian* and the *Daily Mail*[8] refer to another obvious disciplinary failing on behalf of the Abbey

> Dr Neary also wants a friend to accompany him to the hearing. But the abbey authorities have rejected Mr Field, Labour MP for Birkenhead and a Privy Counsellor, allegedly saying Dr Neary could only be represented by another abbey employee.[9]

The media realised that the row threatened to embroil the Abbey in the kind of turmoil that had recently engulfed other cathedrals, in particular, the trouble at Lincoln with Dr Brandon Jackson,[10] and the dispute at St Paul's over the appointment of the Revd Lucy Winkett as a minor canon.[11]

---

[8] *Guardian (London)*, 31 March 1998, Guardian home page, pg. 6. *Daily Mail (London)*, 31 March 1998, pg. 7.

[9] For the importance of allowing a person to have a friend or colleague present during the disciplinary hearing, see *Practical Church Management,* pg. 109.

[10] For the dispute at Lincoln Cathedral, see *Daily Mail,* 20 July 1995, pg. 1, 6, 7; *Daily Mirror,* 18 July 1995, pg. 3; *Daily Telegraph,* 22 July 1997, pg. 8; 14 January 1998, pg. 6; 14 January 1998, pg. 6; 20 July 1995, front page; 21 July 1995, pg. 9; 24 July 1995, pg. 2; 4 March 1995 pg. 5; 4 March 1995, pg. 5; *Guardian,* 6 March 1995, Guardian Home Page, pg. 4; 22 July 1997, home page, pg. 4; *Sunday Times,* 30 March 1997, home news; *The Times,* 22 July 1995, home news; 22 July 1997, home news; 30

The details of Dr Neary's alleged offence were still obscure, but Mr Field is quoted as believing that the affair should have been resolved without Dr Neary being barred from his duties. However the report in the *Sunday Times* for 5 April gives more detail than was available a week earlier.

> Neary and his wife act as agents for the abbey choir, and concert fees are channelled through a business bank account separate from abbey funds. Carr is said to be incensed that the abbey did not profit from certain overseas tours.

By this time the Abbey choirboys had been banned from seeing either Dr or Mrs Neary.[12]

Dr Neary took advice initially from Cherie Booth QC, who specialises in employment law. The involvement of the Prime Minister's wife added to the media excitement over the story.[13]

3. EFFORTS TO NEGOTIATE A SETTLEMENT

In addition to Judge Compston's offer, an offer to mediate was made in February by Lord Weatherill, former speaker of the House of Commons, and a senior official at the Abbey. This offer

---

December 1995, home news; 5 July 1996, home news.

[11] For the dispute at St Paul's Cathedral, see *Daily Telegraph,* 13 February 1997, pg. 1; *Sunday Times,* 11 May 1997, home news. 'St Paul's faithful walk out in row over woman priest'.

[12] *Sunday Times,* 5 April 1998, Sunday, Home news. According to the programme *The Abbey Story* (part 1), broadcast on BBC Radio 4 on 10 June 1999, the newspapers supplied to Westminster Abbey Choir School had stories about the dispute excised, so that the boys had to telephone their parents to find out what was happening.

[13] *Sunday Times,* 5 April 1998, Sunday, Home news. Cherie Booth QC only acted in the initial stages of the dispute. At the trial, the Nearys were represented by Patrick Elias QC. There would have been embarrassing political implications for the Prime Minister's wife to take on a case involving the Queen.

was not accepted.[14] The Revd Colin Semper, former canon treasurer of the Abbey, also tried to achieve a reconciliation, but apparently the Dean refused to discuss the plan.[15] One choir school parent urged the Bishop of London, the Rt Revd Richard Chartres, who is also Dean of the Chapels Royal, to intervene. He responded

> The Dean of the Chapels Royal and the Bishop of London have no standing whatsoever in Westminster Abbey and this is frequently made very clear.[16]

On 17 and 21 April, two without prejudice meetings were held at solicitors' offices in an attempt to reach a settlement.[17] One possibility discussed was a short-term reinstatement to allow Dr Neary to stay at the Abbey for a few months, and then 'go quietly', but no settlement was reached.[18]

4. DISMISSAL

The negotiations failed. On 22 April, Dr and Mrs Neary were dismissed by the Dean and Chapter for gross misconduct. They were accused of taking advantage of their position 'to further their own financial gain'. Dr Neary denied all the allegations, and announced his intention to appeal to the Queen, who is Visitor of the Abbey, a royal peculiar under her direct jurisdiction.

---

[14] *Mail on Sunday,* 19 April 1998, pg. 3.

[15] *Sunday Times,* 6 September 1998, home news.

[16] *The Times,* 21 April 1998, home news.

[17] *Church Times,* 11 December 1998, news, pg. 2; David Green, 'Near(l)y Justice', Relational Justice bulletin, issue 4, October 1999, pg. 8 (The Relationships Foundation, Cambridge, 1999).

[18] *The Times,* 21 April 1998, home news. It appears that this offer was suggested by the Dean and rejected by Dr Neary, rather than vice-versa. According to the Dean's letter to *The Times,* 12 December 1998, pg. 23, Dr Neary rejected all offers.

The Dean and Chapter now gave more details of the dispute to the press. The Abbey auditors had raised questions about a company, Neary Music Ltd, that appeared in the Abbey accounts, but which had been set up in 1997 without the knowledge of the Dean and Chapter. The Dean said

> Dr Neary was not open with the Dean and Chapter over his using of the abbey (*sic*) name and its choir. Dr Neary behaved in such a way that it is now impossible for the Dean and Chapter to trust him.[19]

The Dean said Neary Music Ltd had been set up in April 1997 without the knowledge of the Abbey authorities to handle choir contracts and retain surplus funds. Mrs Neary was the sole director and Dr Neary the company secretary.

> It was used to handle monies for the abbey (*sic*) choir's Oslo tour, concerts at the Barbican and the National Gallery in 1997. It was also party to a recording contract. In addition it received fixing fees for abbey events.[20]

Canon Michael Middleton, the Abbey treasurer, said

> No one knew that fixing fees were being taken by Mrs Neary on abbey (*sic*) events. Neary Music Ltd paid Mrs Neary a £1,500 dividend. It is not about the money. It is about what the money represents. We run our affairs here on business lines, but at the same time we are a religious organisation, a college where we operate on the basis of trust. It is far more serious when that trust is eroded than the question of a few pounds.[21]

In their leading articles, both *The Times* and the *Daily Telegraph* made the following comments regarding the Dean. *The Times* commented[22]

---

[19] *The Times*, 23 April 1998, home news.

[20] *The Times*, 23 April 1998, home news.

[21] *The Times*, 23 April 1998, home news.

[22] *The Times*, 24 April 1998, feature: 'Out of tune'.

Dr Carr's methods of proceeding could hardly have been more high-handed. After a decade of highly praised service, Dr Neary and his wife were suspended overnight, causing the cancellation of the abbey's justly celebrated concert for Holy Week. Declining offers of mediation by such experienced officers of the abbey as Lord Weatherill, the former Speaker, the dean ordered the investigation, conducted the disciplinary hearing on Maundy Thursday, relayed the findings to the Chapter and, as primus inter pares, won their assent to dismissal.

Dr Carr has acted within his rights. Because the abbey is a Royal Peculiar under the direct jurisdiction of the Queen, no cleric has a chairman's power to intervene. But he has acted neither with Christian humility, nor in the interest of the Church's already wretched reputation for handling disputes. The Abbey has problems enough without this poisoning of the air.

Similarly, the *Daily Telegraph* remarked[23]

[Dr Neary's] dismissal betrays a Dean determined to bring everything under his control. Such a drive to concentrate power will not attract the best musicians to one of the top cathedral jobs in the country. It has already caused much unhappiness at the Abbey. And, for a Christian institution, it has set a poor example.

The Times further commented

To suggest dishonesty in this austere president of the Royal College of Organists is an act of exaggeration so dramatic as to suggest a broader agenda. This affair has more to do with the power struggle between the clerical and musical sides of great cathedrals than with the minutiae of abbey accounts. Dr Carr's record in church politics is that of a zealous but abrasive moderniser determined to establish his executive authority; and in these hermetic hierarchies,

---

[23] *Daily Telegraph,* 23 April 1998, leading article pg. 25, entitled 'Lincoln revisited?'

where principles and passions collide, deans and organists have ever been rivals.[24]

Beyond the bland denial of all allegations, the details of Dr Neary's defence were never disclosed to the press. From the determination[25] of Lord Jauncey it is clear that they claimed that the new company had been set up on professional advice a year earlier, and was no secret. They said that any fixing fees they received related to events which were not promoted by the Abbey, and they denied any dishonesty in relation to them. The total sum involved was approximately £13,900.[26]

5. THE APPEAL TO LORD JAUNCEY

The Queen referred the appeal to the Lord Chancellor, who appointed the retired Law Lord, Lord Jauncey of Tullichettle, to hear the appeal. Lord Jauncey held a preliminary hearing on 10 July, and both parties agreed not to comment on the matter until the case was resolved.[27]

Grandees rallied to assist Dr Neary as character witnesses. Among them were Sir Edward Heath, the former Conservative prime minister and an accomplished organist, Frank Field MP, the Rt Revd John Taylor, the former bishop of Winchester, the Very

---

[24] *The Times*, 24 April 1998, feature: 'Out of tune'.

[25] Lord Jauncey used the word 'determination' rather than 'judgment'. The reason appears from the opening paragraph.

> A Petition dated 3rd July 1998 has been presented to Her Majesty The Queen as Visitor of the Collegiate Church of St Peter, Westminster, ('the Abbey') by Dr Martin Neary requesting that She should resolve a dispute between him and the Dean and Chapter. Her Majesty has appointed me to be her Commissioner for the purposes of exercising Her visitatorial jurisdiction to determine the Petition.

[26] £11,900 received over the period 6th April 1994 and December 1996, and £1,998 during 1997.

[27] *Exeter Express & Echo*, 10 July 1998, pg. 8; *Birmingham Post*, 11 July 1998, pg. 7.

Revd Michael Mayne, former Dean of Westminster, the Revd Colin Semper, the former canon treasurer of the Abbey, and John Gummer MP, former UK Secretary of State for the Environment and Minister of Agriculture, Fisheries and Food.[28]

Friends continued their efforts to try to resolve the dispute. Some parents of the boy choristers made a number of requests to Dr George Carey, archbishop of Canterbury, to intervene, but he refused, saying that he had no standing in the dispute.[29] Dr Carey initially supported Dr Carr's handling of the dispute, but later he was reported to have changed his mind.[30]

However any settlement proved elusive. Dr Neary wanted a public recognition of his honesty, and this the Dean and Chapter were unwilling to make.[31] Despite the enormous strain on Dr Neary's family, and the very large legal costs,[32] he was determined to clear his name.

---

[28] *Sunday Times*, 6 September 1998, home news; *Independent*, 9 November 1998, comment, pg. 3. The determination makes no reference to the evidence of any of these people.

[29] *Sunday Times*, 6 September 1998, home news.

[30] *Sunday Times*, 6 December 1998, home news.

[31] Letter to the author from Dr and Mrs Neary dated 25 February 2003.

[32] Dr and Mrs Neary's legal costs were around £200,000. £95,000 of this sum came from a support group to help them fight their case, but Dr and Mrs Neary had to fund the balance themselves. Dr Carr did not have to risk his own money: the Abbey's legal costs all came out of Abbey funds. Questions were subsequently asked in Parliament about this: see Hansard for 23 June 1999, column 1234. Estimates of £250,000–£400,000 have been suggested for the Abbey's costs: *Church Times*, 11 December 1998, pg. 1; Christopher Compston, 'Fighting for Justice', Relational Justice bulletin, issue 2, April 1999, pg. 3 (The Relationships Foundation, Cambridge, 1999).

The hearing began on 11 September, and lasted 12 days.[33]

The Nearys' situation attracted a high-profile campaign of support. More than 1,200 people signed a petition to the Queen calling for Dr Neary's reinstatement after the hearing.

6. THE RESULT

On 9 December 1999, Lord Jauncey's 52 page determination was published.[34] He held that the Dean and Chapter were justified in dismissing Dr and Mrs Neary. His conclusion was as follows:

> For some three and a half years Dr and Mrs Neary ran a business whose principal income earning assets were the lay vicars and the choristers. They derived profits from this business in the shape of fixing fees and surpluses on events involving the choir. They did not tell anybody in the Abbey what they were doing. They disclosed to no-one there that they and not the Abbey authorities were entering into some contracts on behalf of the choir... By these activities and their silence during this long period they were in clear breach of their duty of fidelity to the Abbey. They used their position as Organist and Music Department Secretary to make secret profits over a prolonged period and they entirely failed to inform the Abbey authorities of what they

---

[33] *London Evening Standard,* 9 September 1998, pg. 7; *Church Times,* 11 September 1998, home page. The start of the appeal was put back two days to allow Dr Carr more time to prepare: BBC news on-line at *www.churchnet.org.uk/news/files3/news124.html.* The length of the hearing is referred to in Lord Jauncey's determination.

[34] Lord Jauncey's determination is summarised best in *The Times,* 10 December 1998, home news, pg. 9; *Guardian (London),* 10 December 1998, Guardian Home Page, pg. 7; *Daily Telegraph (London),* 10 December 1998, Thursday, pg. 10; *Church Times,* 11 December 1998, pg. 1. The full text of the determination is available at *jus-tus.anglican.org/resources/misc/jauncey98.html.* See also the report *Neary v Dean of Westminster* [1999] IRLR 288, (1998) 5 Ecc LJ 303.

were doing, notwithstanding the fact that there were ample opportunities so to do and no good reason for not doing so. I consider that this conduct was such as fatally undermined the relationship of trust and confidence which should have subsisted between them and the Abbey. I am therefore satisfied that the Dean and Chapter were justified in summarily dismissing them.

Lord Jauncey emphasised that the Abbey's case was based on impropriety, not dishonesty. He was critical of the manner in which the disciplinary proceedings were handled.[35]

The Abbey's attempt to convene a disciplinary hearing at such short notice without a detailed statement of the case being made against the Nearys must score gamma minus on the scale of natural justice.

Lord Jauncey ended his determination with a comment about the possibility of the matter being resolved by agreement

I find it surprising that neither the Precentor, Canon Fenton, nor the Dean, notwithstanding his explanation, asked Dr Neary directly about the fund and its operation as soon as they were aware of its existence. Had they done so and had the parties been prepared to discuss openly and frankly the Abbey's concerns, to acknowledge that serious mistakes had been made and to consider the reasons therefor, it might perhaps have been possible to avoid the present unhappy situation with all its attendant publicity and to have reached a rather less dramatic resolution of their differences.

Some press reports of the result accepted Lord Jauncey's finding that there had indeed been gross misconduct by the Nearys, and that the Dean and Chapter were justified in dismissing them.[36] Other reports ignored the main result and concentrated on Lord Jauncey's criticism of the Dean. Reactions included that 'it

---

[35] Pg. 47–8 of the transcript.

[36] *Church Times,* 18 December 1998, pg. 15; *Church Times,* 24 December 1998, pg. 15; *Daily Express,* 18 December 1998, Jenni Murray.

was an Establishment cover up', even that 'Lord Jauncey was got at'.[37]

Judge Compston has since written that while Lord Jauncey may have got the law right, many people think the eventual outcome unjust.[38]

Lord Jauncey's determination is, in the author's view, somewhat odd, for two reasons: his circular definition of what amounts to gross misconduct, and his treatment of the Neary's conduct as, effectively, dishonest. First, gross misconduct. Dr Neary's agreement with the Abbey provided that it could be terminated immediately in the event of gross misconduct. Lord Jauncey concluded from an analysis of the law that gross misconduct does not require dishonesty. According to Lord Jauncey, gross misconduct includes 'any conduct which must so undermine the trust and confidence which is inherent in the particular contract of employment that the master should no longer be required to retain the servant in his employment'. This amounts to saying that a person whose contract says they may be dismissed for gross misconduct may be dismissed if their conduct so undermines the trust and confidence in the relationship that the employer may dismiss them: which is of course a circular definition. This gave Lord Jauncey considerable freedom in reaching his conclusion.

Second, dishonesty. Lord Jauncey emphasises at the outset that the Abbey's case against the Nearys was based on impropriety and not dishonesty. Yet he considered that the Nearys' 'lack of openness' about their fixing business, and their 'secret' profits were sufficient for gross misconduct. There are, of course, de-

---

[37] *Church Times*, 18 December 1998, home page.

[38] Christopher Compston, 'Fighting for Justice', Relational Justice bulletin, issue 2, April 1999, pg. 3 (The Relationships Foundation, Cambridge, 1999). A response to Christopher Compston's article appeared in the following issue: David Green, 'Near(l)y Justice', Relational Justice bulletin, issue 4, October 1999, pg. 8.

grees of dishonesty, but as dishonesty was not part of the Abbey's case, it is odd that Lord Jauncey confused matters by referring to a lack of openness and to 'secret' (a tendentious word) profits. It seems, with respect, to be an attempt to justify by a back door the conclusion Lord Jauncey decided to reach.

Lord Jauncey's conclusion on the Nearys was adverse. He held that no employer should be required to tolerate this behaviour, particularly from someone who was the organist of Westminster Abbey. This was the view of the Dean and Chapter. One of the most senior judges in the country agreed.

7. THE AFTERMATH

Dr Carr spoke out after the determination. His comments as reported in the *Guardian*[39] and *Church Times*[40] indicate that he did not accept Lord Jauncey's criticism of the Abbey's conduct. He said he could see no way in which the Abbey could have conducted the matter differently. It followed legal advice to the letter, and did try to negotiate a settlement with the Nearys at an early stage. He acknowledged that the Abbey had lessons to learn from a process likely to leave it with hundreds of thousands of pounds of legal costs, but saw this as a management issue:

> We have to put systems in place which do not destroy the trust we place in our staff but which would pick out anything which was going awry earlier.

> We have followed the letter of the law from the start. The moment financial irregularities are suspected, you have to suspend people. We were not the people who initiated the appeal proceedings - we have to respond to the petition served against us. We acted both properly and inevitably. In that sense, we couldn't have done things differently.

---

[39] *Guardian (London)*, 10 December 1998, Guardian Home Page, pg. 7.
[40] *Church Times*, 11 December 1998, pg. 1, 2.

Dr Carr saw every other aspect of the determination as a vindi-
cation of the Abbey's system of administration and constitution.
Despite his championing of cathedral reform, he rejected any suggestion that royal peculiars should be reformed.[41]

In a letter to *The Times*,[42] Dr Carr denied Lord Jauncey's view
that matters could have been resolved less dramatically.

> As for vindictive management, the Dean and Chapter
> throughout have strictly followed legal advice. And the
> 'less dramatic solution' of which Lord Jauncey speaks, was
> also sought by the Dean and Chapter: for 11 hours we ne-
> gotiated but Dr Neary rejected all offers and appealed to
> the Queen. The Dean and Chapter then had no choice: we
> were cited as respondents and had to respond.

The *Guardian* wrote:

> What many in the church will be pondering this weekend is
> the wider question of how much damage has been done to
> its credibility. The answer has to be: an enormous amount.
> Again and again, the questions asked are: how can people
> call themselves Christians and behave like this? Where is
> the humility, where is the forgiveness, where is the com-
> passion about which they spend so much time talking and
> praying? The answer to many is that these pompous clerics
> don't practise what they preach, and are just a bunch of
> hypocrites.[43]

Church Times commented that when trust went, the rest followed.

> It was natural for the Dean and Chapter to consult their
> lawyers over behaviour that they suspected but did not
> know to be misconduct; similarly, few would blame the

---

[41] This comment should be seen in the light of his comments in May 1999
when the new Commission to examine the royal peculiars was announced: *Church Times*, 21 May 1999, pg. 7.

[42] *The Times*, 12 December 1998, pg. 23.

[43] *Guardian (London)*, 12 December 1998, Guardian Home Page, pg. 4.

Nearys for seeking legal help when they were summarily suspended and dismissed. The law, however, as well as being clear-sighted in its purpose, is hard-hearted in its execution. Once the abbey allowed its hands to be tied by the lawyers, it was actively inhibited from pursuing charitable relations with the Nearys, and for this it must take some blame. But by the time this juncture was reached the damage had already been done. Those without experience of life in a religious community cannot appreciate how vital is the element of trust. Once gone, it is almost impossible to restore, and the best recourse is to put aside the question of right or wrong and simply get out.[44]

In February 1999, it was reported that the Dean had agreed to pay Dr Neary an unspecified figure, despite Lord Jauncey's determination. The deal was negotiated by Lord Weatherill acting as conciliator. The payment was to be made without accepting any liability.[45] In fact, although terms were agreed in principle,[46] no contract was signed. The Dean subsequently withdrew from the agreement on the grounds that the Abbey's lawyers had apparently advised against it.[47]

8. LESSONS TO BE LEARNED

In suggesting that there are some lessons to be learned from the dispute, the author is well aware of the danger of hindsight. It is easy to say after the event that matters should have been han-

---

[44] *Church Times*, 18 December 1998, home page.

[45] *Evening Standard*, 11 February 1999, pg. 1. The report says that Dr Carr was bowing to pressure from senior clerics in agreeing to make the payment.

[46] The terms were that Dr Neary was to be made organist emeritus, he was to be paid his salary from the time of his suspension up to the date of Lord Jauncey's determination, and his pension was to be paid as though he had stayed on at the Abbey until he was 65.

[47] *The Abbey Story* (part 2), broadcast on BBC Radio 4 on 17 June 1999.

dled differently. The author is also very much aware of the considerable experience and high-standing of the institutions and people involved, and of the difficulties involved in handling such a high-profile dispute. The following points are therefore made with some deference, and are certainly not intended in any way to be personally critical of any of the parties.

a) Management principles or Scriptural principles

The first lesson is whether the strict application of management principles applies to Christian employment, or whether this should be tempered by some other Christian principles.

The Dean took the position that as a matter of management, when dishonesty is suspected, you must suspend an employee pending a hearing to determine the facts. The solicitor who advised the Dean and Chapter has made the point that they followed the code of disciplinary proceedings developed by ACAS.[48] That may be good business practice in a commercial organisation, but public opinion seems to have been that in the case of Westminster Abbey it was not appropriate to have an immediate suspension, in the week leading up to Easter, with the attendant publicity, and where the amounts involved were not large.

What are the 'other Christian principles' which should have been applied? They have already been referred to in chapter 1.[49]

> If your brother sins against you, go and show him his fault, just between the two of you. If he listens to you, you have won your brother over.

> But if he will not listen, take one or two others along, so that 'every matter may be established by the testimony of two or three witnesses.'

---

[48] David Green, 'Near(l)y Justice', Relational Justice bulletin, issue 4, October 1999, pg. 8.

[49] See pg. 6.

If he refuses to listen to them, tell it to the church; and if he refuses to listen even to the church, treat him as you would a pagan or a tax collector.[50]

The first step may well be to approach the wrong-doer on a personal basis, preferably one-to-one. No one else should be informed, certainly not the press or the public. Many problems can be resolved, one-to-one, especially if the investigation is handled appropriately.

In the BBC Radio 4 program *The Abbey Story*[51] it was reported that there had been occasions in the last 10 years or so where dishonesty had been found among the Abbey staff, and where matters had been resolved on an informal personal basis, without the employee losing his job. Within a religious community, management practices do not necessarily need to be run on commercial lines. More Christian, more 'gentlemanly' ways of handling matters are appropriate.

If a one-to-one fails, the second stage should be an internal investigation, within the organisation; but again, a private matter, with no publicity. If this fails, it may be appropriate to take the third stage, to 'tell it to the church', in other words, go public about the matter.

It seems that Dr Carr did not take step 1, but instead went straight to a mixture of steps 2 and 3. His suspension of Dr Neary on 20 March 1998 was a public act. For a whole week more, it was perhaps not too late to retrieve the situation. However, on 27 March, the Receiver General wrote to the parents of the choristers informing them of the dispute,[52] and this led to the press reporting the matter on 30 March.

---

[50] Matthew 18:15–17.

[51] *The Abbey Story* (part 1) broadcast on BBC Radio 4 on 10 June 1999.

[52] The author has seen a copy of the letter.

b) *Fair disciplinary procedures*

If matters could not be resolved informally on a one-to-one basis, the next step might or should have been a private internal investigation. The Abbey disciplinary procedures clearly failed in this regard. If the disciplinary proceedings had been conducted differently, the result might still have been Dr Neary's dismissal. The appeal by Dr Neary to the Queen was an expression of dissatisfaction not only at the result, but also at the process; and the public sympathy for Dr Neary was likewise fuelled by the perceived defects in the disciplinary process. If the process had been seen by Dr Neary and the press to have been fair, he would not have had such overwhelming public support and sympathy, and may have accepted the decision if it had been against him.

Lord Jauncey criticised the Abbey for attempting to convene a disciplinary hearing at short notice without a detailed statement of the case being made against the Nearys. Another criticism was the refusal to allow Dr Neary to have anyone other than an Abbey colleague to represent him at the initial disciplinary hearing.

Judge Compston has referred to the lack of independence of the disciplinary process. In his letter to *The Times* at the time:

> In this country we are presumed innocent until proved guilty. Furthermore, a fair trial demands that the judge is independent.

> Rightly or wrongly, the Dean will be seen to have made up his mind on Dr Neary. Therefore neither he nor the Chapter should continue to chair the investigation. An independent tribunal is needed – and needed now. Surely Buckingham Palace should now intervene and a senior judge should be found.[53]

Writing in a similar mould a year later, Judge Compston said:

> [the disciplinary hearing] was heard by the Dean who had already suspended the Nearys. He could hardly go back on

---

[53] *The Times*, 1 April 1998.

that. Moreover, the Canon Treasurer who prosecuted later decided, as a member of chapter, on their guilt! A very elementary breach of natural justice.[54]

Whatever the defects in the internal procedures in Westminster Abbey, no-one can say that the complete re-hearing of the appeal by Lord Jauncey was anything but independent and fair. Whether the hearing of the appeal erred on the issue of proportionality is perhaps another matter, discussed below.

c) Broken trust can be restored

Even if gross misconduct is proved at a disciplinary hearing, a tribunal still has to consider whether it is appropriate to dismiss the employee. In its case before Lord Jauncey the Abbey emphasised the importance of mutual trust and confidence between individuals. Lord Jauncey held that Dr Neary's conduct struck at the root of the trust and confidence between Dr Neary and the Dean and Chapter, and therefore the Dean and Chapter were entitled to dismiss him. Entitled maybe, but it did not follow that they should have done so. The Dean's action may have been right in law, but the possibility of reconciliation should also have been considered.

In 1698 a similar situation at the Abbey involving an even more famous organist than Dr Neary was handled rather differently. In that year the Chapter discovered that the Abbey organist and composer Henry Purcell had sold places in the organ loft to spectators. Like Dr Neary, Purcell had been making secret profits. The Chapter demanded that he hand the money he received from these sales over to them, giving him only two days in which to do so

> And in default thereof his place to be declared to be null and void. And it is further ordered that his stipend or sal-

---

[54] Christopher Compston, 'Fighting for Justice', Relational Justice bulletin, issue 2, April 1999, pg. 3 (The Relationships Foundation, Cambridge, 1999).

ary due at our Lady Day last past be detained in the hands
of the Treasurer untill further order.

Not surprisingly, Purcell complied with the demand, and his
musical reputation continued unblemished at the Abbey.[55] The
same option was never given to Dr Neary.

In his attempts to negotiate a settlement, Judge Compston
asked the Nearys whether they would be willing to pay back to
the Abbey any sums which a proper accounting showed was due.
They said they would be more than willing to do so, or to pay the
money over to the Musicians Benevolent Fund, if the Abbey felt
that that was more appropriate.[56]

If in the seventeenth century, an incident involving secret
profits could be put right by the restoration of the money wrongly
taken, why not in the twentieth?[57] Trust is clearly very important;
but broken trust can be restored. This should especially be so in a
Christian context, where all parties should be aware of the Christian imperative of forgiveness.[58] Trust was restored in the case of
Purcell. Trust could have been restored in the case of Dr Neary.

If the Dean and Chapter believed Dr Neary had been dishonest
when they dismissed him in April, by September their case
against the Nearys was based on impropriety and not dishonesty.
Surely it would have been sufficient for the Dean to have said that

---

[55] *The Oxford Companion to Music*, by Percy Scholes (Oxford University
Press, 1970), article on Henry Purcell. See also *London Evening Standard*, 9
December 1998, pg. 20.

[56] The Nearys made the same point in the radio program *The Abbey Story*
(part 2), broadcast on BBC Radio 4 on 17 June 1999.

[57] Both trust law and criminal law have developed very considerably
between the 17th and the 20th centuries. The Chapter's perception of
Purcell's misdeeds was coloured by the legal development of the 17th
century, and it could be argued that this is a ground for distinguishing
Purcell's case from Dr Neary's.

[58] For example, Colossians 3:13.

Dr Neary had been dismissed in April because the evidence then suggested that Dr Neary had been dishonest, but that later it became clear that Dr Neary had not been dishonest, although the fixing fees clearly should have been paid to the Abbey? On that basis, Dr Neary could have returned to the Abbey, honour would have been restored, the world would have been pleased that the dispute had been resolved, and trust could have been re-established.

As the Rt Rev Hugh Montefiore[59] wrote in the *Church Times*[60]

> Where there are faults on both sides, what should Christians do? Reconciliation is at the heart of the Christian gospel. It can take place only when all parties admit their faults, and start again in a new relationship of trust and openness. The party initially wronged has to take the first step in reconciliation. Why could this not happen at the Abbey? It might put a strain on the parties concerned, but that is the challenge of the gospel.

d) A sense of proportion

Under the Civil Procedure Rules 1998 claims under £15,000 are normally allocated to the fast track procedure, unless the trial is likely to last more than a day.[61] The hearing before Lord Jauncey took twelve days, with leading counsel on both sides, and the total legal costs estimated at up to £600,000.[62]

The amount at stake was £13,900. With no disrespect to Lord Jauncey – the trial pre-dates the Woolf reforms of 1999 – robust modern case management should not allow a trial of this nature to grow so out of proportion to the amount at stake. The overrid-

---

[59] Bishop Montefiore is the former bishop of Birmingham.

[60] *Church Times*, 18 December 1998, pg. 9 (letters). Bishop Montefiore's analysis is criticised in the *Church Times*, 24 December 1998, pg. 9.

[61] CPR rule 26.6(4). References to particular rules are usually abbreviated as CPR rule XX, or even CPR r. XX.

[62] For the costs, see pg. 63, fn. 32.

ing object of the court now is to deal with cases justly, and this involves

> (a) ensuring that the parties are on an equal footing;
> (b) saving expense;
> (c) dealing with the case in ways which are proportionate –
>> (i)   to the amount of money involved;
>> (ii)   to the importance of the case;
>> (iii) to the complexity of the issues; and
>> (iv) to the financial position of each party;
> (d) ensuring that it is dealt with expeditiously and fairly.[63]

With the possible exception of (c)(ii), all these point to a speedy and simple resolution of the case.

e) Attempts to mediate

It is a fundamental axiom of mediation that the mediator must be neutral as between the parties. A mediator who is seen to judge or criticise the conduct of a party, especially if he or she makes that judgment or criticism public, is most unlikely to be accepted as a suitable mediator by the party who has been criticised.

This may well be the reason why the Dean refused the offer by Judge Compston to mediate. Both Judge Compston's letter in *The Times*[64] and his private letter to the Dean are critical in tone, and this may be one reason why the Dean did not accept the Judge's offer to meet him. It is not known whether the same applies for the approaches by Lord Weatherill and the Revd Colin Semper in April 1998.[65]

The attempts to settle in the solicitors' offices were serious, or they would not have taken 11 hours. According to the Dean and

---

[63] CPR rule 1.1(2).

[64] *The Times*, 1 April 1998.

[65] Lord Weatherill was involved in the settlement negotiations in February 1999, after Lord Jauncey's determination.

Chapter's solicitor, the negotiations failed because the Nearys would not accept that they were guilty of doing anything wrong.[66] Whether at this stage, the possibility of using an outside mediation service was discussed is not known. Nor is it known whether this was discussed at any later stage.

f) The conflict triangle

The Westminster Abbey case is a good illustration of three different aspects of many disputes. When the matter came before Lord Jauncey, he was primarily concerned with the substantive dispute between the parties: whether or not Dr Neary had kept the fixing fees without the knowledge and approval of the Abbey authorities. One aspect of the dispute was thus the factual problem which needed to be resolved. Another aspect was the relationships and people involved. Lord Jauncey held that the breach of trust by Dr Neary was sufficient to undermine the trust between the parties, and so entitled the Dean and Chapter to dismiss him. The third aspect of the dispute was procedural: how the dispute was handled, a subject on which Lord Jauncey made criticism of the Abbey.

These three aspects, the substantive dispute, the relationships involved, and the management of the resolution process, are key to mediation practice. Mediators refer to what is known as the conflict triangle containing three elements: the problem, the people, and the process.[67] This is shown in figure 1.

---

[66] David Green, 'Near(l)y Justice', Relational Justice bulletin, issue 4, October 1999, pg. 8 (The Relationships Foundation, Cambridge, 1999).

[67] Jennifer Beer and Eileen Steif, *The Mediator's Handbook*, 3rd edn. (Gabriola Island, BC, Canada, New Society Publishers, 1997), pg. 14.

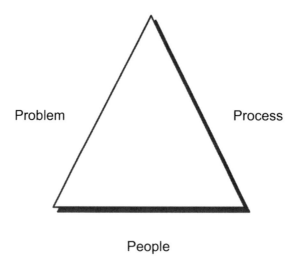

Problem   Process

People

Figure 1. The conflict triangle

The problem side of the triangle represents the key factual elements of the dispute – for example, in the Westminster Abbey dispute, whether or not Dr Neary had kept the choir fixing fees without telling the Abbey that he was doing so and obtaining its approval.

The people side of the triangle represents the personal relationships involved – in the Westminster Abbey case, the breakdown of trust between Dr Carr and Dr Neary.

Lastly, the process side of the triangle represents the way the dispute is handled – in the Westminster Abbey case, the circumstances surrounding the original suspension, and how the dispute was managed thereafter. If the Abbey had handled the dispute differently, the result may well have been different; and much of the emotive content would have been absent.[68] Process is thus important, not just in itself, but because it may affect the outcome.

This concept of the conflict triangle is central to this book. A mediator needs to look at the facts of the dispute, the feelings of the participants, and the form the mediation process should take. Any lasting resolution must recognise all three sides of the conflict. Church disputes typically involve all three elements: problem, people, and process. Mediators need to find ways to resolve the substantive issues between the parties; to deal with the underlying relationship difficulties between them; and to devise a process which includes all necessary parties, and which is both fair and acceptable to all involved, and thus assist the parties to arrive at a negotiated settlement acceptable to all.[69]

9. THE FUTURE

In May 1999 a new commission was set up under the chairmanship of Professor Averil Cameron, the Warden of Keble College, Oxford, to look into the organisation, management and accountability of each of the royal peculiars, i.e. Westminster Abbey, St George's Chapel, Windsor, and the Chapels Royal.[70] This new commission was seen as the natural successor to the Howe Commission on Cathedrals. The Howe Commission had been charged with examining the running of cathedrals, and resulted in the Report of the Archbishops' Commission on Cathedrals,[71] and the Cathedrals Measure 1999.

---

[68] As Lord Jauncey himself indicates on the last page of his determination.

[69] This will be developed fully in later chapters.

[70] See *Church Times*, 21 May 1999, pg. 7.

[71] The Report of the Archbishops' Commission on Cathedrals (London, Church House Publishing, 1994). For a review by Eric Kemp, see 3 Ecc LJ 343.

The Cameron report was published in March 2001.[72] One of its main recommendations is to set up a standing commission for the royal peculiars, to exercise visitorial functions on behalf of the sovereign. This would satisfy the need for a complaints procedure conducted by persons external to the institution itself, one which would ensure compliance with the rules of natural justice, and the right to a speedy, fair and open hearing.[73] One particular benefit from the proposed standing committee deserves quoting in full:

> We now touch on some of the other benefits which we see as flowing from the new Standing Commission. While the primary purpose of the new body would be to perform Visitorial functions on the Sovereign's behalf, it would also be able to give informal advice to the Deans and Chapters on contentious matters, and thereby perhaps prevent grievances reaching the point at which they give rise to a formal appeal. Mediation is now a principle which is increasingly recommended, especially for dispute settlement in cases relating to charities, and it is at least possible (though we express no view on the point) that if such a body had been in existence in 1998, and been able to perform a mediating role, the need to appoint Lord Jauncey of Tullichettle might never have arisen.[74]

It is to be hoped that these new procedures, if adopted,[75] will help the Church of England to avoid such disputes in the future.[76]

---

[72] *Report of the Review Group on the Royal Peculiars* (London, Church House Publishing, 2001), also available at *www.open.gov.uk/lcd/majrep/royalp.htm*.

[73] *Report of the Review Group on the Royal Peculiars*, chapter 7 paragraph 12.

[74] *Report of the Review Group on the Royal Peculiars*, chapter 7 paragraph 20.

[75] The Lord Chancellor's Department issued a *Consultation paper on the recommendations of the Review Group on the Royal Peculiars* (London, Lord Chancellor's Department, 2001). The consultation paper was published

on the Lord Chancellor's Department web site *www.lcd.gov.uk/consult/royal/rrroyal.htm*. Responses were sought by 1 October 2001.

[76] For reference, the following is a list of 155 newspaper reports referring to the Neary dispute, all 1998 unless stated otherwise.

Bath Chronicle, 12 September, News, pg. 7;

Belfast News Letter, 1 July, Wednesday, News, pg. 18;

Birmingham Post, 31 March, Tuesday, pg. 1; 11 July, Saturday, pg. 7; 27 August, Thursday, pg. 12; 10 December, Thursday, pg. 18;

Bristol Evening Post, 18 June, pg. 36; 7 December, News, pg. 2; 10 December, News, pg. 39;

Church Times, 3 April, pg. 1, 3 (Dr Neary threatened with sack); 9 April, pg. 3, letters 7 (Holy week concert cancelled); 17 April, pg. 2 (meeting about Neary); 24 April, pg. 1 (Dr Neary to appeal to Queen); 1 May, pg. 5 (support for Dr Neary); 8 May, pg. 23 letters; 15 May, pg. 2, letters, pg. 9 (choir parents criticise Carr); 26 June, pg. 2 (Special Commissioner to hear case); 17 July, pg. 2 (Lord Jauncey to hear case), photo pg. 3; 4 September, pg. 2 (Neary hearing set to begin); 11 September, pg. 3 (hearing begins, and likely to cost £250,000); 23 October, home page; 11 December, news, pg. 1, 2 (Dr Neary loses appeal), article on past conflict, pg. 12; 18 December, home page, pg. 15 (Psst! Wesley won); 24 December, letters, pg. 15 (Choose your angle); 21 May 1999, pg. 7; 4 June 1999, news, pg. 3.

Daily Express, 18 December, Jenni Murray.

Daily Mail, 31 March, pg. 7; 23 April, pg. 25; 11 May, pg. 24; 12 May, pg. 24; 10 December, pg. 13; 10 December, pg. 35; 6 April 1999, pg. 13;

Daily Telegraph, 31 March, Tuesday, pg. 2; 3 April, Friday, pg. 9; 5 April, Sunday, pg. 25; 10 April, Friday, pg. 12; 23 April, Thursday, Leading Article, pg. 25; 23 April, Thursday, pg. 1; 7 May, Thursday, pg. 1; 8 May, Friday, pg. 14; 11 May, Monday, pg. 7; 12 September, Saturday, pg. 16; 6 October, Tuesday, pg. 11; 12 October, Monday, pg. 4; 10 December, Thursday, pg. 1; 10 December, Thursday, pg. 10; 10 December, Thursday, pg. 11; 10 December, Thursday, pg. 33; 11 December, Friday, pg. 28; 12 December, Saturday, pg. 25; 19 May 1999, Wednesday, pg. 11;

Evening Chronicle (Newcastle, UK), 7 May, Thursday, Edition 1, pg. 6;

Evening Herald (Plymouth), 26 May, pg. 18;

Evening News (Edinburgh), 7 May, Thursday, pg. 8;

Evening Standard, 30 March, pg. 1,2; 31 March, pg. 11; 2 April, pg. 7; 3 April, pg. 2; 3 April, pg. 7; 7 April, pg. 14; 22 April, pg. 1; 23 April, pg. 4; 24 April, pg. 16; 7 May, pg. 1; 8 May, pg. 27; 11 May, pg. 1; 13 May, pg. 4; 13 July, pg. 2; 9 September, pg. 7; 9 December, pg. 20; 9 December, pg. 4; 10 December, pg. 7; 21 December, pg. 15; 23 December, pg. 60; 24 December, pg. 5; 11 February 1999, pg. 1; 12 February 1999, pg. 2; 18 May 1999, pg. 2;

Express & Echo (Exeter), 10 July, pg. 8;

Guardian, 31 March, Guardian Home Page, pg. 6; 3 April, Guardian Home Page, pg. 4; 4 April, Guardian Home Page, pg. 5; 23 April, Guardian Home Page, pg. 1; 26 May, Guardian Features Page, pg. 2; 7 September, Guardian Home Page, pg. 6; 10 September, Guardian Home Page, pg. 9; 10 December, Guardian Home Page, pg. 1; 10 December, Guardian Home Page, pg. 7; 12 December, Guardian Home Page, pg. 4; 12 December, Guardian Home Page, pg. 5;

Independent, 3 April, Friday, Features, pg. 19; 3 April, Friday, News, pg. 6; 11 April, Saturday, News, pg. 6; 23 April, Thursday, News, pg. 3; 24 April, Friday, News, pg. 3; 29 April, Wednesday, Comment, pg. 16; 6 September, Sunday, News, pg. 13; 11 October, Sunday, Title Page, pg. 1; 12 October, Monday, News, pg. 10; 9 November, comment, pg. 3; 10 December, Thursday, News, pg. 13; 15 December, Tuesday, Comment, pg. 2; 12 February 1999, Friday, News, pg. 3; 25 April 1999, Sunday, News, pg. 8;

Journal (Newcastle, UK), 23 April, Thursday, Edition 1, pg. 14; 10 September, Thursday, Edition 1, pg. 18; 10 December, Thursday, Edition 1, pg. 14;

Mail on Sunday, 19 April, pg. 3;

Observer, 5 April, The Observer News Page, pg. 23; 5 April, The Observer News Page, pg. 27; 26 April, The Observer News Page, pg. 5;

Scotsman, 10 December, Thursday, pg. 5; 11 December, Friday, pg. 8;

Sunday Telegraph, 13 December, Sunday, pg. 33; 20 December, Sunday, pg. 28; 25 April 1999, Sunday, pg. 16;

Sunday Times, 5 April, Sunday, Home news; 12 April, Sunday, Features; 10 May, Sunday, Features; 10 May, Sunday, Home news; 28 June, Sunday, Home news; 30 August, Sunday, Home news; 6 September, Sunday, Home news; 11 October, Sunday, Home news; 6 December, Sunday, Home news; 13 December, Sunday, Features; 20 December, Sunday, Home news; 14 February 1999, Sunday, Home news; 11 April 1999, Sunday, Home news;

The Times, 30 March, Monday, Home news; 31 March, Tuesday, Home news; 1 April, letters; 21 April, Tuesday, Home news; 23 April, Thursday, Home news; 24 April, Friday, Features; 24 April, Friday, Home news; 7 May, Thursday, Home news; 12 May, Tuesday, Features; 3 July, Friday, Features; 31 August, Monday, Features; 12 September, Saturday, Home news; 6 October, Tuesday, Home news; 10 December, home news, pg. 1; 10 December, home news, pg. 9; 11 December, Friday, Features; 12 December, letters to the editor, pg. 23; 19 December, Saturday, Features; 26 December, Saturday, Features; 7 January 1999, Thursday, Features; 12 February 1999, Friday, Home news; 24 March 1999, Wednesday, Features; 15 April 1999, Thursday, Features; 3 May 1999, Monday, Features; 4 May 1999, Tuesday, Features; 28 May 1999, Friday, Home news;

Western Daily Press, 23 April, pg. 8; 18 June, pg. 6; 10 December, News, pg. 3.

Chapter 3

CHURCH DISPUTE RESOLUTION IN THE UNITED KINGDOM

1. TYPES OF CHURCH DISPUTE

B efore looking at different models of mediation, an analysis is needed of the types of church disputes which arise in practice. Such an analysis of the problem is required before possible solutions are considered. Chapter 1 briefly described the various methods used to identify the types of church dispute which arise in practice.[1] A number of methods were used for this purpose.

First, a search was conducted using *Lexis* of newspaper reports of church disputes over the period 1993 to 1999.[2] A database was built up of all these reports, and a preliminary categorisation was made of the various disputes which arose during this period. A search was also conducted of law reports and legal textbooks for cases which arose during this period.[3] Second, the author corresponded with all archdeacons and diocesan secretaries in England,[4] seeking their views on how church disputes can best be re-

---

[1] See pg. 48.

[2] All newspaper reports available on the *Lexis* database were used for this purpose. Also a manual search was conducted of the *Church Times.*

[3] Searches were carried out in two computer databases, *Lexis*, and Sweet & Maxwell's *Current Legal Information*. A manual search was also conducted of the entire series of the Ecclesiastical Law Journal. The legal textbooks used were those concerned with ecclesiastical law, in particular Mark Hill, *Ecclesiastical Law*, 2nd edn.

[4] The text of the letters sent to archdeacons and diocesan secretaries is set out in appendix 2. There were 59 replies to the author's letter requesting information: 38 from archdeacons, 2 from bishops, 17 from diocesan sec-

solved in practice. The responses to this survey indicated the types of disputes with which archdeacons and diocesan secretaries found themselves involved. Third, the author relied on his personal professional involvement in this area as a barrister, and as a former churchwarden. Fourth, the author was part of the planning team for and helped to lead an interdenominational conference on church conflict in 1999.

The outcome of this research is presented in this chapter.

In some cases research had to extend before 1993, in order to understand the background to some of the modern disputes. The history of well over 100 recent disputes has been examined in detail. They cover a variety of churches and Christian organisations in the UK. In addition to Church of England disputes, disputes in the Episcopal Church of Scotland,[5] the Church of Scotland (which is Presbyterian),[6] the Church in Wales, the Episcopal Church in

---

retaries, and 2 from other diocesan officers. The replies cover 31 of the 43 dioceses, i.e. 72 per cent.

[5] There are two main churches in Scotland: the Church of Scotland, which is the national Church of Scotland and is commonly referred to as the Kirk, and the Episcopal Church of Scotland, known also as the Scottish Episcopal Church. The Episcopal Church of Scotland is governed by its bishops and its Synod, and is part of the Anglican Communion. For the constitutional position of the Episcopal Church of Scotland, see Ivor Guild, 'Synodical Government in the Scottish Episcopal Church', 4 Ecc LJ 493.

[66] Each church in the Church of Scotland is governed by its Kirk session, a meeting of its elders. Kirk sessions are grouped in Presbyteries, rather as Church of England parishes are grouped in dioceses. The National Assembly of the Church of Scotland corresponds to the General Synod of the Church of England. The Church of Scotland is not part of the Anglican Communion. For the constitutional position of the Church of Scotland, see C.R. Munro, 'Does Scotland have an established Church?', 4 Ecc LJ 639, and Frank Cranmer, 'Church-State Relations in the United Kingdom: A Westminster View', 6 Ecc LJ 111.

Ireland, the Baptist Union, the Methodist Church, and the Roman Catholic Church are included.

A distinction should be made between church disputes that are internal and those which are external. Internal church disputes are those within the Church itself: external disputes are those between the Church and non-members.[7] Some external disputes are primarily concerned with church matters; others are not. Bell ringing frequently causes annoyance to non church-members, but is primarily a church matter.[8] The disputes about marching past various churches in Northern Ireland are disputes between two communities, in which religion plays a part, but is not primarily a church matter. For this reason the mediation of the Northern Ireland disputes is not considered (though the Good Friday agreement of 1998 followed an extended period of political mediation).

---

[7] The definition of membership is not clear-cut within the Church of England: see James Behrens, *Confirmation, Sacrament of Grace* (Leominster, Gracewing, 1995), pg. 75–80. In one context membership gives the right to vote, in another it may refer to the right to receive Holy Communion.

[8] Bellringing may cause a dispute between a church and people outside the congregation, who object to the noise: see R.H. Bloor, 'Clocks, bells and cockerels', (1995) 3 Ecc LJ 393, Thomas Watkin, 'A happy noise to hear? Church bells and the law of nuisance' 4 Ecc LJ 545; Sarah Thomas and Thomas Watkin, 'Oh Noisy Bells Be Dumb' (1995) Journal of Planning and Environmental Law 1097. For a recent example in which the author appeared as counsel, see *Calvert v Gardiner* [2002] EWHC 1394, [2003] 7 Ecc LJ 99, a claim in nuisance concerning the bells of St Mary's Parish Church, Down Saint Mary, Crediton, Exeter. The claimant's cottage was some 27 yards from the church, and he complained that their noise aggravated his ulcerative colitis. An earlier incident in the same dispute is referred to in Sarah Thomas and Thomas Watkin, 'Oh Noisy Bells Be Dumb' (1995) JPL 1097, at pg. 1105.

In general reports of disputes outside the UK have not been studied, even where they have been reported in the UK press.[9]

For the purpose of this book therefore, church disputes are not just confined to internal disputes between members of a local church congregation. Church disputes include any dispute with which the Church is involved, both with its own members, and with outsiders where they concern Church matters. The Church should be a witness to non-believers in the way it handles disputes. Christians are to be 'salt' and 'light' in all areas of their lives.[10]

The majority of church disputes fall into the 15 categories shown in figure 2.

To keep this chapter within a reasonable length, only very brief details of the cases mentioned are included here, sufficient to demonstrate the types of dispute which arise. However two farcical disputes concerning church bells deserve a fuller mention, if only for light relief.[11]

---

[9] For church disputes abroad, see chapter 7, 'Mediation in the Anglican Communion', which covers the Anglican Church in Australia, Canada, Hong Kong, New Zealand, South Africa and the USA.

[10] Matthew 5:13-16. Compare Mark 9:50, where having 'salt' is linked with being at peace with one other.

[11] The first of these bell disputes is a dispute about worship and doctrine, and so falls in that category. As Mrs Mather's actions resulted in damage to church property, it can conveniently be placed in the church property category. Arguably the *St Swithin's* case indicates a need for a separate category for torts such as the tort of nuisance: see pg. 88, fn. 8. It would then be possible to include the defamation and personal injury categories within the one torts category. The classification used in this chapter is preferred, because not all church people will appreciate the range of wrongs included in the legal term tort. Similarly, Halsbury's Laws of England 4th edn., vol 14, par. 582 fn. 3 categorises nuisance caused by church bells under the category of church property.

Type of dispute
1. alterations to church buildings and graveyards
2. church governance: disputes between a church and the diocesan authorities or the Bishop
3. personality conflicts: e.g. disputes between clergy working in a team, usually involving six people or less
4. pastoral breakdown
5. disputes over forms of worship/doctrine
6. gay or gender issues
7. racial discrimination
8. employment disputes
9. minor discipline matters, not involving sexual allegations
10. property disputes
11. financial disputes
12. defamation
13. personal injury
14. commercial contract disputes
15. tax disputes

Figure 2. Types of church dispute

In the village of Staffin, on the Isle of Skye, two churches are in earshot (literally) of each other, one belonging to the Free Presbyterian Church of Scotland, the other belonging to the Episcopal Church of Scotland. The strict Free Presbyterian Church frowns on the use of bells and other musical instruments. The minister of the Free Presbyterian church was in dispute with the minister of the Episcopal Church over the Episcopal Church's bells, which started ringing around 15 minutes or so into the Free Presbyterian Church service. The Free Presbyterian Church minister believed that the ringing drowned out his sermon, and disturbed the Sabbath peace.[12]

The second case about church bells is that of Midge Mather and *St Swithin's Church, Compton Bassett*. Mrs Mather, a sprightly 64-year-old, had been involved in a long-running dispute with the PCC of St Swithin's church, over the peals from the twelfth century church tower 100 yards from her home. Eventually she took matters into her own hands. One night she armed herself with a crowbar and a hacksaw, smashed down the 500-year old oak door to the bell tower, and sawed through the bell ropes. She was later prosecuted and convicted for causing criminal damage.[13]

Some disputes are tragic. In *St Marien Church, Hamburg, Germany*, two worshippers had feuded for eight years over who sat in the end seat of row 43. Eventually one resolved the dispute by taking an axe to church, and killing the other during a church service.[14]

Newspaper reports are not always factually accurate, and sometimes present a one-sided view of a dispute. Wherever pos-

---

[12] *The Sunday Mail*, 30 November 1997, pg. 35. This bell dispute would fall in the 'worship and doctrine' category of dispute.

[13] *The Times*, 29 July 1996, home news; *Sunday Times*, 4 August 1996, News Review, pg. 8; *Daily Telegraph*, 6 August 1996, pg. 4; *The Times*, 6 May 1997, home news; *Evening Standard*, 17 September 1997, pg. 5; *The Glasgow Herald*, 18 September 1997, pg. 8; *Guardian*, 18 September 1997, pg. 4; *The Times*, 18 September 1997, pg. 3; *The Times*, 19 September 1997, pg. 3. This bell dispute is not a dispute about worship and doctrine (Mrs Mather did not attend St Swithin's), so it is classified as a dispute about church property: see pg. 88, fn. 8, and pg. 89, fn. 11.

[14] *Daily Mirror*, 16 December 1994, pg. 19. Another tragic case is *St James, Hockwold, near Thetford, Norfolk* (Mr and Mrs Dallimore) described below under the heading of defamation.

sible several sources have been consulted when summarising a dispute, so as to avoid presenting a distorted or inaccurate view.

Many church disputes are not reported in the newspapers, nor do they reach the law reports. In some cases this is because a dispute which might have been newsworthy if it had continued was in fact resolved. In other cases it is because the type of dispute is itself not inherently newsworthy: it may be too petty, or it may be more in the nature of a commercial than a Christian dispute. For obvious reasons, churches do not like their disputes to be made public. It is not therefore possible by the means adopted to obtain comprehensive statistical evidence as to the number of disputes in any category, or the relative size of one category compared to another. However, the responses from diocesan secretaries and archdeacons indicate that the types of dispute mentioned in this chapter are typical, and cover most of the types of disputes which arise.[15]

Each of the categories of dispute indicated will now be discussed.

a) *Alterations to church buildings and graveyards*

Alterations to church buildings and graveyards belonging to the Church of England are generally subject to the faculty jurisdiction.[16] In many cases faculty applications are uncontentious. In other cases, the local church and the diocesan advisory committee may be in disagreement as to the suitability of the proposed

---

[15] The responses from the survey in chapter 7, 'Mediation in the Anglican Communion', which covers the Anglican Church in Australia, Canada, Hong Kong, New Zealand, South Africa and the USA, also confirm that my list is both typical and comprehensive.

[16] A faculty is a permission to effect some alteration to a church building, its contents or to its churchyard. See further, pg. 36. Cathedrals and some peculiars are not subject to the faculty jurisdiction: G.H. and G.L. Newsom, *Faculty Jurisdiction of the Church of England*, 2nd edn. (Sweet & Maxwell, 1993), pg. 1.

works, or there may be opposition from English Heritage, the Victorian Society, or some national amenity society.[17] The congregation itself may be divided as to whether the work should be carried out.

A range of different parties may be affected by these disputes. Thus *Holy Trinity, Freckleton*[18] was a dispute between relatives of the deceased and the vicar over a proposed inscription on a gravestone. In *Sherborne Abbey, Dorset*,[19] the proposed works were opposed by the Victorian Society. In all the other cases mentioned, the congregation was divided as to whether the works should proceed.

Disputes under this category include what should be the inscription on a headstone;[20] the installation of a lavatory;[21] the re-

---

[17] If the church or the churchyard is of archaeological interest, notice of a faculty application has to be given to national amenity societies and the local planning authority: Faculty Jurisdiction Rules 2000, SI 2000/2047, rule 13.

[18] See *In re Holy Trinity Churchyard, Freckleton* [1994] 1 WLR 1588, (1994) 3 Ecc LJ 350.

[19] *Sherborne Abbey, Dorset.* Newspaper reports include *The Times*, 24 March 1995, home news; *Daily Mail*, 24 March 1995, pg. 20; *Guardian*, 11 July 1995, pg. 7. See *Re St Mary the Virgin, Sherborne* [1996] Fam 63.

[20] *Holy Trinity, Freckleton.* Newspaper reports include *The Times*, 12 July 1994, home news; *The Times*, 13 July 1994, features; *Sunday Times*, 17 July 1994, home news. See *In re Holy Trinity Churchyard, Freckleton* [1994] 1 WLR 1588, (1994) 3 Ecc LJ 350. The archdeacon of Northampton (Peterborough) commented that the most vitriolic disputes are often about memorials in churchyards, and they are the most difficult to resolve where one of the parties has no real contact with the Church at all.

[21] *St John the Baptist, Great Rissington, Gloucestershire.* Newspaper reports include *The Times*, 9 January 1993, home news; *Daily Telegraph*, 9 January 1993, pg. 3; *The Times*, 18 February 1993, home news; *Daily Telegraph*, 18 February 1993, pg. 4. For a similar dispute, see *St Peter and St Paul, Oxton, Notts*, reported in *Daily Telegraph*, 20 December 1995, pg. 21.

placement of church windows;[22] and re-ordering (the relocation or removal of fixtures, fittings and ornaments in a church).[23] Removal of pews is a particularly contentious matter.[24] One case concerned the erection of a gargoyle;[25] another, a statue of the Virgin Mary;[26] and one, a dispute over the installation of a number of High Church furnishings to which an evangelical member of the congregation objected.[27] Several archdeacons referred to

---

[22] *Sherborne Abbey, Dorset.* See pg. 93, fn. 19. A similar dispute is *St Mary's, Bilbury, Gloucestershire,* reported in *Daily Telegraph*, 10 October 1992, pg. 4.

[23] *St Luke's, Maidstone,* reported in Sunday Times, 14 August 1994, home news. For the Court of Arches judgment, see *In re St. Luke the Evangelist, Maidstone* [1995] Fam 1. See also *Re St Helen's, Bishopsgate* (1993) 3 Ecc LJ 256; (1993) 12 Consistory and Commissary Court Cases, Case 23, concerning a grade 1 listed building in the City of London. The approach taken in *Re St Helen's, Bishopsgate* was expressly approved in *Re St Luke the Evangelist, Maidstone* [1995] Fam 1, 9A–B, *Re St Mary the Virgin, Sherborne* [1996] Fam 63, and *Re Wadsley Parish Church* (2001) 6 Ecc LJ 172.

[24] *St Nicholas, Wells-Next-the-Sea,* reported in Guardian (London), 10 July 1998, Guardian Home Page, pg. 4.[24] The removal of pews and replacing them with chairs is a typical example of an area leading to conflict: James Behrens, *Practical Church Management* (Leominster, Gracewing, 1998) at page 247. A similar dispute is *St Peter and St Paul, River, Kent,* reported in *Daily Telegraph*, 30 October 1997, pg. 4, and as *Re St Peter and St Paul, River* (1997) 5 Ecc LJ 130.

[25] *St Peter's, Oundle,* reported in *The Times,* 19 October 1996, home news; *The Times*, 9 November 1996, home news; *Independent,* 19 November 1996, pg. 1.

[26] *St Mary's, Cottingham,* reported in *The Times,* 29 November 1993, home news; *Independent,* 11 March 1994, pg. 2; *Daily Telegraph,* 11 March 1994, pg. 2. The case is reported as *Re St Mary the Virgin, Cottingham* (1994) 3 Ecc LJ 347. For the subsequent history, see *The Sunday Telegraph,* 8 May 1994, pg. 13.

[27] *Re St Nicholas, Arundel* (2002) 6 Ecc LJ 290, a case in which the author appeared as counsel. For a commentary on the 'more common' in-

disputes arising from alterations to church buildings, including refurbishments;[28] and churchyard disputes.[29]

b) Church governance

Church governance disputes arise between a church and the diocesan authorities or the Bishop. These can arise from a number of causes. Perhaps the most serious cases are those which lead to a parish or group of parishes opting out of episcopal oversight, and in effect running their affairs independently of the Church of England hierarchy. In 1995, in Swaffham in Norfolk, the bishop dismissed the Revd Kit Chalcraft, a priest-in-charge who had been divorced twice, and who announced his intention to marry for a third time. This led to five of the churches in his care defecting from the diocese, and running their own affairs independently. The conflict continued until 2002, when Mr Chalcraft was once again licensed by the bishop, and the five churches were reintegrated into the diocese.[30] A less dramatic case was that of *St Ninian's, Whitby*, a privately owned chapel, licensed for Church of

---

stances where the faculty jurisdiction falls to be invoked, see Mark Hill, *Ecclesiastical Law*, 2nd edn. (Oxford University Press, 2001) pg. 206.

[28] Archdeacon of Canterbury; archdeacon of Southend (Chelmsford); archdeacon of Plymouth (Exeter); bishop and archdeacon of Ludlow (Hereford); archdeacon of Hampstead (London); Archdeacon of Northolt (London); archdeacon of Northumberland (Newcastle); archdeacon of Northampton (Peterborough); archdeacon of Man (Sodor and Man).

[29] Bishop and archdeacon of Ludlow (Hereford); archdeacon of Rochdale (Manchester); archdeacon of Northampton (Peterborough).

[30] The case of the Revd Kit Chalcraft of Swaffham, Norfolk is reported in *Daily Telegraph*, 27 February 1995, pg. 5; *Independent*, 3 March 1995, home section, pg. 4; *Guardian*, 6 March 1995, home page, pg. 1; *Guardian*, 27 September 1995, home page, pg. 7; *Daily Telegraph*, 4 March 1996, pg. 4; *Church Times*, 1 March 2002, pg. 4, 'Breakaway group is back in the fold'.

England services, whose congregation opted to join the new Anglican Catholic Church.[31]

The cases of *Jesmond Parish Church*[32] and *St Oswald, Walkergate*[33] both concerned homosexuality. Both churches are evangelical, and took exception to the stance taken by the Bishop of Newcastle on whether all homosexual activity is sin, to the extent of refusing to accept the Bishop's episcopal authority.

The cases mentioned above were widely reported in the press. A number of disputes under this head are not newsworthy, but still very important to the parishes concerned. Such conflicts between parishes and the diocese often centre on disputes over appointments of clergy, the scale of refurbishments to parsonages, and the calculation of an individual parish contribution to the common fund.[34] As an example, the *Eltisley Parish* dispute arose

---

[31] The Anglican Catholic Church broke away from the Church of England over the ordination of women. See *Guardian,* 16 May 1994, home page, pg. 4; *The Times,* 24 February 1998, home news.

[32] *Newcastle Evening Chronicle,* 18 June 1997; *The Newcastle Evening Chronicle*, 15 November 1997, local news, pg. 9; and correspondence published in Jesmond Parish Church's web site: *www.church.org.uk.* See also the following articles in the *Church Times* for 1998: 30 January, pg. 1, 3 (unlicensed priest appointed); 6 February, pg. 3 (does not pay full quota); 13 February, pg. 9 (letters); 20 February, pg. 7 (Newcastle gives pledge on gays), pg. 8 (leader comment).

[33] *Newcastle Journal,* 8 December 1997; *Church Times*, 19 June 1998, pg. 3; *Church Times,* 24 July 1998, pg. 7; *The Times,* 4 August 1998, home news, pg. 6; *Church Times*, 14 August 1998, pg. 6. The Ed Moll dispute at St Oswald, Walkergate is reported in *Gill v Davies* (1997) 5 Ecc LJ 131; and the full judgment is printed in Mark Hill, *Ecclesiastical Law,* 2nd edn. pg. 707.

[34] Letter from the diocesan secretary for Truro. He said that in all of these cases, the conflict is either resolved or at least defused through the conciliatory efforts by the diocesan secretary, the diocesan registrar, the chairman of the diocesan board of finance, the archdeacons and the

over the proposed appointment of a team vicar who was separated from her husband.[35] The archdeacons and diocesan secretaries referred to disputes over the parish share (quota);[36] the sale of a vicarage;[37] the extent of repair and refurbishment to a vicarage;[38] clergy deployment and appointments (this includes disputes over patronage);[39] diocesan governance;[40] and pastoral reorganisation.[41] Disputes about child protection procedures also come in this category, as diocesan requirements are sometimes seen as impractical by the churches which have to put them into practice.[42]

---

bishops. In practice it has meant a lot of time being spent on visiting parishes and sitting down to discuss the issues with them. The diocese is trying to involve the rural deans in a rather more active role, particularly in seeking agreements with parishes on paying common fund arrears.

[35] *Ely Ensign* May 1998, *ely.anglican.org/ensign/e9805/index.html*; *Church Times*, 18 September 1998, pg. 5; *The Sunday Telegraph*, 20 September 1998, pg. 10.

[36] Bishop and archdeacon of Ludlow (Hereford); archdeacon of Northampton (Peterborough); diocesan secretary for Truro.

[37] Archdeacon of Lincoln.

[38] Diocesan secretary for Truro.

[39] Bishop and archdeacon of Ludlow (Hereford); diocesan secretary for Truro.

[40] Archdeacon of Northumberland (Newcastle), referring in particular to the St Oswald, Walkergate dispute.

[41] Archdeacon of Northampton (Peterborough). In the diocese of York, disputes over pastoral reorganisation have been avoided by good communication practice. 'The situation has been quite transformed by encouraging the deanery synods to have the fullest possible discussions beforehand, before the pastoral committee working parties move in' (Archdeacon of York).

[42] The diocesan secretary for Lichfield and the archdeaconry of Croydon (Southwark diocese) reported conflicts concerning these procedures.

A number of disputes arise under the topic of suspension of presentation.[43] *St Luke's, Kingston* was a case where the church-wardens challenged the bishop's of Southwark's plans for pastoral reorganisation.[44] In November 1995 Brooke J granted Gregory Fordham, one of the churchwardens, permission to seek judicial review of the bishop's decision to withdraw financial support for an incumbent priest for their parish.[45] A similar dispute over suspension of presentation arose between the patron of Penshurst and the Bishop of Rochester in 2000. Judicial review proceedings were issued, but the parties then agreed to have the dispute resolved by arbitration.[46]

Church governance disputes also arise at the local level, over the conduct of elections and the annual parochial church meeting.[47]

c) Personality disputes

Within a team ministry, or the dean and Chapter at a cathedral, personality conflicts can prevent individuals working together properly. Perhaps the most famous, or infamous, recent case under this head is the long-running dispute at Lincoln Cathedral between 1988 and 1997 involving the Dean, the Very Revd Dr

---

Child protection procedures were also specifically mentioned in the CEDR conference as an area of conflict.

[43] For suspension of presentation, see the Pastoral Measure 1983, section 67, and James Behrens, *Practical Church Management*, at page 269.

[44] *The Times,* 16 October 1995, home news; *Guardian,* 20 October 1995, pg. 12; *Daily Telegraph,* 23 October 1995, pg. 9; *Guardian,* 14 November 1995, pg. 10; *The Times,* 14 November 1995, home news.

[45] *The Times,* 16 October 1995, home news; *Guardian,* 20 October 1995, pg. 12; *Daily Telegraph,* 23 October 1995, pg. 9; *Guardian,* 14 November 1995, pg. 10; *The Times,* 14 November 1995, home news.

[46] The author was counsel for the patron in the *Penshurst* dispute.

[47] Archdeacon of Northolt (London); diocesan secretary for Salisbury; archdeacon of Southend (Chelmsford).

Brandon Jackson, the subdean, Canon Rex Davis, the bishop of Lincoln, the Rt Revd Robert Hardy, and the other canons at the cathedral.[48]

Disputes between vicars and their organists are legion.[49] Vicars sometimes feud with their churchwardens,[50] or with the choir.[51]

---

[48] *The Times*, 22 July 1995, home news; *Daily Telegraph*, 4 March 1995 pg. 5; *Guardian*, 6 March 1995, pg. 4; *Daily Mirror*, 18 July 1995, pg. 3; *Daily Mail*, 20 July 1995, pg. 1, 6, 7; *Daily Telegraph*, 20 July 1995, front page; 'The Big Story', broadcast on ITV on 20 July 1995; *Daily Telegraph*, 20 July 1995, front page; *Daily Telegraph*, 21 July 1995, pg. 9; *Daily Telegraph*, 24 July 1995, pg. 2; *The Times*, 30 December 1995, home news; *The Times*, 5 July 1996, home news; *The Times*, 5 July 1996, home news; *Sunday Times*, 30 March 1997, home news; *The Times*, 22 July 1997, home news; *Guardian*, 22 July 1997, home page, pg. 4; *Daily Telegraph*, 22 July 1997, pg. 8; *Daily Telegraph*, 14 January 1998, pg. 6; *Church Times*, 16 January 1998, pg. 3; *Daily Telegraph*, 4 March 1995, pg. 5; *Guardian (London)*, 6 March 1995, Guardian Home Page, pg. 4; *Daily Telegraph*, 14 January 1998, pg. 6. Another cathedral personality dispute was that at *St Paul's Cathedral, Dundee*, the case of the Revd Miriam Byrne: see *The Times*, 30 May 1998, pg. 10; *Church Times*, 5 June 1998, pg. 2; *Guardian (London)*, 16 November 1998, home page, pg. 3; *Church Times*, 20 November 1998, pg. 3; *The Times*, 30 May 1998, pg. 10; *Scotland on Sunday*, 15 November 1998, pg. 8; *Guardian (London)*, 16 November 1998, home page, pg. 3; *Scotland on Sunday*, 15 November 1998, pg. 8; *Sunday Times*, 15 November 1998, News, pg. 28; *The Scotsman*, 28 April 1999, pg. 5; *Church Times*, 4 December 1998, pg. 9 (letter); *Church Times*, 25 June 1999, news, pg. 3; *The Aberdeen Press*, 16 November 1998, religion, pg. 9; *Guardian (London)*, 16 November 1998, home page, pg. 3; *The Scotsman*, 16 November 1988, pg. 3; *The Aberdeen Press*, 16 November 1998, religion, pg. 9; *The Scotsman*, 22 April 1999, pg. 20; *The Scotsman*, 22 April 1999, pg. 20; *Church Times*, 30 April 1999, news, pg. 5; *The Scotsman*, 28 April 1999, pg. 5.

[49] *In Tune With Heaven, the Report of the Archbishops Commission on Church Music* (London, Church House Publishing and Hodder & Stoughton, 1992) addresses the resolution of such conflicts at paragraphs 557–559 and 634. *All Saints, Beeston Regis, Norfolk* is one of many such dis-

Sometimes the personality dispute involves various members of the congregation, such as the dispute at *St Mary's, Langham*.[52] At one level this dispute was about the removal of a number of Victorian pews, and various other alterations to the church building. At another level, the dispute was a personality clash between various members of the village, and what might appear to be rather insensitive behaviour by the rector. In other cases, the breakdown is just between the members of the team.[53]

The archdeacons and diocesan secretaries referred to a number of disputes under this head: conflict between the parish priest and members of his congregation;[54] complaints against clergy;[55] breakdowns in trust following insensitive changes;[56] the parish

---

putes. See *Daily Mail (London)*, 26 April 1994 pg. 15; *The Times*, 26 April 1994, home news.

[50] One such dispute is *Holy Trinity Church, Silksworth, Sunderland*, reported in *The Northern Echo*, 4 April 1996, pg. 10.

[51] As in *St Michael's, Oulton*, a dispute reported in *Daily Mail (London)*, 17 July 1998, pg. 33. The archdeacon of Croydon wrote saying that organists and church choirs are a main source of irritation and conflict in churches. He said there is a 'choir culture' which seems more interested in singing music than Christian worship, and this needs to be challenged honestly and patiently by the clergy.

[52] *Guardian (London)*, 20 March 1996, Guardian home page, pg. 5.

[53] For example, the *Tayside team ministry* dispute. See *Daily Mail*, 12 July 1997, pg. 23.

[54] Archdeacon of Aston (Birmingham); archdeacon of Canterbury; diocesan secretary for Lichfield; archdeacon of Middlesex (London); archdeacon of Northumberland (Newcastle); Norwich diocesan counsellor; archdeacon of Lambeth (Southwark); archdeacon of West Ham (Chelmsford).

[55] Archdeacon of Aston (Birmingham); archdeacon of Tonbridge (Rochester).

[56] Archdeacon of Craven (Bradford).

100

priest's relationship with the PCC;[57] the parish priest's relationship with the churchwardens;[58] problems within team and group ministries;[59] personal relationship problems focused on a single issue;[60] serious pastoral breakdown;[61] personality clashes,[62] and clergy personal problems such as marriage difficulty, alcoholism, depression, laziness, and 'running out of steam'.[63]

d) Pastoral breakdown

Pastoral breakdown is where the relationships between the vicar and a significant number of his or her congregation have reached a low ebb. By definition, these cases involve a large number of people, and there is an overlap with the previous category of personality conflict. Some of the cases involve priests who suffer from alcoholism[64] or mental sickness;[65] others involve

---

[57] Archdeacon of West Cumberland (Carlisle); archdeacon of Lindisfarne (Newcastle).

[58] Archdeacon of Southend (Chelmsford); Norwich diocesan counsellor.

[59] archdeacon of West Cumberland (Carlisle); archdeacon of Barnstable (Exeter); bishop and archdeacon of Ludlow (Hereford).

[60] Archdeacon of West Ham (Chelsmford); bishop and archdeacon of Ludlow (Hereford).

[61] Archdeacon of Hackney (London); archdeacon of Basingstoke (Winchester).

[62] Archdeacon of Rochdale (Manchester).

[63] Archdeacon of Aston (Birmingham); archdeacon of Lindisfarne (Newcastle); archdeacon of Tonbridge (Rochester); archdeacon of Wiltshire (Salisbury).

[64] The archdeacon of Lindisfarne wrote to say he had been involved in one serious dispute in the diocese of Newcastle where the clergyman involved was suffering from drink addition.

[65] The archdeacon of Tonbridge wrote to say she had helped to resolve one case where the parish priest was suffering from a severe depressive illness. There was a happy outcome to this case. With the help of his doctor the priest's medication was carefully prescribed, and his health

101

priests who simply fall out with a significant number of their congregation.

St Peter's Church, Ropley is in the last category. A breakdown in
trust over the incumbent's autocratic manner, and controversy
over his marriage to his curate, led to a split in the congregation,
which mediation was unable to resolve.[66] The *Gaulby Group Benefice* dispute was another such case. At one level there was concern
about the incumbent's 'excessively evangelistic style in the pulpit'.
At another level, there was no doubt concern about his conviction
before magistrates for indecent exposure, even though this conviction was subsequently set aside on appeal. The dispute was
finally resolved by a pastoral scheme which split his benefice into
two. The legality of this scheme was challenged by the incumbent, but the scheme was upheld by the Privy Council.[67]

---

improved; and the archdeacon helped the parish support the vicar
through this period. 'There have been no further complaints in the past
two years.'

[66] See *Guardian*, 16 May 1994, home page, pg. 4; *The Times*, 24 February 1998, home news; *The Times*, 20 January 1997, 'worshippers desert
vicar who married his curate'; *Guardian*, 4 January 1997, home page,
pg. 10; *The Times*, 16 October 1995, pg. 3; *The Times*, 10 December 1995,
pg. 6; *Daily Telegraph*, 10 December 1996, pg. 2; *Guardian (London)* 4
January 1997, home page, pg. 10. The author corresponded with the
Winchester Diocesan Registry concerning the mediation efforts, and received letters dated 15 June and 21 July 1999.

[67] The criminal case is reported at *Cheeseman v DPP* [1992] QB 83. In the
law reports his name is misspelled, and there is no mention that he is a
priest; *The Times*, 18 March 1999, home news, pg. 7; *Birmingham Evening
Mail*, 18 March 1999, pg. 7; *Church Times*, 19 March 1999, pg. 1 and pg. 3.
The Privy Council decision is reported as *Cheesman v Church Commissioners* [2000] 1 AC 19; (1999) 5 Ecc LJ 305. For earlier reports in the *Church
Times*, see *Church Times*, 9 February 1996 pg. 3 ('new row at Burton Ov-
ery'); 26 April 1996 pg. 5 ('more trouble at APCM'); letters 3 May 1996
pg. 9; letters 10 May 1996, pg. 9; 23 January 1998, pg. 5 ('the reorganisa-

e) Disputes over forms of worship/doctrine

Many disputes arise as a result of an attempt by a vicar to bring about change in the form of services. Often these involve an attempt to bring modern forms of evangelical or charismatic worship into a traditional congregation. Typical of many is the dispute at *Newport Parish Church*, where the minister introduced a more evangelical style of worship, with a 'praise band', and this led to a split in the congregation and the resignation of the organist.[68] *St Mary's Wroxham* was a case where the majority of the choir resigned in protest at having to sing modern hymns.[69] At *St Thomas the Apostle, Glaisdale, North Yorkshire*, the 'old versus new' music dispute split the congregation, and led to the closure of the church.[70] Similarly, at *St Mark's, Broadwater Down, Kent*, the exercise of charismatic gifts[71] and the 'Toronto Blessing'[72] were at the heart of the dispute.[73]

---

tion approved'); *Church Times*, 18 December 1998, pg. 2 (Privy Council hears appeal).

[68] *Daily Mail*, 26 February 1999, pg. 5.

[69] *The Times*, 10 October 1996, home news; *Daily Telegraph*, 10 October 1996, pg. 8.

[70] *Daily Mail (London)*, 10 November 1994, pg. 23.

[71] The 'charismatic gifts' are described in 1 Corinthians 12:1-11 and 14. The most controversial (both in New Testament times and now) is probably the 'gift of tongues'.

[72] The 'Toronto Blessing' is an extraordinary thing to watch. Members of the church (sometimes quite respectable members of the church!) suddenly find themselves laughing or weeping uncontrollably during the service. They may fall down on the floor, move their limbs about wildly, and make odd noises. Those who speak in favour of it say that this is the work of the Holy Spirit, and cite similar occurrences throughout Christian history. Those who speak against it give all sorts of other explanations as to what is going on.

[73] *The Times*, 11 May 1996, home news. The archdeacon of Man (Sodor and Man) reported that in 1996 there had been a major pastoral break-

Worship issues (services, music, and churchmanship) were mentioned by several archdeacons as a source of conflict.[74]

f) Gay or gender issues

There is an overlap between this category and two of the previous categories. To some, the ordination of women, and gay Christians and gay priests are all theological issues, and should be treated as a dispute over doctrine. To others, as has been seen, these disputes raise the issue of church governance. But the number of disputes under this head is sufficient to justify a category of their own.

Gay disputes include the cases already mentioned of *Jesmond Parish Church, Newcastle*, and *St Oswald, Walkergate*. Gay issues were not mentioned by the archdeacons in their letters to the author, which may suggest that the subject is not as important as the media would like to make out; but at the CEDR[75] conference, gay issues were specifically raised in the context of equal opportunities.

Disputes arising from the ordination of women include *St Mary's, Colkirk*, where the pro-ordination views of the new vicar led to a split in the village and the closure of the church.[76] The

---

down in one parish when the incumbent had been influenced by the Toronto Blessing. The bishop had become involved, and the archdeacon had tried to mediate. Sadly it failed, and a large part of the congregation left. Gradually the situation in that church was easing.

[74] Archdeacon of West Ham (Chelsmford); Archdeacon of Northolt (London); archdeacon of Rochdale (Manchester), archdeacon of Aston (Birmingham); archdeacon of Northumberland (Newcastle); archdeacon of Lynn (Norwich); archdeacon of Man (Sodor and Man); archdeacon of Croydon (Southwark).

[75] For CEDR, see pg. 48, fn. 198.

[76] *The Times* report of 30 December 1996 is confused. It says that the Parochial Church Council forced the incoming vicar to resign, which seems extraordinary. The short report in *The Times* for 28 December 1996

Revd Paul Williamson launched a series of legal actions against various bodies in the Church of England[77] to oppose the legislation permitting the ordination of women, until he was eventually declared a vexatious litigant.[78] The appointment of the Revd Lucy

---

seems to be more accurate. It appears that the Parochial Church Council opposed the appointment of a new vicar who backed the ordination of women as priests.

[77] He also brought proceedings for leave to seek judicial review of the Church in Wales concerning the ordination of women: *R v Dean and Chapter of St Paul's Cathedral and another ex parte Williamson*, Queen's Bench Division (Crown Office List) CO/992/97 (hearing date 22 August 1997) (1997) 5 Ecc LJ 129 and [1998] COD 130.

[78] The judgments in most of the cases concerning Mr Williamson are available on *Lexis*, and some are also reported elsewhere. In chronological order, these are as follows:

- *R v Archbishop of Canterbury and Another, ex parte Williamson*, Court of Appeal (Civil Division), *Independent* 9 March 1994, (hearing date 1 March 1994). The judgment is set out in Mark Hill, *Ecclesiastical Law*, 2nd edn., pg. 672.

- *Reverend Williamson v Archbishop of Canterbury and Others*, Chancery Division, *The Times* 25 November 1994, *Independent* 14 December 1994, (hearing date 11 November 1994).

- *R v Archbishop of Canterbury, ex parte Williamson*, Queen's Bench Division (Crown Office List), CO/2149/95, (hearing date 15 March 1996).

- *The Revd Williamson v The Archbishop of Canterbury and Others. R v The Bishops of Bristol, ex parte The Revd Williamson. R v The Presidents and Representatives of the House of Bishops, ex parte the Revd Williamson*, Court of Appeal (Civil Division), (hearing date 5 September 1996).

- *Re Williamson*, Queen's Bench Division (Crown Office List), CO/1159/97, (hearing date 10 July 1997).

- *R v Attorney General, ex parte Williamson*, Queen's Bench Division (Crown Office List), CO/1159/97, (hearing date 16 July 1997).

- *R v Dean and Chapter of St Paul's Cathedral and another ex parte Williamson*, Queen's Bench Division (Crown Office List), CO/992/97,

Winkett as a minor canon at St Paul's Cathedral in 1997 led to a split between various members of the existing clergy at St Paul's.[79] Yvonne Craig describes a conflict among cathedral clergy concerning the duties of their new colleague, a woman priest, and shows how the conflict was resolved by mediation.[80] Dr Miriam Byrne's controversial appointment to Dundee Cathedral led to members of the congregation leaving the cathedral.[81] The breakdown in the relationship between the Revd Nicola Jay and her parish, the combined benefice of *St Philip and St James, Kimblesworth, County Durham*, involved several issues as well as gender.[82]

(hearing date 22 August 1997), reported at (1997) 5 Ecc LJ 129 and [1998] COD 130.

- *HM Attorney General v Williamson*, Court of Appeal (Civil Division), (hearing date 6 March 1998).

[79] *Daily Telegraph*, 13 February 1997, pg. 1; *Sunday Times*, 11 May 1997, home news. 'St Paul's faithful walk out in row over woman priest'.

[80] Yvonne Craig, *Peacemaking for churches* (London, SPCK, 1999), pg. 22.

[81] Not only was she a woman, which upset the traditionalists opposed to the ordination of women as priests, but she was a former Roman Catholic nun, who had married a monk, and then divorced to remarry. When this became known, some traditionalist members of the Episcopal Church of Scotland left the cathedral to join other congregations soon after her appointment. George Greig, the cathedral's honorary chaplain for 13 years, resigned at her appointment: *Guardian (London)*, 16 November 1998, home page, pg. 3.

[82] The causes of the *St Philip and St James, Kimblesworth, County Durham* dispute included a pastoral reorganisation, changes made by Mrs Jay after her appointment, the closure of a church because of disrepair, and what appears to have been a petty row. Gender plainly played a part because she was one of the first woman priests in Durham. Some of her parishioners considered that her relationship never got off the ground. See reports in *Church Times*, 29 May 1998, pg. 7; *Newcastle Journal*, 14 May 1998, regional news, pg. 9; *Newcastle Journal*, 21 May 1998, regional news, pg. 19; *Newcastle Journal*, 1 June 1998, regional news, pg. 7.

g) Racial discrimination

A number of disputes involve a racial element. The dispute involving the Revd Eve Pitts (who is black) and the team ministry at *St Nicholas, King's Norton, Birmingham* was much publicised on account of her colour, but the real dispute was a personality conflict between the members of the team.[83] In *Hackney Marsh* in East London, one of the main issues in the dispute was the relationship between the black female curate, the Revd Urmila Patel, and the other members of the team ministry, and also her relationship with various members of the congregation.[84] Racial discrimination was mentioned as a concern at the CEDR conference on church conflict in October 1999. Racial discrimination can be a crime under the Race Relations Act 1976.[85] Whether or not there is much racial discrimination in the strict sense of the 1976 Act, it is clear that a racial element is involved in many disputes where one or more of the parties is from a racial minority.

h) Employment disputes

Many employment disputes involve the church authorities and just one employee, e.g. the dismissal of the organist of *Crathie Kirk, Balmoral.*[86] In some cases many employees can be affected, and

---

[83] *The Times,* 3 March 1997, home news; *Church Times,* 7 March 1997 pg. 1 (photo), pg. 3; 14 March 1997, pg. 9 (letters); 21 March 1997, pg. 2 (petition presented to bishop Mark Santer), pg. 9 (letter); 27 March 1997, pg. 9 (letter); 13 June (service of reconciliation, to which Eve Pitts claims she was not invited); Church Times, 13 February 1998, pg. 3; 20 February 1998, pg. 9 (letter).

[84] The Revd Michael Clark, who was appointed in 2000 by the Bishop as facilitator for this dispute, provided helpful background information to the author.

[85] James Behrens, *Practical Church Management,* pg. 94.

[86] *The Glasgow Herald,* 17 March 1997, pg. 3; *Daily Mail (London),* 17 March 1997, pg. 3. *The Times,* 17 March 1997 report 'Organ row threatens

the dispute is more in the nature of industrial action. The dispute between the Dean of St Paul's Cathedral and 18 virgers,[87] despite its ecclesiastical setting, was a typical employment grievance concerning pay and conditions.[88] The dispute in the Episcopal Church of Scotland board of communication was an industrial dispute about the proposed redundancy of one-third of the staff.[89] Another dispute involving large numbers concerned the redundancy of 200 volunteers at Salisbury Cathedral.[90]

The prevalence of employment disputes was borne out by archdeacons and diocesan secretaries. One diocesan secretary said that his diocese faced a complaint to an employment tribunal from a female lay worker.[91] Two archdeacons identified an unprofessional approach to good employment practice for church employees, e.g. the failure to have a proper job description for a church administrator, as a source of conflict.[92]

i) Discipline

Discipline covers a spectrum including criminal conduct and serious moral failings such as adultery; issues of principle over

---

royal patronage of Balmoral church'; *The Scotsman*, 22 April 1997; *Daily Mail (London)*, 12 May 1998, pg. 24; *The Times*, 9 May 1998, features.

[87] St Paul's retains the original spelling for verger, referring to the man or woman who carries a *virge* or rod of office.

[88] *Daily Telegraph*, 9 November 1992, pg. 8. For the role of the verger (or virger) more generally, see James Behrens, *Practical Church Management*, chapter 7.

[89] *The Scotsman*, 19 May 1998, pg. 10; *Edinburgh Evening News*, 19 May 1998, pg. 2; *The Scotsman*, 20 May 1998, pg. 10; *The Glasgow Herald*, 24 December 1998, pg. 5; *The Glasgow Herald*, 4 May 1999, pg. 11.

[90] *Church Times*, 19 March 1999, home page; *The Times*, 23 April 1999, pg. 3; *The Times*, 30 April 1999, features 'cathedral dispute'.

[91] The diocesan secretary for Lichfield.

[92] Archdeacon of Northolt (London); archdeacon of Rochdale (Manchester).

church governance, involving perhaps issues of worship and doctrine, and a challenge to episcopal authority; and less serious cases where there has been some pastoral failing by the clergyman.

Examples of clergy discipline cases widely reported in the media include church trials against clergymen accused of sexual misconduct, one in England,[93] and one in Wales;[94] a case where a Church of Scotland minister was disciplined for conducting business activities;[95] and a dispute where a leading minister and theology professor of the Free Church of Scotland was almost made the subject of a heresy trial.[96] These cases were all very expensive.[97] Many minor discipline cases are handled quietly, are not

---

[93] The case of the Very Revd Dr Brandon Jackson, dean of Lincoln Cathedral, accused of an improper sexual relationship with a former verger, a Miss Verity Freestone. He was acquitted. For newspaper reports, see *Daily Mail*, 20 July 1995, pg. 1, 6 and 7. For a commentary on the procedure, see *Under Authority, Report on Clergy Discipline* (London, Church House Publishing, 1996).

[94] The disciplinary trial of the Revd Clifford Williams, found guilty of adultery with a parishioner, and various other offences. See *R v Provincial Court of the Church in Wales ex parte Williams*, 23 October 1998, *Lexis* report, and (1999) 5 Ecc LJ 217. See also *Williams v Bishop of Bangor* (1999) 5 Ecc LJ 304.

[95] The Revd Tom Logan. The case is of legal interest, in that it established that in Scotland decisions by the church on matters of doctrine, worship, government and discipline are not subject to review by the civil courts: *Logan v Presbytery of Dumbarton* [1995] SLT 1228, *The Times*, 23 May 1995.

[96] Professor Donald Macleod. For newspaper reports, see *Daily Telegraph*, 18 April 1996, pg. 4; *Independent (London)*, 18 April 1996, news, pg. 3; *Sunday Times*, 6 October 1996, home news; *The Scotsman*, 31 October 1996, pg. 8; *The Edinburgh Evening News*, 14 May 1998, pg. 8.

[97] Dr Brandon Jackson's trial cost £99,825: see *Under Authority, Report on Clergy Discipline*, pg. 117. The Revd Clifford Williams' trial cost £309,000: see Church Times, 1 October 1999, news, pg. 5.

headline news, and are relatively inexpensive. For example, a dispute concerning the parish priest's handling of a convicted sex-offender who had joined a congregation was handled by a formal, but private, hearing by the bishop.[98]

A number of cases which also fall into other categories are perceived as raising issues of discipline, e.g. *St John the Baptist, Kidderminster*. The Revd Charles Raven was in dispute with his bishop over the bishop's stand on homosexuality.[99] Mr Raven saw the dispute as a matter of doctrine. The Bishop of Worcester saw Mr Raven's being willing to work within the terms of his licence as a matter of discipline.[100] The *Kidderminster* dispute 'is not an isolated storm in a tea-cup but a vivid and highly charged expression of widely felt tensions'.[101]

Discipline includes discipline of the laity. The *St Kenelm, Clifton upon Teme* dispute arose when the choirmaster refused to allow a person to sing in the choir because she ran a new age shop, which the choirmaster considered incompatible with Christianity.[102] Discipline of the laity also includes refusal of the sacrament. In the Church of England this is limited to cases of grave

---

[98] The diocese was Lichfield. The Bishop's report was sent to the author by the diocesan secretary.

[99] *Church Times*, 16 June 2000 pg. 1. 'Kidderminster goes critical. Rebel priest stands firm and rejects Bishop's compromise offer'.

[100] Correspondence (by email) between the Bishop of Worcester and the author during 2000, when the possibility of the author acting as mediator in the dispute was under consideration. In the event, no mediation took place. The dispute continued until 2002: *Church Times*, 29 June 2001 pg. 3. 'Kidderminster vicar to stay on, unlicensed'; *Church Times*, 1 February 2002 pg. 4. 'Raven flies C of E nest as his contract ends'.

[101] Peter Fisher, '*Koinonia* and Conflict', *Theology*, November/December 2001, 420 at 424.

[102] *Daily Telegraph*, 11 February 1995, pg. 3.

and immediate scandal to the congregation.[103] This form of discipline is still being used, albeit infrequently, principally in cases of sexual misbehaviour, but also where the parties are involved in some conflict.[104] The former Lord Chancellor, Lord Mackay of Clashfern, was disciplined by the Free Presbyterian Church of Scotland for attending a requiem mass for a colleague.[105]

Cases where there are serious sexual allegations against one of the parties are not generally considered appropriate for mediation: if the allegations are proved, discipline is called for.[106]

---

[103] Canon B 16.

[104] See Tom Culver, '*Canon B 16: excommunication in the Church of England*' (University of Wales unpublished LLM Dissertation, Cardiff Law School, 1996). In a lecture in 2000 to the Ecclesiastical Law Society Mr Culver gave the then up-to-date figures for the use of this provision. Of 26 occasions where the sacrament had been refused, 21 were for sexual sin, and 6 were for conflict. (Presumably one occasion was for both).

[105] In 1989, the Associated Presbyterian Church of Scotland was formed following the furore when Lord Mackay of Clashfern, the then Lord Chancellor, and the Free Presbyterians' highest-profile elder, was disciplined by hard-liners for attending a requiem mass for Lord Wheatley, a former court of session judicial colleague. Lord Mackay was suspended for six months, and later left the church. This led to 14 ministers, almost half of the church's clergy, and almost half of the Free Church's 6,000 members crossing over to form the Associated Presbyterian Church: *Sunday Times*, 21 January 1996, home news; *The Scotsman*, 15 May 1998, pg. 8.

[106] *Under Authority, Report on Clergy Discipline*, paragraph 8.32 argues also that some offences amount to an offence against the Church generally, and a penalty should be imposed if they are proved. One of the case studies in *Under Authority* (at page 88) involves sexual allegations, and there is no mention of the word mediation. There is also concern that the confidential nature of the mediation process would be seen as a cover-up.

111

Chapter 7 will show that this is not an absolute rule world-wide.[107]

j) Property disputes

Property disputes cover many areas. The issue over the Forsyth bequest was which of two church denominations was entitled to a bequest.[108] The *Chipping Sodbury* dispute concerned a right of way.[109] The *Hutten Buscel* dispute concerned a sycamore tree which was damaging a church, and later a dispute with the diocesan authority over permission to sell a valuable silver trophy to pay for restoration works.[110] The *Grange Road Baptist Church* dispute concerned a club which met on church premises.[111] The *St Mary's, Whitby* dispute concerned the use of the churchyard for a costume parade.[112]

Property disputes frequently arise between churches and local or other authorities exercising statutory powers. The *Hutten Buscel* dispute was one such. Another concerned the exercise of compulsory purchase powers by the Manchester City Council over

---

[107] For example, in Bendigo (Australia), the diocese's sexual harassment protocol and its Ecclesiastical Offences Act both provide for mediation. It may be a matter of degree. Minor touching may be one thing; sexual intercourse another.

[108] *The Scotsman*, 15 May 1998, pg. 8.

[109] *Western Daily Press*, 18 April 1998, pg. 5; *Bristol Evening Post*, 20 April 1998, 'Church path feud turns to law'.

[110] *Daily Mail (London)*, 8 December 1994, pg. 17; *Church Times*, 30 July 1999, News, pg. 2; *Church Times*, 19 November 1999, News, pg. 2.

[111] *The Northern Echo*, 12 March 1997, pg. 5; *The Northern Echo*, 17 September 1997, pg. 50; *The Northern Echo*, 25 January 1999, pg. 6.

[112] *Daily Telegraph*, 13 June 1997, pg. 3. The story first appeared in Focus, the newsletter for the evangelical church Holy Trinity, Brompton in West London.

two churches owned by the Methodist Church.[113] In *St Michael's, Highworth, near Swindon* the PCC came into conflict with the local planning authority over proposals to install floodlights to illuminate the church.[114]

Three dioceses identified churchyards as a source of conflict;[115] and one, the use of church bells.[116]

k) Financial disputes

Reimbursement of parochial working expenses to the incumbent is an area which causes frequent conflict.[117] So does the allocation of clergy working expenses where parishes are combined.[118] There is an overlap between this category and the Church governance category over such items as the scale of re-

---

[113] The dispute came to court over the issue whether the Methodist Church was entitled to interest on the compensation due under the Compulsory Purchase Act 1965. Both Buckley J at first instance and the Court of Appeal decided that the Methodist Church was entitled to such interest: *Halstead v Manchester City Council* [1998] 1 All ER 33.

[114] *Western Daily Press*, 13 August 1998, news, pg. 5. For one consistory court's approach to floodlighting see *Re St Peter and St Paul, Wantage* (1999) 5 Ecc LJ 306.

[115] Bishop and archdeacon of Ludlow (Hereford); archdeacon of Rochdale (Manchester); archdeacon of Northampton (Peterborough).

[116] Diocesan secretary for Salisbury. This was the case of Midge Mather and the bells at Compton Bassett.

[117] In the diocese of Bath and Wells, the diocesan secretary reported frequent conflict on the question of reimbursement of parochial working expenses to the incumbent. Money of course is quite often an emotive area in which conflict can arise. The diocesan secretary considered that conflict often arose from an arrogance on the part of the incumbent, and an unwillingness to provide the sort of detail in the atmosphere of transparency which is now prevalent in charity finance and the commercial world generally.

[118] Archdeacon of Northumberland (Newcastle).

furbishments to parsonages, and the calculation of an individual parish contribution to the common fund. Financial disputes can arise over innumerable areas connected with how the church spends the church budget. Similarly, disputes can arise with vicar and warden trusts connected with the church.[119] A typical financial dispute arose at one church when the PCC turned down the vicar's request for a car and a computer.[120]

Financial disputes sometimes involve allegations of theft or embezzlement. Criminal cases are outside the scope of this book, as they need to be dealt with through the proper criminal process. Any attempt to resolve the dispute by mediation to avoid a criminal trial would risk being seen as a 'cover-up'. A form of mediation known as victim-offender mediation may however be appropriate after conviction, as a means of enabling the victims to express their needs and feelings, and for the offenders to accept and act on their responsibilities.[121]

l) *Defamation*

One church defamation case receiving considerable publicity was the case of the Dallimores.[122] One Rebecca Dallimore made accusations of satanic ritual abuse against her parents Valerie and

---

[119] For example, in one case in which the author was professionally involved, the dispute was as to the amount the trustees would contribute to the repair of the tower.

[120] *St Cyrus and St Julietta, Luxulyan, Bodmin*, reported in *The Times*, 11 December 1993, home news.

[121] For victim-offender mediation, see Marian Liebmann, *Mediation in Context* (London, Jessica Kingsley Publishers, 2000), chapter 8. In particular restorative justice (another name for victim-offender mediation) is finding favour with those involved with youth crime: see *Mediation Magazine* (Bristol, Mediation UK, 2001) issue 67 (September 2001), pg. 1.

[122] *Sunday Times*, 5 June 1994, home news; *Guardian*, 15 November 1995, pg. 11; *Daily Telegraph*, 13 July 1996, pg. 13; *Church Times*, 13 November 1998, pg. 7

David Dallimore during a healing ceremony at the home of the Revd Arthur Rowe, the vicar of St James' Church in Hockwold, near Thetford, Norfolk. The matter received widespread publicity as a result of an article published in the *Lynn News* following an interview with Mr Rowe. A criminal investigation by the police against the Dallimore parents was dropped, and the parents then sued Mr Rowe for defamation.

Less dramatic was the *King's Christian Fellowship, Tavistock* dispute, which arose out of public prayers made by the pastor for two divorced single mothers in the congregation. The two women claimed that the prayers amounted to slander, and demanded an apology.[123]

m) Personal injury

According to *The Churchyards Handbook*,[124] the largest number of claims made against churches results from persons, either visitors or regular members of the congregation, slipping, tripping or falling on paths, steps or in other parts of the churchyard.[125] Churches should of course take out third-party insurance against such a risk.[126]

---

[123] *Daily Telegraph*, 27 January 1997, pg. 5.

[124] *The Churchyards Handbook* (London, Church House Publishing, 2001) pg. 128.

[125] In *Rigby v Incumbent and churchwardens of St Peter's Church (Yately)* [1998] CLY 337 Mrs Rigby sustained a knee injury in a slipping accident, and brought legal proceedings against the church. (The report does not state whether the incident took place in the church or the churchyard.) Another personal injuries case involving a church is *O'Sullivan v Church of Ireland*, noted in Practice and Procedure 1998, 1 (Feb.), 13 (London, Round Hall/Sweet & Maxwell, 1998).

[126] See James Behrens, *Practical Church Management*, chapter 21.

n) Commercial contract disputes

There are many cases where professionals have been employed by a church, and some dispute has arisen about the quality of the work done or the fees charged. Repair work may have been done badly, an alteration may be found to have some design flaw, building work may have gone over budget, or a solicitor's fees may be higher than was expected. Similarly, a church may find itself in a normal commercial dispute with a supplier of goods, if the goods turn out to be faulty. Diocesan secretaries are often contacted by churches involved in such disputes.[127] These disputes do not usually get reported in the newspapers. Only occasionally do they raise some legal issue, so as to be reported in the law reports.[128]

o) Tax disputes

Several cases have arisen where churches have got into a dispute with Customs and Excise over whether building work was standard or zero rated for VAT.[129] These disputes are different from the majority of church disputes, in that there is no personality conflict or human element involved. No-one has done any-

---

[127] This information comes from the former diocesan secretary for London, Christopher Smith.

[128] One such claim between builders and a church, arising out of restoration works, is *William Tompkinson v The Parochial Church Council of St Michael* (1990) 6 Const LJ 319. Another, a claim by a church against a firm of architects, arising out of alleged defects in design, is *Lancashire and Cheshire Association of Baptist Churches Inc v Howard & Seddon Partnership (a firm)* [1993] 3 All ER 467. A church claim in respect of negligent tax advice by a barrister is the case of *Liverpool RC Diocese v Goldberg* [2001] 1 All ER 172. The claim was settled after the draft judgment was circulated to the parties: *Liverpool RC Trustees Inc v Goldberg (No. 3) (Practice Note)* [2001] 1 WLR 2337.

[129] For an explanation of the main VAT principles relevant to churches, see James Behrens, *Practical Church Management*, chapter 27.

thing wrong: this sort of tax dispute is morally neutral.[130] In *St Paul's, Brentford*, liability for VAT turned on whether the work was an 'alteration' or an 'enlargement' of an existing church.[131] In *Emmanuel, Wimbledon*,[132] the issue was whether there had been an 'enlargement of' the church or an 'extension to' the church. In *Holy Trinity, Heath Town, Wolverhampton*,[133] the issue was whether certain building and electrical works which were to be carried out were repairs, which are standard rated, or alterations, which are zero rated. In *St Andrew's Church, Ealing*,[134] the issue was again whether works to the tower of the church were alterations or re-

---

[130] Tax disputes can, of course, arise from tax evasion, which is a criminal offence, rather than tax avoidance, which is not.

[131] *Customs & Excise Commissioners v London Diocesan Fund* [1993] STC 369 concerned the replacement of St Paul's, Brentford, by a new church. The old tower with its spire remained, but 90 per cent of the rest of the old church was destroyed to make way for the new building. The issue was whether the work amounted to an 'alteration' or 'enlargement' of an existing church, which would have been zero rated, or was essentially a new building, which would be standard rated. The tribunal held that the new church was essentially a new building, and therefore was standard rated.

[132] *Carrophil Ltd v Commissioners of Customs and Excise*, 1 April 1993, reported only on *Lexis*. The appellant was the building company that had carried out works to Emmanuel Church, Wimbledon to provide accommodation for the Sunday School. Enlargements are standard rated, extensions zero rated. The tribunal held that the new Sunday School was an extension to the church, rather than an enlargement, and accordingly the building works were zero rated.

[133] *PCC of Holy Trinity Church (Heath Town, Wolverhampton) v Commissioners of Customs and Excise*, 18 October 1995, reported only on *Lexis*.

[134] *PCC of St Andrew's Church Eakring v Commissioners of Customs and Excise* [1998] BVC 2117, also reported on *Lexis*.

pairs. In *St Dunstan's Roman Catholic Church*,[135] the issue was whether a garage built on the church grounds was to be used for a charitable purpose, which would mean the garage should be zero rated, or for a private purpose, which would mean it should be standard rated.

VAT disputes are not all about the construction of buildings. In 1999 the Dean and Canons of Windsor lost an appeal against a tribunal decision that they must continue to pay VAT on admission charges to St George's Chapel, Windsor.[136]

Tax disputes can arise in areas other than VAT. In *Battle Baptist Church v Inland Revenue Commissioners*,[137] the issue was whether the church was eligible for gift aid where subscribers sent letters purporting to cancel loans they had made and convert them to gifts.

2. FEATURES OF CHURCH DISPUTES

a) *Complexity*

Not all church disputes can conveniently be placed in one category. Many disputes are complex, involving two if not more categories. Many disputes have a number of causes which go back years, and which may have nothing to do with the present incumbent. Some disputes may arise out of one isolated action or proposal, but many disputes have more than one cause.[138] One of

---

[135] *Re St Dunstan's Roman Catholic Church, Southborough v Commissioners of Customs and Excise* [1998] V & DR 264. For a case comment, see Butterworths Tax Journal 1998, 465, 21–22.

[136] *Church Times,* 10 January 1999, news; *Dean and Canons of Windsor v Customs and Excise Commissioners* [1999] BVC 2010.

[137] *Battle Baptist Church v Inland Revenue Commissioners* [1995] STI 694.

[138] For example, *St Philip and St James, Kimblesworth, County Durham* involved a dispute with the diocese over church organisation, changes made – perhaps too quickly – by Mrs Jay after her appointment, a con-

the reasons church conflicts are often difficult to resolve is because they are often complex.[139]

Several disputes mentioned in this chapter come into a number of categories: in particular, church governance seems to be linked to a number of the other categories.

i church governance – discipline – personality dispute

The trial of the Very Revd Dr Brandon Jackson, the Dean of Lincoln Cathedral, was a discipline matter, but was linked to a bigger problem at the cathedral arising out of a personality conflict between the Dean and the subdean. Equally, the Lincoln dispute can be seen as raising an issue of church (or cathedral) governance.

ii church governance – employment

The Westminster Abbey dispute[140] in 1998 is at one level an employment dispute; at another level it raises questions of church governance.[141]

iii church governance – discipline

Likewise, the dispute involving the Revd Kit Chalcraft in Norfolk[142] was a discipline matter, but became a matter of church

---

cern by the parishioners that they did not have a church to worship at (it was closed for repairs), a concern that Mrs Jay was not ministering to the parishioners' needs, and a petty argument about hand-shaking at a communion service.

[139] See 'Why is conflict so difficult?' in David B. Lott (ed.) *Conflict Management in Congregations* (Bethesda, Maryland, USA, Alban Institute, 2001) pg. 8.

[140] *Neary v Dean of Westminster* [1999] IRLR 288, (1998) 5 Ecc LJ 303. The case is discussed in detail in chapter 2, 'The Westminster Abbey dispute".

[141] Arguably, it might also fall within the 'personality conflicts' category.

[142] See pg. 95, fn. 30.

governance. The Revd Tom Logan's dispute[143] was a disciplinary matter, but raised an important constitutional right concerning church governance.

iv church governance – discipline – gay or gender issues – worship and doctrine

It may be argued that the various disputes about homosexuality show the categorisation at its weakest. *Jesmond Parish Church, Newcastle*[144] and *St Oswald, Walkergate*[145] led to a major confrontation between the church and the bishop of Newcastle over the issue of episcopal oversight. Episcopal oversight could be said to be a matter of church governance. But in the *Kidderminster* dispute,[146] the bishop saw the issue as one of church discipline, whilst Mr Raven saw the issue as a matter of doctrine.

Often different issues are of different importance and value to different parties to a dispute. The giving of an apology may be regarded as costing nothing, but the receipt of an apology may be fundamental to continuing negotiations. Mediators are well used to exploring each issue with each party to identify value differentials: something of positive value to one party and little cost to another could lead to movement, and may even be the gesture that leads to resolution of the dispute.[147] The fact that the disputes about homosexuality are viewed differently by bishops, evangelicals, and no doubt by homosexuals themselves, is an encouraging factor, suggesting that a solution to these disputes may indeed be found by mediation. The fact that the gay issue straddles a num-

---

[143] See pg. 98, fn. 44.

[144] See pg. 96, fn. 32.

[145] See pg. 96, fn. 33.

[146] See pg. 110, fn. 99.

[147] *Mediator Training Course Handbook* (London, CEDR, 1997), pg. 58.

ber of other categories neither weakens this conclusion, nor indicates that gay issues are not capable of resolution by mediation.[148]

v Property disputes – alterations to church buildings and graveyards – worship and doctrine

Not all property disputes concern the fabric of the church building, but there is an obvious link between the category for faculty disputes, which are described as disputes about church buildings and graveyards, with other property disputes. Many faculty disputes involve delicate issues of theology and churchmanship, and so faculty disputes are linked to worship and doctrine.[149] The various disputes about bells come under these categories.[150]

---

[148] There is no reported English case of a successful mediation of a gay issue. However there is a gay dispute in Belgium which seems to be moving towards mediation. The dispute is between the Roman Catholic Archbishop, Cardinal Danneels, and a gay priest, Rudy Borremans, who is living with another man. The case is reported in the Belgian newspaper *Gazet van Antwerpen* of 29 August 2001. A Belgian member of the Ecclesiastical Law Society, Willy Bogaert, provided this information.

[149] James Behrens, *Practical Church Management*, pg. 315. As an example, *Re St Helen's, Bishopsgate* (1993) 3 Ecc LJ 256; (1993) 12 Consistory and Commissary Court Cases, Case 23, concerned how to restore a church which had been bomb-blasted by the IRA. The case can be seen as a dispute over churchmanship – whether to restore the Victorian high church architecture which was there before the bomb, with its sacramental emphasis on the sanctuary, or to restore the Reformation style church which was there before the 1850s, with its emphasis on the pulpit. The Victorian Society and English Heritage wanted the former, the evangelical congregation wanted the latter. The Chancellor decided in favour of the congregation. Another faculty case which explicitly concerned churchmanship was *Re St Nicholas, Arundel* (2002) 6 Ecc LJ 290.

[150] In particular, 'worship and doctrine', and 'property'.

vi No need for a 'Cathedrals' category

There have been many disputes at cathedrals and royal peculiars: the Lincoln Cathedral dispute with Dr Brandon Jackson;[151] at Westminster Abbey, the dispute with Dr Neary;[152] the dispute at St Paul's Cathedral, Dundee with the Revd Miriam Byrne;[153] the dispute at St Paul's Cathedral, London concerning the Revd Lucy Winkett;[154] the dispute at St Paul's Cathedral, London concerning the virgers;[155] and the dispute at Salisbury Cathedral concerning the volunteer workers.[156] This suggests that cathedrals and royal peculiars should perhaps be a separate category. This is not necessary, as there is no common theme to these disputes other than the fact that they took place at these establishments, nor was there any common management failing. Indeed the Salisbury Cathedral dispute[157] was handled well, and was quickly resolved.

vii Usefulness of the categorisation

The categorisation into 15 types of dispute is therefore, it is submitted, helpful. It forms the basis of the survey into the use of mediation in the Anglican Communion which follows (chapter 7). As the responses to that survey show, this categorisation is not the only way of looking at the disputes which arise. In particular, a number of the responses to that survey categorised disputes not by reference to the problem, but by reference to the people involved. Thus, for example, a dispute between the parish priest and the PCC may be treated as one category, whether the subject matter of the dispute is the church building, worship, finance,

---

[151] See pg. 57, fn. 10.

[152] See chapter 2.

[153] See pg. 99, fn. 48.

[154] See pg. 58, fn. 11.

[155] See pg. 108, fn. 88.

[156] See pg. 108, fn. 90.

[157] See pg. 108, fn. 90.

church government, or whatever. Church disputes involve both an issue which needs to be resolved, and the people affected by that issue. The 15 types of dispute is a categorisation of the former, and to some extent it may appear to ignore the latter.[158]

b) Numbers of parties involved

One reason for the complexity of many church disputes is the number of parties involved, each of whom may have a different perception of the underlying problem. It is one thing to mediate a dispute between two or three people; a very different approach may be called for when a problem affects a whole community. A person seeking to help resolve a complex dispute involving several parties or a community needs to understand how to manage conflict in groups. This is more than just knowing how to chair a meeting; it may involve, for example, developing and proposing a new process or procedure for group decision-making. Chapter 6 will examine this in detail.

c) The conflict triangle

The concept of the conflict triangle was introduced in chapter 2. The survey in this chapter indicates that church disputes involve all three elements in the triangle.

i Problem issues

The substantive dispute is of course important, and is how this chapter has sought to categorise disputes.[159] But many church disputes also involve issues of human relationships; and the process for handling each dispute is also important, not just for its own sake, but because it may affect the outcome.

---

[158] To some extent only. The names chosen for two of the 15 categories, personality disputes and pastoral breakdown, indicate that these categories are primarily disputes about relationships. The three elements of the conflict triangle are considered further in section c) below.

[159] See fn. 158 above.

ii People issues

It is clear that many disputes involve the emotions of the people concerned. Indeed, where a dispute touches matters of faith, this is likely to be the case. It is the task of the mediator to recognise, acknowledge, and handle such emotions. A mediator seeking to resolve a dispute needs to find out what the dispute is really about, not just what it appears to be about. The root cause of a dispute may not be what the parties first tell the mediator that they are arguing about. The failure by Mrs Jay[160] to shake hands with two members of her congregation at a service would not lead most normal people to feel that they had been snubbed, and to tell the vicar that he was not wanted. Plainly there was hurt and resentment which went deeper than this. Many single issue disputes concerning, for example, the organ, the use of rites in public services, or boundaries for people's responsibilities, may conceal a problem in personal relationships.[161] Dealing with hurts and resentments is covered in both chapter 5, 'Community mediation', and chapter 6, 'Consensus-building mediation'.

iii Process issues

The news reports frequently point to a lack of proper management of the dispute, when matters first become contentious. The secular world knows that how a dispute is handled is almost as important as the outcome that is reached. The next section of this chapter is therefore about management issues of church disputes.

---

[160] *St Philip and St James, Kimblesworth, County Durham,* see pg. 106, fn. 82.

[161] Archdeacon of West Ham (Chelsmford); bishop and archdeacon of Ludlow (Hereford).

3. MANAGEMENT ISSUES OF CHURCH DISPUTES

The letters to all archdeacons and diocesan secretaries in England,[162] stated that the author was trying to build up a picture of (a) how conflicts can be avoided before they start, (b) how they can best be resolved in practice, and (c) what lessons can be learned from those disputes which could not be resolved. The letters asked for each diocese's experience in this area, and whether the diocese had people trained in mediation available to assist in resolving church disputes. The following management issues were identified in the responses.

a) Involvement of Church hierarchy

The survey confirms that archdeacons, rural deans and bishops are often the first point of contact when things go wrong.[163] The responses show that these people put considerable effort and time into helping to resolve disputes which come to their attention. In some cases, their efforts appear to succeed.[164] In other cases, the bishop's attempts to mediate failed.[165] In some cases, the result of the bishop's or archdeacon's intervention is not recorded.[166] Where the dispute has involved a bishop, the intervention of an archbishop has sometimes succeeded in resolving the issue,[167] and

---

[162] The text of the letters sent to archdeacons and diocesan secretaries is set out in appendix 2.

[163] See James Behrens, *Practical Church Management,* pg. 250.

[164] Cases where the bishop or archdeacon's intervention has resolved a dispute include *St Philip and St James, Kimblesworth, County Durham; Eltisley Parish;* and *St Cyrus and St Julietta, Luxulyan, Bodmin.*

[165] Notably, the dispute at Lincoln Cathedral. Other examples where mediation attempts appears to have failed include *St Mary's, Langham; St Michael's, Oulton; Westminster Abbey; Swaffham, Norfolk;* and *St Peter's Church, Ropley.*

[166] The result of intervention by the bishop or archdeacon in the dispute at Holy Trinity Church, Silksworth, Sunderland is not recorded.

[167] e.g. St Oswald, Walkergate.

sometimes has not.[168] Sometimes an archbishop has refused to intervene.[169]

b) Early intervention to prevent escalation

A number of responses indicated the need for the archdeacon to intervene as early in the dispute as possible, before attitudes harden, and the level of conflict rises.[170] Early intervention does not always succeed in preventing a dispute escalating, but it is usually an advantage.[171] By intervening early, archdeacons can listen to both sides, and defuse tension.[172]

---

[168] e.g. at Lincoln cathedral, and arguably St Ninian's, Whitby.

[169] e.g. Jesmond parish church (The Revd David Holloway).

[170] Archdeacon of Canterbury; archdeacon of Hackney (London); archdeacon of Northolt (London). The archdeacon of Wisbech (Ely) commented on the need to prevent parties taking up entrenched positions: 'the deeper they dig their trenches, the less they can see.' The concept of the level of a conflict is discussed in chapter 6, 'Consensus-building mediation'.

[171] The archdeacon of Canterbury reported that in one dispute his early intervention failed to prevent a painful consistory court. In the second, he went in with a management consultant, and after many conciliation meetings there was a service of penitence for everybody as paving the way to a fresh start in the church.

[172] The archdeacon of Southend (Chelmsford) commented that archdeacons can also encourage early consultation which is particularly helpful in building cases. Widespread consultation both within the parish and with the DAC about proposed building works is very helpful in preventing conflict arising: see Mark Hill, *Ecclesiastical Law*, 2nd edn., pg. 180–183.

c) Management time

Many archdeacons spoke about the considerable time they and others spent in dealing with conflict.[173] The letter to the archdeacons did not ask for statistics, but the responses suggest that most archdeacons and diocesan secretaries seem to be handling two or three cases of conflict at any one time. There are typically six disputes in any one diocese at any one time.[174] Multiply that over

---

[173] Diocesan secretary for Blackburn, 'quite a slice of the bishop's, archdeacons' and his own time'; contrast the archdeacon of Aston (Birmingham), 'he did not want to give the impression that it was necessary to spend a great deal of time on such disputes'; archdeacon for Westmorland and Furness (Carlisle), 'constantly involved in the process of mediation'; archdeacon of West Ham (Chelmsford), 'quite a bit of time'; archdeacon of Horsham (Chichester), 'constantly find themselves mediating'; bishop and archdeacon of Ludlow (Hereford), 'often'; archdeacon of Lincoln, 'a lot of his time'; a diocesan counsellor in Norwich, 'from time to time'; archdeacon of Northampton (Peterborough), 'archdeacons do spend a great deal of their time resolving conflicts within parishes and disagreements between clergy and laity. This is extremely time-consuming'; archdeacon of Man (Sodor and Man), 'resolving disputes takes up a good deal of his time'; diocesan secretary for Truro, 'a lot of time being spent on visiting parishes and sitting down to discuss the issues with them' (this may be more preventative than curative).

[174] *Church Times*, 8 October 1999, page 3 quotes the author as giving the figure of six disputes per diocese at the CEDR conference 'Mediating Church Conflict' on 5 October 1999. In fact it was given it as part of a press release on 23 September 1999 shortly before the conference. The figure of six disputes per diocese is reached on the basis that each diocese has on average three archdeacons, and each archdeacon has two current disputes he is handling. This is a very conservative estimate. The author suspects that the number of more than trivial disputes is much higher than this. The diocesan secretary for London had a shelf of about 20 files representing current disputes when the author visited him; and the archdeacon of West Ham (Chelmsford) said that he had been drawn into three quite serious church conflicts in the course of the pre-

the 43 dioceses, and over 250 disputes at any one time represents a large amount of management time.

d) Human resources available to resolve conflict

Some dioceses regard resolving disputes as a pastoral matter, and therefore appropriate for archdeacons, to the exclusion of almost everyone else.[175] But in the majority of dioceses a variety of people gave their services to the Church to assist resolving disputes, apparently with some success. The Church calls upon a wide range of human resources for this service. In addition to the obvious categories of the bishop and archdeacons, the list includes a whole range of diocesan staff, clergy and lay people, and both Christian and secular organisations. Specific mention was made in the responses of the following (there is some overlap between the categories):

i diocesan staff

diocesan secretaries,[176] the chairman of the diocesan advisory committee,[177] a network of link people with deaneries for disputes regarding parish share,[178] the diocesan communications officer,[179] diocesan office staff,[180] diocesan support ministers (e.g. the agricultural chaplain, the social responsibility officer, and the local

---

vious week. There are 112 archdeacons divided between the 42 dioceses in England and Wales, and a further seven archdeacons for the diocese in Europe: see the *Church of England Year Book* (London, Church House Publishing, 2001).

[175]Bishop of Exeter; diocesan secretary for Chichester; diocesan secretary for Europe.

[176] Diocesan secretary for Bath and Wells; diocesan secretary for Blackburn; diocesan secretary for Salisbury; diocesan secretary for Truro.

[177] Bishop of Hereford.

[178] Bishop of Hereford.

[179] Archdeacon of Walsall (Lichfield).

[180] Bishop of Hereford.

ministry officer)[181] the diocesan director of ministry and training,[182] diocesan counsellors,[183] a diocesan officer for continuing ministerial education,[184] a diocesan adviser on pastoral care and counselling,[185] bishop's senior staff,[186] a diocesan pastoral secretary,[187] a diocesan registrar,[188] and a chairman of the diocesan board of finance.[189]

ii clergy

a retired priest running a conciliation service,[190] parish priests in the diocese,[191] rural deans,[192] a wise nun,[193] a retired archdeacon,[194] an archdeacon's wife,[195] and many in the diocesan staff category above.

---

[181] Bishop of Hereford.

[182] Archdeacon of Northumberland (Newcastle).

[183] Diocese of Norwich (working for the Norwich board of social responsibility).

[184] Archdeacon of Lynn (Norwich).

[185] Archdeacon of Rochester.

[186] Archdeacon of Tonbridge (Rochester).

[187] Diocesan secretary for Salisbury.

[188] Diocesan secretary for Truro.

[189] Diocesan secretary for Truro.

[190] Archdeacon of Canterbury.

[191] Archdeacon of West Cumberland (Carlisle).

[192] Archdeacon of West Cumberland (Carlisle); archdeacon of Southend (Chelmsford); bishop of Hereford.

[193] Archdeacon of Southend (Chelmsford).

[194] Archdeacon of West Cumberland (Carlisle).

[195] Archdeacon of Rochester.

iii lay people and organisations

family advisers,[196] management consultants,[197] outside consultants,[198] local authority and community organisations,[199] consultants for team ministries,[200] Christian organisations dealing with conflict,[201] the Charity Commissioners,[202] ACAS,[203] individuals skilled in mediation.[204]

The survey shows that there is a whole network of persons available to assist in mediation, some of whom are already acting in other capacities for the diocese, while others are brought in as and when the need arises.

e) Different roles of the archdeacon

Many responses to the survey showed that mediation was alive and well in diocesan practice. Other responses showed a preference for other forms of dispute resolution. So for example,

---

[196] Archdeacon of Birmingham.

[197] Archdeacon of Canterbury.

[198] Archdeacon of West Cumberland (Carlisle).

[199] Newham's Conflict and Change Provision, referred to by the archdeacon of West Ham (Chelmsford); Milton Keynes Community Mediation Service (Oxford).

[200] Bishop of Hereford; archdeacon of Hackney (London).

[201] The London Mennonite Centre, recommended by the archdeacon of Canterbury and the archdeacon of Newark (Southwell); The Upside Down Trust, recommended by the archdeacon of Barnstable (Exeter) and the archdeacon of Newark (Southwell); the Guild of Centurions (Peterborough).

[202] Bishop of Hereford.

[203] Diocesan secretary for Lichfield.

[204] The archdeacon of Lambeth (Southwark) recommended two particular individuals. The archdeacon of York had 'one or two' people.

some archdeacons saw themselves more as trouble-shooters,[205] others as mediators,[206] others as combining the two roles.[207] Some archdeacons and bishops seem to prefer a semi-formal judicial process.[208] Many responses specifically refer to disputes being 'settled', or resolved (other than by formal or informal judicial process), and the advantage of this.[209]

Some archdeacons see their role as bishop's officer as a hindrance to acting as a mediator, because of the bishop's disciplinary role.[210] Parishes associate the archdeacon with the church hierarchy, which is not a help if the dispute is between the parish church and the diocese.[211] In consequence, many dioceses are now using for such disputes other persons as mediators, persons who have no juridical role in the diocese: in particular, rural deans, di-

---

[205] Archdeacon of Aston (Birmingham); bishop of Ludlow (Hereford), archdeacon of Lindisfarne (Newcastle); archdeacon of York. See also the response of the diocesan secretary for Sheffield.

[206] Archdeacon of Canterbury ('honest broker'); archdeacon of Westmorland and Furness (Carlisle); archdeacon of West Ham (Chelsmford); archdeacon of Wisbech (Ely) (who used the mediation jargon 'win-win'); archdeacon of Barnstable (Exeter); bishop of Ludlow (Hereford); archdeacon of Walsall (Lichfield); archdeacon of Northolt (London); archdeacon of Rochdale (Manchester); archdeacon of Northumberland (Newcastle); archdeacon of Northampton (Peterborough); archdeacon of Sodor and Man.

[207] Archdeacon of Rochester; archdeacon of Southend (Chelsmford); archdeacon of Tonbridge (Rochester).

[208] Archdeacon of Aston (Birmingham); diocesan secretary for Lichfield.

[209] Diocesan secretary for Blackburn; archdeacon of Wiltshire (Salisbury); archdeacon of Walsall (Lichfield); archdeacon of Hampstead (London).

[210] Archdeacon of Aston (Birmingham); archdeacon of Lambeth (Southwell).

[211] Archdeacon of West Cumberland (Carlisle); archdeacon of Northumberland (Newcastle).

131

ocesan staff, and outside mediators.[212] As the archdeacon of Chelmsford said, there is an informality about being in touch with the rural dean, whereas once things get into the archdeacon's domain, it almost certainly becomes more formal. Some archdeacons recognise the value of mediation, but prefer to send in others as mediators rather than take this role themselves, or to use outside bodies.[213] It was encouraging to see a chancellor asking the archdeacon to assist in resolving a faculty dispute.[214]

Disputes about the allocation of parish share are, on one level, a dispute between the parish and the diocese, but on another level, a dispute as between the various parishes in a deanery. In some dioceses, the archdeacon has successfully acted as mediator in disputes about the parish share;[215] other dioceses prefer to use other persons to help resolve such disputes.[216]

f) Financial implications

The financial implications of conflict in the churches are mainly hidden costs, not costs which can specifically be allocated to conflict. It is clear that most conflict resolution is handled in-house, by senior clergy (in particular, bishops and archdeacons), and others on the diocesan staff. There may be some incidental costs, for example travelling expenses incurred in visiting the parishes concerned, and there are undoubtedly costs such as telephone calls which would be met by the diocese in any event, but in the main, no additional fees are paid specifically for dispute resolu-

---

[212] Bishop of Hereford; archdeacon of Lynn (Norwich); Diocesan secretary for Truro; and many others.

[213] The archdeacon of Newark (Southwell).

[214] Archdeacon of Hampstead (London). For another case settled by the same chancellor (now, the Dean of the Arches), see James Behrens, *Practical Church Management*, pg. 322-3.

[215] Diocesan secretary for Truro; the archdeacon of Northampton (Peterborough).

[216] The archdeacon of Ludlow (Hereford).

tion. None of the dioceses said that it had a person 'on the pay-roll' as mediator. Likewise, no diocese had plans to appoint such a person.[217]

Direct costs might be payable to some of the lay people and organisations mentioned on page 130. Some of the family advisers, management consultants, outside consultants, individuals and organisations may give their services to the Church free of charge; or they may be paid for these services. The survey did not reveal whether or not, nor the extent to which, dioceses had to pay for the benefit of their expertise. Nor was it clear whether the individuals and organisations which the dioceses used for mediation were Christian.[218]

Costs cannot always just be contained within existing resources. Some diocesan staff clearly have the time to assist in resolving disputes: others are too busy to carry out this role.[219] In such cases, if conflicts are to be resolved, either external mediators need to be brought in,[220] or additional staff have to be employed. Many conflicts are about church finance, and so the resolution of

---

[217] Diocesan secretary for Lichfield, and the archdeacons of Stoke-upon-Trent and Walsall (both Lichfield); diocesan secretary for Blackburn; archdeacon of Lincoln; archdeacons of Hackney and Middlesex (both London); archdeacon of Manchester; archdeacon of Northampton (Peterborough); archdeacon of Tonbridge (Rochester); diocesan secretary for Salisbury; diocesan secretary for Sodor and Man.

[218] A mediator does not judge between the parties, so it is not a Scriptural requirement that the mediator be a Christian. However, judges of church disputes should be Christians: see 1 Corinthians 6:1–8. (Thus, the Ecclesiastical Jurisdiction Measure 1963, s. 2(2) states that before appointing a lay person as chancellor the bishop shall satisfy himself that the person to be appointed is a communicant.) The survey in chapter 7, 'Mediation in the Anglican Communion', found that clergy were used in 66% of cases, and professional mediators in 34% of cases.

[219] Diocesan secretary for Sheffield.

[220] Which the diocesan secretary in Sheffield said would be invaluable.

such conflicts has a direct financial effect either on the parish or on the diocese concerned. Where conflict is not resolved, dioceses may be involved in expensive litigation. The legal fees and costs of bringing intractable disputes to final resolution are considerable, and beyond the purse of many parishes.[221]

The survey reveals the need for a cost-benefit analysis of different approaches to dispute resolution. The existing use of senior clergy to resolve disputes may seem expensive in terms of human resources; but even senior clergy are paid at a lower rate than many professionals in secular employment, so it may be more economic to use them in this role rather than outside mediators.

The financial cost of providing additional training for clergy and laity also needs to be examined. Again, a cost-benefit analysis is needed. The benefits of additional training should be fewer disputes, and better and quicker resolution of those disputes which cannot be avoided.[222] Putting a monetary figure on this is not the whole story: the Church should be seen as a community where disputes are rare; but where they do happen disputes should be resolved efficiently, fairly, and in a manner which is consonant with the Church's mission.

4. OTHER ISSUES

a) Dispute avoidance

Many of the disputes follow controversial or what appear to be insensitive appointments. Some of these disputes could have been avoided by suitable preparation of the parties before the appointment became effective. In others, the appointment was bound to provoke problems.

---

[221] Archdeacon of Northolt (London). For typical legal costs, see 'Financial cost' pg. 478.

[222] See further, 'Training', pg. 137 below.

A lack of knowledge of church law[223] seems to be a factor leading to disputes. In particular, church law frequently requires proper consultation before changes are made, and there are numerous cases where a failure to consult parishes or staff properly before changes were made led to a dispute.[224] This points to a need for better education of both priests and laity, and for proper management of parishes.

b) Church management

A number of responses drew attention to bad management practice leading to conflict. Examples used in the survey, in their own words, include: lack of proper records and procedures for parochial working expenses;[225] mishandling the chairing of meetings[226] not handling differences of opinion objectively and dispassionately[227] poor presentation[228] bad communication[229] bad management[230] bad business practices[231] wrong leadership style[232] neglect to follow proper PCC procedures[233] ignoring the

---

[223] A lack of knowledge of other areas of law which impinge on church life, in particular employment law, is also a factor.

[224] As in *St Mary's, Cottingham; St Mary's, Langham; St Peter's Church, Ropley;* and the *Church of Scotland board of communication.*

[225] Diocesan secretary for Bath and Wells.

[226] Archdeacon of West Cumberland (Carlisle); diocesan secretary for Salisbury.

[227] Diocesan secretary for Salisbury.

[228] Archdeacon of Wisbech (Ely).

[229] Diocesan secretary for Bath and Wells; diocesan secretary for London; archdeacon of Hackney (London); archdeacon of Northolt (London).

[230] Diocesan secretary for London.

[231] Diocesan secretary for London.

[232] Archdeacon of Hackney (London).

[233] Archdeacon of Hackney (London); diocesan secretary for Salisbury.

PCC or standing committee before making changes;[234] an unprofessional approach to good employment practice for church employees such as administrators;[235] lack of sensitivity;[236] wrong ways of working for PCCs;[237] writing the wrong sort of letter;[238] and failure to comply with requirements such as child protection procedures.[239]

Bad management practices typically lead to disputes in three of the 15 categories of dispute: personality conflicts, pastoral breakdown, and employment disputes. Bad management practices can fuel a breakdown in personal relationships, and vice-versa. For example, in the field of employment within the church, the lack of a proper job description frequently leads to a breakdown in trust between the priest and the church administrator or the organist.[240] Many cases of problems within a team ministry are caused by failure to have specific job descriptions within the team.[241] Similarly, a lack of proper communication or leadership skills can lead to a breakdown in trust between the priest, the PCC, and other members of the congregation.[242]

Management is also important in the handling of disputes. A single issue conflict can escalate until it overwhelms a whole range of parochial activities and personalities if it is badly han-

---

[234] Archdeacon of Hackney (London); archdeacon of Northolt (London); archdeacon of Rochdale (Manchester).

[235] Archdeacon of Northolt (London); archdeacon of Rochdale (Manchester).

[236] Archdeacon of Rochdale (Manchester).

[237] Diocesan secretary for Norwich.

[238] Archdeacon of Wiltshire (Salisbury).

[239] Archdeacon of Croydon (Southwark).

[240] Archdeacon of Rochdale (Manchester).

[241] Archdeaconry of Barnstable (Exeter).

[242] Archdeacon of Hackney (London); archdeacon of Tonbridge (Rochester).

136

dled by the leadership.[243] As has been seen, the process of handling a dispute may affect its outcome.[244]

c) Training

Bad management is, or at least should be, avoidable by the use
of appropriate training. Similarly, bad management should be
comparatively easy to put right, again by suitable training.
Broken relationships are more difficult to restore; but it is part of
the gospel that they can be. Single-issue disputes should be the
easiest type of conflict to resolve; but it is well-known to experienced mediators, and the survey bears this out, that many single-
issue disputes are merely the presented issue, hiding much
deeper, pastoral, concerns.[245]

The survey reveals implications for training, both of laity,
clergy, diocesan staff, and in particular archdeacons. Such training should be both preventative and restorative: prevention of
conflict where possible, and management of conflict where not.

Both clergy and lay church officers are likely to require training
in many of these matters. They should be at least aware of all of
them. The author's *Practical Church Management* covers some of
these areas, but dioceses may need to consider including many of
these topics as part of the continuing ministerial education of
clergy, and as part of the training for lay church officers. A number of dioceses run training sessions for new churchwardens, PCC
secretaries and PCC treasurers.[246] Others involved in training who
should encourage these principles are vicars training curates, directors of post-ordination training, and rural and area deans giv-

---

[243] Archdeacon of Northumberland (Newcastle).

[244] See pg. 1.

[245] Archdeacon of Northumberland (Newcastle); archdeacon of Ludlow
(Hereford).

[246] Diocesan secretary for Sheffield. Similar courses are offered in a
number of other dioceses.

ing guidance to new incumbents.[247] They are also matters for clusters of parishes within dioceses to monitor in the mutual support they give to clergy in a neighbourhood.[248]

Secondly, training should be given to those most called upon to manage church conflict. Several archdeacons said that they and others should be trained in conflict management.[249] It is encouraging that several archdeacons have plainly thought deeply and read widely about the subject of conflict resolution. It is also most encouraging that conflict management is now beginning to be taught: at theological college and as part of post-ordination training,[250] and in one diocese[251] for the bishop's senior staff and rural deans.[252] Archdeacons and others should at least be made aware that there are trained skilled mediators who can offer very considerable help.[253] Training can be informal: one archdeacon reported that regular meetings of archdeacons and diocesan secretaries are the places where one learned most.[254]

d) Pastoral theology

Lastly, the survey reveals a considerable wisdom on the part of many senior clergy (and others) on the subject of dispute resolu-

---

[247] Archdeacon of Hackney (London).

[248] Archdeacon of Hackney (London).

[249] Archdeacon of West Cumberland (Carlisle); archdeacon of West Ham (Chelmsford); archdeacon of Stoke-upon-Trent (Lichfield); archdeacon of Hackney (London).

[250] Archdeacon of Canterbury.

[251] Archdeacon of Rochester.

[252] Albeit only as a one-off event.

[253] Archdeacon of Lambeth (Southwark).

[254] Archdeacon of Westmoreland and Furness (Carlisle). The archdeacon of Tonbridge (Rochester) said that the diocese had held a helpful training morning on conflict resolution for the bishop's senior staff and rural deans.

tion. Much of this wisdom has been acquired by experience. As mentioned in the section on training,[255] conflict management is now beginning to be taught to clergy and senior clergy. A pastoral theology of conflict management is developing, which can only be for the good.[256]

---

[255] Pg. 137.

[256] As has already been seen in Chapters 1 and 2, theology underpins church dispute resolution. For this reason, theology will form a significant part of the assessment of the different mediation models considered in chapters 4, 5 and 6; and in the survey in chapter 7, 'Mediation in the Anglican Communion' a number of bishops see mediation in theological or pastoral terms rather than as a legal process.

Chapter 4

COMMERCIAL MEDIATION

Til that the pale Saturnus the colde,
That knew so manye of aventures olde,
Foond in his olde experience an art
That he ful soone hath plesed every part.
As sooth is seyd, elde hath greet avantage;
In elde is bothe wysdom and usage;
Men may the olde atrenne and noght atrede.
Saturne anon, to stynten strif and drede,
Al be it that it is agayn his kynde,
Of al this strif he gan remedie fynde.[1]

---

[1] Geoffrey Chaucer, *The Canterbury Tales*, 'The Knight's Tale'
(lines 2,443–52), (London, Penguin Books, 1996).

In David Wright's translation:
>   Till bleak old Saturn, versed in stratagems,
>   Was able, from his long experience,
>   To find an answer satisfying both.
>   The old, in fact, have a great advantage:
>   Wisdom, experience, belong to age.
>   You can outdo the old, but not outwit.
>   Though it's not Saturn's nature to discourage
>   Terror and contention, he was quick
>   To find a remedy for the whole dispute.

Geoffrey Chaucer, *The Canterbury Tales*, translated by David Wright
(Oxford University Press, 1985). Saturn's 'remedy' is not a suitable
precedent for modern mediators. He engineered the death of one of the
contesting parties in a riding accident.

1. INTRODUCTION

This Chapter and the next two chapters describe three different models of mediation used for the resolution of secular disputes. This Chapter discusses the commercial model of mediation, which is used by lawyers for the resolution of commercial disputes. Chapter 5 discusses the community mediation model used by local community mediation services to resolve neighbourhood disputes. Chapter 6 discusses consensus-building mediation used by organisations such as the Environment Council for the resolution of disputes involving communities and other large groups of people. It will be seen that each of these models has potential for resolving church disputes, but that each model is more appropriate for some types of church dispute than for others. It will also be seen that each model emphasises one side of the conflict triangle in particular. Thus the commercial model emphasises the problem side of the triangle, the community model emphasises the people side, and the consensus-building model emphasises the process side. It is this fact which will point the way to selecting the most appropriate mediation model for each of the 15 types of dispute discussed in chapter 3.[2]

2. THE MODEL FAMILIAR TO LAWYERS

The commercial model of mediation is perhaps the mediation model best known amongst lawyers, and much has been written about it already in standard legal textbooks and legal encyclopaedias. For example, Atkin's Court Forms is a standard reference source for all civil litigation practitioners. It comprises 151 titles spread over 65 volumes. Volume 6(2) covers two subjects: alternative dispute resolution, and arbitration.[3] The alternative dispute resolution section extends to 190 pages, and divides the subject into the following sections: introduction, the nature of ADR processes, the types of ADR available, mediation, ADR and the UK courts, settlement agreements, structured settlements, and

---

[2] See figure 15 on pg. 333. As the table shows, the 15 types of dispute do not fall into three neat categories. In nine of the 15 types of dispute, the choice is clear. But in six types of dispute, there is a choice between two models depending on the circumstances.

[3] New volumes and reissued volumes of Atkin are issued several times a year. Many volumes have had to be updated following the changes brought about by the Civil Procedure Rules 1998. The volume on alternative dispute resolution and arbitration was reissued in 1998.

ADR and mediation contract clauses. A procedural chart
(page 62) shows the various steps leading, on the one hand, to a
successful end to the mediation, and on the other to the dispute
continuing in the hands of solicitors. The volume contains a
number of forms suitable for use in ADR processes, for example,
contract clauses to encourage parties to mediate when a dispute
arises, request forms for mediation, and terms for the appointment of a mediator. The volume includes no less than 30 appendices covering various published materials and guidelines, such
as 'The Academy of Experts' Guidelines for Mediation', and 'A
guide to the RICS Dispute Resolution Service', the 'Academy of
Experts' Code of Conduct for Mediators', and the 'Central London
County Court Mediation Scheme note for mediators'. Lastly, the
volume lists the names and addresses of the main providers of
ADR services in the UK.

Similarly, several legal textbooks have been written either devoted entirely to commercial mediation, or which contain a chapter on commercial mediation as part of some wider subject. An
example in the former category is *Commercial Dispute Resolution:
an ADR practice guide*,[4] written by three directors of CEDR; an example in the latter category is the *Handbook of Arbitration Practice*
by Bernstein, Tackaberry, Marriott and Wood,[5] part 11 of which is
entitled 'alternative dispute resolution'.

It is perhaps misleading to head this section 'the model familiar to lawyers'. Some lawyers are familiar with, and keen supporters of, mediation. Some have trained as mediators, and combine this with their legal practice. Others shun mediation like the
plague. ADR to some means 'Alarming Drop in Revenue';[6] and

---

[4] *Commercial Dispute Resolution: an ADR practice guide* (London, Butterworths, 2nd edn. 1999).

[5] *Handbook of Arbitration Practice* by Bernstein, Tackaberry, Marriott and
Wood (London, Sweet & Maxwell, 1998).

[6] *Mediator Training Course Handbook* (London, CEDR, 1997), pg. 138.

many litigation lawyers, both barristers and solicitors, see mediation as the scourge of their practice.

3. THE CIVIL PROCEDURE RULES 1998

It is however becoming increasingly difficult for litigation lawyers to stick their heads in the sand about mediation, because the Civil Procedure Rules 1998 (which came into force in April 1999), and several practice directions made pursuant to the rules, require the court actively to consider ADR. Parties and their advisers are therefore open both to criticism and to sanctions such as costs if they neglect to do so.[7]

Thus, the very first rule in the new CPR, Part 1, headed 'overriding objective' includes the Court's duty to manage cases (Rule 1.4), and this includes

> encouraging the parties to use an alternative dispute resolution procedure if the court considers that appropriate and facilitating the use of such procedure.[8]

Similarly, Part 26, covering Case Management, includes the power of the court to stay the action to allow the parties to use ADR.

> A party may, when filing the completed allocation questionnaire, make a written request for the proceedings to be stayed while the parties try to settle the case by alternative dispute resolution or other means.[9]

The *Chancery Guide* chapter 17[10] is entitled Alternative Dispute Resolution, and states

---

[7] *Dunnett v Railtrack plc* [2002] EWCA Civ 303, [2002] 1 WLR 2434; *Cowl v Plymouth District Council* [2001] EWCA Civ 1935, [2001] 1 WLR 803; *Hurst v Leeming* [2002] EWHC 1051; [2002] Lloyd's Rep PN 508.

[8] CPR rule 1.4(e).

[9] CPR rule 26.4(1).

[10] *Civil Procedure* (also known as *The White Book*) (London, Sweet & Maxwell, 2003) Vol. 2 par. 1–1.

17.1   While emphasising the primary role of the Court as a forum for deciding cases, encourages parties to consider the use of ADR (such as, but not confined to, mediation and conciliation) as a possible means of resolving disputes or particular issues.

17.2   The settlement of disputes by means of ADR can:

(a)   significantly help litigants to save costs;

(b)   save litigants the delay of litigation in reaching finality in their disputes;

(c)   enable litigants to achieve settlement of their disputes while preserving their existing commercial relationships and market reputation;

(d)   provide litigants with a wider range of solutions than those offered by litigation; and

(e)   make a substantial contribution to the more efficient use of judicial resources.

17.3   The Court will in an appropriate case invite the parties to consider whether their dispute or particular issues in it, could be resolved through ADR. The Court may also adjourn the case for a specified period of time to encourage and enable the parties to use ADR and for this purpose extend the time for compliance by the parties or any of them with any requirement under the CPR or this Guide or order of the Court. The Court may make such order as to the costs that parties may incur by reason of the adjournment or their using or attempting to use ADR as may in all the circumstances seem appropriate.

17.4   Legal representatives in all cases should consider with their clients and the other parties concerned the possibility of attempting to resolve the dispute or particular issues by ADR and they should ensure that their clients are fully informed as to the most cost effective means of resolving their dispute.

17.5   Parties who consider that ADR might be an appropriate means of resolving their dispute or particular issues in the dispute, may apply for directions at any stage.

17.6   The Clerk to the Commercial Court keeps some published information as to individuals and bodies that offer ADR services. (The list also includes individuals and bodies that offer arbitration services.) If the parties are unable to agree upon a neutral individual, or panel of individuals, for ADR, they may refer to the Judge for assistance.

The Guide to Practice in the Central London County Court Business List, section G,[11] headed Alternative Dispute Resolution, states

> The Central London County Court operates a Mediation Service whereby Mediations lasting up to 3 hours take place in private in small conference rooms at 4.30 p.m. on weekdays and in addition the Manager of the Business List keeps some published information as to individuals and bodies that offer ADR Services. (The list will also include individuals and bodies that offer arbitration services.) If the parties are unable to agree upon a neutral individual or panel of individuals for ADR, they may by consent refer to the Judge for assistance in reaching such agreement. The Business List Judge will not, however, recommend any individual or body because it would be inappropriate to do so.

The Commercial Court Guide section G[12] deals with alternative dispute resolution, in terms almost identical to those quoted from the Chancery Guide.[13]

---

[11] *Civil Procedure* (2001 edition), Vol. 2 par. 2C–333. This is not printed in the 2003 edition.

[12] *Civil Procedure* (2003 edition), Vol. 2 par. 2A–100.

[13] The terms are so similar that one plainly was used as a precedent for the other.

The Practice Direction for the Court of Appeal, Paragraph 11,[14] provides as follows:

ALTERNATIVE DISPUTE RESOLUTION (ADR)

A pro bono scheme commenced in 1997. The scheme has to take into account the fact that cases which have already been tried at first instance raise different issues, so far as ADR is concerned, to cases which have yet to be tried.

The scheme has recently been refined. Now in appropriate cases, as soon as an appeal set down with the Civil Appeals Office, a letter of invitation to consider ADR, signed by the Master of the Rolls, is sent to the parties' solicitors. The letter encloses an explanatory leaflet and a response form. A member of staff is available to answer queries, provide general information and help with specific cases.

The supervising Lords Justices responsible for particular categories of work are vigilant in their case management for those cases that appear suitable for referral to ADR. Recently a very substantial commercial appeal was compromised as result of a referral by the supervising Lord Justice. Equally, presiding Lords Justices are able to propose a referral to ADR at the determination of appeals which otherwise will lead to a re-hearing or the issue of further proceedings.

Legal aid covers the costs of ADR for an assisted party.

Further information is available from the Civil Appeals Office, Royal Courts of Justice, Strand, London, WC2A 2LL (tel. 020 7936 6486).

So, not only is mediation provided for as part of the general Civil Procedure Rules 1998, applicable across the whole frame of

---

[14] Practice direction for the Court of Appeal (Civil Division) (RSC PD 59), printed in The Civil Court Practice 2001 (London, Butterworths, 2001).

civil litigation, but it is also specifically mentioned in the guides issued by three major divisions of the civil litigation system, and as a scheme administered by one very busy and important county court.[15]

4. A SLOW TAKE-UP

Prior to this new support for ADR in the Civil Court procedures, the take-up of mediation services by the legal profession and by clients was very low, but where it was taken up, the success rate was high. The statistics for five mediation schemes are shown in figure 3.

Scheme	Commercial Court	Court of Appeal	Medical negligence	Planning system	Central London County Court
Cases where mediation offered		250	56	212	4,500
Cases mediated	67	12	12	48	160
% take up		5%	21%	23%	4%
Satisfactory resolution	60		11	31	99
% success rate	90%		92%	65%	62%

Figure 3. Statistics for five mediation schemes

---

[15] Since the main research for this book was undertaken a number of other local courts have developed their own mediation schemes: Leeds, Manchester, Exeter, Birmingham, Guildford and Norwich.

a) *The Commercial Court*

The first of these schemes is that set up in 1993 for use in the Commercial Court. The original practice direction of 1993 for use in the Commercial Court encouraging the parties to consider ADR had no effect on the commercial legal world.[16] No cases were referred to mediation by the Commercial Court between 1993 and 1996. In 1996 a power to adjourn the case at the option of the judge was introduced and applied.[17] In the period from June 1996 to July 1998, ADR orders had been made in at least 67 cases, of which in only 7 cases did the parties fail to attempt ADR or fail to achieve settlement.[18]

---

[16] The scheme was established by a Practice Statement in 1993: see Practice Statement (Commercial Cases: Alternative Dispute Resolution) [1994] 1 WLR 14, by which judges could encourage the use of ADR.

[17] See Practice Statement (Commercial Cases: Alternative Dispute Resolution) (No. 2) [1996] 1 WLR 1024.

[18] See *Alternative Dispute Resolution – a Discussion Paper* (London, Lord Chancellor's Department, 1999), annex B. Slightly different figures, but to the same effect, are quoted by Mr Justice Colman in an interview in the Law Society's Gazette of January 8, 1998, quoted in Brown and Marriott, *ADR Principles and Practice*, 2nd edn. (London, Sweet & Maxwell, 1999) pg. 33. According to the report, over 100 adjournment orders for ADR had been made and in the overwhelming majority of cases settlement appears to have been reached. For a recent assessment, see Professor Hazel Genn, *Court-based ADR initiatives for non-family civil disputes: the Commercial Court and the Court of Appeal* (London, Lord Chancellor's Department Research series no. 1/02, March 2002). Copies of the report can be seen on the LCD website on *www.lcd.gov.uk*. Professor Genn found that out of 233 cases where mediation had been ordered by the Commercial Court, only 5 per cent subsequently went to trial.

b) *The Court of Appeal*

Similarly, the ADR scheme set up by the Court of Appeal led to only a trickle of actual mediations. In the period from November 1998 to March 1999, parties in 250 cases were sent information about the scheme and, of these, both sides agreed to mediation in 12 cases.[19]

c) *Medical negligence*

The NHS medical negligence mediation pilot scheme (the Oxford Scheme)[20] was launched in 1995 in two NHS regions – Anglia and Oxford, and Northern and Yorkshire. It was anticipated that up to 40 cases would be mediated over a two-year period, but the scheme was extended for an additional year when the number of referrals remained low. By the end of the third year a total of 12 cases had been mediated, and settlement reached in 11 of them. In addition, there were 44 other cases identified by the research team in which mediation had been suggested to the opposing side, 14 of these were on-going referrals at the close of the scheme. The 12 mediated cases involved a host of medical specialities, but half involved obstetrics and gynaecology. Proceedings had been issued in just four cases, and five claimants had already pursued their grievance through NHS complaints procedures. All the mediations took place within one day. They took between four

---

[19] See *Alternative Dispute Resolution – a Discussion Paper*, annex B. For a recent assessment, see also Professor Hazel Genn, *Court-based ADR initiatives for non-family civil disputes: the Commercial Court and the Court of Appeal*. The statistics were not so good as for the Commercial Court. 38 appeals were mediated, but only half settled at the mediation or afterwards.

[20] See Linda Mulcahy, *Mediating medical negligence claims* (London, HMSO, 1999). Copies are also available from Adrian Landon, Complaints and Clinical Negligence Policy Unit, NHS Executive, Tel: 0113 254 5679, and at *www.doh.gov.uk/mediation/index.htm* and *www.doh.gov.uk/mediation/mediation.pdf*.

and eleven hours to complete, the average being just over seven hours. Financial settlement was reached in all but one of the cases, with the average settlement being just over £34,000, and the settlement range £5,000 to just over £80,000. A number of additional 'remedies' were granted, including apologies, extensive explanations of medical decisions and the rationale for treatment decisions, new treatment plans, and information about a foetus' place of burial.

Following this pilot study, the NHS Litigation Authority 'has adopted a positive policy of encouraging and funding mediation in appropriate cases'.[21]

d) Planning disputes

A pilot scheme for mediation in the planning system was commissioned by the Department of the Environment, Transport and the Regions in 1998 as part of its Modernising Planning Initiative. The scheme ran from December 1998 to December 1999. There was very limited take up from local authorities being offered a part in the pilot scheme (of the 70 who responded only 32 offered to participate). From the 212 enquiries which continued past the initial stage, 52 mediations were arranged, representing an acceptance rate of nearly 25 per cent.[22] Four of these were cancelled, leading to 48 effective mediations.[23] Satisfactory outcomes were agreed at 31 of these mediations. On this basis, 65 per cent of the mediations in the pilot project can be considered successful

---

[21] *Guide to Mediating Clinical Negligence Cases* (London, Clinical Disputes Forum/CEDR, October 2001) par. 4.7. The Guide is also available through the Clinical Disputes Forum and CEDR websites – *www.clinical-disputes-forum.org.uk* and *www.cedr.co.uk*.

[22] *Mediation in the Planning System* (London, Department of the Environment, Transport and the Regions, June 2000), paragraph 3.7.4. The report is also available at *www.planning.detr.gov.uk/mediation/index.htm*.

[23] Paragraph 3.10.2 of the report.

as achieving an outcome.[24] The case categories of those that went forward to mediation was largely householder/minor dwelling, and the most common focus was design. The report concluded that the process is welcome, whatever the outcome.

> Whatever the outcome, in only five cases has there been any dissatisfaction with the mediation process itself on the part of applicants. In general, there has been considerable appreciation expressed of the benefits of mediation in getting everyone around the table in a relaxed atmosphere.[25]

The report said that mediators need not be planners.

> 5.6.2. The success of a mediator very much depends on his or her personal qualities and the use of basic mediation techniques rather than on any detailed knowledge of the planning system. For instance, 96 per cent of householder applicants stated that they found the mediator courteous, helpful and a good listener and seven remarked that the mediation was the first occasion, that, in relation to the case in hand, anyone had really listened to them.

> 5.6.3. It is critical for a mediator to understand and empathise with the aspirations of the parties, to encourage both parties to resist going over past history time and time again, to look at the situation as it now stands and to consider possibilities for the future. No specific professional planning skills are required for that. Some knowledge of planning is useful in coming to terms with possible solutions, but the presence of a representative of the local planning authority should ensure that no solutions could ever be arrived at which are unacceptable in planning terms.

The report recommended the encouragement of mediation, that a permanent service should be established, and a guide for best practice for mediation in planning should be produced.

---

[24] Paragraph 4.2.1 of the report.

[25] Paragraph 5.2.1 of the report.

e) The Central London County Court

The scheme at the Central London County Court started in May 1996. Parties to defended cases above the small claims limit to which automatic directions applied were offered mediation. This scheme was evaluated by Professor Hazel Genn of University College, London during 1998, and comprised data from the commencement of the scheme up to July 1998.[26] During the period of her study, mediation was offered in 4,500 cases, but only 160 mediations (3.6% of the cases where mediation was offered) took place. She found that 62% of mediated cases reached a settlement at the mediation appointment and that mediation achieved earlier settlement.[27] Only four personal injury cases were referred to mediation during the pilot study period, although personal injury cases comprised almost half of the cases offered mediation. This compares unfavourably with the experience in the United States, Canada and Australia where a substantial proportion of all personal injury and medical negligence cases are referred to mediation or another ADR process.[28] Contract, goods/services disputes and debt cases had the highest levels of demand although the joint acceptance rate was less than ten percent. The joint demand for mediation was *lowest* when both parties had legal representa-

---

[26] Professor Hazel Genn, *The Central London County Court Pilot Mediation Scheme Evaluation Report* (London, Lord Chancellor's Department Research Series number 5/98, July 1998). An executive summary appears at Professor Hazel Genn, *The Central London County Court Pilot Mediation Scheme Evaluation Report* (2001) 67 Arbitration 109 (London, Chartered Institute of Arbitrators, 2001), and *www.open.gov.uk/lcd/research/1998/598esfr.htm*.

[27] See *Alternative Dispute Resolution – a Discussion Paper*, annex B.

[28] See the *Response by the General Council of the Bar to the Lord Chancellor's Department's discussion paper on ADR* (London, General Council of the Bar, 2000), paragraph 3. No greater precision is given of 'a substantial proportion'. For a brief summary of some of the ADR schemes abroad, see *Handbook of Arbitration Practice* by Bernstein, Tackaberry, Marriott and Wood (London, Sweet & Maxwell, 1998), page 596.

tion. Acceptance of mediation was highest among disputes between businesses.

Interviews by Professor Genn with solicitors rejecting mediation revealed:

- lack of experience and widespread ignorance of mediation among the legal profession;
- apprehension about showing weakness through accepting mediation within the context of traditional adversarial litigation;
- evidence of litigant resistance to the idea of compromise, particularly in the early stages of litigation.

However the scheme is continuing, and 120 mediations took place under it during 2001.[29]

f) The trend

These statistics make depressing reading for those already converted to the benefits of mediation. However, the trickle of cases in the early and mid-1990s has now become a steady stream, albeit not yet a flood. In the years after 1996, commercial solicitors were forced to sample mediation. As time passed, more and more became willing to 'jump before being pushed'. It is now the case that litigation solicitors in commercial firms both in London and in provincial England and Wales have real experience of

---

[29] See *www.open.gov.uk/lcd/civil/adrpilfr.htm* for a user-friendly introduction to the scheme. The statistics for 2001 were supplied to the Chartered Institute of Arbitrators in February 2002. During 2001 the author was appointed as mediator in two disputes under the scheme: a £20,000 building construction dispute, and a £18,000 dispute for the professional fees of an expert witness.

ADR, and look upon it as the preferred route to resolution of a dispute.[30]

Since the CPR, the take-up has increased considerably, but it is still comparatively small. A MORI survey conducted between February to March 2000 to assess the impact of the new CPR found that more than 50 per cent of the lawyers interviewed had not been involved in mediation since the CPR took effect.[31] Personal experience suggests that whereas in 1998 few solicitors had experienced an actual mediation, many have now experienced several.

One of the factors which has tipped the balance is the enthusiasm and knowledge of the court. Commercial and Chancery judges now actively support ADR. Mr Justice Coleman[32] and Mr Justice Lightman[33] have both spoken at a CEDR annual conference, and have developed the case law in this area. [34]

Between 1990 and 2000 CEDR has undertaken more than 1,000 mediations. Of these, around half were conducted in the year up to March 2000, a 100% increase on the 252 conducted in the preceding 12 months. The other major player, the ADR Group, re-

---

[30] See the *Response by the General Council of the Bar to the Lord Chancellor's Department's discussion paper on ADR* (London, General Council of the Bar, 2000), paragraph 11.

[31] *CEDR Civil Justice Audit* (London, CEDR, April 2000), pg. 48.

[32] A judge of the Commercial Court.

[33] A judge of the Chancery Division.

[34] In *Hurst v Leeming* [2002] EWHC 1051; [2002] Lloyd's Rep PN 508, Lightman J held that a party who refuses to go to mediation would normally be penalised in costs. In *Cable & Wireless plc v IBM United Kingdom Ltd* [2002] EWHC 2059 (Comm Ct); [2002] 2 All ER (Comm) 1041, Colman J ordered a stay of proceedings until Cable & Wireless had complied with a contractual agreement to refer disputes to ADR.

ports a three-fold increase over the same period; it dealt with 123 mediations in the six months up to March 2000.[35]

The number of bodies offering dispute resolutions services is increasing every month.

> Old players, like CEDR and the ADR Group, have now been joined by young Turks: the Panel of Independent Mediators (PIM), Dispute Mediation, Association of Mediation Solicitors, and the London Mediation Service to name just a few which have sprung up over the last year or so.[36]

For example, in June 2000, the Lawyers Christian Fellowship newsletter announced 'a new Christian Mediation & Arbitration Service'.[37]

More and more people are being trained as mediators. CEDR trains 350 mediators a year. CEDR is careful to emphasise to people before they go on its training course[38] that it cannot guarantee newly-qualified mediators any mediation work following their qualification. This has caused some discontent amongst CEDR trained mediators, especially as CEDR has recently introduced a continuing professional development scheme, under which mediators who wish to remain registered with CEDR must be able to demonstrate that they have carried out a minimum number of mediations in each three-year period. Even if there is not yet mediation work for these recently-trained mediators, they

---

[35] *Solicitor's Gazette (London, the Law Society)*, 30 March 2000, page 30.

[36] *Solicitor's Gazette (London, the Law Society)*, 30 March 2000, page 30.

[37] *Lawyers Christian Fellowship Newsletter*, May 2001, pg. 1. (The Lawyers Christian Fellowship, 33 St James' Square, Bath BA1 2TT). The service is Resolve, Unit 3, Newhouse Business Centre, Old Crawley Road, Horsham, West Sussex. The author attended and spoke at a one-day conference held by Resolve in March 2001 to publicise its work.

[38] The CEDR five-day mediation training course costs over £3,000.

are usually enthusiastic about the process, and can explain it and encourage its use to their clients.

5. GOVERNMENT INTEREST

Governments both in this country and abroad are expressing great interest in mediation, and wide consultation is taking place with providers of mediation services, mediation training organisations, the public, court users, lawyers, and statutory bodies providing dispute resolution procedures. For example, in November 1999 the Lord Chancellor's Department issued a 49 page consultation document 'Alternative Dispute Resolution, a discussion paper', and in May 2000 it published a summary of the responses to the consultation document.[39] Most recently, in 2002 the Lord Chancellor's Department research programme published an evaluation of the use of ADR in dealing with disputes in the Commercial Court and the Court of Appeal.[40]

a) Australia

In Australia, the National Alternative Dispute Resolution Advisory Council (NADRAC) was established in October 1995 to provide independent advice to the Commonwealth Attorney-General. Amongst other publications, it has published a 200-page discussion paper *Issues of fairness and justice in alternative dispute resolution*,[41] a 78-page report *Primary dispute resolution in family*

---

[39] *Alternative Dispute Resolution – a Discussion Paper.* The summary of the responses received to the discussion paper is at *www.open.gov.uk/lcd/consult/civ-just/adr/adrrespfr.htm.*

[40] Professor Hazel Genn, *Court-based ADR initiatives for non-family civil disputes: the Commercial Court and the Court of Appeal.*

[41] *Issues of fairness and justice in alternative dispute resolution* (Australia, National Alternative Dispute Resolution Advisory Council (NADRAC), November 1997).

law,[42] and a 149-page consultation document *The Development of Standards for ADR Discussion Paper*.[43]

NADRAC's discussion paper on issues of fairness and justice includes the subject of imbalance of power. It will be seen that this is an important issue in some church disputes.[44] The paper discusses strategies to address barriers to fairness and justice in alternative dispute resolution for a large number of different user groups. The user groups include: where gender is an issue; where one party comes from a cultural minority; where age is a factor – particularly, children, adolescents and elderly people; people with disabilities; persons with minority sexual preferences – both lesbians and gay men; persons living in rural and remote communities; and where there are socio-economic power differences. Thus, to take but one example, one of the suggestions made to deal with perceived bias in cases of gender discrimination is to use co-mediation, i.e. both a male and a female mediator working together. The paper referred to an evaluation report on the Family Court Mediation Service, in which 149 cases were mediated in a 12 month period. It was there reported that approximately 88% of parties considered having a male and female mediator with both legal and social science training made a significant and positive difference to the handling of the proceedings.[45]

NADRAC's *The Development of Standards for ADR Discussion Paper*[46] does not refer to church disputes as such. But the more the Church adopts mediation, the more important it will be for the

---

[42] *Primary dispute resolution in family law* (Australia, National Alternative Dispute Resolution Advisory Council (NADRAC), March 1997).

[43] *The Development of Standards for ADR Discussion Paper* (Australia, National Alternative Dispute Resolution Advisory Council (NADRAC), March 2000).

[44] See pg. 209.

[45] *Issues of fairness and justice in alternative dispute resolution*, pg. 62.

[46] *The Development of Standards for ADR Discussion Paper.*

Church to address the issues set out in this report. Thus, for example, one chapter summarises the main arguments both for and against having standards. In favour of standards it is argued that they lead to greater practitioner accountability; to greater consumer choice; and to greater credibility of ADR, its practitioners, and its service providers. As against this, it is argued that the existence of documented standards will restrict those who wish to practice ADR and will limit competition; that there is no current need for standards given the wide choice of ADR practitioners; that it may not be possible to draft standards which apply to every possible type of ADR and context; and that standards hinder creativity in the way disputes can be resolved. NADRAC is of the view that the development of standards would permit the promotion of the objectives of ADR, minimise dissatisfaction with its operation, promote service provider and practitioner accountability, and promote the appropriate use of ADR. The consultation paper asks whether readers agree that standards are needed for ADR.

Other chapters in the discussion paper cover the content of standards, attaining standards, maintaining standards, enforcement of standards, and options for regulation. There are various bodies offering accreditation for mediation in the UK, but none is run specifically by or for Churches.[47] The Church will need to consider whether the standards set by these secular bodies are sufficient for Church mediations, or whether the Church should have different standards.

---

[47] CEDR and the ADR Group are two commercial organisations offering training and accreditation. Local mediation centres within the umbrella of Mediation UK offer accreditation for community mediation training. The training course run by the United Reformed Church (described later in this chapter) does not lead to accreditation.

b) USA

In the USA, in June 1999 a first draft for a Uniform Mediation Act appeared.[48] The proposed Act is the product of drafting efforts by two separate but co-operating drafting committees, one representing the American Bar Association (which is working through the Section of Dispute Resolution), and the other representing the National Conference of Commissioners on Uniform State Laws. The project's web site[49] includes drafts, 'Frequently Asked Questions', and comment/participation opportunities. The August 2001 final draft[50] has 15 parts, including sections on mediation confidentiality, loss of privilege, mediator disclosure to a court or other authority, non-party participation in the mediation, electronic signatures, and the summary enforcement of mediated settlement agreements.

The August 2001 final draft was officially adopted by the full National Conference on Uniform States Laws at its August 2001 meeting in West Virginia. Only three states, Arkansas, North Dakota, and Virginia, voted against adoption of the Act. The American Bar Association House of Delegates then voted to endorse the Act at its February 2002 meeting. The Uniform Mediation Act is currently being considered by individual states for adoption.[51]

c) South Africa

Traditional forms of dispute resolution which, for present purposes, may be termed ADR processes, have long existed in rural

---

[48] The text of the Draft is available from the National Conference of Commissioners on Uniform State Laws, 211 E Ontario Street, Suite 1300, Chicago, Illinois 60611, USA. It is also available on the internet at *www.pon.harvard.edu/guests/uma*.

[49] *www.pon.harvard.edu/guests/uma*.

[50] *www.law.upenn.edu/bll/ulc/mediat/med01AM.htm*.

[51] For the latest information, see *www.ronkelly.com*.

South Africa.[52] Unofficial dispute resolution has furthermore been the norm in metropolitan areas for as long as these areas have existed. The earliest unofficial people's courts were the civic associations with dispute-settlement functions which were found in 1901 in the township of Uitvlugt in the Cape Town area.

In the latter part of the 1970s the people's courts were generally known as makgotla and should be distinguished from the politicised people's courts that could be found in the mid-1980s. In 1989 new structured people's courts emerged. They are today successfully functioning as community courts.

Many different institutions, governmental and non-governmental, have over the years tried to address the question of integrating, controlling, acknowledging or formalising these institutions. The State's efforts to control these alternative institutions through the establishment of advisory boards, urban and community councils and town councils proved unsuccessful. More recently, attempts have however been made by a number of non-governmental organisations to introduce more appropriate forms of dispute resolution to communities. Examples of such initiatives are those being conducted by the Community Dispute Resolution Trust and the Community Peace Foundation. These initiatives have met with mixed degrees of success.

Commercial arbitration has long been part of the dispute resolution framework in South Africa and in other Western countries. It is well established in South Africa. The Alternative Dispute Resolution Association of South Africa (ADRASA) and more recently the Arbitration Federation of South Africa (AFSA) have been significant attempts to institutionalise private commercial arbitration and, to a much lesser extent, mediation. Similar initiatives exist in the field of engineering and construction.

---

[52] *Alternative Dispute Resolution*, (South African Law Commission, Issue Paper 8, Project 94, 1997, ISBN 0–621–27319–8), paragraph 2.13.

In the 1970s the major shift that took place in industrial relations gave rise to a need for more appropriate forms of dispute resolution in the workplace. This need was filled at the time by the Independent Mediation Service of South Africa (IMSSA) which was instrumental in introducing forms of mediation and arbitration. The success of this initiative has been borne out by the extensive reliance on mediation and arbitration in the Labour Relations Act 1995[53] and by the establishment of the Commission for Conciliation, Mediation and Arbitration to carry out these functions.

South Africa has enacted an act dealing with ADR.[54] ADR practitioners in South Africa felt that the concept behind this legislation, fixing statutory rules for the conduct of mediation and appearing to limit it to minor cases, was inappropriate and untimely. Nevertheless it has remained on the statute book.[55] In 1997 the South African Law Commission published a consultation paper on alternative dispute resolution.[56] No new statute has been published covering the whole of South Africa, but Uganda has recently reformed the framework for alternative dispute resolution, the result being the Arbitration and Conciliation Act 2000.[57] Part five of the Act focuses on conciliation.

---

[53] See the Labour Relations Act 1995, part VII, especially section 135. Section 135 has since been slightly amended by the Labour Relations Amendment Act 1996 (No 42 of 1996) and the Labour Relations Amendment Act 1998 (No 127 of 1998).

[54] The Short Process Courts and Mediation in Certain Civil Cases Act No 103 of 1991.

[55] Brown and Marriott, *ADR Principles and Practice*, 2nd edn., pg. 442.

[56] *Alternative Dispute Resolution*, (South African Law Commission). The report is also available at *www.law.wits.ac.za/salc/issue/ip8.html*.

[57] Arbitration and Conciliation Act 2000, Act No 7 of 2000. This repealed the Arbitration Act 1930, Cap. 55, which was enacted in 1930.

6. A FRAMEWORK FOR THE PROCESS

The commercial mediation model has five phases:

- preparation

- opening

- exploration

- negotiation

- conclusion.

a) Preparation

There are various important stages in a commercial mediation process, before the mediator meets either of the parties. This is a key feature distinguishing a commercial mediation from the community mediation model championed by Mediation UK. In the community mediation model, the mediator sees each of the parties in turn, right from the outset.

The key steps are as follows:

- securing the agreement of both parties to mediate.

- agreeing the identity of the mediator.

- agreeing the fees payable to the mediator, and any mediation institution such as CEDR or the ADR Group.

- entering into a formal written contract for the mediation service. This will cover amongst other matters, the conduct of the mediation, the impartiality of the mediator, the confidentiality of what is said at the mediation, costs, and that any settlement needs to be recorded in writing before it is binding.

- agreeing practical matters such as the date and venue, and refreshments.

- checking that each party will have present at the mediation someone with sufficient authority to settle the dispute, and who will be representing each party at the mediation.

- preparing a case summary with supporting documents (if appropriate) and submitting these to the mediator in advance. CEDR's usual practice is to ask the parties to exchange these summaries, the ADR Group's usual practice is that they are not exchanged. This difference in practice illustrates the flexibility of the process and, in the author's personal experience, both work well.

CEDR's experience is that these initial administrative arrangements take on average eight hours for each mediation. Much time is spent on the telephone in dealing with the parties' concerns about the process, fixing the practical arrangements, and in selecting and agreeing the identity of the mediator. Where more than two parties are involved in the dispute, the administration time involved can be even more. CEDR's Mediator Training Course Handbook says that mediators who administer their own cases should expect to spend at least as much time in the preparation stage as in the actual mediation.

The ADR Group operates the following system when requested to arrange a mediation. The party who refers the matter to the ADR Group is asked to complete a form stating the parties to the dispute; a brief description of the dispute; details of the legal representatives (if the parties have appointed them); and whether mediation has been discussed and agreed upon between the parties.

The ADR Group case manager then contacts all the parties to discuss the dispute briefly. He or she outlines the procedure that will be followed, establishes whether there are any time limits or deadlines that have been imposed by the court or any other party, and whether there is any other aspect that needs urgent attention. If the other side has not agreed or indeed are not keen to mediate, the case manager will seek to persuade them – usually success-fully.

The ADR Group then selects one or perhaps two suitable me-diators, and sends details of their experience to each party. The ADR Group tries to find mediators with expertise relevant to the dispute, with a suitable level of experience, and in the right loca-tion.

The parties are asked to confirm to the ADR Group case man-ager their preferred choice of mediator, to provide a list of avail-able dates (in the approaching three to four week 'window'), and their preferred choice of venue. In many cases, the mediator's own premises are used, but this may not be possible.

The principle that the parties should be free to select their me-diator has a parallel with the Roman law principle of party auton-omy over the selection of a judge. Under the Roman law *legis actio* and formulary system procedure, after an initial hearing before the magistrate, a dispute was referred to another person, an *arbiter* or *iudex*, not a state official but a private person. The parties could agree upon a judge of their own choice, or if they could not, one was chosen from the magistrate's list (*album iudicum*) of suitable citizens. The parties always retained the right to reject a judge who did not suit them.[58] From this developed the canon law principle of *recusatio judicis*, a refusal of, or exception to a judge upon any suspicion of impartiality,[59] and the modern common

---

[58] See W.W. Buckland, *A Text-Book of Roman Law from Augustus to Justin-ian*, 3rd edn. revised by Peter Stein (Cambridge University Press 1968), pg. 607; H.F. Jolowicz and Barry Nicholas, *Historical Introduction to the study of Roman Law*, 3rd edn., pg. 178; Andrew Borkowski, *Textbook on Roman Law*, 2nd edn. (London, Blackstone Press, 1997), pg. 69.

[59] See Wharton's *Dictionary of Jurisprudence* (London, Stevens & Sons, 1876) (*sic*). For its use in Canon law see R. H. Helmholz, *Canon Law and the Law of England*, (London, Hambledon Press, 1987), chapter 2. For a warning in the Apocrypha against the danger of judicial bias, see Ecclesiasticus 8:14.

law principle of a judge recusing himself on the grounds of possible impartiality.[60] Thus, parties can object to a judge or arbitrator if there is a real danger of bias,[61] and similarly to the appointment of a mediator who is not seen as impartial.

The case manager then liaises with all the parties and with the mediator to establish a suitable date, time and venue for the mediation. He or she also checks who will be attending the mediation, so that a suitable number and the right size of rooms can be booked.

The case manager discusses the subject of costs with the parties. The costs for a mediation are usually borne equally between the parties, but any costs split is acceptable so long as the parties are in full agreement. The mediation is normally scheduled to last 3 to 5 hours, unless the case manager thinks it will last longer, and the deposit is then payable.

The parties are sent a mediation agreement, which must be signed and returned to the ADR Group before the mediation day.

Once the case manager has arranged the date, time and venue of the mediation, the parties are requested to prepare a position statement which outlines details of the dispute, the reason for deadlock and what each party hopes to achieve out of the media-

---

[60] For a modern instance where the judge (Lord Hoffmann) should have recused himself, see *Reg. v. Bow Street Metropolitan Stipendiary Magistrate, Ex parte Pinochet Ugarte (No. 2)* [2000] AC 119.

[61] *Locabail (UK) Ltd v Bayfield Properties Ltd (Leave to Appeal)* [2000] QB 451 (and conjoined cases); *Save and Prosper Pensions Ltd v Homebase Ltd* [2001] L & TR 11 (arbitrator's firm had acted for associated company of a party in the arbitration, *held*: arbitrator disqualified from acting). Contrast *Weatherill v Lloyds TSB Bank Plc* [2000] CPLR 584 (No danger of bias where judge oblivious that he held small shareholding – 570 shares out of five-and-a-half billion issued – and where he had immediately disposed of these shares towards the end of the trial when he discovered the fact).

tion. This document is not intended to be a negotiation tool, nor are the parties requested to set minimum or maximum 'settlement positions'. The position statement and any accompanying documentation that either party seeks to rely upon at the mediation is then forwarded to the mediator, who will be able to identify the principle issues and areas of the dispute prior to the mediation.

The mediator is encouraged to contact the parties prior to the mediation to introduce himself or herself and to discuss any fears or enquiries they may have concerning the process that will be followed on the day. The mediator may also request that the parties prepare additional documentation.

It is not necessary for a mediator to have the same command over the detailed facts of a dispute as an arbitrator or a judge. Preparation time is typically between three and five hours. In a multi-million pound dispute involving several parties, preparation time might be greater, but even in the most complex case will be no more than 20 or 25 hours. The hearing time of most commercial mediations is one day, though it can be a very long day, extending from 9 am to 11 p.m. or even later. Various special mediation schemes are limited to a specific number of hours. Thus, the Central London County Court mediation scheme is strictly limited to three hours. (The lights in the building go out at 7:30 prompt. It is said that many settlements are reached at 7:29!). A scheme for charity disputes organised jointly by CEDR and the NCVO is limited to five hours. A CEDR scheme for the Housing ombudsman is limited to four hours.

In commercial mediations, the parties are usually represented by solicitors or barristers at the mediation. This is largely because lawyers have been involved in the handling of the claim before the parties decided to try mediation, and especially if court proceedings have already been commenced, it is sensible that the lawyers should be available to advise the clients confidentially about any proposed settlement, and to assist in drafting it. In many of the special scheme mediations run by CEDR, the parties are not legally represented at the mediation, though there is no rule on the matter. Indeed, one of the key things about mediation is that it is a very flexible process. In commercial mediations, other parties are sometimes present: in particular, experts and insurers.

b) *Opening phase*

The mediation process itself involves the mediator winning the confidence of the parties, so that he or she can help them find common ground, and eventually enable them to reach a settlement. It involves several different roles, and many skills. He or she must be

- a manager of the process, a 'chairman', but not a dominating one.

- a communicator, reading the party's feelings about the case, and showing empathy to emotions. An example occurred in a claim by a purchaser of a business against the vendor for fraudulent misrepresentation. At the start of the first private session with the vendor, the mediator said, 'it cannot be pleasant being accused of fraud'; to which the vendor commented 'it's the first time in my life'. It was apparent from the vendor's body language (a lowering of the shoulders) that this question had caused him to relax.

- a reality tester. The mediator will studiously avoid giving legal advice and appearing to act as judge. Yet the mediation is possibly the first time some of the legal arguments in the case have been tried out on a neutral third party, and so the mediator's reaction to these arguments often carries great weight both with the party and with his lawyers. If a mediator can point to difficulties in a party's evidence, it becomes easier to persuade the party to alter his assessment of the likely outcome if the matter were to proceed to a trial, and in consequence to adjust his negotiating stance. Indeed, it could be said that the

169

best way to get two parties to settle is to persuade each one that they are going to lose.

- a 'sponge' for emotions, allowing the parties their 'day in court'. In some medical negligence cases, what the patient wants as much if not more than money is to hear the hospital authority accept responsibility for what went wrong, and to hear from them that steps are being taken to make sure that the same mistake does not happen again to someone else.

- a problem solver. It is always a delight when a settlement can be reached which involves the parties placing their trust in each other once again, for some continuing business relationship. A settlement sum of £500,000 may not be acceptable to one party, but a sum of £250,000 coupled with an incentive scheme under which there is a commission for future work totalling £250,000 (or even more) may be quite another matter.

The opening session of a commercial mediation is slightly formal. The 'nitty gritty' takes place later, in the private sessions with each of the parties. But the opening session is important, and should not be omitted just to speed up the process. In particular, it enables the mediator to set his seal of authority on the day's proceedings, and it enables the parties and their representatives to present their points in their own way, without any constraints save for a sensible time limit (typically 10 minutes per party), and being restrained and unprovocative in delivery.

The mediator starts by explaining his role, and the procedure for the day.[62] He then invites each party to make a presentation.

---

[62] The following is an outline of a typical opening by a mediator in a commercial dispute.

Role

The mediator thanks the parties for coming, and explains his or her own role:

The mediator is present to help negotiations, not as a judge. The mediator is not there to impose any solution on the parties.

The mediator is a chairman – to keep up momentum during the day.

The mediator is neutral – The mediator is not there to express views on the merits, but may test the parties' views.

The mediator explains the two levels of confidentiality. Everything said in the mediation is private to the mediation, and is not to be repeated outside the mediation. Nothing which is said to the mediator by one party will be repeated to the other party unless the mediator is specifically authorised to say it. Throughout the day the mediator will regularly check with one party what the mediator may or may not say to the other party.

The mediator thanks the parties for the case summaries and any agreed sets of documents which he has read.

Mediation agreement

The mediator checks that the mediation agreement has been signed, and if not, has it signed. It is usual to emphasise some of the key terms which are agreed:

that the mediation is without prejudice and confidential;

the parties have authority to settle;

there is no settlement until matters are finalised in a written agreement;

the parties are free to withdraw at any time, but the mediator will encourage them to continue for as long as he considers it likely to be constructive.

Outline of procedure

The mediator sets ground rules for each party's opening statement.

They should be no longer than 10 minutes.

There should be no interruptions by the other side.

It does not matter who speaks for each party, whether the lawyer or the client.

The mediator may remind the parties that he or she has read their case summaries and the pleadings in the action, so they do not need to repeat what they have already said. Instead, he encourages the parties simply to summarise their key arguments and the merits of their case in a non-confrontational way.

171

In commercial mediations, these are usually made by the lawyers if they are present. Sometimes however it is very effective for one party personally to express how he feels about what has happened, as this will often help the healing process, and show the other party that the complaint is genuine.

There may be questions which follow, but these are usually brief. It is usual to break up into private sessions (known as caucuses) after the joint meeting.

The mediator reminds them that he is not a judge, so they are here to persuade the other party, not the mediator, of the strength of their case.

The mediator reminds them that everything is without prejudice, so they can be open and make concessions if this may help to progress negotiations.

The mediator then explains that he or she will see each party in turn, in private, so that the mediator can explore with them the underlying interests and issues in the case. The mediator emphasises that everything said to him or her at these private sessions is confidential.

The mediator explains that eventually, hopefully, the parties will reach agreement, and this will be set out in writing and signed by the parties.

Points re approach to mediation

Lastly, the mediator may try to encourage the parties by pointing to some of the merits of the mediation process:

It enables the parties to focus on the present and the future, not to dwell on the past.

It enables the parties to look to their commercial interests, not just their strict legal rights.

Options may be available for settlement which would not be available in litigation. This gives room for creative and lateral thinking.

The parties should be positive – There is a good chance of settlement. (CEDR advertises a 90% success rate.)

c) Exploration

The next stage is a succession of private meetings (caucuses) with each party in turn. Several elements are present here. The mediator needs to build relationships with the parties, so that they can start to be open about the strengths and weaknesses of the case. The mediator needs to allow the parties to express their real feelings, and show their emotions about the case. The mediator needs to show that he recognises and understands how the parties feel on these issues. The mediator needs to demonstrate *empathy* rather than *sympathy*: he must remain unbiased, and not emotionally involved himself, but he must show understanding and an ability to associate with how the parties feel.

In commercial disputes, it may not be thought that emotions play a significant part in a dispute which on paper is about money; but emotions are often present even in such cases. A professional negligence action, whether the negligence is that of a doctor, a solicitor or an accountant, often involves human suffering beyond merely financial loss. In a breach of contract claim, trust may have been betrayed, and confidence broken. Parties who were in business together for many months or years may now be at loggerheads. Allegations may have been made in the proceedings which are harmful to any future relationship, and if a solution is to be considered which involves such relationships being restored, such feelings need to be recognised, and allowed to be expressed. This is particularly relevant to church disputes, the majority of which are more concerned with people and relationships than with money.

The caucus is a place where the mediator can discuss with the parties more than just the merits of the case. In particular he or she will try to look at the wider picture of their commercial and personal interests. The written statements of case and the legal arguments may not reveal the real concerns of the parties. For example, one party may not wish to lose face before his colleagues. A party may not wish to have questions asked about the anticipated cost of the litigation at its forthcoming annual general meeting. One party may be desperately concerned at the financial consequences if it loses the action. An elderly party arguing over the ownership of a house may actually find the house too big a responsibility, and want to move to something smaller.[63] The expression *hidden agenda* sounds sinister, but many parties may have concerns which go beyond what the dispute appears to be about at first sight. The caucus is the time when these can be discussed confidentially with the mediator. The survey in chapter 3 of diocesan practice in the Church of England showed that the same principle applies to Church disputes: many single-issue disputes hide deeper, pastoral, concerns.[64]

The caucus is also a place where the mediator starts to examine some of the difficulties in the case, to challenge the parties' expectations in the litigation. In theory, a good mediator need not be an expert in the subject matter of the mediation; and certainly there are many good mediators who are not trained lawyers. But it is often helpful if the mediator does have practical experience of the type of dispute in which the parties are enmeshed. A mediator who is a lawyer can readily appreciate some of the evidential or legal difficulties which each side faces, and discuss them with the parties and their advisers. Although a mediator should not give his own view of the law or the merits, in practice many mediators come close to adopting an evaluative role on some of the issues in the case. A mediator may well point out some aspect of the evidence which is weak, and ask the party how he feels the judge might react to it. This is often a perhaps less than subtle hint by the mediator as to where his own views lie.

In a mediation expected to take a whole day, a typical caucus session may last 20 to 30 minutes. Anything longer is likely to

---

[63] For example, this was the position of the author's client Mrs Collings prior to the Court of Appeal hearing in *Collings v Lee* [2001] 2 All ER 332.

[64] See pg. 137.

cause the other party to start to get worried. After one or two caucus sessions with each party, the mediator needs to change the emphasis to how the dispute is to be resolved. We are now moving into the next stage, the negotiation stage of the mediation.

d) Negotiation

In some commercial disputes, the mediator may find at this stage that he is simply acting as a courier, to convey offers and counter-offers from one party to the other. A deal may well be reached by this means. In other cases, a joint session may be appropriate; a session with, say, just the lawyers; or a session with two out of three parties together, so that the common issues between them can be discussed, and a proposal put to the third party. Sometimes a brainstorming session may be needed to see a way round a particular difficulty: this can be very helpful if all parties are trying to work towards a solution.

In commercial mediations, there may come a time when there appears to be deadlock. A defendant is convinced the claim is only worth £100,000, but the claimant is convinced it is worth £300,000. A whole host of strategies may be employed to see if the deadlock can be broken:[65]emphasising the parties commercial interests in the proposed settlement; 'expanding the cake' by finding some added feature which makes a deal worthwhile; breaking down the problem into components, and reaching agreement on parts of the claim first; these are but examples of techniques which may help. The guidance notes for mediators published by the British Academy of Experts[66] identifies the following 'techniques' for this stage of the mediation:

---

[65] A helpful table of possible remedies for various common types of deadlocks is to be found in Andrew Acland, *Resolving disputes without going to court* (London, Century Business Books, 1995) pg. 172–174.

[66] See in Atkin's Court Forms, 2nd edn. vol. 6(2) (1998 issue), page 178.

i Obtain Movement

- Explore alternative solutions and trade-offs.

- Re-establish priorities of the parties.

- Communicate the possibility of movement.

- Create doubts in parties' minds concerning the strength of their positions.

- Ensure each party understands the position of the other party by re-stating their cases.

- Express proposals as hypothetical questions to avoid rejection except in principle.

- Deflate unreasonable or extreme demands and positions.

- Narrow differences.

ii Obtaining Agreement

- Develop the habit of agreement.

- Emphasise progress, issues settled and the pace of movement.

- Stress consequences of failure.

- Make suggestions and exert pressure for agreement.

- Avoid back-sliding.

- If appropriate, make final suggestions and recommendations.

- Try to end on a positive note.

e) Conclusion

If it becomes clear no agreement will be reached, the mediator should terminate the mediation. But the mediator will still seek to keep the channels open for further mediation or negotiation, and will contact the parties to see if anything further can be done.

Many disputes which do not settle on the day of the mediation, do settle within a week or so afterwards.

If agreement is reached, the mediator, or the parties' lawyers, should draft a written agreement, and have all the parties sign it. It is perhaps trite, but needs to be said that the agreement should be clear, unambiguous, simple, and comprehensive. Drafting even a comparatively short agreement can take half-an-hour or more, and this can be frustrating if the mediation has already gone late into the evening. The Central London County Court Form MD8A 'Points for consideration when drafting mediation settlement terms',[67] gives the following helpful guidance:

- If the agreement involves the payment of money, consider: how much? by whom? to whom? by when? in what instalments? carrying interest?

- Does the agreement reached include terms other than paying money? If so, are these clearly set out? Is there a timetable for them to be carried out?

- Is this agreement meant to take effect now, or at some future time? Does either party really need a 'cooling-off period', to think about, or take advice on, the agreement before it becomes binding?

- What agreement have the parties reached as to the costs of the litigation and the mediation? Is either party legally-aided? If so, are they aware of the implications of that on any settlement money received?

- Is this settlement intended to bring to an end all relevant litigation between the parties? If so, does the agreement expressly state this? Has each party got the necessary authority to settle?

---

[67] Central London County Court Form MD8A 'Points for consideration when drafting mediation settlement terms', printed in Atkin's Court Forms, 2nd edn. vol. 6(2) (1998 issue), page 183.

7. SUCCESS RATE

Commercial mediation has a high success rate. As Atkin's Court Forms[68] states

> Statistics for an activity as confidential as mediation are inevitably difficult to obtain and open to doubt, but all the authoritative bodies quote success rates for mediation of between 75 and 95%. Even mediations which fail and are terminated by the mediator or one of the parties, frequently enable later settlement as a result of the discussions which have taken place and so help avoid the full costs of litigation.

In the early years of mediation in this country people sought to try to identify the types of case for which mediation was appropriate, it being thought that mediation was appropriate for only a few types of case. Now the emphasis is the other way round: to identify those cases for which mediation is not appropriate, the presumption being that it is appropriate for most types of dispute. So, for example, Rix J's annual report on the Commercial Court for 1998[69] states

> It is wisely said that most categories of litigation are suitable for ADR and that the trick is to identify the case in which ADR is not appropriate rather than to try to identify the categories of case for which it is.

That said, the category of cases in which mediation has been and is used effectively is almost endless. The following are examples: agency claims; banking, insurance and financial services; charity and trusts; church disputes; commercial contracts; community – environmental; company disputes; construction projects; defamation[70]; education; employment; family – divorce; fran-

---

[68] See in Atkin's Court Forms, 2nd edn. vol. 6(2) (1998 issue), page 25.

[69] *Annual report on the Commercial Court* [1999] 2 Lloyds 802, pg. 804.

[70] See Richard Shillito, 'Mediation in libel actions' New Law Journal 2000, 150(6921), 122–123. A draft protocol encouraging early settlement, arbitration and mediation to prevent unnecessary libel cases going

chises; housing; industrial – employment; intellectual property
and information technology; international disputes; landlord and
tenant, and housing; partnership; personal injury; planning; professional negligence; small claims – car repairs; and trade unions.[71]

---

to court has been launched by a committee of libel experts assembled by
the Law Society. Jeremy Fleming, 'Libel protocol to cut litigation.' Law
Society Gazette 2000, 97(5), 4.

[71] This list is compiled from a number of sources: in particular, the
author's personal experience, information published by CEDR, and textbooks on ADR. CEDR's *Cutting the Cost of Conflict: Highlights 1997–1998*
(London, CEDR, 1999) lists mediations arranged by CEDR in the following areas: accounting, shipping/oil, shares, banking/finance, professional negligence, construction/engineering, pensions, partnership,
medical negligence, intellectual property, insurance/reinsurance, contract (sale of goods), contract (supply of services), information technology and telecommunications, and employment. Russell Caller, *ADR and
Commercial Disputes* (London, Sweet & Maxwell, 2001). *ADR and Commercial Disputes* has one chapter on each of the following types of dispute: banking and finance disputes, commercial property disputes, employment disputes, franchising disputes, insolvency disputes, insurance
related disputes, IT disputes, landlord and tenant disputes, partnership
disputes, shipping disputes, and probate and trust disputes. Brown and
Marriott, *ADR Principles and Practice*, 2nd edn. has one chapter on each
of the following types of mediation: civil and commercial mediation,
divorce and family mediation, employment mediation, mediation of
community and neighbourhood disputes, and mediation of environmental and public policy issues. A similar variety can be seen from
some of the commercial mediations in which the author has been involved:

- a claim for defective computer goods,
- an international sale of goods dispute concerning the motor trade,
- fees claimed by a consultancy firm,
- fees claimed by an expert witness,
- a housing dispute involving a Jewish charity,

179

In Lord Irvine's Inaugural Lecture to the Faculty of Mediation and ADR[72] the Lord Chancellor stated

> I think the use of ADR in administrative cases is of necessity limited. There may be more to be gained from the development of the ombudsman system, though I appreciate that ombudsmen are more concerned with the resolution of grievances, than with the resolution of disputes over conflicting rights.

A cynic would comment that a government minister would say that about disputes with the government. Yet the experience of the United States suggests that cases which set the rights of individuals against the state often raise very sensitive issues, and it may be right for the government to tread cautiously in this area.

Mediation is not much used for tax disputes. But there is no reason in principle why, for example, a VAT dispute between a trader and HM Customs & Excise, an income tax dispute with the Inland Revenue, or an inheritance tax dispute with the Capital Taxes Office, should not all be suitable for resolution by mediation.[73]

- a claim against two firms of accountants for professional negligence,
- a claim for breach of warranty arising out of the sale of a business,
- a doctors' partnership dispute,
- flood damage to a factory caused by burst pipes,
- an internet web-site dispute,
- a claim for wrongful dismissal,
- a will dispute
- disputed membership of a charity.

[72] 27 January 1999. Available at *www.open.gove.uk/lcd/speeches/1999/27-1-99.htm*.

[73] There are reports from counsel who specialise in such work that HM Customs & Excise and the Inland Revenue are both amenable to resolving disputes by mediation. Most tax disputes are resolved by negotia-

Two established cases where mediation is said not to be appropriate are, first, where a party desires to establish a precedent for the future, and second, where a party needs the immediate protection of the court by, for example, obtaining an injunction. Yet, even in this latter case, an injunction is often granted as an interim measure pending the full determination of the issues. Once an interim injunction is granted to preserve the status quo, it may often be appropriate for the parties then to seek mediation to attempt to resolve the substantive issue. Similarly, a party may need to issue proceedings to protect its position under the Limitation Act 1980. Once the claim has been issued, an order can be obtained[74] for the action to be stayed while the parties seek to resolve the dispute by mediation. In such cases, the courts and mediation both have a role in resolving the dispute.

Mediation is not appropriate where one party has no genuine interest in settlement. Sometimes a party will mis-use the mediation process, coming to the mediation not with any proposals or intention to negotiate, but in order to see more of the strength of the other side's case. If a mediator realises this is the position, he should confront that party (privately), and say that he proposes to end the mediation immediately unless the party is willing to negotiate. Some commercial clients, in particular insurers, are now very familiar with the mediation process, and some now seek to use it for this improper purpose; mediators need to be alive to this new trend.

There are cases where there is no real dispute that the debt is owing, but one party simply can't or won't pay. In such cases, even if a sum is agreed at the mediation, the person to whom the payment is to be paid may have to obtain a judgment and then enforce it in order to achieve payment. However, such cases may still be appropriate for mediation, as the mediator may be able to

---

tion, and HM Customs and Excise and the Inland Revenue regard mediation as simply a form of assisted negotiation.

[74] Under CPR Part 26.

181

agree instalment terms on an acceptable basis; and a clear settlement agreement can usually be enforced by a summary procedure, rather than having to litigate the original dispute, with its
attendant delay and expense.[75] (In some cases a claimant may be
able to obtain summary judgment under CPR Part 24, but he must
be able to prove that the defence has no real prospect of success.
If there appears to be a conflict of evidence on an important issue,
the court will usually refuse summary relief.)

   There is also considerable debate on when is the best time in a
dispute to seek to resolve it by mediation. The earlier the matter
is mediated, the less costs have been incurred in the litigation, but
also the issues may not have been revealed, and the parties may
not have any real idea of the strengths of their case. If a matter is
only sent to mediation shortly before the trial, then the evidence is
ready, and the issues are clear, but the parties have had the costs
and hassle of possibly years of litigation. In many disputes, costs
can become disproportionate to the amount which is at stake. The
Civil Procedure Rules 1998 seek to address this problem by allo-
cating cases to one of three tracks, the small claims track, the fast
track, and the multi-track, with different levels of complexity in
procedure, and different levels of fees allowed, for each track.
This addresses the problem of disproportionate costs to some extent, but legal fees are still a matter of major concern to all but the
very rich, the very poor (who qualify for legal aid), and those who
are insured or have their fees paid by some trade union or other
organisation. In the NHS medical negligence mediation pilot

---

[75] See CPR Part 40.6 for consent orders generally. Where proceedings
are to be stayed on agreed terms to be scheduled to the order, the draft
order should be drawn so as to read as follows: 'And the Claimant and
the Defendant having agreed to the terms set forth in the schedule
hereto, it is ordered that all further proceedings in this claim be stayed,
except for the purpose of carrying such terms into effect. Liberty to apply as to carrying such terms into effect.' This form of order is called a
'Tomlin Order'.

scheme, the 'information threshold' for referral to mediation was most commonly identified as being the point where expert advice on the claim had been received by one or both of the parties.

8. FINANCIAL COST

The cost of mediating a commercial dispute is relatively expensive, but it is usually much less than cost of litigation. In broad terms a one-day mediation (and few last more than one day) costs each party less than the cost of one day in court. The two major mediation providers, the ADR Group and CEDR have different charging structures, and it is not easy to see at a glance what the overall total cost will be; but generally, CEDR works out cheaper than the ADR Group for low value claims, and the ADR Group works out cheaper than CEDR for high value claims. A smaller organisation, the Centre for Business Arbitration, generally works out the cheapest of all, especially for large claims.

CEDR's fee schedule[76] for commercial mediations includes mediator contact with parties before the mediation, mediator preparation, an eight-hour mediation day, and management support for the mediation process. For two-party disputes the fees are as set out in figure 4.

---

[76] For further details, see CEDR's web site at *www.cedrsolve.com/*

Value of Claim	Total Mediation Fee	Fee per Party	Extra Days	Extra Hours
Up to £50,000	£1,650	£ 825	n/a	£150/hour
£50 – 150,000	£2,600	£1,300	£1,560	£150/hour
£150 – 300,000	£3,800	£1,900	£2,280	£250/hour
£300 – 700,000	£4,600	£2,300	£2,760	£250/hour
£700,000 – 1m	£5,200	£2,600	£3,120	£300/hour
£1m – 2.5m	£5,800	£2,900	£3,480	£300/hour
£2.5m+	negotiable			

Figure 4. CEDR fee schedule (two-party disputes)

For three- and four-party disputes fees are higher than two-party rates due to the extra management and preparation time required.[77] This is shown in figure 5. Any extra hours required are charged at the same two-party hourly rate.

---

[77] Where there are more than four parties fees are charged on a case-by-case basis.

Value of Claim	Total Mediation Fee	Fee per Party (3 or 4)	Extra Days
Up to £50,000	£2,145	£715 / £536.25	n/a
£50 – 150,000	£3,380	£1,126.66 / £845	£2,028
£150 – 300,000	£5,000	£1,666.66 / £1,250	£3,000
£300 – 700,000	£6,000	£2,000 / £1,500	£3,600
£700,000 – 1m	£6,800	£2,266.66 / £1,700	£4,080
£1m – 2.5m	£7,600	£2,533.33 / £1,900	£4,560
£2.5m+	negotiable		

Figure 5. CEDR fee schedule (three- and four- party disputes)

The ADR Group's fee is normally a fixed fee payable per hour of mediation time. This is £125 per party, or £175 in the case of a central London based mediator. (The ADR Group is based in Bristol.) For three or more party disputes, the fee is calculated on a two party basis plus 15 per cent for each additional party (the same as CEDR).

The ADR Group charges for preparation at the rate of £75 per hour, the first hour being free. A proportionately higher fee is charged for Central London mediators (£105 per hour.)

The fees for the Centre for Business Arbitration[78] as shown in figure 6.

---

[78] Centre for Business Arbitration, 11 Old Square, Lincoln's Inn, London WC2A 3TS.

Dispute value	Fee for 1/2 day per party	Fee for full day per party
under £50,000	£400	£550
£50,000 – £99,999	£500	£750
£100,000 – £199,999	£550	£850
£200,000 – £499,999	£650	£1,050
£500,000 – £999,999	£725	£1,200

Figure 6. Centre for Business Arbitration fee schedule

In practice the fees charged for most mediations organised by the Centre for Business Arbitration are now based not on the amount which is in dispute, but on the hourly charge of the mediator, together with a straight £250 administration fee for the Centre. A typical one-day mediation (say, eight hours) where the mediator charges an hourly rate of £150, allowing, say, three hours for preparation, thus costs around £2,000, shared between the parties.[79]

In a commercial case, a party who is represented by solicitors (and in some cases, a barrister as well) will have additional fees to pay. Solicitors usually charge an hourly rate. Barristers vary, some charging an hourly rate, others a fixed fee. The ADR Group's fee structure brings home to the parties that every hour of mediation is costing £125 for the mediator, and probably a

---

[79] 11 hours at £150, plus £250 administration, totals £1,900. In addition, travel and incidental expenses are payable. On costs assessments, solicitors' time spent travelling is allowed at one-half their normal hourly rate. Similarly, some mediators charge half their normal hourly rate for time spent travelling.

similar amount, if not more, for each party's solicitor.[80] The solicitor will also charge for the time preparing for the mediation: this includes preparing the case summary for the mediator, preparing what the solicitor proposes to say in the opening joint session, and making sure the solicitor has up-to-date figures for the costs incurred and estimates for the future likely costs in the case. This may amount to several hours' chargeable time. A solicitor who goes into a mediation unprepared is doing his client a dis-service. Finally, there may well be the costs of hotel accommodation if that is where the mediation is taking place.

The above fees are for normal commercial disputes. CEDR administers some special schemes at a reduced cost. Of particular interest is the scheme it administers jointly with the National Council for Voluntary Organisations (NCVO) for voluntary organisations and charities. Typical disputes which are mediated under this scheme include internal disagreements in a governing body, employment disputes, landlord and tenant problems, intellectual property questions concerning publications or a logo, and commercial disputes concerning the organisations products and services.

Mediations under the CEDR/NCVO scheme are limited to five hours, and the fee structure charged is as follows:

---

[80] £125 per hour is an average hourly rate for a solicitor with less than 4 years' post qualification experience. The *Supreme Court Costs Office Guide to the summary assessment of costs*, revised by senior costs judge Peter Hurst, February 2001 (London, Crown Copyright, 2001) gives guideline hourly charging rates for solicitors for 2001 ranging from £60 to £100 for trainee solicitors, from £86 to £180 for solicitors with up to four years' experience, and £120 to £335 for solicitors with over 4 years' experience. The table is broken down by locality, the cheapest solicitors being on the Wales & Chester circuit, the Western Circuit, and the North Eastern Circuit, and the most expensive solicitors being those in the City of London and those close to the Royal Courts of Justice, Strand, London WC2.

- For a small organisation (with an income of under £250,000 per annum), the cost of mediation is £150 (with a subsidy of £350).

- For a medium organisation (with an income of between £250,000 and £2,000,000 per annum), the cost of mediation is £300 (with a subsidy of £300).

- For a large organisation (with an income over £2,000,000 per annum), the cost of mediation is £700 (with no subsidy).

The sliding scale of costs reflects CEDR's own charging principles, albeit at a lower rate. The sliding scale of support available reflects the desire to give most support to those very small organisations who are in need of the service.

These costs are for internal disputes only. For disputes between one organisation and another, the normal CEDR fees usually apply.

In addition, each party may well have its own hidden costs in attending the mediation, in particular the cost of its own management time. However, the management time spent in mediation is usually time well spent in comparison to the considerably greater management time which would be involved if the dispute went to court.

In the 1980s and early 1990s, mediation was referred to as a 'win-win' option. A more realistic description would perhaps be 'pain-pain'. Commercial mediation is not cheap, and success cannot be guaranteed. A mediation which fails to produce a settlement becomes yet another four-figure sum in the eventual legal costs which the client usually has to pay. Yet if commercial mediation continues to have the high success rate that pilot studies have shown, and if mediation standards are maintained, it normally makes good commercial sense to try to resolve a dispute by mediation. The best alternative to a negotiated settlement is usually considerably more pain, both financial, and personal: financial, in the cost of the litigation, and in the loss of management time; personal, in the loss of opportunity to heal relationships and open opportunities for future business. And as the last sentence shows, a party's personal and financial interests may often be linked.

9. APPLICATION OF THIS MODEL FOR THE CHURCH

a) *What types of church dispute*

Mediation is a very flexible process, but some models are better for one type of dispute than another. It is perhaps helpful to consider the use of this model for the 15 main types of church dispute analysed in chapter 3.

i *Alterations to church buildings and graveyards*

Disputes in this category frequently involve the whole community, both members of the church, and non-churchgoing members of the community. Frequently such disputes also involve statutory bodies such as English Heritage. Although a dispute concerning an alteration to a church sometimes involves the congregation dividing into two 'camps', those for and against a particular alteration, in many cases such a simple division is not possible, and the objectors may all have different reasons for objecting to a particular proposal, or a particular part of a proposal. Such disputes do not readily fall into what is basically a two-party model for mediation. The commercial dispute usually involves a small number of parties, though multi-party mediations are increasing. In its *Cutting the Cost of Conflict: Highlights 1997–1998*[81] CEDR reported that multi-party mediations rose from 11% in 1996/1997 to 16% of total cases in 1997/1998.

A mediation involving more than two parties almost invariably takes longer than one involving just two parties. Each additional party adds to the time taken to mediate a dispute. There will be very long waiting times while the mediator attempts to see all the

---

[81] *Cutting the Cost of Conflict: Highlights 1997–1998* (London, CEDR, 1999).

189

parties in turn. In construction disputes, which seem to be one of the few types of claims where there may be several parties, this difficulty is sometimes met by the use of more than one mediator; and this approach may be appropriate for this sort of church dispute. Yet what is often required is a means of developing a procedure so that all the members of the congregation are satisfied with the process. The standard commercial model for mediation needs to be adapted considerably before it can be used for large congregational disputes, such as when a controversial reordering of the church is proposed. We will see later that the Mennonites have developed a mediation model which is appropriate for large congregational disputes, and it differs considerably from the commercial model presented in this chapter.

Some disputes involving graveyards do not involve the whole community. The dispute at *Holy Trinity, Freckleton*[82] was one such, being a dispute between relatives of the deceased and the vicar of a church over a proposed inscription on a gravestone. This mediation model would have worked well for such a dispute: a representative for the relatives on one side, the vicar (or someone representing the diocese) on the other side.

ii Church governance

Some of the disputes concerning church governance were disputes where a whole community feels resentful about the manner in which the diocesan authorities have attempted to enforce compliance with some church policy or law against the incumbent. The dispute in *Swaffham, Norfolk* is an example.[83] While the dispute was initially just between the bishop and one priest, it developed into a community dispute. The commercial mediation model might have been appropriate in the initial stages of the dispute, when it was simply an issue between the bishop and Mr

---

[82] See *In re Holy Trinity Churchyard, Freckleton* [1994] 1 WLR 1588, (1994) 3 Ecc LJ 350.

[83] See pg. 95, fn. 30.

Chalcraft. The commercial model is clearly not an appropriate model once the dispute spread to the whole community.

The *Abbotsford Parish* dispute between the Revd Tom Logan and the Scottish Presbytery[84] which sought to suspend Mr Logan from his ministry was suitable for this model of mediation. There is no reason why a large organisation cannot be represented at a mediation by one or two members: the critical issue is whether those members have authority to agree to a settlement on behalf of the organisation without referring back to it. The Presbytery could have authorised one or two representatives to attend the mediation, and to negotiate and conclude a suitable agreement on behalf of the Presbytery. Alternatively, the Presbytery could have authorised the representatives to negotiate, but not to conclude a final agreement. In that case, the agreement would not become binding until the Presbytery had formally agreed to adopt it.[85]

The cases of *Jesmond Parish Church*[86] and *St Oswald, Walkergate*[87] were both disputes between a congregation and the diocesan

---

[84] *Logan v Presbytery of Dumbarton* [1995] SLT 1228, *The Times*, 23 May 1995. See pg. 109, fn. 95.

[85] A similar situation arose in one of the author's commercial mediations. The settlement proposed was outside the authority of one of the parties present at the mediation, and final agreement had to await approval from a parent company.

[86] *Newcastle Evening Chronicle,* 18 June 1997; *The Newcastle Evening Chronicle*, 15 November 1997, local news, pg. 9; and correspondence published in Jesmond Parish Church's web site: *www.church.org.uk.* See also the following articles in the *Church Times* for 1998: 30 January, pg. 1, 3 (unlicensed priest appointed); 6 February, pg. 3 (does not pay full quota); 13 February, pg. 9 (letters); 20 February, pg. 7 (Newcastle gives pledge on gays), pg. 8 (leader comment).

[87] *Newcastle Journal*, 8 December 1997; *Church Times*, 19 June 1998, pg. 3; *Church Times*, 24 July 1998, pg. 7; *The Times*, 4 August 1998, home news, pg. 6; *Church Times*, 14 August 1998, pg. 6. The Ed Moll dispute at St Oswald, Walkergate is reported in *Gill v Davies* (1997) 5 Ecc LJ 131; and

191

authorities concerning episcopal authority. The *Jesmond* dispute is at the time of writing still unresolved. The dispute over Ed Moll at *St Oswald, Walkergate* was resolved by mediation. Ed Moll personally attended the mediation with the bishop, and the congregation was ready to support him in any agreement which he reached in good conscience at that mediation. So, although *St Oswald, Walkergate* involved a whole congregation, there was one representative who plainly could represent that congregation in the mediation.[88]

Mediation was used, but failed, in the case of *St Peter's Church, Ropley*, where the incumbent's controversial marriage to his curate led to a split in the congregation.[89]

Disputes arising from the use of the bishop's power to suspend presentation under the Pastoral Measure 1983 are suitable for this model of mediation. The dispute usually involves the following parties: two parish representatives (often, but not necessarily, the church wardens), the patron or a representative from the patronage board, and the bishop.[90] Another reason why this type of dispute is particularly suitable for this model of mediation is that solicitors are often involved: if the dispute is not resolved, there is the legal remedy of judicial review open to the parties.

iii Commercial contract disputes

Little needs to be said under this heading. Such disputes are the stuff of commercial mediation, and therefore any church dis-

---

the full judgment is printed in Mark Hill, *Ecclesiastical Law*, 2nd edn. (Oxford University Press, 2001) pg. 707.

[88] The author recommended mediation in another dispute raising similar issues, the *Kidderminster* dispute, see pg. 110.

[89] See pg. 102, fn. 66.

[90] One such dispute where mediation was recommended was the *Penshurst* dispute, see pg. 98.

pute in this category should be suitable for the commercial mediation model.

iv Defamation

The commercial model of mediation is starting to be used in defamation disputes.[91] Defamation actions by definition involve alleged damage to the claimant's reputation. Similar considerations arise in commercial fraud cases, for example where a purchaser of a business claims that the vendor dishonestly misled him as to the profitability of the business. A damaged reputation can sometimes be restored by a suitable public notice.[92] Once the wording of this has been agreed, the mediation can move to the stage of negotiating a suitable figure to compensate the claimant for any actual loss he has suffered.

v Discipline

As has been seen, discipline covers a spectrum including criminal conduct and serious moral failings such as adultery, issues of principle, and less serious cases of pastoral failure.[93]

CRIMINAL CONDUCT / SERIOUS MORAL FAILING

Mediation is not appropriate as a means of avoiding the normal criminal process where a crime has been committed: to do so would be to usurp the proper functions of the criminal justice

---

[91] See pg. 103, fn. 70.

[92] A typical notice would be as follows.

> The action proceeding in the High Court of Justice between X and Y has been settled on confidential terms acceptable to all parties. X wishes to state that it now accepts that the allegations of fraud and deceit made in those proceedings were without foundation and are unreservedly withdrawn.

The words 'now accepts' is a face-saver for Y, as it does not state that Y was wrong at the time to think X dishonest.

[93] See pg. 108, and the section 'Complexity' on pg. 118.

system, and would bring the Church into disrepute. Nor is mediation appropriate in cases of alleged serious moral failing, such as the accusations of adultery made against the Revd Clifford Williams[94] and Dr Brandon Jackson.[95] Such cases are an offence against the Church generally, and if the offence is proved, a penalty should be imposed.[96]

ISSUES OF PRINCIPLE

The fact that a dispute involves doctrine does not prevent it being mediated: issues such as the ministry of women in a particular church have been resolved by mediation.[97] The commercial model is therefore suitable for the *Kidderminster* type dispute.[98] There may be some personal element involved, but the key issue in that case is how to reconcile the parties' different theological convictions on homosexuality with the duty of canonical obedience.

LESS SERIOUS CASES

Mediation is appropriate for less serious cases of discipline.[99] Section 12 of the Clergy Discipline Measure 2003 provides that the bishop may direct that an attempt be made to use mediation to resolve the complaint, and a timetable for the mediation is then set out in section 15 of the Measure.[100] A complainant may in

---

[94] See pg. 109, fn. 94.

[95] See pg. 109, fn. 93.

[96] *Under Authority, Report on Clergy Discipline* (London, Church House Publishing, 1996), pg. 81.

[97] See pg. 106, fn. 80.

[98] See pg. 110, fn. 99.

[99] *Under Authority, Report on Clergy Discipline*, pg. 81.

[100] The measure uses the word 'conciliation' rather than 'mediation'. *Alternative Dispute Resolution – a Discussion Paper* (London, Lord Chan-

some circumstances be fully satisfied by an apology and an expression of willingness to handle a situation differently in future.
If so, the mediation model in this chapter is suitable for the task
though, as mentioned below, a more informal model may be better.

Where the main issue is how to restore the broken trust or relationship between the parties, following some misconduct by the
clergyman, the commercial model of mediation is likely to be too
formal. The community model described in chapter 5 has much
more emphasis on transforming relationships than does the commercial model, and the more informal community model is therefore better suited to such discipline cases.

vi Employment disputes

Most employment disputes are over the position of one person:
the dispute involving Dr Neary at Westminster Abbey is typical,
save for the fact that it involved such public figures and suffered

---

cellor's Department, November 1999) Annex A describes *conciliation* as
follows:

> Conciliation is a procedure like mediation but where the third
> party, the conciliator, takes a more interventionist role in
> bringing the two parties together and in suggesting possible
> solutions to help achieve an agreed settlement. The term
> 'conciliation' is gradually falling into disuse and the process is
> regarded as a form of mediation.

A similar definition is given by the Australian National Alternative Dispute Resolution Advisory Council (NADRAC). According to
NADRAC's definition, a conciliator has more of an advisory role than a
mediator, and the conciliator may suggest terms for settlement, but not
impose them on the parties: *Alternative Dispute Resolution Definitions*
(Australia, National Alternative Dispute Resolution Advisory Council
(NADRAC), March 1997). The *Response by the General Council of the Bar
to the Lord Chancellor's Department's discussion paper on ADR* (London,
General Council of the Bar, 2000), paragraph 14 states 'mediation and
conciliation should not be distinguished as to meaning'.

from so much publicity. In 1999 CEDR reported that 5% of its cases were employment disputes.[101] One example is given by CEDR in its quarterly publication *Resolutions*.[102] In that case the managing director of an engineering company claimed £600,000 damages for wrongful dismissal.[103] The dispute began in April 1997, and proceedings were issued in October 1997. In 1999 the case was stayed by the High Court so that the parties could attempt mediation. The parties contacted CEDR and the mediation commenced six weeks later, producing a settlement in one day.

vii Financial

Financial disputes are the mainstay of commercial mediation, and therefore this model is well suited to their resolution.

viii Forms of worship, and doctrine

Issues such as the choice of music, the use of charismatic gifts, and the ministry of women can split a congregation. Where the dispute is essentially a community dispute, then what has been said about finding a suitable process to resolve it applies here too. But in some cases, the sides in the dispute can be represented by a small number of key protagonists, and mediation using the model shown in this chapter can be used to resolve the issues.

ix Gay or gender issues

Some gay or gender issues involve very personal matters, and are therefore not best suited to this model of mediation. Where the dispute encompasses other categories such as discipline, as in

---

[101] *Cutting the Cost of Conflict: Highlights 1997–1998* (London, CEDR, 1999).

[102] *Resolutions*, Issue 24 (London, CEDR, 1999), pg. 4.

[103] Coincidentally, the figure quoted in chapter 2, 'The Westminster Abbey dispute', as the legal costs of the Neary dispute.

the *Kidderminster* dispute,[104] and the personal element is not so important, this mediation model may be useful.

x Personality conflicts and pastoral breakdown

This model of mediation is much used in cases where there is a dispute essentially between two people. It is less useful in cases where the dispute is between one person and a whole community. So, for example, the dispute at Lincoln Cathedral was a classic case where mediation was attempted, although it failed to produce a solution. The dispute in St Paul's Cathedral, Dundee over the Revd Miriam Byrne was at one level a dispute between Mrs Byrne and her congregation. Yet at another level it was a dispute between Mrs Byrne and the bishop of her diocese. According to the *Church Times,* the dispute between Mrs Byrne and her bishop was resolved following mediation by Archbishop Tutu, though later reports suggest that the dispute with the congregation still continued.[105]

The dispute at All Saints, Beeston Regis, Norfolk was a classic case of a breakdown in relationship between the vicar and the organist. Such two party disputes are very suitable to mediation using the commercial model. The dispute at St Mary's, Langham was one between the whole community and the vicar, and related to the vicar's management style. Mediation was attempted – the archdeacon acted as mediator – but the dispute was not resolved. The important feature when mediating a dispute involving a community is to find a process under which all members of the community feel their interests and views are represented, so that the process is fair and they are content with the outcome. It is a very different process from the two-party model of mediation presented in this chapter.

---

[104] See pg. 110, fn. 99.

[105] See pg. 68, fn. 42.

xi Property disputes

Disputes between two parties such as over the Forsyth bequest
are suitable for the commercial model. A dispute such as the dispute at Wickwar, Chipping Sodbury, involving a number of people claiming to use a right of way, is less easy to mediate.
Mediation might be suitable if the persons who claimed the right
of way would agree to act through one representative at the mediation, and be bound by any agreement reached at the mediation. But generally, mediations concerning public rights are not
suitable to this model.

Disputes with local authorities is another area where mediation
is unlikely to be useful. It is not usual for planning officers and
other public authority officers to attend a mediation over their
recommendations concerning a property. In the case of planning
matters, this is usually because the planning officer does not himself have power to grant or refuse planning permission: he merely
makes a recommendation to the council which is considering the
application.

xii Personal injury and tax disputes

The commercial model of mediation is well established as an
alternative to personal injury litigation. Similarly, the professional
and commercial approach of this model is well suited to the
resolution of tax disputes.

xiii Summary

So we may conclude that many of the types of church dispute
identified in chapter 3 are suitable for this model of mediation.
The main type of dispute which are not suitable for this model are
where the people and process sides of the conflict triangle are
more important than the problem side. The three most obvious
categories where this applies are personality conflict, pastoral
breakdown, and congregational disputes over proposed building
works. In a personality conflict, the factual disputes may be in-

significant in comparison to the need to rebuild the relationship between the parties. In a pastoral breakdown or a case of congregational disagreement over a building project, there are likely to be numerous different interests, and the disputants cannot easily be represented by a small number of persons. Such disputes require a different process, one which enables all parties to feel their interests have been heard, acknowledged, and respected, so that all parties are then content to abide with the outcome.

b) Resources, human and financial

Most commercial disputes are mediated by commercial mediators, that is solicitors, accountants, surveyors, and other professionals, who expect to be paid for their services. The fees payable to the two main commercial institutions CEDR and the ADR Group have already been set out.[106] The fees cover the administration cost charged by the institutions, and the fees paid to the mediators themselves. It is not easy to establish how much mediators themselves earn from the process, but in 2000 the *Solicitors Gazette* stated as follows:

> A CEDR mediator can expect to earn between £450 and £2,500 a day depending on the size and complexity of case and their experience. ADR Group mediators are paid a minimum of £405 to undertake a mediation, and £135 for each hour after the first three hours, although a spokesman for the company said the rates were often considerably higher.[107]

The fees paid by CEDR to mediators for a mediation under one of its special schemes are significantly less. The fee paid by CEDR to a mediator to mediate a dispute under the CEDR/NCVO scheme is £250.

A number of professional mediators operate independently from CEDR and the ADR Group, and in most cases their charges

---

[106] Pg. 183.

[107] Solicitor's Gazette, 30 March 2000, page 31.

are somewhat less expensive than the full CEDR and ADR Group rates.

The Church may wish to give more emphasis to mediation as a means of resolving disputes, but balk at paying such high rates for mediation services. There are two alternatives. The first is to train a number of volunteers, clergy, and diocesan staff to act as mediators. These persons can then act independently from any mediation organisation, either for nothing as part of their Christian service, or for a nominal fee as a part of their normal church duties, or at appropriate higher rates: the second is to seek to establish some special scheme or rates with one of the main mediation providers.

The difficulty with the second of these two options is that the Church quite naturally would wish to ensure that whoever CEDR or the ADR Group recommends as mediator is not only experienced as a mediator, but also has some understanding of the Church and is sympathetic to Christian values. Following the CEDR conference of October 1999, CEDR wrote to all its accredited mediators to identify those who are suitably qualified and who would be willing, if asked, to offer help in resolving disputes within or between faith communities. The result of this survey is a list of 45 mediators, who described themselves as shown in figure 7.[108]

---

[108] There is probably considerable overlap between the various Christian categories listed here. No mediators described themselves as Muslims.

Anglican	1	Hindu	1
Christian	21	Jewish	7
Christian and wider spiritual beliefs	1	Roman Catholic	5
Church of England	9	Total	45

Figure 7. CEDR survey of accredited mediators

However, only five of these 45 stated that they had already acted as mediator in a 'faith' dispute.

Perhaps the key factor in mediation is the choice of the mediator. Plainly, the CEDR survey has not produced a significant number of mediators with actual experience of mediation of church disputes. This suggests that the Church should not at this stage in general approach CEDR for mediators for its disputes.

In contrast, the survey in chapter 3 of the current diocesan practice in the Church of England has shown that in the majority of dioceses there already exists a number of people who give their services to the church to assist resolving disputes, apparently with some success. The list includes the bishop and archdeacons, a whole range of diocesan staff, clergy, lay people, Christian and secular organisations. Some of these people are already acting in other capacities for the diocese, others are brought in as and when the need arises. In many cases, these people no doubt acted at no additional cost to the church, but costs cannot always just be contained within existing resources. As discussed in chapter 3, some diocesan staff clearly have the time to assist in resolving disputes, while others are too busy to carry out this rôle. In such cases, if conflicts are to be resolved, either external mediators need to be brought in, or additional staff have to be employed.

The Church needs to consider whether this is best left on an *ad hoc* basis, or whether it is to be organised either more centrally or at diocesan level. It raises again the importance of training for mediators, and whether special training for Christian mediators should be organised by the Church or by an organisation such as CEDR for the Church.

c) Adapting the formal model for Church mediations

The commercial mediation model is very flexible, but it is a somewhat formal process, and perhaps daunting to those who have not experienced it. There is a general misapprehension that the mediator will decide issues for the parties, or that the parties will be pressurised into agreeing something which they will afterwards regret. There is sometimes a perception that suggesting mediation shows weakness. As the use of mediation grows in the commercial and legal world, so many of these difficulties will disappear. It is still relatively new and unfamiliar in this country.

The formal commercial mediation model needs to be made more flexible for use in a church dispute. The approach for some church disputes will need to be very informal. This is particularly relevant in the early stages of the mediation framework described above.[109]

i Preparation

SECURING AN AGREEMENT TO MEDIATE, AND IDENTIFYING THE MEDIATOR

Sometimes parties do not know how to suggest mediation to the other party. An approach can be made directly, or by one side inviting a mediator to approach the other side to attempt to secure an agreement to mediate the dispute. If one party does wish to make the approach directly, it is helpful to emphasise the reasons for proposing mediation rather than litigation, for example the

---

[109] See 'A framework for the process', pg. 164.

saving in cost, and the wish to avoid court proceedings if possible. Some parties are concerned that by suggesting mediation, they are indicating that they consider their own case is weak. Now commercial mediation has become well established, suggesting mediation should not carry this connotation, but a party can make it clear that it is suggesting mediation as a suitable means of resolving the dispute, not because it considers its own case is weak. The letter should suggest suitable mediators, or mediation organisations which can supply a mediator. There may also be practical matters to be covered while the parties attempt to resolve the dispute, such as an agreement to extend the time for some action to be taken, and agreeing what (if anything) may be said to the congregation or other interested parties.

FEES

Whether fees are paid depends on who is the mediator, on the formality of the process, and on the policy issues discussed under the heading *Resources, human and financial* above.[110]

A MEDIATION CONTRACT

If the mediation is arranged through an agency such as CEDR, there will be a mediation contract. In cases where the parties approach the mediator directly, and no fee is paid, it may not be necessary or appropriate to have any form of formal contract. If the mediation is a dispute, say, between a churchwarden and an organist, who have fallen out with each other over their respective roles in the church, the dispute is not about money but about personal relationships. No mediation contract may be required. Yet it is submitted that even in these cases, a letter should be written to confirm the practical arrangements for the day, so that people's time is not wasted.

---

[110] Page 199.

PRACTICAL MATTERS

A neutral venue needs to be found. It may be a person's home, or some rooms in the church, or an office. Commercial mediations often take place in a number of rooms hired in a hotel. In the main, experience of these is that they are impersonal and depressing, but that is a personal view! Refreshments need to be planned, depending on the time which the mediation is expected to take.

PREPARING A CASE SUMMARY

It is extremely helpful to ask the parties to set out the issues they would like to be mediated. In a commercial mediation, these case summaries are often prepared by each party's solicitors. In a church mediation, this would be the exception. But if the mediator knows something about the dispute before he arrives at the mediation, he can think about it and plan more effectively. Asking the parties to write something focuses their attention on the issues, rather than the people; and this is a very useful step in helping to resolve the issues.

ii *The opening phase of the mediation*

The mediator needs to establish with the parties what is to happen, the procedure for the day, and stamp his authority on the process. An opening statement by the mediator is likely to be much shorter than in a commercial model, but needs to cover a number of elements. The mediator will mention his independence, and perhaps his experience as a mediator of church disputes. He will cover the procedure for the day, and discuss any ground rules which the parties consider useful. He will mention the confidentiality of the process, and emphasise that it is voluntary, so a party can leave at any time if it is not helping. He will state that if agreement is reached, the mediator will record it in writing for the parties to take away at the end.

Some mediators may wish to consider opening with a prayer. If the mediator is an ordained minister, this will appear natural, and unlikely to cause any difficulty. If the mediator is not ordained, he needs to be confident that this will not cause any embarrassment to the other parties. Some mediators may be accustomed to extemporary prayer; others may wish to use one of the collects from the Book of Common Prayer. The collects for Quinquagesima Sunday (the Sunday before Lent), and for the 19th and 22nd Sundays after Trinity are all suitable for such an occasion.[111] The collect for Quinquagesima Sunday[112] asks God to send his Holy Spirit and to pour into our hearts 'that most excellent gift of charity, the very bond of peace', which therefore encourages reconciliation. The collect for the 19th Sunday after Trinity[113] asks God that his 'Holy Spirit may in all things direct and rule our hearts'; thus encouraging the parties to allow God to guide them in the mediation. The collect for the 22nd Sunday after Trinity[114]

---

[111] The text of these collects is set out in the Appendix. Further examples of suitable prayers are given in Yvonne Craig, *Peacemaking for churches* (London, SPCK, 1999), pg. 89.

[112] Quinquagessima Sunday is the Sunday before Lent. The collect for Quinquagessima in the Book of Common Prayer is as follows:
> O LORD, who hast taught us that all our doings without charity are nothing worth; Send thy Holy Ghost, and pour into our hearts that most excellent gift of charity, the very bond of peace and of all virtues, without which whosoever liveth is counted dead before thee: Grant this for thine only Son Jesus Christ's sake. Amen.

[113] The collect for the 19th Sunday after Trinity (from the Book of Common Prayer):
> O GOD, for as much as without thee we are not able to please thee; Mercifully grant, that thy Holy Spirit may in all things direct and rule our hearts; through Jesus Christ our Lord. Amen.

[114] The collect for the 22nd Sunday after Trinity (from the Book of Common Prayer):
> LORD, we beseech thee to keep thy household the Church in continual godliness; that through thy protection it may be free from all

asks God 'to keep thy household the Church in continual godliness; that through thy protection it may be free from all adversities, and devoutly given to serve thee in good works', thus encouraging the parties to seek to heal what is a church conflict.

The parties' opening statements are very important. In church disputes, there is likely to be a lot of anger, frustration and other emotions; and these opening statements allow the parties to express such feelings. The opening statements may well cover broader areas than the parties set out in their letter or written summary. Opening statements in a church dispute are usually made by the parties themselves, rather than by their advisers as in a commercial mediation. The mediator can then see straightaway the sort of feelings that lie behind the dispute between the parties

iii Exploration

The exploration phase is likely to follow the commercial model, although there is likely to be more exploration of feelings than in many commercial disputes. Skilful questioning can help to explore the underlying issues, and these may be seen differently by the different parties. For example, in a case where a parish rejects the bishop's authority because of his liberal stand on homosexuality, the parish may see the main issue as making a stand for strict Scriptural principles, whereas the bishop may see the main issue as one of church order. Emotions may be relevant: in many disputes anger is present, and the mediator needs to know how to diffuse this when it surfaces.

iv Negotiation

The exploration and negotiation phases are fluid, and the parties will pass from one to the other and back again. Many mediators use a flip-chart to list the main issues in the dispute. It may be possible to resolve some of the issues early on in a mediation,

---

adversities, and devoutly given to serve thee in good works, to the
glory of thy Name; through Jesus Christ our Lord. Amen.

and crossing them out on the flip-chart is an encouragement to show the progress which is made during the day.

v Conclusion

If and when all the matters are resolved, it is useful to record what has been agreed in writing. In a commercial mediation, this will be a formal agreement, often drafted by the lawyers for the parties, as it is usually intended to create proper legal relations which can be enforced in court if necessary. Most church disputes will not need this formality. But it is helpful to record the agreement, even though not in legal language. So, for example, the agreement might read as follows:

On 13th June 2000 John Walker (the churchwarden) and James Mackinsey (the organist) agreed the following points.

James will consult with the PCC and members of the congregation over the proposal to change the choir robes. Costings will be obtained, but the final decision is to await the appointment of the new vicar

John will raise with the PCC the issue of the use of inclusive language in hymns, and seek the views of the congregation on this issue also.

John will ......

James will ......

And they both sign it at the bottom.

d) Length of the mediation process

Mediation involves giving each party the opportunity to express how they see the dispute, and then working patiently with each one in turn to see how it can be resolved. The process takes several hours. Mediations of commercial disputes frequently take a full day, sometimes stretching late into the evening. The Central London County Court mediations are limited to three hours. The charity mediations organised by CEDR jointly with the NCVO are

limited to five hours.[115] The average length of the mediations in
the NHS medical negligence mediation pilot scheme was seven
hours. Mediations under the Housing ombudsman scheme administered by CEDR last for up to four hours. The ADR Group
normally schedules mediations to last for three to five hours,
though in one commercial mediation arranged by the ADR Group
where the author attended as counsel, the mediation lasted
from 9.30 am until 8.45 p.m., and no resolution was reached.

It is a truism that commercial disputes are in the main about
money. Perhaps that is why they seem to take longer to mediate
than other types of dispute. The survey of the types of church
dispute does include examples of commercial disputes, but in the
main, church disputes are not about money. One would hope
therefore that most church disputes can be mediated in half a day
or less, rather than a full day. This of course should make it considerably easier to schedule a mediation into the busy timetables
of the participants.

Yvonne Craig states[116] that mediations of church disputes often
take about two hours. Certainly some mediations may be capable
of mediation in this time, but more serious disputes may well take
longer. It may be appropriate to schedule a two-hour mediation
in the first instance, with the option of a second session at a later
date if necessary. This accords with the results of the survey of
mediation in the Anglican Communion in chapter 7. There the
trend is towards holding a number of 2–4 hour meetings, rather
than trying to do everything in one session. The survey also
found that the average mediation time for a church dispute is 13
hours. So, there is plainly much diversity.

---

[115] Some charity disputes involve numerous parties. In such cases, much
more time may be needed to negotiate a settlement. The mediation of
one charity dispute in 2001 in which the author represented one of the
parties lasted for two full days.

[116] Yvonne Craig, *Peacemaking for churches*, pg. 50.

e) Imbalance of power

Litigation can sometimes be used oppressively by one party with considerably more resources than another. Although legal aid redresses the balance somewhat in favour of the very poor, there are few individuals who can comfortably risk several thousand pounds, sometimes several tens of thousands of pounds, in litigation; and yet for large institutions or companies such sums, while not to be risked recklessly, do not constitute a significant proportion of the overall wealth of the organisation. The Civil Procedure Rules 1998 redresses the balance somewhat. So, CPR Part 1 requires the court to deal with each case in ways which are proportionate to the financial position of *each* party.[117] As the commentary in *Civil Procedure* states

> In the 'Access to Justice' Reports[118] it was said that one of the defects in the civil justice system was the 'lack of equality' between the powerful, wealthy litigant and the under-resourced litigant and amongst the specific objectives of the reforms proposed in those Reports was the need to establish 'equality of arms' between the parties involved in civil cases so as to ensure, so far as possible, that there should be 'a level playing field between litigants of unequal financial or other resources' (see *Final Report*, pg. 2 and 146 and *Interim Report*, pg. 26). It was said that financially stronger and more experienced parties could exploit rules of court so as to intimidate weaker parties by spinning out proceedings and escalating costs.[119]

The new procedures intended to redress this balance include case management, with simpler, less expensive, procedures for low value cases, and strict limitations on costs in such cases.

---

[117] Rule 1.1 (2) (c)(iv).

[118] Lord Woolf, *Interim Report on Access to Justice* (London, HMSO, June 1995), and Lord Woolf, *Final Report on Access to Justice* (London, HMSO, July 1996).

[119] *Civil Procedure*, vol. 1 par. 1.3.6.

It is sometimes argued that mediation is not appropriate in cases where there is a large imbalance of financial power. Yet a claim may have wider implications for an organisation than just the money at stake in the particular dispute. The adverse publicity which litigation may bring to a client may be more important than winning a particular dispute.[120] A number of respondents to the Lord Chancellor's Department's ADR Discussion Paper[121] considered that a mediator should be able to redress any imbalance of power.[122]

Most church disputes are not about money, and very few lead to litigation. Although there may be perceived to be an imbalance of financial power between, on the one hand, the parish, and on the other, the diocese, this difference only results in the diocese having an advantage over the parish in those few cases where litigation may be a real possibility.

Where the diocesan authorities do however have a considerable advantage over the parish is in the area of legal knowledge and experience. So, for example, a bishop is likely to deal with suspension of presentation[123] several times during the course of a year, whereas it is a unique experience for each parish where the power is to be exercised. The timetable for effective opposition to a proposed suspension is tight: a response to the bishop's proposal must be formulated within 28 days by the parish. The parish may seek advice from the diocesan registrar, and yet it was probably the diocesan registrar who drafted the notice proposing

---

[120] In the author's professional practice, publicity has been an important consideration for a whole variety of clients, from building societies to computer suppliers.

[121] *Alternative Dispute Resolution – a Discussion Paper* (London, Lord Chancellor's Department, 1999).

[122] See the ADR Discussion Paper Summary of Responses, paragraph 14. This is available at *www.open.gov.uk/lcd/consult/civ-just/adr/adrrespfr.htm*.

[123] Under s.67 of the Pastoral Measure 1983.

suspension for the bishop; so the diocesan registrar may find himself advising the opposing sides in a dispute. If the bishop overrules the parish's objections and serves a notice of suspension, the parish must either accept the situation or instruct solicitors to advise it. A bishop's decision to suspend can be overruled by judicial review,[124] but only one such case has come before the court. The cost to the parish of challenging such a decision is likely to be several thousand pounds, and is unlikely to be contemplated unless there is a wealthy benefactor in the parish who is willing to pay for the litigation.[125]

Mediation may well be a suitable means of resolving such a dispute. Again, the issues in a disputed suspension go beyond just the parties themselves. Disputes involving the exercise of bishops' powers may raise sensitive political issues, as the recent controversy concerning the Churchwardens Measure 2001 demonstrates.[126] The Church does not like washing its dirty linen in public. In one disputed suspension case, the matter was resolved eventually by both parties agreeing to abide by an expert determination,[127] but mediation was proposed as an alternative.

f) Training and standards

Maintaining standards is a matter to be addressed by all professions. Many professions choose self-regulation, and mediation is one such. This is a current issue in both Australia[128] and Eng-

---

[124] As in the case of *St Luke's, Kingston*.

[125] Such as Lord de L'Isle in the *Penshurst* dispute.

[126] See James Behrens, 'The Churchwardens Measure 2001', 6 Ecc LJ 97.

[127] The *Penshurst* dispute, see pg. 46. By agreement, the papers were sent to Sheila Cameron QC for her decision.

[128] *The Development of Standards for ADR Discussion Paper* (Australia, National Alternative Dispute Resolution Advisory Council (NADRAC), March 2000).

land.[129] Mediators trained by bodies such as CEDR in order to maintain their accreditation status have to fulfil CPD (Continuing Professional Development) requirements.

The Church has as yet no centralised training for mediators, nor is mediation part of any post-ordination training program, though disputes management is now part of such training, and is also beginning to be taught at theological college.[130] For persons wishing to train as mediators, the main providers of suitable training are as follows:

- CEDR and the ADR Group;
- Local community mediation services;
- The East Midlands Synod of the United Reformed Church; and
- The London Mennonites.

The CEDR training is a five-day residential course, and costs £3,450 plus VAT.[131] The last two days are assessed, and accreditation is only given to those who pass the assessment. The proportion who succeed is about two-thirds. Persons are taught the commercial model of mediation outlined in this chapter. One of the example mediations used for the role-plays which form part of the training is a claim by a church against an architect for negligent design of a building project for the church. But, this example apart, the course makes no reference to church disputes.

Mediation UK does not itself train mediators, but acts as an umbrella body for local mediation initiatives which themselves provide training. These services usually specialise in one or more areas of mediation involving neighbour disputes, mediation be-

---

[129] *Alternative Dispute Resolution – a Discussion Paper* (London, Lord Chancellor's Department, 1999), section 8, 'Quality control'.

[130] See pg. 138 fn. 250, pg. 293, and pg. 344.

[131] This is the cost of the November 1999 course. A non-residential course in December 1999 costs £2,850 plus VAT.

tween victims and offenders (restorative justice), and conflict resolution work with schools and young people (peer mediation). Other work includes conflict resolution in the workplace, health service and other institutions. Mediation UK has over 500 members consisting of individuals and organisations.[132] Mediation UK believes that everyone should have access to a good mediation service which is free of charge. The community mediation training course prepared by Mediation UK is a five day course.[133] The training is usually free of charge – but persons going on these courses have to agree to do a number of hours (unpaid) work as mediators for the local mediation service after they have completed their training.

The United Reformed Church course runs for two days. It is based on the CEDR model, and costs £85. The participants who went on the two-day URC course attended by the author were all conscious at the end of the course of their lack of experience, and felt the need to have further practice before using what they had learned in a real case.

The URC East Midlands Synod plans to train all the ministers and one lay person in each congregation within the East Midlands province. There are 158 congregations in the Synod with 61 stipendiary and 19 non-stipendiary ministers for these congregations. In the five years their two-day course has been running, they have trained 78 people. Initially the course was directed solely to members of the URC. More recently the course has become more ecumenical. The course in June 2000 attended by the author was one of a pair of courses with twelve people on each: five URC ministers, seven lay URC members, eight Church of

---

[132] Mediation UK's *Annual Report 2001* (Bristol, Mediation UK, 2001) breaks down the membership as follows: 262 organisation members comprising 140 community services, 63 victim-offender services, and 59 schools; and 241 individual members.

[133] An alternative course is available being six three-hour evenings, and one weekend.

England vicars, three lay Church of England members, and one from the House Church Movement. There were five women and seven men on the first course, and six women and six men on the second. The ages ranged from early 20s to late 60s. They were all white.

The London Mennonites run a five-day course on church mediation. The course costs £400 for persons sponsored by an organisation, or £300 for self-paying individuals. The courses started in 1996, and for the first four years there was one course a year. In 2000 and 2001 two courses a year were held. There have been between 25 and 30 people on each course. As at September 2001 over 160 people have attended one of the London Mennonites courses. They have come from over 15 different denominations and over 10 different countries.[134]

Mention has been made of the steady growth of mediation services since 1989, both commercial services and ones openly Christian.[135] There are more Christian initiatives in the pipeline: for example, one in the diocese of Canterbury,[136] and one which is being set up by the Yorkshire Baptist Association.[137]

10. CONCLUSION, AND A MUSICAL ANALOGY

The commercial model of mediation is a suitable framework for most church disputes involving a small number of parties. It is not suitable for use in congregational disputes with numerous people. In most cases the commercial model is likely to need

---

[134] *Bridging the Gap, the Bridge Builders Newsletter*, Issue no. 1 (London, Bridge Builders (The London Mennonites) September 2001).

[135] See for example pg. 157, fn. 37.

[136] Mediation for Kent Churches, organised by Professor Alan Hay, 8 South Canterbury Road, Canterbury, Kent CT1 3LJ (email a.hay@tinyworld.co.uk). This has links to the United Reformed Church, Methodist and Baptist Churches, and the Quakers in the Kent area.

[137] The contact is the Area Superintendent, Ernie Whalley.

'softening', in the sense of being made more informal. But the model is very flexible, and can easily be adapted to different church needs. Like jazz playing, the basic harmonic structure remains constant, but what each player puts on top varies with each performance.

The commercial model can be used in 'legal' disputes where one or more parties has already instructed lawyers, such as disputes over church governance, or commercial disputes between a church and an outside organisation. It can be used for one-to-one disputes involving, for example, employment issues, and some minor discipline matters. It is less useful for 'community' disputes involving a breakdown in the relationship between the whole parish and its priest: though even in such cases, there may well be spokesmen who can represent the various different views in the parish, and so enable the mediation to take place effectively between a small number of participants. It is also not best suited to what is primarily a personality dispute.

The model can be used in cases where there might appear to be an imbalance of power between the participants. It is not suitable for cases where a serious crime has been committed or some serious wrongdoing requiring disciplinary action has occurred.

A recent development is the use of the Internet for commercial mediation. It may well be convenient for the parties to use email to correspond with each other and with the mediator before the face-to-face mediation takes place. That apart, it is not considered that what is known as 'on-line mediation' has anything to offer the Church. This topic is considered fully in Appendix 1.

The jazz player improvises not only the notes but also the rhythm. The commercial model is geared towards one session lasting up to a day, in some cases two to three days. Many church disputes should be capable of mediation using this model in four hours or less, but even this length may require the model to be adapted somewhat. It may be more convenient to arrange two sessions of, say, two hours each, rather than one session of four

215

hours. Although some momentum may be lost by this process, some progress towards a solution should be apparent to both parties within the first two-hour period.

Lastly, the model raises a number of other issues:

- who is to train the jazz player?
- how much training does he or she need?
- how much is he or she to be paid?
- and with more and more players joining the band, does there need to be a conductor?

Chapter 5

COMMUNITY MEDIATION

But right anon the worthy knyght bigan,
Whan that he saugh that al the peple lough,
Namoore of this, for it is right ynough!
Sire pardoner, be glad and myrie of cheere;
And ye, sire hoost, that been to me so deere,
I prey yow that ye kisse the pardoner.
And pardoner, I prey thee, drawe thee neer,
And, as we diden, lat us laughe and pleye.
Anon they kiste, and ryden forth hir weye.[1]

---

[1] Geoffrey Chaucer, *The Canterbury Tales*, 'The Pardoner's Tale'
(lines 960–68) (London, Penguin Books, 1996). In David Wright's translation:

    But at this point the worthy knight cut in,
    For he saw the others had begun to laugh.
    'Let's have no more of this; that's quite enough!
    Now, Mister Pardoner, smile and cheer up!
    As for you, Mister Host, come, my dear chap,
    I beg you, shake hands with the pardoner.
    And you, come over here, Pardoner, pray,
    And let's all laugh and have fun as before.'
    At this they shook hands, and rode upon their way.

Geoffrey Chaucer, *The Canterbury Tales*, translated by David Wright
(Oxford University Press, 1985).

1. HISTORY OF COMMUNITY MEDIATION

a) Early community mediation services

Community mediation developed in the UK in the 1980s.[2] The earliest scheme was the Newham Conflict and Change Project, London, formed in 1983. It was started by two ministers with parishes in Newham, and is still continuing. Its current projects include a conciliation service for local people, education development work supporting local schools, a consultancy service, and training in conflict resolution techniques. Other early schemes include the Southwark Mediation Centre, London (1984), Sandwell Mediation and Reparation Scheme, West Midlands (1985), the Edgware Mediation Service (1984), and the Stoke Newington Reconciliation Unit (1985).[3] Of these, the

---

[2] For a full account, see Marian Liebmann, *Community and Neighbour Mediation*, (London, Cavendish Publishing, 1998), chapter 2. For shorter accounts see Marian Liebmann, *Mediation in Context,* (London, Jessica Kingsley Publishers, 2000), chapter 1; Brown and Marriott, *ADR Principles and Practice*, 2nd edn. (London, Sweet & Maxwell, 1999), chapter 12.

[3] See Marshall, T. *Reparation, Conciliation and Mediation*, (London, Home Office Research and Planning Unit, Paper 27, 1984); and a similar survey

Southwark and Sandwell schemes are still continuing, but the Edgware and the Stoke Newington services both failed to attract sufficient funding to survive.

In the early 1990s the number of community mediation services increased rapidly, but thereafter has remained fairly constant.[4] This is shown in figure 8.

year	services		year	services
1991	59		1996	110
1992	64		1997	135
1993	77		1998	135
1994	81		1999	134
1995	94		2000	134

Figure 8. Growth of community mediation services

---

one year later: Marshall, T. and Walpole, M. *Bringing People Together: Mediation and Reparation Projects in Great Britain*, (London, Home Office Research and Planning Unit, Paper 33, HMSO, 1985).

[4] These figures are taken from Mediation UK *Annual Reports 1991–2000*. For the figures to 1997, see also Marian Liebmann, *Community and Neighbour Mediation*, pg. 27. Some estimation is necessary because it is not always possible from the annual reports to say whether a particular service is involved in community mediation as opposed to some other form of mediation – for example, victim-offender mediation. Marian Liebmann, *Mediation in Context*, pg. 26 says that the number of community mediation services in August 1999 was 124, which is lower than the 135 listed in the 1999 annual report. But it is clear from the reports that the general picture has not changed over the last four years.

219

Several of the mediation services in the UK were started by Quakers. Figure 9 lists a number of these services.

- Kingston Friends Mediation, Kingston-on-Thames, Surrey.

- Lambeth Mediation Service, London.

- Leap Confronting Conflict, Finsbury Park, London.

- EMU Promoting Schools Project, Londonderry.

- Mediation Dorset.

- West Midlands Quaker Peace Education Project.

- CRISP (Conflict Response in Schools Programme), Middlesborough.

- Face To Face, Neighbourhood Mediation in York.

- The Hope Project, Stourbridge.

Figure 9. UK mediation services started by Quakers[5]

Although started by Quakers, most of these services do not contain the words 'Quaker' or 'Friends' in their name,[6] and are completely secular, offering mediation services to individuals and schools of any or no religious persuasion. This Quaker involvement is encouraged by Quaker Peace and Service, which is one of the four central committees of the Quaker structure in the UK. The primary function of Quaker Peace and Service is to work for peace and against violence, helping to build institutions of peace

---

[5] Valerie Clements of Quaker Peace and Service kindly provided this information.

[6] Quakers are also known as the Religious Society of Friends.

at all levels, from neighbourhoods to the international level.[7] It therefore encourages community mediation services, and Quaker involvement in such undertakings. Quaker involvement is discreet – Quakers are opposed to proselytising and therefore do not publicise their religion – but Quakers and Quaker involvement permeates the community mediation movement in the UK. Thus, for example, at Mediation UK's AGM in 2000 there were about 45 people present, amongst whom the author was introduced to four Quakers. Similarly, the main training book on community mediation used in the UK[8] adopts much material from the training book in community mediation developed by the Quakers in the USA;[9] and the training materials produced by Camden Mediation Service included some devised by Kingston Friends Mediation.

b) The establishment of a national organisation

Mediation UK was founded as FIRM (Forum for Initiatives in Reparation and Mediation) in 1984. Its original emphasis was very much concerned with work in the criminal justice arena.[10] In 1991 the organisation changed its name to Mediation UK, and moved its national office from Beaconsfield to Bristol. After 1991, the focus of the work shifted to civil justice and community safety, with a very rapid rise in the number of community mediation

---

[7] Anthony Bradney and Fiona Cownie, *Living without law; an ethnography of Quaker decision-making, dispute avoidance and dispute resolution* (Aldershot, Ashgate, 2000) pg. 65–66.

[8] Mediation UK, *Training Manual in Community Mediation Skills* (Bristol, Mediation UK, 1995, reprinted 1999).

[9] Jennifer Beer and Eileen Steif, *The Mediator's Handbook*, 3rd edn. (Gabriola Island, British Columbia, Canada, New Society Publishers, 1997). The 1st edition was published in 1982, the second edition in 1994.

[10] FIRM originated as an informal group of probation officers, academics, and victim support workers.

services, which were essentially dealing with conflicts between neighbours.

Funding for the first five years was always tenuous, with the majority of funding coming from Quaker charitable trusts, notably Joseph Rowntree and various Cadbury trusts. Between 1995 and 1998 Mediation UK received statutory funding from the Department of Environment (Environmental Action Fund), and in 1999 it received a substantial three-year grant from the National Lottery Charities Board. Its total income in the year 1999–2000 was £326,000, of which the largest single grant was £132,000 from the National Lottery Charities Board. Mediation UK's role is summarised in its annual report as follows:[11]

> Mediation UK is a registered charity which promotes and supports community mediation. It is at the hub of a national network of mediation services in local communities. These services usually specialise in one or more areas of mediation involving neighbour disputes, mediation between victims and offenders (restorative justice) and conflict resolution work with schools and young people (peer mediation). Other work includes conflict resolution in the workplace, health service and other institutions. Mediation UK does not deal with family (i.e. divorce and separation) or commercial disputes. There are other organisations dealing with these matters with whom Mediation UK meets in the Joint Mediation Forum.
>
> Mediation UK seeks to
> - Raise awareness of mediation as a constructive means of resolving conflict.
> - Provide information and advice on community mediation issues.
> - Encourage and support the establishment of new mediation services.

---

[11] Mediation UK *Annual Report 2000* (Bristol, Mediation UK, 2000), pg. 4. The author is a director and the company secretary of Mediation UK.

- Set practice standards for mediators and mediation services.
- Accredit both mediators and mediation services.
- Act as the national voice for our members and community mediation in general.

The relationship between community mediation services and Mediation UK is both direct and indirect. At the direct level, Mediation UK provides accreditation, training support, and advice for individual local mediation services. At the indirect level, Mediation UK acts as a spokesman to encourage national and local government to support and fund community mediation projects. As an example of its work on a national level which affects local mediation services, Mediation UK has taken a leading role in helping to establish the Mediation Quality Mark awarded by the Legal Services Commission for the new Community Legal Service.[12]

2. THE OBJECT OF MEDIATION: RESOLUTION OR TRANSFORMATION?

Mediation UK's training manual in community mediation skills published in 1995 is one of the standard training manuals used by community mediation services in the UK.[13] The model of community mediation available from many mediation services follows very much the pattern set forth in this manual. However, over the last three years, this pattern is changing. Community mediation is currently going through a change of emphasis as a result of the 'transformation' theory which has revolutionised community mediation in the USA since 1995. The transformation theory has not altered the overall structure of the process, rather its objective. This change of objective affects the content of what takes place during mediation, and, therefore, its outcome. In essence, transformative mediation is people-orientated, rather than

---

[12] Mediation UK *Annual Report 2000*, pg. 11.

[13] Mediation UK, *Training Manual in Community Mediation Skills*.

problem-orientated. Transformative mediation aims to transform the parties to a dispute rather than to resolve the dispute itself. Transforming the parties may lead to resolving the dispute; but under the transformation theory the object of mediation is transformation of the parties, not resolution of the dispute.

The classic exposition of the transformation theory is that of Bush and Folger. In their book *The Promise of Mediation*[14] they describe two main elements in transformation: empowerment and recognition. The need for empowerment arises because when we are in conflict, we are often 'weak', in the sense of being confused, fearful, and unsure of what to do. One aim of mediation is to enable people to become calmer, more confident, more organised, and more decisive – and thereby 'empowered' to take control of the situation.[15] A party is empowered

- when they understand more clearly what their goals and interests are in the situation

- when they understand the options available to them

- when they learn better how to listen to the other party, to communicate with the other party, to organise and to analyse issues.

- when they are able to assess fully the strengths and weaknesses of their own position and the position of the other in the dispute.

The second main goal in transformative mediation is recognition. When in conflict, disputing parties typically feel threatened, attacked, even victimised by the conduct of the other party. As a result, they are focused on self-protection; they are self-absorbed, defensive, suspicious, hostile to the other party, and incapable of

---

[14] Robert Bush and Joseph Folger, *The Promise of Mediation* (San Francisco, Jossey-Bass, 1994).

[15] Robert Bush and Joseph Folger, *The Promise of Mediation*, pg. 85.

seeing beyond themselves to the needs and interests of the other party. Transformation aims to move a party from self-absorption to recognition; to being more open, attentive, and responsive to the perspectives and situation of the other party.[16]

A party gives recognition

- when they first even consider looking at the dispute from the other party's point of view

- when they decide to attempt to look at the dispute from the other party's point of view

- when they actually try to see things from the other party's perspective

- when they are willing to reinterpret past events in the light of the other party's perspective

- when they admit to the mediator, even privately, that they now see things in a different light

- when they openly say to the other side that they understand the other side's position; especially when they are able to express that position verbally to show that they understand it

- when they accompany such a statement of new understanding with an apology of some kind

- when in the light of this new understanding they agree to make some accommodation to the other party, either towards resolving the dispute, or towards their future relationship.

In terms of the conflict triangle of problem, people and process, resolution concentrates on the *problem*, while transformation concentrates on the *people*. In moving from dispute resolution to dispute transformation, community mediation has shifted its emphasis from *problem resolution* to *people transformation*.

---

[16] Robert Bush and Joseph Folger, *The Promise of Mediation*, pg. 88.

This is partly a change in emphasis: the transformation element has always been present in community mediation, but the aim of resolution has until recently been at the forefront. Thus, for example, the Mediation UK handbook states

> Mediators encourage people to understand something of the other side's views.[17] [transformation]

But this is balanced by the next sentence

> Generally, when people go to a mediation service, they get a real chance to move the dispute forward. [resolution]

It has been noted that many church disputes involve deeper issues than those which the parties first describe as being the immediate problem. Resolving the immediate problem may not deal with these deeper issues. However, transforming the parties may deal with these deeper issues, and this may be far more significant than resolving the particular dispute which brought them to mediation.

Such deeper, emotional, issues can surface in community mediation, and it would be wrong to suggest that the resolution model ignores these matters. But where they do surface, the resolution model tends to sideline such issues, regarding them as suitable for some forum other than mediation.

> Loneliness, depression and loss all play a part in making minor irritants into major problems and, while it is important not to be seen to minimise the complaint, it may be necessary to explore the possibility of work in this area by referral to another agency, as an alternative or in addition to continuing the mediation process, subject to the party's consent.[18]

This suggests that the transformation model may be more suitable for church disputes than the resolution model of community

---

[17] Mediation UK, *Training Manual in Community Mediation Skills*, pg. 48.

[18] Mediation UK, *Training Manual in Community Mediation Skills*, pg. 46.

mediation. Plainly, the transformation theory needs to be looked at closely, to assess its suitability for church disputes.

The transformation theory is presented by Bush and Folger in secular, but moral, terms. They argue that transformative mediation has the potential for moral improvement for the participants.[19] They see *dispute resolution* as an objective of an individualist world-view, whereas *dispute transformation* is essentially part of a relational world-view.[20]

> By their choice between the problem-solving and transformative approaches, people in the mediation movement are deciding whether mediation will remain one more institution in an individualist society or become a foundational part of a different relational society that is not a utopian dream but a gradually emerging reality.... Not just the mediation movement but the entire society stands at a cross-roads, choosing which path to take.[21]

Christians may feel uncomfortable with this secular argument that adopting transformative mediation will lead to a moral improvement in society.[22] However the concepts of empowerment and recognition are thoroughly Christian. In the *Magnificat*[23] Mary sings of God's empowerment of her, and of his 'lifting up' the humble.[24] The Church recognises the work of the Holy Spirit

---

[19] Robert Bush and Joseph Folger, *The Promise of Mediation,* pg. 30–31, 230–231.

[20] Robert Bush and Joseph Folger, *The Promise of Mediation,* pg. 236–7.

[21] Robert Bush and Joseph Folger, *The Promise of Mediation,* pg. 259.

[22] It is one thing to create better relations between two people; it is quite another to restore relations in a whole community, or in society as a whole.

[23] Luke 1:46f.

[24] Many scriptural passages have the theme of God empowering a person for a particular purpose: Isaiah 61:1; Exodus 4:15; Judges 14:6 to name but three examples. A similar theme is expressed in 2 Chroni-

in empowering followers of Jesus Christ.[25] Similarly, Christians are called to *recognition*, in Christ's challenge to love our enemies, to do good to those who hate us, and to pray for those who persecute us.[26]

One ethical problem about the transformative theory is that the parties come to mediation expecting one thing and getting another. They come expecting a means of resolving the dispute, but not appreciating what may be involved in that process. They do not come realising that the mediator's objective is not the same as their own; and that the mediator hopes to achieve that objective by encouraging them to change as individuals, whether or not this leads to a resolution of the dispute. From a legal position, it could be argued that the mediator is not providing what he contracted to provide.[27] In answer to this charge, it is highly questionable whether there is any contract between the parties and the mediator or service provider. First, unlike many models of family, civil or commercial mediation, parties in community mediation are not ordinarily asked to sign an agreement setting out the terms and ground rules on which the mediation will take place.[28] Second, as

---

cles 14:11 where King Asa prays 'LORD, there is no one like you to help the powerless against the mighty'.

[25] Romans 8:6–16; 23–27.

[26] Matthew 5:44; Luke 6:27, 35; Galatians 5:14. This was very strange teaching to those who heard it. Jesus' words (Matthew 5:43–44) were 'You have heard that it was said, `Love your neighbour and hate your enemy.' But I tell you: Love your enemies and pray for those who persecute you'. The sentence does not end at the end of verse 44, but continues in verse 45: 'that you may be sons of your Father in heaven. He causes his sun to rise on the evil and the good, and sends rain on the righteous and the unrighteous.' Jesus' reason for his instruction was that this is God's nature, and we should be like God. As verse 48 states, 'Be perfect, therefore, as your heavenly Father is perfect.'

[27] Brown and Marriott, *ADR Principles and Practice*, 2nd edn., pg. 11.

[28] Brown and Marriott, *ADR Principles and Practice*, 2nd edn., pg. 288.

228

the service is provided free of charge, it is difficult to see what consideration could be said to be provided by the parties. Third, the whole emphasis on the process is that it is intended to be informal and 'non-legal', which negates the suggestion that the parties have entered into legal relations.

This disparity between how the parties may see mediation and how the mediator sees it means that when a party asks the mediator how the mediator is going to help resolve the dispute,[29] the mediator has to be extremely delicate in the way he answers the question. An answer to the effect that the mediator will help to transform the parties by empowerment and recognition would almost certainly put an end to the process. What the people in dispute want, or think they want, is understanding and resolution.

Yet there are problems in the resolution approach too. First, Bush and Folger describe how resolution-orientated mediators tend to make global assessments of parties' circumstances, focusing on the facts of the problem as presented by the parties rather than the reactions of the parties to each other during the mediation process. The overall relationships between the parties and how these can be improved are ignored. There is a tendency to categorise a dispute as, for example, a 'noise dispute', and to ignore more subtle concepts such as how the parties communicate with each other, and what human relationships may be involved.

Secondly, by their selection of the areas which they consider can be resolved, resolution-mediators have a tendency to influence the selection of topics which form the discussion at the mediation and eventually form part of any settlement terms. Part of the mediation process is to establish a number of issues which can be discussed, and resolution-mediators tend to drop concerns that cannot be treated as problems. Thus, for example, the Quaker Mediation Handbook has one page listing types of things which

---

[29] A question which is often asked.

can be negotiated, and concerns which 'can be discussed but not negotiated' and which are therefore 'unmediatable'.[30] These unmediatable issues are listed as

> beliefs, principles and values, child-raising, attitudes, anger, personal style, what happened, hurt feelings, perceptions, management style, interpretations, prejudices, trust, blame, fault, [and] right.

Similarly, the Mediation UK training manual[31] lists feelings about the other party or the situation, values, attitudes, interpretations of reality, and motives, as topics which cannot be mediated.

Yet the transformative approach would say that many of these matters *are* mediatable. Perceptions can be altered, once parties give recognition to each other, or where a disempowered party is empowered. Hurt feelings and anger can be healed by recognition, for example, in the form of an apology. Trust can be restored when parties are empowered so as not to feel vulnerable. Personal or management styles can be altered when one party gives recognition to the other. Transformative mediators can offer possible reinterpretations of parties' actions and motives: the skill lies in suggesting that alternative interpretations are possible without pressuring parties to move from their views.[32] Many more examples can be given.

The third problem arises from the statistics-driven materialistic world which sees success only in terms of concrete settlements, rather than improved human relationships. Resolution-mediators find themselves drawn into this world-view, leading them to

---

[30] Jennifer Beer and Eileen Steif, *The Mediator's Handbook*, 3rd edn., pg. 117. This is quoted in the Mennonite training book by Carolyn Schrock-Shenk (ed.), *Mediation and Facilitation Training Manual*, 4th edn. (Akron, Pennsylvania, Mennonite Conciliation Service, 2000), pg. 176.

[31] Mediation UK, *Training Manual in Community Mediation Skills*, pg. 186.

[32] Robert Bush and Joseph Folger, *The Promise of Mediation*, pg. 269–270.

push for a 'settlement', to maintain their personal 'success rate'. Report forms for mediation organisations usually require the mediator to state whether settlement was reached, and if not, why not. Especially where mediators are paid rather than working on a charitable basis, a good settlement-rate establishes a person as a successful mediator: mediators sometimes refer to their settlement-rates when seeking further mediation work.[33] Funders for mediation service providers likewise have a tendency to assess the success of services in terms of settlement-rates, and require statistics of these rates as a condition for further funding.

Public perception still sees mediation in settlement-rate terms. The table in chapter 4 showing statistics for five pilot mediation projects contains an official 'success rate' for four out of the five projects. The projects regard 'success' as a settlement reached at the mediation session. Yet there is some evidence that the transformative approach is also seen as important. The report for the pilot scheme for mediation in the planning system concluded that the process is welcome, whatever the outcome.

> Whatever the outcome, in only five cases has there been any dissatisfaction with the mediation process itself on the part of applicants. In general, there has been considerable appreciation expressed of the benefits of mediation in getting everyone around the table in a relaxed atmosphere.[34]

This is a key difference between the philosophy behind commercial and community mediation. Commercial mediation remains dispute-orientated, with settlement regarded as the main objective; community mediation until recently has been likewise dispute-orientated, but is now moving fast towards being person-orientated, with transformed relationships being the ultimate ob-

---

[33] By contrast, barristers are forbidden to advertise their success rates: *Code of Conduct for the Bar* (London, The General Council of the Bar of England and Wales, 1998), paragraph 308.2.

[34] Paragraph 5.2.1 of the report.

jective – but public perception of mediation is only starting to appreciate this change.

Bush and Folger argue that resolution-mediation and transformation-mediation are fundamentally distinct and inconsistent. One cannot, they believe, integrate the two approaches, for example, by adding to the problem-solving approach an emphasis on empowerment and recognition, or by swapping from one approach to the other during the course of a mediation session.[35] They argue that the core practices of each approach are inconsistent, and it is effectively impossible for mediators to employ both sets of practices together. The Mennonite[36] training manual takes issue with them over this.

> The mediation we promote in this manual does not fit cleanly into either the [resolution model or the transformation model] but carries many elements of both.[37]

The Mennonite model looks for ways to resolve the particular dispute between the parties, but it also looks at ways to transform their relationship by addressing the hurts and misunderstandings between them. The Mennonite model sees transformation as relating not just to the people in conflict, but to the whole social and structural situation in which the conflict arises. The Mennonite approach is thus to focus both on transformation and on resolution, and also to look at the wider picture. During a mediation session, the Mennonite model encourages the mediator to keep focused on two main paths: problem solving, and healing, and to swap between the two during the course of a mediation as may be appropriate.[38] But the Mennonite model is also concerned about

---

[35] Robert Bush and Joseph Folger, *The Promise of Mediation*, pg. 108.

[36] The Mennonites are a Christian Anabaptist denomination.

[37] Carolyn Schrock-Shenk (ed.), *Mediation and Facilitation Training Manual*, 4th edn., pg. 158; also pg. 18.

[38] Carolyn Schrock-Shenk (ed.), *Mediation and Facilitation Training Manual*, 4th edn., pg. 177.

issues of power and oppression, and mediators are taught by the Mennonites to be on the look-out for circumstances where more fundamental social or structural transformation is called for instead of or in addition to mediation. In such cases mediation should be refused, or only offered if the parties agree also to some process to deal with the underlying broader problem.

> The goal is not to get the parties to the negotiation table or even to reach a mutually agreed upon settlement. It is to establish more just, equitable and peaceful relations. Transformation of social structures and systems that create conflict must also be included in our goals.[39]

3. THE COMMUNITY MEDIATION PROCESS

a) How a community mediation service operates

The process of community mediation is described, as it is practised by Camden Mediation Service in London. Camden Mediation Service started in 1995. The Camden Mediation Service model is based on the model recommended by Mediation UK, and Camden Mediation Service is itself accredited by Mediation UK as a mediation service provider. Where appropriate, comparisons are made with the mediation model taught by the Mennonites and the Quakers, as these are very similar to the secular community model.[40] The Camden Mediation Service has taken the

---

[39] Carolyn Schrock-Shenk (ed.), *Mediation and Facilitation Training Manual*, 4th edn., pg. 90.

[40] Quakerism has its roots in Christianity, and there are many Quakers who regard themselves as Christians; but there are also many who do not. The Quakers are members of the Council of Churches for Britain and Ireland (which as an objective fact may indicate that they should be considered a denomination), but many Quakers are, in effect, universalists, emphasising the common spiritual thread running through a wide variety of outward forms. Quakerism has no creed. See generally Anthony Bradney and Fiona Cownie, *Living without law*, chapter 2.

transformational model of mediation fully on board, and teaches it to new volunteer mediators.[41]

As various aspects of the model are described, how well these might apply to church disputes will be discussed. At the end a global comparison between commercial and community mediation will be made to assess the suitability of community mediation as a model for mediating church disputes.

Referrals to a community mediation service are either by one of the parties to the dispute, or by some third party agency. For example, many neighbour disputes between council tenants are referred to the Camden Mediation Service by the estate officer at the District Housing Office for Camden.

Camden Mediation Service collects basic details of the case, and summarises how the service works and what will happen next. If the referring party wishes to proceed, Camden Mediation Service opens a file for the case, and allocates it to two of the volunteer mediators who work for the service. Mediation for Camden Mediation Service is always co-mediation, so there are always two mediators assigned to a case.

Co-mediation increases the opportunity for ethnic, gender, and age balance between the mediators and the participants. Co-mediators are frequently chosen to reflect the attributes of the disputants, and this often enhances rapport and trust. Having two mediators provides an additional set of eyes and ears, insight and experience; and it also provides a means of apprenticeship for inexperienced mediators. Co-mediating offers some security to the mediators (and also to the parties), particularly when home visiting. It provides also a safeguard in the event of any complaint.

---

[41] The author participated on a six-day training course run by Camden Mediation Service in October 2000. The Camden Mediation Service training course gave considerable emphasis to recognition and empowerment.

In the case of church mediations, it is often difficult to find one mediator whom the parties are all willing to trust as mediator. For example, if the dispute is between a member of the congregation and the priest, the lay person may prefer the mediator to be a lay person, while the priest may prefer to have someone who is ordained. Having two mediators, one lay, the other ordained, is often a way through this difficulty. Similarly, where gender is an issue in the church dispute, the parties may be willing to accept two mediators, one of each gender. A third problem is whether the mediator should be an 'insider', someone from within the fellowship or within the church structure; or whether he should be an 'outsider', someone from outside the immediate fellowship, possibly even outside the denomination. The experience of the Mennonites is that having a team where one mediator is an insider and the other an outsider is often acceptable to the parties, and provides both comfort and balance, to enable the parties to trust the mediation process.

The mediators working for Camden Mediation Service are all volunteers, and all have been through a six-day assessed training course, involving a combination of lectures, role-plays, and discussions. Mediation UK's training manual sets out a standard course providing 40 hours training. The standard mediation training course with the Mennonites is five days.[42] The training course for Camden Mediation Service is free, but there is an expectation that mediators will give about three hours a week of voluntary time to working for the Camden Mediation Service and attending Camden Mediation Service events, for a period of two years after training. The Mennonite five-day course costs £400.

---

[42] The Mennonite training course covers the 'community' style of mediation in three days. The Mennonite training course does not cover the subject of home visits, but treats the mediation as beginning when the parties meet at a face-to-face mediation. The last two days of the Mennonite course are spent dealing with group facilitation, i.e. handling large congregational disputes, and power issues.

235

As a comparison, the CEDR five-day commercial mediation course costs approximately £3,000.

b) Stage 1: Initial contact with the first party

Once the two mediators are assigned to the case, they make contact with one of the parties, and arrange a home visit. Ideally this should be arranged within one week from the mediators being assigned the case.[43] Although both resolution-mediators and transformation-mediators see home visits as a key part of the community mediation model, they see the purpose of such visits differently. Resolution-mediators see the home visits as an opportunity for the mediators 'to see the situation at first hand as well as establishing contact on the party's own ground'.[44] The occasion is also an opportunity

> to establish a working relationship with the party and get a full story of the dispute and its history. It is often apparent that the initial complaint in the referral is only part of the issue and the party may want to talk about matters not directly associated with the conflict with the neighbours.[45]

In short, resolution-mediators see the purpose of the home visits as two-fold: first, as an opportunity for 'story-telling' (literally, telling the story, not fabricating it); second, as an opportunity to

---

[43] This instruction appears on the standard letter Camden Mediation Service writes to its mediators when assigning a new case to them. Camden Mediation Service aims to complete its cases within 60 days from first referral, and in most cases does so well within this period. As an example, the first case in which the author acted as mediator for Camden Mediation Service was referred to Camden Mediation Service on 1/11/2000, the author was appointed on 7/11/2000, home visits took place on 16/11/2000 and 23/11/2000, and a mediation session took place on 5/12/2000, just over one month after the case was referred to Camden Mediation Service.

[44] Marian Liebmann, *Community and Neighbour Mediation*, pg. 45.

[45] Marian Liebmann, *Community and Neighbour Mediation*, pg. 45.

236

build rapport, to aid the mediation process. The process is seen as the first step at resolving the problem.

In contrast, transformation-mediators see the home visit as the beginning of the process of enabling a shift in perspective to take place, so that the parties are able to listen effectively to each other, hearing what the other person has to say, which enables them to accommodate the other person's viewpoint.[46]

The difference is subtle. The structure of a home visit conducted by a mediator trained in the traditional model may be almost identical to the structure of a home visit conducted by a mediator trained in the transformation model. But the aims of the two types of mediators are different, and this is bound to affect the content of the home visit, the questions that are asked, and the way the mediator steers the discussion. The resolution-mediator is aiming to get the parties to meet in a face-to-face mediation. For the transformation-mediator, a face-to-face mediation is but one option. The transformation-mediator is much more on the lookout for opportunities for recognition and empowerment than in seeking to persuade the parties to come to a face-to-face mediation. The transformation-mediator seeks to enable the party to deal with the conflict, to understand the options available, and to encourage a change in attitude and perceptions. One outcome of the home visits, for example, may be that the two parties are enabled to discuss the dispute with each other, and resolve it, without the need for further mediation. Transformative mediation may thus empower the parties to resolve their dispute themselves.

The resolution-mediator walks a thin line between pressurising and encouraging the parties to come to a mediation session. The

---

[46] *Mediation Visits – Purpose* (London, Camden Mediation Service training materials, 2000).

parties may need to look at alternatives before making their decision. They may need time to think things over.[47]

Resolution-mediators may become discouraged if their efforts to encourage the parties to meet at a face-to-face mediation are unsuccessful. As transformation-mediators do not see a face-to-face mediation as the objective of the home visits, they are less concerned if no face-to-face mediation ensues.

Empowerment and recognition comes about during a home visit through the building of trust and confidence, in the process and in the mediators. In many cases, one party to a dispute feels undermined. By listening in a non-judgmental way, mediators help the party relax, help build their self-esteem, and help increase their confidence. Mediators help the parties explore options in a confidential discussion, thus empowering them. Similarly, once confidence is established, mediators are able to encourage the parties to try to see the problem from the other party's perspective, and parties are enabled to do so without feeling vulnerable or exposed. Realising that they have a choice whether or not to take matters to a face-to-face mediation, and consciously making the decision one way or the other, is itself empowering, and a step towards the transformation of the party and perhaps also resolving the dispute.

The initial contact with the first party can be illustrated by figure 10. The key steps are shown in the central vertical path: the home visit, which builds trust and leads to transformation. Helping to build trust are two side elements: the neutral environment, and the use of key mediation skills. As trust is established, the two side elements of recognition and empowerment lead to a transformation and change of perception.

---

[47] Mediation UK, *Training Manual in Community Mediation Skills*, pg. 169 is entitled 'Encouraging them to mediate'.

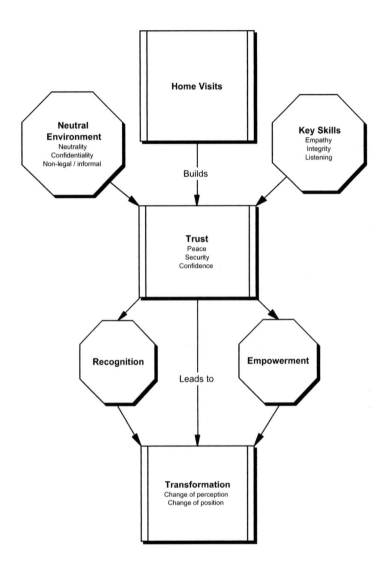

Figure 10. Home visits

i Neutral environment

The neutral environment is not simply the fact that the visit is taking place in the party's home. It expresses the fact that the meeting is informal, confidential, and that the mediator is not there as judge. Although the first party will have received a leaflet from the Camden Mediation Service describing the service, it is important for the mediators to emphasise that mediation is an informal process. Mediators have no legal powers or authority, but are simply there to use their skills to see if they can assist the parties. One mediation service handout cited in the Mediation UK handbook suggests the following format for explaining this to the parties

> We don't have any legal powers or authority, but what we do is to try and help in situations where there seems to be some dispute or problem between neighbours. We don't take sides in a dispute, but we want to listen to what everyone has to say, then see if we can help improve the situation in any way.[48]

The handbook refers to the three Ns.

– non-legal: no legal power, no authority

– neighbour dispute: the type of situation mediators deal with

– neutral: mediators do not take sides.

An introduction by a transformation-mediator might be along the following lines

> Let me explain what we do. We are not part of the Council. The Camden Mediation Service is an independent service. We go to each side to hear what each side has to say, and we give you the opportunity to talk about the problem to-

---

[48] Mediation UK, *Training Manual in Community Mediation Skills*, pg. 159, taken from a Lambeth Mediation Service handout. This is suggested in the context of the visit to the second party, but the same applies to the first party visit also.

gether. We are not here to take sides. We offer a process for you to discuss with the other side the issues, and hopefully resolve some of them. You can decide what you want to say to the other side.

ii Confidentiality

It is also important that the party understands that the meeting is confidential. Strictly, nothing said by one party to a mediator may be repeated to the other party, or to any third party, except with that party's permission. A mediator cannot even be compelled to give evidence in court of what was said at the mediation.[49] One paragraph from page 238 of the judgment in this case is succinct and authoritative.

> A substantial and, to our knowledge, unquestioned line of authority establishes that where a third party (whether official or unofficial, professional or lay) receives information in confidence with a view to conciliation, the courts will not compel him to disclose what was said without the parties' agreement: see *McTaggart v McTaggart* [1949] P. 94; *Pool v Pool* [1951] P. 470; *Henley v Henley* [1955] P. 202; *Theodoropoulas v Theodoropoulas* [1964] P. 311; *D. v National Society for the Prevention of Cruelty to Children* [1978] A.C. 171, 191E, 226F, 236G.

The paragraph refers to conciliation, but the court said that this term includes mediation. The only exception recognised by this case is where a party makes a clear statement at the mediation admitting that he or she has in the past caused or is likely in the future to cause serious harm to the well-being of a child; and even then the judge would exercise a discretion and will only admit the evidence where the public interest in protecting the child's interests outweighs the public interest in preserving the confidentiality of attempted conciliation. The case was in the context of family litigation, but the principle is general. Similarly, documents disclosed on a without prejudice basis during the mediation cannot

---

[49] *In re D. (Minors) (Conciliation: disclosure of information)* [1993] Fam. 231.

241

be used by either party in any subsequent litigation between the parties.[50]

Confidentiality occasionally raises ethical issues for mediators, where they feel that certain information should be disclosed to some third party, but they do not have permission to disclose it. For example, it may be apparent during a home visit that an elderly party is mentally ill. In such circumstances, should the mediation service alert the local mental health unit? In one case, the mediator realised that the party he was visiting bore a striking resemblance to a photo-fit of a wanted criminal. The party mentioned he was about to leave the country. The mediator was concerned whether or not he should inform the police. In such circumstances, Camden Mediation Service's policy is that confidentiality may need to be broken to the limited extent of the mediator discussing the matter with the director of the mediation service, so that the mediation service can decide on the correct course, and take responsibility for any complaint made subsequently by the party. Once the mediator has raised the matter with Camden Mediation Service, the matter becomes Camden Mediation Service's decision, rather than the mediator's.[51]

---

[50] *Instance v Denny Bros Printing Ltd (Interim Injunction)* (Pat Ct) [2000] FSR 869.

[51] In the photo-fit case, the director of the mediation service did decide to alert the police. The police then investigated and found that the party, although he did look like the photo-fit picture, had nothing to do with the crime. No complaint was made by the party against the Camden Mediation Service for taking this course. Surely Camden Mediation Service's decision in this case was wrong? It is one thing to break confidentiality where there is evidence given at the mediation of, for example, child abuse; it is quite another for the mediator to form his own judgment about a matter not connected with the mediation, and to pass that information on to the police. Such a disclosure by a mediator (or a mediation service) would not be permitted under section 8 of the Uniform Mediation Act in the USA.

iii Informality

Also important is the informality of the visit, and the emphasis by the mediators of their impartiality. They are not there to judge, nor to act as witnesses, but plainly they do see the inside of the party's home, and get a feel for the person's living conditions. Part of community mediation training is how to achieve impartiality between the parties during the face-to-face mediation; but impartiality is also important in the context of the home visit. Impartiality involves being non-judgmental, respecting personal boundaries, and not treating the person as a stereotype. Mediators need to be aware of their own prejudices, yet recognise and respect the other person's different values and beliefs. A mediator needs to be aware of prejudice in all its forms: these include race, gender, sexual orientation, religion, age, and class. The following are stereotype reactions to situations mediators may meet when visiting, reactions which they must guard against:

- Clean houses mean nice people

- Noisy children have inadequate parents

- Smokers are feckless and irresponsible

- Angry people are a nuisance

A mediator needs to be able to prevent stereotyping by acknowledging differences, by affirming individuality, and by appreciating diversity.

iv Key skills

The second main element to building trust is the use of mediation skills. The most important of these are active listening, exploring options without advising; establishing empathy; respect; and integrity.

v Active listening

Active listening means:

– Encouraging: 'Tell us some more about ...'

– Acknowledging: 'Yes, I understand ...'

– Checking: 'Am I right that you feel very angry about ...'

– Clarification: 'I don't quite understand why ... Could you explain ...'

– Affirmation: 'That is really helpful.'

– Empathy: 'I can understand why you are worried about this.'

– Summarising: 'Tell me if I have got this right. You said that ...'

– Asking open questions, rather than 'cross-examining'. 'How did you feel about that?'

– Balance: You may need to 'draw them out', but then do not interrupt them.

– Body language: an open body posture, appropriate physical proximity, eye contact, appropriate facial expression, affirmative gestures, and stillness.

vi Empathy

Empathy is not the same as sympathy. Empathy means being aware of and understanding what someone is feeling; sympathy is feeling it yourself. Empathy involves putting yourself in the shoes of the other party, and seeing the situation through their eyes. It involves communicating your understanding to the other party in an effective and appropriate response. If empathy is offered by the mediator, the party feels understood and less isolated. However, if sympathy is offered, the mediator's impartiality is impugned.

244

vii Integrity

Integrity involves the listener in being open to his or her own feelings as much as possible, avoiding all facade or expertise or superiority. As the Camden Mediation Service training materials states

> In order to be congruent or genuine towards another, you must first be congruent or genuine towards yourself.

This is consistent with the Christian requirement to love our neighbours *as ourselves*.[52] Integrity involves being aware of one's own prejudices and preconceptions, and consciously putting them to one side, so as to react with an open mind to the party. It involves constant monitoring and training, which is why mediation services seek to develop a support mechanism for mediators, including meetings, support groups, mentors, informal and social activities, continuing training, and periodic appraisals.[53]

viii Summary

To summarise, at the home visit the mediators explain their role, and encourage the party to describe the dispute as they see it. By active listening and other mediation skills they seek to begin the process of transformation in the party, empowering them to understand and examine the options in the dispute; and encouraging them to examine the dispute from the other party's perspective. Some parties are nervous about the whole process, but meeting the mediator privately in their own home builds up trust and makes them more at ease. Most home visits last 30–45 minutes. At the end of the visit, the party may decide that they do not want to proceed further with the mediation service. If this is so, the file will be closed. If the party does want to proceed, then

---

[52] Leviticus 19:18; Matthew 22:39; Romans 13: 9; Galatians 5:14; James 2: 8.

[53] Mediation UK, *Training Manual in Community Mediation Skills*, pg. 301–2 lists methods of providing support. See also Marian Liebmann, *Community and Neighbour Mediation*, pg. 125–128.

the mediators will explain that they will be visiting the other party, and if both parties are willing to meet in a face-to-face mediation, then a meeting will be arranged at a convenient time and in a neutral place. In the case of the Camden Mediation Service, face-to-face mediations take place in the Camden Mediation Service premises. Dates and times are suggested, telephone numbers obtained if not already known, and the visit brought to an end.

c) Stage 2: First contact with the second party

Potentially the visit to the second party could be antagonistic, because the second party may be the one who has been complained about, and who has not themselves contacted the mediation service. In practice, this is less of a problem than might appear, for two reasons. First, in many cases, the reference to mediation is not by the first party but by a neutral agency such as the local authority housing department. Second, the mediation service contacts the second party to inform them that mediation has been suggested, and asks them to confirm that they are willing to see a member of the service. Mediation services are generally experienced in explaining to parties the benefits of mediation, and further, that a home visit is impartial, confidential, and not-legally binding, and this encourages the second party to see the mediators.[54] Plainly, if the second party is unwilling to see the mediators, then the mediation process will stop, though sometimes further visits may be made to talk through the first party's options. In 'most cases'[55] the second party is willing to see the mediators, and is sometimes very relieved that action is possible on a problem which is as upsetting to them as to their neighbour.

Assuming the second party is willing to meet the mediators, the form of the visit to the second party is very much the same as

---

[54] For advice on how to persuade the second party to mediate see also Jennifer Beer and Eileen Steif, *The Mediator's Handbook*, 3rd edn., pg. 140.

[55] Marian Liebmann, *Community and Neighbour Mediation*, pg. 47.

the visit to the first party. There is an introduction by the mediators, there is then conversation in which the second party explains how they see the situation, and discussion of the options available, including the possibility of a face-to-face mediation.

The introduction by the mediators again emphasises the three Ns,[56] and confidentiality. Confidentiality may be reinforced by the mediators refusing to act as a messenger between the parties. Frequently a party wants the mediator to tell the other side something. The proper reply is to say, 'you will have an opportunity to tell them this at the mediation session'. This both reinforces what confidentiality means in practical terms, and encourages transformation by stimulating direct communication between the parties.

In visiting the second party, the mediators must be careful how much they appear already to know about the dispute. They are frequently under some pressure to reveal more of the issues complained about than is appropriate. Some mediators are reluctant to disclose even that they have already seen the first party. If they disclose matters said to them by the first party they will be in breach of their promise of confidentiality to that party, and they also risk appearing to have taken sides, and therefore of not being impartial.

To summarise, the home visit to the second party and any further parties follows very much the same format as the visit to the first party. Resolution-mediators tend to use the home visit as an opportunity to build trust, and to start the process of resolving the dispute. So they give the parties 'uninterrupted time'[57] to discuss the problem as they see it, and then encourage the party to come to a face-to-face mediation. The resolution-mediators' object is to establish a working relationship with the party and to get a

---

[56] Non-legal, neighbour disputes, and neutrality: see pg. 240.

[57] Mediation UK, *Training Manual in Community Mediation Skills*, pg. 181. Jennifer Beer and Eileen Steif, *The Mediator's Handbook*, 3rd edn., pg. 34.

full story of the dispute and its history.[58] Transformation-mediators are interested in developing an interaction with the party, getting the party to talk, and empowering them where necessary so that they are able to discuss options, and start to consider matters from the other side's perspective. The conversation is dynamic, with both the mediator and the parties discussing options and looking at possible ways forward. The result may or may not be that the second party wants to take things further at a face-to-face mediation.

A word should be said about note-taking at home visits. Mediators do take notes during the home visits, but these are usually brief. They will include names, addresses and telephone numbers if these are not already known. Camden Mediation Service encourages mediators to list the main issues which the party discusses, but not the detailed facts; and also the mediators' impressions of the feelings that are involved. The notes are not used as evidence, because the home visits are confidential, and the notes made during them are therefore confidential. The notes made by the mediators are merely an aide-memoir for them of the main topics which have been discussed, to help them, for example, in planning the face-to-face session.

d) Stage 3: Face-to-face session

Before the parties arrive for the face-to-face mediation some preparation is necessary. In some cases, the mediators will be different from those who prepared the case by visiting the parties: the practice here differs between services. In the Camden Mediation Service the mediators are the same people as those who visited the parties in their homes. The author considers this to be the better practice, as the mediators have already built up trust with the parties during the home visits, whereas new mediators will have to start this process from scratch. If the mediators did not carry out the home visits, the visitors need to brief the mediators

---

[58] Marian Liebmann, *Community and Neighbour Mediation*, pg. 45, 47.

as to what took place. In all cases the mediators need to discuss how they are to share their roles during the mediation session; predict what might go wrong, and what they can do to prevent this; decide how the mediation room should be arranged; and discuss anything else which needs to be considered before the parties arrive.

In some mediation services there is also a receptionist or observer present throughout the mediation session.[59] In the Camden Mediation Service the role of the observer is to act as receptionist, to assist the mediators with practical matters, and to provide feedback at the end of the session. He or she prepares the mediation room with the necessary number of chairs, paper and pens, water and glasses. The observer meets and greets the parties, organises tea and coffee as required, deals with any photocopying, and sees the clients out at the end of the session. The observer is present in the mediation room throughout the session, observing the process in silence, and taking notes for the final feed-back to the mediators. At the end of the mediation, after the clients have left, the observer gives feed-back to the mediators on how the process went, on teamwork, on the reactions of the clients, and any general views on the session.

One of the matters to be considered by the mediators before the parties arrive is the seating arrangements. A variety of seating arrangements is possible.[60] One or more parties may wish to have a supporter present, and this adds to the number of people in the

---

[59] The observer role is mentioned in Mediation UK, *Training Manual in Community Mediation Skills*, pg. 166. No mention is made of the observer role in Marian Liebmann, *Community and Neighbour Mediation*, Brown and Marriott, *ADR Principles and Practice*, 2nd edn., chapter 12, or Carolyn Schrock-Shenk (ed.), *Mediation and Facilitation Training Manual*, 4th edn.

[60] For diagrams of suitable seating arrangements, see Mediation UK, *Training Manual in Community Mediation Skills*, pg. 167, Jennifer Beer and Eileen Steif, *The Mediator's Handbook*, 3rd edn., pg. 29.

mediation room. One party may be feeling intimidated or physi-
cally threatened, and the seating will need to be arranged to give
that party a sense of safety. An example of a seating arrangement
used for a mediation involving three parties is shown in figure 11,
and illustrates some of the dynamics which need to be considered.[61]

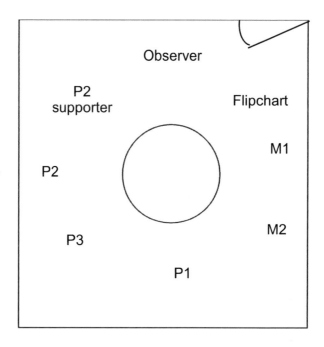

Figure 11. Community mediation seating arrangement

---

[61] This diagram appears somewhat middle-class and professional. The
flip-chart is not essential, but is helpful in many mediations.

This dispute arose because P1 and P3 were both complaining about noise made by P2.[62] P1 was elderly and somewhat frail, and during our home visit complained also of verbal abuse from P2. P2 wished to bring a friend to support her at the mediation. This friend had taken a prominent role in previous discussions between the parties, there was concern that she should not interfere during the mediation session. The friend was therefore placed next to P2, but in the corner so that she did not take too prominent a position round the table. The observer needed to be near the door for access. P1 and P3 were placed adjacent to each other, so that they supported each other, and to achieve a balance with P2 and her supporter. P1 was placed between P3 and M2, rather than between P3 and P2, because of P1's age and because of the allegations of verbal abuse. M1 and M2 sat together so that they could both watch the interaction between the clients without having to move their position. The flip-chart was placed near to M1 and adjacent to the door, to make the best use of space in a room that was a little on the small size.

The face-to-face mediation can be divided into the following sections: the opening by the mediators, the opening statements by the parties, identifying the issues with the parties, working on the issues one at a time in discussion or working on healing relationships, building up areas of agreement and recording the agreement in writing if this is appropriate, closure and follow-up.

i The mediators' opening

The opening by the mediators is very much shorter and less formal than the opening session of a commercial mediation. It begins with a welcome, and introduces the people present in the room. The mediators will check whether first names are to be used. They introduce the observer and explain his or her role, and check with all parties that it is all right for supporters to be pres-

---

[62] P1, P2, P3 stands for Party 1, Party 2 and Party 3. Similarly M1 and M2 stands for Mediator 1 and Mediator 2.

ent. (The Camden Mediation Service checks with the parties beforehand when any of them wants to bring a supporter, so this
point does not usually cause any difficulty.)

The mediators then explain the process: that mediation is an
opportunity for the parties to look at the issues they have, and to
talk about them. The mediators explain that mediation is voluntary, and that it is confidential. That means that the mediators
will keep the information heard confidential, and that they cannot
be called upon to give evidence anywhere else about what is said
at the mediation.[63] They explain that the process is informal,[64] and
that the session may last for two to three hours.

Mediators usually then seek to gain the parties' agreement to a
number of ground rules for the conduct of the mediation. These
include respecting one another, for example not using abusive
language, not interrupting someone when they are speaking, and
agreeing that the mediators can stop the session at any time. The
Camden Mediation Service has a no-smoking ground rule,[65] and
also requests that all mobile phones are switched off. The parties
may suggest other ground rules which they feel would be appropriate.[66] The mediators explain that it may be useful for them to
meet separately with each party to discuss matters which arise

---

[63] Nor can any of the parties be called upon to give evidence as to what
is said during the mediation.

[64] The Camden Mediation Service guidelines recommend saying that
mediation is 'non-binding' 'which means that only the clients can enforce any outcomes. Mediation does not stop the clients from taking any
other action.' These guidelines were written by a non-lawyer, and they
probably refer to the fact that even if the parties come to an agreement,
this agreement is not intended to have formal contractual effect.

[65] It is not obvious why this rule assists the mediation process.

[66] Mediation UK, *Training Manual in Community Mediation Skills*, pg. 179
suggests the following additional ground rules: openness, patience, remaining seated, and allowing the mediators to remain in control of the
session.

during the course of the session, and that anyone can ask for this if they would like to discuss something privately.

Some American transformation-mediators argue that by suggesting particular ground rules mediators are being too directive, too resolution-orientated. They advocate simply asking the parties what suggestions they have about how they and the mediator should have the joint session together. This goes even further than Bush and Folger, who regard, for example, the non-interruption ground rules useful.[67]

ii Opening statements

After any questions have been answered, the mediation moves into the opening statement section, sometimes called 'uninterrupted time'.[68] Even though the mediators[69] have heard each party's story during the home visits, this is an opportunity for each party to explain the situation as he or she sees it to the mediators and to the other party at the same time. The mediators get an overview of the situation and a sense of the personalities and feelings involved when the parties are together. Each party has the experience of being listened to, uninterrupted, perhaps for the first time in the dispute.

The mediators may need to protect each person's uninterrupted time by stopping interruptions. This can be done by reminding the parties of the ground rules they have agreed to. The mediators may suggest that the listening party makes a written note of any points they feel are important so that they can address them when it is their turn to speak.

---

[67] Robert Bush and Joseph Folger, *The Promise of Mediation*, pg. 264. They see the non-interruption rule as providing an opportunity for transformation: see below, pg. 254.

[68] See pg. 247, fn. 57.

[69] Or the persons conducting the home visits.

Mediators sometimes summarise each person's statement, to check that the parties are satisfied that they have been heard correctly. Summarising is a skill which involves more than the ability just to précis the words used by the speaker. It involves an appreciation of the speaker's feelings, and of what is left unsaid as well as what is said. It also helps the mediators to start to identify the issues which need to be addressed.[70]

In transformative mediation, non-interruption remains an important ground rule; but Bush and Folger use it to provide an opportunity for transformation. Bush and Folger encourage listeners to take a proactive stance, marking down new information which they did not know before, or things they did not realise about the other party but that are now evident from hearing the other's opening statement. They then turn to the listener and ask what he or she heard in the other party's statement. This empowers the parties to expect that they might learn something new during the mediation. It encourages each party to give recognition to what the other party has said, and encourages each party to recognise that they have been understood by the other side as well as by the mediator.[71]

iii Identifying the issues

The mediators will then attempt to make a list of the main issues which have arisen in the opening statements onto the flip-chart or a sheet of paper. The mediators will seek agreement on these issues from the parties, and invite the parties to suggest changes or add any which have been left out. Topics may need to be rephrased using words which are impartial: 'How visitors are welcomed' works better than 'Steven's rude language'. In one mediation the author used the all-purpose 'communication problems' instead of 'how to make complaints', and the parties understood what this referred to; but if an issue is not expressed

---

[70] Robert Bush and Joseph Folger, *The Promise of Mediation*, pg. 269.

[71] Robert Bush and Joseph Folger, *The Promise of Mediation*, pg. 265.

with sufficient clarity, it cannot be worked through to a conclusion.

As already explained, resolution-mediators regard many relational issues or issues which involve emotions as not suitable for mediation. Transformation-mediators however regard such issues as the stuff of life.[72] The Mennonites, who combine both resolution and transformation in their model, likewise look for relational and emotion-based issues as well as purely factual issues.[73]

iv Working on the issues, or healing relationships

The next step is where the transformation model differs markedly from the resolution model. Although both models advocate taking one issue at a time (with some flexibility), the approach is very different. Transformation-mediators see their role as getting the parties talking and listening to each other. Both body language and spoken language are used here. For example, if one party is directing all their words to the mediator, the mediator can look at the other party, to encourage the speaking party to do the same. Or the mediator might say 'I think you need to say this to [the other party]'.

The transformation-mediator needs to affirm and encourage the parties. If one party is silent for a time, they may be feeling disempowered, and the mediators need to address the reason for this, and what can be done about it.

The transformation-mediator seeks to foster recognition by encouraging each party to look at the issue from the perspective of the other party, and by ensuring that both parties are listening to each other. The transformation-mediator will encourage the parties to explore possible options for resolution or for how they see

---

[72] See pg. 229.

[73] See pg. 232.

the way forward. Statements of regret or apology should always be acknowledged and affirmed.

The transformation-mediator sees the ultimate purpose of mediation as improving communication between the parties. Transformation mediation aims to foster good communication in the mediation session, and to encourage, even to teach, the parties how to communicate in a new way, so that they can keep to this level or at least an improved level of communication in their future contacts with each other. In this way the parties are empowered to resolve any future difficulties before they escalate into conflicts.

The resolution-mediator sees the ultimate purpose of mediation as resolving the dispute which brought them to mediation. Whereas transformation-mediators are actively looking for the underlying emotions, and how these can be transformed, resolution-mediators simply handle emotions when they appear, rather than aim to bring them to the surface. One is proactive, the other reactive. The CEDR mediation training for commercial mediation is plainly reactive:

> it is important that the Mediator recognises, copes with and, where necessary, manages each Party's expression of emotion.[74]

This has major significance for church disputes. There is a common theme in church disputes of the presented issue not being the real issue between the parties, and mediators of church disputes need to examine the history of the relationships between the parties to heal underlying concerns.

Transformative-mediation sees dealing with these underlying relationship issues as often more significant than resolving just the presenting factual dispute. But the basic six-day training from Camden Mediation Service gives little guidance as to how in practice to bring about a transformation when relationship issues

---

[74] *Mediator Training Course Handbook* (London, CEDR, 1997), pg. 36.

surface, beyond encouraging each party to listen to and understand how the other party sees the situation. It is assumed that once this takes place, relationships will be transformed. In some cases they are, but a lot more could be taught as part of the community model on the subject. Actively eliciting feelings, and then enabling them to be transformed takes both confidence and practice; and Camden Mediation Service failed to provide proper training for this.

There are several reasons why Camden Mediation Service appears to be weak in this area. First, Camden Mediation Service teaches that mediation is an art rather than a science: there is no one right way to handle every situation, and Camden Mediation Service is cautious about being prescriptive. Second, community mediation is explicitly secular, and there is either a reluctance to get involved in, or simply a lack of understanding of, a subject which (many Christians would argue) has a spiritual dimension. Third, there is concern that if inexperienced mediators handle situations wrongly great distress and indeed offence could be caused, and legal claims might be made against the mediation service. Fourth, there is a distinction between mediation and counselling, and Camden Mediation Service does not feel it to be Camden Mediation Service's role to teach therapy and counselling skills.[75]

A mediator does not need the skills and expertise of a counsellor in handling emotions. Mediation should not be confused with counselling or any process that deals with the resolution of personal emotional issues. A mediator must however have the ability to cope with the emotions expressed by the parties in a way that accepts them normally and non-judgmentally. A mediator needs to be able to work sensitively with parties in exploring issues and concerns underlying those that they present in the me-

---

[75] Brown and Marriott, *ADR Principles and Practice*, 2nd edn., pg. 242 discusses this in the context of family mediation, but the principle is general.

diation; and a mediator needs to be able to handle emotions or strength of feeling in the best way either to help resolve the dispute or to transform the parties.[76]

It is here that the Mennonite mediation model scores over the community mediation model. The Mennonite model sees problem-solving and healing of emotions as equally important, and mediators are trained to do both.

> This stage consists of alternating back and forth between these two tasks.[77]

The Mennonite healing model aims to enable the parties to state their feelings directly to each other, and to know they have been understood and respected, which often provides opportunities for healing. An example of the process would be as follows:[78]

Step 1: paraphrasing feelings and encouraging impact statements:

> 'I have a sense, Mary, that it has been quite a struggle for you since your husband died. Can you tell us a little more about this'.

Or

> 'Mary, what was the impact of this on you personally.'

Step 2: encouraging paraphrasing by the other party:

> 'George, I'd like to ask you to say to Mary in your own words, what you understand her to be saying just now.'

Or

> 'George, tell me what you hear Mary saying.' Then:

> 'George, would you mind just turning to Mary, and tell her directly what you just told me.'

---

[76] Brown and Marriott, *ADR Principles and Practice*, 2nd edn., pg. 331.

[77] Carolyn Schrock-Shenk (ed.), *Mediation and Facilitation Training Manual*, 4th edn., pg. 177.

[78] Carolyn Schrock-Shenk (ed.), *Mediation and Facilitation Training Manual*, 4th edn., pg. 177–80.

Step 3: checking this has been understood;

> 'Mary, do you think George has understood what you were saying?'

When one party realises that the other party really understands the hurt he or she has been through, frequently conversation between them moves onto a new level. This is especially so if both parties have suffered some emotional hurt, and each party can be encouraged to address the other in this way. The result can be dramatic. The parties suddenly talk freely, straightforwardly. A new relationship is formed.

This is just an example of the Mennonites training in this field. The subject has to be handled delicately and not rushed. Sometimes the mediator may ask a party to give some idea of what they need in order to let go of their feelings.

> 'Is there anything else that you need to put this behind you?'

Or

> 'Is there anything else which will enable you to let go of this?'

In the role plays during the five-day Mennonite training course, the author found himself playing the part of a young church youth leader who lacked confidence when confronted by the dominating parents of some of the children in the church. The parents were complaining about the way the youth leader ran the youth group. In the mediation the mediators skilfully got the youth leader to speak out his feelings to one of these parents, where they were acknowledged, and responded to in a way which released the fear, empowered the youth leader, and dramatically altered the relationship. This was only a role play, but the effect of the process was quite extraordinary.

v Building areas of agreement

Where mediators focus on problem solving, this usually involves first identifying the parties' interests as opposed to their

259

positions. The difference between positions and interests is that positions focus on each party's perceived solution, whereas interests focus on the problem and the reason for the party's perceived solution. A position is the party's solution to the problem – party B's dog must go; the interest is why it has to go – it barks at night preventing party A's sleep. When parties focus on interests rather than positions, they discover that they may have interests in common – the dog is useful because it deters burglars. This helps the parties work together for a solution which may suit both parties – moving the dog to another room, different arrangements to look after the dog so that it is not bored, feeding the dog at a different time, buying a cat to keep the dog company, etc.

The classic illustration of the difference between interests and positions is two cooks arguing over who is to have an orange. Both of them want it, they both want it now, and there is only one orange. Their positions appear irreconcilable until you ask why they each want it. One cook then says she needs the flesh and the juice for a fruit salad, the other needs the rind for a cake: when the mediator discovers this, the conflict is resolved.

Exploring interests helps parties in a number of ways: it empowers each party by encouraging each party to look at their real needs in the situation; it also encourages each party to understand the interests of the other party and to give recognition to them. The parties may discover that they share a number of interests, and this enables them to look for solutions that meet the interests of both parties.

The next stage is to generate options, and then to evaluate and choose between them to find a mutually acceptable solution.

Community mediators are trained to be hesitant about suggesting solutions themselves. There are good reasons for a mediator holding back: holding back means trusting that the parties understand their situation better than the mediator does. The mediator's obvious solution may not be feasible or feel right to the parties. If a mediator hands the parties a solution, the parties may

feel stupid, petty, or ungenerous in not having offered it themselves. If the mediator makes the suggestion, the parties may feel
uncomfortable in saying no to the mediator. If the solution is
theirs, the parties have more stake in making it work; but if it is
the mediator's solution, the parties see it as the mediator's fault if
it fails.[79]

Similarly, a mediator should be careful not to give advice, beyond referring parties to other agencies such as the Citizens Advice Bureau, the Council housing department, or solicitors, when
considering the options available. Sometimes this can raise ethical
difficulties for a mediator. If, for example, the mediator is by
training a lawyer, he or she may be aware that one party appears
to be ignorant of their legal rights, and the other is taking advantage of that fact to obtain more than he would be entitled to if the
matter went to court. Bush and Folger argue that the mediator is
under almost no duty to protect the weaker party from entering
into an 'unfair' agreement.[80] Bush and Folger suggest that in such
circumstances mediators should ask the parties whether they
think their information [which includes legal advice] is adequate
in order to proceed, but they insist that self-determination includes the freedom to make one's own mistakes. 'Unless there is
reason to believe the party lacks the capacity for decision-making,
protecting parties from themselves by insisting on more information is a pitfall that undermines empowerment'. Bush and Folger
recognise that in some cases parties do lack the capacity for decision-making, and say that in such cases the mediator should intervene, perhaps by discontinuing the session. They suggest that
perhaps the most important example is the case where one party
is the victim of past violence by the other. In such circumstances
fear of future harm may negate that party's capacity to engage in

---

[79] Jennifer Beer and Eileen Steif, *The Mediator's Handbook*, 3rd edn.,
pg. 122.
[80] Robert Bush and Joseph Folger, *The Promise of Mediation*, pg. 214.

genuine deliberation and decision-making on issues involving the abuser.

There are a number of ways for a mediator to generate options, other than suggesting them himself.[81] One is to get a number of suggestions, before discussing their merits: a 'brainstorming' exercise. Asking the parties for more ideas; asking each party what they can do to help resolve the issue rather than what the other side can do; encouraging each party to think what the other party would want them to do; encouraging the parties to narrow extreme positions – to find a way in between what they have both suggested; all these are part of the mediator's skills. Questioning about the problem can make it less general and more specific, and enable options to be considered. For example, a general complaint about noise may need to be broken down so that each party's daily routine is examined: if the problem is partly when the noise is played, is there any other time when it would not be so disturbing?

When some options have been suggested, the next step in problem-solving is to explore them. This may be straightforward, with the parties discussing each option in turn with little help from the mediators, and modifying the suggestions when necessary, or it may need guidance from the mediators. The Camden Mediation Service training suggests that mediators should check that solutions satisfy the SMART test: they should be Specific, Measurable, Achievable, Realistic, and Timed.

'Specific' means that the agreement should say exactly what a party will do or will not do in the situation. Non-judgmental language should be used: 'P1 will phone P2 and ask in a non-confrontational way for the radio to be turned down'.

---

[81] Jennifer Beer and Eileen Steif, *The Mediator's Handbook*, 3rd edn., pg. 122; Mediation UK, *Training Manual in Community Mediation Skills*, pg. 232.

'Measurable' means that the parties should be able to see straight away whether things are working.

By 'achievable' is meant that a mediator should not let a party promise more than he can realistically deliver. If necessary, a mediator should scale down a party's offer if the mediator sees it not being practical, or if it involves co-operation from another party who is not present. So, for example, in a complaint about noisy children, it may be appropriate for a party to 'encourage' the children to play in another room.

'Realistic' means that in the areas of lifestyles, people are not going to change overnight. If they like rock music, they are not going to stop liking rock music.

'Timed' means that there should be a timetable for implementation, a date by which the goal is to be achieved.

Agreements tend to be reached on one issue at a time. Some small items may be satisfactorily resolved, even though one or more major points may not be. The mediator builds on the momentum, and notes down points which are agreed as they take place. He encourages the parties, suggests moving to other topics if there appears to be an impasse, stage manages, suggests a break if he thinks it appropriate, and may decide to discuss with the parties separately. The process is not the same as the negotiation of a commercial mediation. In a commercial mediation, the parties usually want a settlement of everything, or nothing at all. If the matter cannot be settled in a commercial mediation, the litigation will continue. In community mediation, there is no litigation, and agreements can be partial. In a community mediation, an agreement which deals only with some of the issues is better than no agreement at all.

It is often useful to put into a mediation agreement what will happen in future when the problem reoccurs. And where most of the accommodation is being made by one party it is helpful to include some recognition or acceptance by the other party, so that the agreement does not seem wholly one-sided:

> P2 will try to reduce the noise of door slamming.
>
> P1 recognises that the noise from music has got better since complaints were made in May.
>
> P1 will express any concerns about noise politely and at the time rather than afterwards. P2 will respond positively.

Unlike commercial mediations, not all agreements reached by the parties need to be recorded in writing. There are good reasons to encourage the parties to write down their agreements: committing oneself on paper is a demonstration of good faith; and a document that is signed and kept is more likely to be remembered and adhered to than a verbal agreement.[82] But there are many cases where this formality is uncomfortable, and suggests a continuing lack of trust, and the fragility of the party's promises. A written agreement may itself become a focus for future disagreement, an instrument of destruction rather than of healing and reconciliation. In such cases, matters should be left fluid and unwritten. A half-way house would be for the mediator to offer to record some of the matters in a closing letter from the mediation service to each of the parties. This has less formality than a written agreement, it helps act as a record, it confirms the good faith of the parties, and its very informality should not detract from the progress which has been made during the mediation session.[83]

Where an agreement is to be recorded in writing, Camden Mediation Service uses an agreement form which starts

> This agreement was reached at a mediation session on [mediation date] between [participants] of [addresses]

---

[82] Marian Liebmann, *Community and Neighbour Mediation*, pg. 56; Mediation UK, *Training Manual in Community Mediation Skills*, pg. 238.

[83] Jennifer Beer and Eileen Steif, *The Mediator's Handbook*, 3rd edn., pg. 122; Mediation UK, *Training Manual in Community Mediation Skills*, pg. 53.

which is just like a legal contract. But at the bottom of the form, below the space for the parties' signatures, the form says

> This agreement is not a legally binding document, but has been reached voluntarily and without prejudice between the above parties.

These words indicate that the agreement reached by the parties is not intended to create a legal contract which can be enforced in court. For this reason, although they should be specific (the first of the SMART requirements), agreements reached at community mediations are written in the parties' own words rather than in formal legalistic language. If the dispute does involve legal issues, the parties can arrange for a lawyer to draft a legal agreement based on the mediation agreement, and this can then be signed as a formal contract if appropriate

In summary, an agreement is an agreement for the parties, not for the mediator. It is not for the mediator to try to force the parties to sign a mediation agreement for the sake of maintaining the mediator's personal success rate. The transformation-mediator knows that agreements are useful and helpful and sometimes needed; but a transformed relationship is better. The transformative approach is to indicate that if the parties agree to take steps to deal with their situation, these steps can be written into a final agreement. But other accomplishments of the mediation can be written up, for example in a closing letter to both parties from the mediation session, even if the dispute was not resolved. These points might include understandings which were reached at the session, new information which was exchanged, and descriptions in the parties' own words of new ways of communicating that were followed in the mediation – new ways that might help them in their discussions after the session.[84]

---

[84] Robert Bush and Joseph Folger, *The Promise of Mediation*, pg. 264.

vi Closure and follow-up

The closing stage of the mediation session involves the mediator summarising what has been achieved at the session, whether or not a written agreement has been reached, and indicating the remaining steps which the service can offer. In some cases it may be appropriate to have a further mediation session. This may well happen if the mediation runs out of time, or the parties become too tired to continue. It may be that one necessary person is not present, and one party wants to discuss the matter with him or her before continuing. In some cases, the parties may want to try out the agreement for a trial period, and then meet again for evaluation and revision. Or one party may want to obtain some information before making a decision at the mediation session. In such cases, if the parties want another mediation session, the mediation can continue on another date.[85]

The mediators have certain tasks once the parties have left, covering three areas: feed-back to themselves, feed-back to the mediation service, and confidentiality. First, and very important, is feed-back to themselves. The mediators discuss with each other and with the observer (if there is one) how the mediation session went. Camden Mediation Service has a very positive and constructive approach to encourage inexperienced mediators: 'there is no failure, only feed-back'.[86] Feed-back to fellow mediators sets standards of practice, recognises existing skills, provides opportunities for future support if needed, and gives mediators an opportunity to learn different styles. Mediators are encouraged to review the entire mediation from the home visits to the end of the mediation session, and to look at the content – for example, their use of language and the way they related to the clients, their neu-

---

[85] Practical matters for the mediator to cover in such circumstances are set out in Jennifer Beer and Eileen Steif, *The Mediator's Handbook*, 3rd edn., pg. 63.

[86] From the author's notes made during the Camden Mediation Service five-day mediation training course.

trality and impartiality, and the way they were able to work on empowerment and recognition. They should look at the other mediator, asking themselves what they liked of what they saw, and what they would have done differently; how they worked as a team, and how they felt they personally handled the mediation. Mediation UK has a suggested evaluation form to be used during feed-back covering a whole range of mediation skills: preparation, introductions, control of the session, ability to empathise, understanding the issues, co-operation with co-mediator, communication skills, fairness, identification and acknowledgement of feelings, creative thinking, speed and helpfulness, competency in dealing with difficulties, summarising, planning next steps, clarification of action, post-visit planning. Camden Mediation Service suggests a more informal approach lasting 15-30 minutes, with the mediators and the observer just discussing orally the various points which occur to them.

The mediators' second task is to report to the mediation service the outcome of the mediation, and whether any further involvement is required. The mediators will also submit any claims for travelling and other expenses to the mediation service at this time. In Camden Mediation Service cases, any official or final communication with regard to cases must come from the Camden Mediation Service office, not from the mediators. The closing letter from Camden Mediation Service can be an opportunity to record matters which were discussed or agreed, or new ways the parties used to relate to each other, even if no formal agreement was reached at the mediation session. Similarly, if the mediation ended after one of the home visits because one or other party did not want to attend a mediation session, the closing letter can be used to remind the party of some of the options which are available other than mediation, and to offer further mediation service if both parties agree. Camden Mediation Service is careful to ensure that what is said in a closing letter does not breach confidentiality, by only including confidential matters which the parties agree with the mediators should be included. Camden Mediation

Service is also careful to maintain impartiality by not including any information which appears to cast blame on either side if the mediation process has failed. Where a housing officer referred the case to mediation and asks Camden Mediation Service the result, Camden Mediation Service might report, for example, that 'one of the parties' was not willing to attend the mediation session, but the letter would not state which party it was. This caution is proper, as otherwise the independence of the mediation service from the housing service is impugned. Mediation services in the USA adopt the same practice.[87]

The third task for the mediators, in keeping with their promise of confidentiality, is to destroy their notes of what was said during the home visits or mediation sessions. Only essential information should be kept, such as the report forms of the home visits and the mediation session, a copy of any settlement agreement, and copies of any correspondence. Even these should be destroyed after a period of time.[88]

Most mediation services have a set follow-up procedure once the mediation has come to an end, whether this occurs after the home visits, or after one or more mediation sessions.[89] In almost all cases the service will write to the parties after a period of time (in the Camden Mediation Service this is between one and two months after the closure letter), inviting them to express any views about the process and the outcome of their contact with the service, and how well any agreement made at the session is working. This provides feed-back to the organisation on how the

---

[87] Under the section 8(a)(1) of the Uniform Mediation Act the mediator may disclose 'whether the mediation occurred or has terminated, whether a settlement was reached, and attendance'. Attendance at a mediation may thus be disclosed, but not non-attendance.

[88] If a settlement is reached and the notes can be destroyed in the presence of the parties, this adds to the symbolic effect of the dispute being resolved.

[89] Brown and Marriott, *ADR Principles and Practice*, 2nd edn., pg. 292.

process has worked, provides statistical information for funders, and allows the service an opportunity to review its procedures. The service can through its follow-up procedures identify any needs for further training, and deal with the (fortunately rare) cases where a complaint is made.[90]

e) Variations

As already indicated, not all disputes go all the way through this process. Either the first or the second party may decide not to continue after the first home visit. Sometimes the parties seem ready to meet, but try to make the practical arrangements difficult. The mediation service needs to balance the need to accommodate people in genuine difficulties, but also needs to set boundaries to avoid being manipulated.[91]

i Shuttle mediation

In some cases it may not be appropriate or possible to bring the parties together for a face-to-face mediation. One of the parties may refuse a meeting, there may be threats, power differences, high levels of distrust, or past harassment or violence. In such cases, the mediation service may decline to act further in the dispute; but an alternative is to use 'shuttle mediation'. Shuttle mediation is where the mediators pay a succession of visits to each party in turn, without them meeting together in a joint session.

Shuttle mediation has some similarity to the private 'caucus' meetings which are standard in commercial mediation but rare in

---

[90] Marian Liebmann, *Community and Neighbour Mediation*, pg. 57.

[91] In one mediation in which the author was mediator, one party said she could only have a home visit between 2 and 3 on a Friday afternoon while her 2 year old daughter was at a play-school, and the visit was to take place not in her home but in a spare room at the play-school. The author discussed the matter with Camden Mediation Service, and Camden Mediation Service said that arrangements would have to be made by the party so that the visit could be at her home.

community mediation. The difference between shuttle mediation and caucuses is that a caucus is just a part of the process, whereas shuttle mediation is the whole process. A commercial mediation consists of a number of joint meetings and caucus meetings all taking place in one session over a day; whereas in shuttle mediation there are no joint meetings, but separate meetings take place over an extended time with the mediators seeing one party one day, and the other party days, perhaps weeks, later.

Community mediation services see shuttle mediation as second best.[92] Progress is slower than face-to-face mediations, and the mediators often have to make several visits to each party before agreement can be reached. However it does have a value in helping to improve communication, and can lead either to a resolution of the dispute, or to a face-to-face mediation when relations have been improved by the shuttle mediation. In one ecclesiastical case between members of a team ministry[93] where the bishop appointed a mediator in February 2000, shuttle mediation over a twelve month period made considerable progress.

There are specific difficulties which need to be addressed in shuttle mediation. Issues of confidentiality need to be sorted out at an early stage to determine what can and what cannot be discussed with the other party. It is important that the mediator does not simply become a message taker between the two parties, but uses his mediation skills to the full, helping the parties to look at interests rather than positions, helping them consider options, looking for ways to empower the parties and for ways to improve recognition.

---

[92] Marian Liebmann, *Community and Neighbour Mediation*, pg. 59. Shuttle mediation received only the briefest of mentions in the Camden Mediation Service five-day training course.

[93] Hackney Marsh in East London.

ii Private meetings

Private or 'caucus' meetings are part of the mediator's armoury, but they are not used in community mediation as a matter of course. In the context of a two-to-three hour mediation, one caucus meeting with each party can take up to half an hour, and this may cause the mediation to run out of time. But there are occasions when a caucus is valuable. A caucus may be useful to support one or other party who is silent, and not contributing to the discussion: the mediators may want to ask the reason privately, and seek to empower the party to take an active role in the rest of the mediation. If one party becomes very angry or distraught, a caucus gives them an opportunity to calm down and recover their composure. A party may prefer to consider their options privately with the mediator, or to reveal some information to the mediator which they do not want the other side to know about. The mediators may need to use a caucus to control the process: if one party is using unhelpful behaviour or language, the mediators can use a private meeting to confront that person and say that the behaviour or language must change if the mediation is to continue. Sometimes a party may threaten to walk out, and a caucus gives the mediators an opportunity to discuss privately with that party the feasibility of continuing the mediation.[94]

iii Multi-party mediation

Many neighbourhood disputes involve more than just two or three people. If a small number of parties are involved in a mediation, the normal format for a community mediation can be followed; but the more parties are involved, the more difficult it is for the mediator to ensure that each party's voice is heard and their interests considered. If a whole group of people is involved, the mediator needs to devise a process in which all members of the group feel included. Although this is considered part of

---

[94] Mediation UK, *Training Manual in Community Mediation Skills*, pg. 223.

community mediation,[95] group process is not part of the standard mediation training offered by Camden Mediation Service; nor is it covered in the Mediation UK training manual. It is however a subject which occupies one whole day of the Mennonites five-day mediation training course.[96]

4. COMPARISON BETWEEN COMMUNITY AND COMMERCIAL MEDIATION

A comparison is needed to see whether one model of mediation is better suited for church disputes generally, or whether the commercial mediation model is better suited to some church disputes, and the community mediation model to others. First, the points of similarity between the two models of mediation are set out, then the differences between them.

a) Points of similarity

i Core mediation skills

The core mediation skills are the same for both types of mediation. These include skills in the three key areas of relating to people, solving problems, and managing the process. In the people category come the active listening skills, the ability to summarise, the ability to build rapport with a party, to develop respect, to show empathy, and using appropriate body language such as eye contact and posture. In the people category comes also the ability to handle emotions, whether anger, fear, distress, jealousy, or whatever; and these can play a part in both community and commercial mediation. Handling emotions includes, for example, the ability to reframe strong language, so that where a

---

[95] For an example of a process in a case involving two groups of about 20 people, see Marian Liebmann, *Community and Neighbour Mediation*, pg. 60–61.

[96] Group process is covered in depth in chapter 5 of Carolyn Schrock-Shenk (ed.), *Mediation and Facilitation Training Manual*, 4th edn.

party makes an unhelpful comment ('he's a liar') the mediator can diffuse strong feelings or broaden perspectives in a constructive way for all parties ('you see it differently from the way he does').

In the problem-solving area for both types of mediation are the ability to help clarify the issues, to help each party to see things from new perspectives, to help generate options, and to help each party evaluate options. In the process area, there is the ability to manage the session, to exercise authority over the process, yet empower each party to be in a position to resolve the dispute. Mediators need to be attuned to sense people's emotions, and to adjust the process accordingly. This will include using joint sessions or caucus sessions, arranging seating, and handling interruptions or disturbances in the best way to resolve power imbalances, outbursts, or other difficult situations. For both types of mediation, the mediator must be able to convey his own independence and impartiality, and win the confidence of the parties.

ii Core mediation personal qualities

This leads to the personal qualities needed by both kinds of mediator. Both types of mediators need to have an understanding of people and situations, they need the ability to learn from experience, they need to be genuine and impartial, they need to be flexible, and they need to have a sense of balance. The mediator's self-assurance and his or her confidence in the process undoubtedly assists the parties to relax and work constructively towards resolving the dispute. Brown and Marriott list four essential attributes or qualities of being a mediator: theoretical understanding of mediation and its dynamics, practical mediation skills, ethical awareness, and emotional sensitivity.[97] These are the same for commercial and community mediation.

---

[97] Brown and Marriott, *ADR Principles and Practice*, 2nd edn., pg. 330–1.

iii Process

Key elements in the process are also the same for both types of mediation. In both cases, mediation is both voluntary and confidential. In both cases, the mediator is independent and impartial. In both cases the general framework for the face-to-face mediation is similar: the mediator seeks to ensure that the parties feel safe and at ease in each other's company; each party then makes an opening statement; the mediator helps to identify the issues; and the mediation then continues using a combination of joint sessions and caucus meetings. In both cases, if agreement is reached, the parties are likely to record it in writing.

b) Points of difference

i The people involved – the parties

But there most of the similarity ends. There are differences in the people involved, the type of dispute, and the process. Taking first the parties to the dispute, most of the people who use a community mediation service are residents in the community. Sometimes people who live outside the local area are referred to the mediation service by some outside agency, but in the case of Camden Mediation Service over 90% of the mediations it conducts are for people living in the London Borough of Camden. In contrast, there is no residential link between the parties to a commercial dispute. Commercial disputes may of course arise within a local geographical area – for example, a person may have a professional negligence claim against a local firm of solicitors – but the disputing parties to a commercial dispute have far less connection to a particular location than do the disputing parties to a community mediation. CEDR is based in London, but handles disputes arising all over the country and abroad.

One model of the Church is as a community of believers.[98] A dispute between members of the same local church therefore has some similarity to the community dispute. But many church disputes are not just internal disputes between members of one local church. For example, there are hierarchical disputes between clergy and the diocesan bishop, and disputes between a church and an outside body.[99]

Community mediation makes a virtue out of ethnic awareness. Cultural diversity is emphasised during the training course of all community mediation services accredited by Mediation UK. Report visit forms for the Camden Mediation Service have an 'ethnic monitoring' section in which the visitors are asked to describe the colour and race of the people they visit. This is in keeping with the egalitarian philosophy of community mediation; but it has no wider purpose than this. Commercial mediation is also aware of ethnic differences, but for a different reason, namely, to make mediators more effective. CEDR offers training in cross-cultural mediation so that mediators know how to relate to different cultures, and realise the different approaches which may be needed in disputes involving different cultures.

In the case of church disputes, ethnic monitoring might serve a rather different purpose, namely, to ensure that each dispute is

---

[98] This is true both theologically and sociologically. In theology it is based on the doctrine of the 'communion of saints', as for example in part of the ninth article of the Apostles' Creed: 'I believe in … the communion of saints.' A sociological analysis of congregations is given in Penny Edgell Becker's *Congregations in conflict* (Cambridge University Press, 1999). She identifies four main models of congregations: houses of worship, family congregations, community congregations, and leader congregations.

[99] See pg. 88 on internal and external disputes, and the categories of disputes considered in chapter 3. An example of a dispute between a church and an outside body would be where English Heritage objects to proposed alterations to a church building.

not looked at in isolation, but is seen in the broader context of the Church's social ministry. Thus if monitoring indicates that a particular type of dispute affects a particular ethnic background within the Church, this may indicate some particular social problem affecting persons of that background. Only when the Church becomes aware of such a social problem can it consider ways to address it other than on a one-to-one basis. Ethnic monitoring of mediation can thus lead to a higher plane of social reform.

ii The people involved – the mediators

Next are the persons who act as mediators. In the case of commercial mediations, these are usually professional mediators, who expect to be paid for their service. In the case of community mediations, they are volunteers in almost all cases giving their time free. Community mediators are far more diverse than commercial mediators. Commercial mediators are usually well educated, white, middle to upper class, employed or self-employed, and experienced in business. CEDR's registered mediators are typically lawyers, surveyors and architects, computer consultants and other professionals. They are mostly male, white, and over 30 years old. In contrast, community mediators come from a whole range of ethnic, religious, cultural, educational and social backgrounds. The ratio of females to males is far greater in community mediation than in commercial mediation, and the age range is also far more diverse in community mediation. On the Camden Mediation Service training course attended by the author there were 15 females and 7 males; ages ranged from under 20 to over 70; some were employed, some self-employed, some were unemployed and claiming social security. 12 were English, one was Italian, one German, one American, one Asian, and the remainder were Caribbeans and Africans. Five (the Caribbeans and Africans) were black. Of those who were open about their religion there were Christians, Muslims, Jews and one Hindu. Camden Mediation Service has a number of mediators who are open about their gay or lesbian sexual orientation. One point of similarity is that both commercial and community mediation seems to appeal to persons in retirement. On the CEDR training course attended by the author in 1998, one member was over 60. Camden Mediation Service has a handful of mediators well into their seventies, including one who has been mediating community disputes for 20 years. Interestingly, Camden Mediation Service mediators do not all live or work in Camden, so they do not necessarily come from the same community as the parties to the dispute. In the London area there are mediation services in Bromley, Camden, Croydon, Ealing, Greenwich, Hackney, Hammersmith and Fulham, Hounslow, Kingston, Lewisham, Newham, Southwark, Tower Hamlets and Waltham Forest, and so people who live or work in parts of London where there is no mediation service and who want to volunteer for this work have to choose a mediation service outside their local community.

The diversity of mediators trained in community mediation is much more suitable for the various types of person involved in church disputes than the very uniform commercial mediator. Although a commercial mediator may match the background of the parties in some church disputes, inner city churches with a mixed colour congregation, and churches where the majority of the congregation are not from a professional background, would find it much easier to find a community mediator from the same culture than a commercial mediator. Although a mediator does not have to be from the same culture as the parties to the dispute, it is much easier for the parties to establish rapport with the mediator when this is the case.

Where a dispute is between members of one church, it may be useful to have as mediator someone from the same community, either from within the same church, or from the geographical neighbourhood. Although in the case of Camden Mediation Service, not all the mediators have connections with Camden, a certain amount of local knowledge is likely to be helpful when discussing options with the parties, and therefore local mediators have an advantage over mediators with no connection with Camden.[100]

In community mediation there are usually two mediators; in commercial mediation only one. This is not an invariable rule: there is no reason why one person cannot act as sole mediator in a community dispute if he and the parties are comfortable with this. Similarly, in large commercial mediations involving numerous parties – a dispute over a major construction project involving architects, quantity surveyors, numerous contractors, sub-contractors, suppliers and the employer is a typical example – it is often essential to have more than one mediator to avoid time being wasted: while the mediator is having a private session with one party, all the others may have nothing to do. One of the reasons why commercial mediations only have one mediator is cost: each commercial mediator expects to be paid. In community mediations, the mediators give their time voluntarily.

The distinction between having one mediator and two is blurred by the apprenticeship system known as pupillage. A newly qualified CEDR mediator has to do two pupillage mediations before he can expect CEDR to put his name forward as a mediator. Pupils are not paid, but many mediators allow their pupil to play a significant part in the mediation, seeing the papers in advance, discussing tactics with the mediator, taking part in the discussions with each party, making suggestions, assisting with drafting any settlement document, and in any other way the mediator may find useful.

Community mediation has a slightly different apprenticeship system. Camden Mediation Service mediators go out on their first case straight after completing the training session, and learn the skills of the job by being paired with a more experienced mediator. After six months, in which they will normally finish about

---

[100] On the usefulness of local knowledge, see Brown and Marriott, *ADR Principles and Practice*, 2nd edn., pg. 334.

four cases, their performance is reviewed, and if it is satisfactory they become fully qualified, and able to handle cases without needing to be paired with a more experienced mediator. Six months should be sufficient to give new mediators sufficient practice of home visits, but, in the author's opinion, gives insufficient experience of face-to-face sessions, as only about one-quarter of cases lead to a face-to-face session.[101]

In the church context, there is no reason in principle why two mediators are required for all disputes. For 'problem' disputes, where a commercial mediation may be appropriate, one commercial mediator should suffice. For 'people' disputes, where a community model is more appropriate, two mediators may be better able than one to achieve rapport with both of the parties, and encourage a transformation of their relationship.

A 'problem' dispute may be illustrated by *Liverpool RC Diocese v Goldberg*.[102] This was a claim for professional negligence by the Diocese against Mr Goldberg QC for tax advice given in 1989. The case is reported on the question whether the claim was barred by the Limitation Act 1980. Mr Goldberg had no personal connection with the Diocese.[103] The claim was purely a professional matter, with no relationship element. If mediation had been suggested, the case would therefore be appropriate for a commercial style mediation, with one mediator. In contrast, the typical employment dispute within a parish where relationship elements are foremost is well suited to the community model, and to two mediators.[104]

---

[101] See pg. 288, figure 12, 'Camden Mediation Service statistics'. The Bristol Mediation statistics on pg. 288 are that only 14% of cases went to a face-to-face mediation.

[102] *Liverpool RC Diocese v Goldberg* [2001] 1 All ER 172.

[103] To emphasise this point, Mr Goldberg QC is Jewish.

[104] Following the trial of the substantive action, the case was settled on confidential terms after the draft judgment was circulated to the parties

iii　The people involved – other persons present at the mediation

In community mediation, there are usually no additional persons present at the mediation apart from the parties and the mediator, an observer, and perhaps one or two 'supporters', persons who are there to give moral support to the parties, but who do not play an active role in the mediation.　In commercial mediations the parties will frequently have their lawyers and sometimes their experts present in addition to the parties.

The role of the lawyer is to advise the client on the strengths and weakness of the case; to act as advocate, presenting the case well at the mediation; to advise on negotiation; and to assist in documenting an agreement if settlement is reached.　The role of experts – accountants, surveyors, doctors, computer experts or whatever the case requires – is similar.　They can assist the party employing them to understand the strengths of its case; they help explain to the mediator (in private session) technical points, and the strengths and weaknesses of their case, so that the mediator can put points to the other side; they help their party consider options for settlement; they may be able to resolve certain issues in discussion with the other side; and they have a tactical role, to show that a party treats the dispute seriously and is prepared to fight the action.　Experts have to be paid for, and at (typically) £1,000 or more for a day, it is no light matter deciding to bring an expert to a mediation; but this fee may be small in the context of a large commercial dispute, and be well worthwhile.　In practice, if expert evidence is likely to be used in the action, it is usual to have the expert there at the mediation.　It is not usually necessary to have an accountant present just to deal with tax advice, but it may be essential to have him on the end of a telephone right up into the evening, so that he can be called if necessary.

---

by the judge: *Liverpool RC Trustees Inc v Goldberg (No. 3) (Practice Note)* [2001] 1 WLR 2337.

In 'problem' church disputes, if the parties have already instructed solicitors, the solicitors would usually wish to attend the mediation. In 'people' church disputes, hopefully the mediation will be taking place before positions have become entrenched and solicitors instructed. If *Liverpool RC Diocese v Goldberg*[105] had gone to mediation, one would expect both Mr Goldberg and the Diocese to have their solicitors present at the mediation, and both sides may well have had their own tax experts also present, as the whole case centred on detailed tax knowledge.[106]

iv   The people involved – the mediation service provider

A mediation service provides a number of functions. Some train and accredit mediators, others rely on their mediators having been trained elsewhere. For example, in the field of commercial mediation, CEDR and the Chartered Institute of Arbitrators provide training in commercial mediation, but the Centre for Business Arbitration (a much smaller organisation than CEDR and the Chartered Institute) does not provide training for mediators. Most community mediation services provide training for their volunteers before sending them out as mediators. Camden Mediation Service is typical in this.

The second function is to provide the necessary back-up administration for mediations. Mention has been made[107] of CEDR's estimate that each mediation takes on average eight hours of administrative time before the parties meet the mediator. This includes attempting to persuade one or more parties to attend a mediator, agreeing the identity of the mediator, agreeing fees, arranging practical matters such as the date, the time, and the location, and ensuring that the written case summaries are delivered on time. There is less administrative back-up for a community

---

[105] *Liverpool RC Diocese v Goldberg* [2001] 1 All ER 172.

[106] A tax expert present at the mediation would be appropriate in this case, because the case centres on tax advice.

[107] Pg. 165.

mediation, but there are still case files to be opened, telephone calls and correspondence. For example, although the mediators contact the parties to arrange the date and time for the home visits, once a visit is arranged Camden Mediation Service writes a confirmation letter to the party and to each mediator confirming the date and time.

The figures for Camden Mediation Service give an example of the total cost of providing a community mediation service. The total income of Camden Mediation Service for the year ended 31 March 2000 was £70,465.[108] The principal source of income was an 'arms-length' service agreement with the London Borough of Camden from whom Camden Mediation Service received £57,000. Other grants were received from the Tudor Trust, the Freemasons' Grand Charity, Hampstead Wells and Camden Trust, and Lloyds TSB Foundation for England and Wales. The expenditure over the year was £57,000 in salaries (three full-time employees), £900 in volunteer training, and £11,000 in other operating costs.

The annual review for Camden Mediation Service for the period April 1998 to March 1999[109] records that Camden Mediation Service had 147 referrals in the 1998/99 year. Dividing the £70,465 cost of running the service by 147 indicates that the administrative cost of each case is £479.35, or nearly £500.

One would hope that no diocese would have to deal with 147 disputes in the course of a year. But if my estimate is right that each diocese has typically six on-going disputes at any one time,[110] that is more than 250 in total over the country. An overall budget of £125,000 a year in administration costs to resolve this

---

[108] These figures come from the Camden Mediation Service Annual Review 1999–2000 (Camden Mediation Service, 2000).

[109] Camden Mediation Service Annual Review 1999–2000 (Camden Mediation Service, 2000)

[110] *Church Times*, 8 October 1999 pg. 3 reporting my remarks at the CEDR conference on 5 October 1999 on managing church conflict.

number of disputes is still small in comparison to the £600,000 in legal fees spent in the Westminster Abbey dispute,[111] or even a conservative estimate of £5,000 to £10,000 per case for more ordinary disputes.

v The type of dispute

Community mediation recognises that conflict stems not just from tangible difficulties such as noise or boundary disputes, but also from issues such as inequality, differences in life style, culture, background, age, the lack of communication skills, all of which can be addressed by mediation. Commercial mediation concentrates on tangible issues; factual rather than relational differences; matters which, if the dispute is not settled, would be appropriate for a court hearing.

While some church disputes raise one or more concrete issues, many raise a number of intangible matters involving emotions and relational matters. The surface dispute often hides a number of deeper issues between the parties, and these need to be addressed if a mediated solution is not to be simply a 'quick fix'. The transformative model of community mediation, aiming for an improved relationship between the parties, rather than a concrete solution to the particular problem which brought the parties to mediation, is more suited to such cases than the commercial model.

Some church disputes do not involve relational matters either at all or to any degree. A hierarchical dispute between a parish and the diocesan authority may be one such; so may be a dispute over who owns a particular property, a commercial dispute concerning an item purchased by the church, a claim for personal injury suffered on the church premises, a tax dispute between the

---

[111] *Neary v Dean of Westminster* [1999] IRLR 288, (1998) 5 Ecc LJ 303. See chapter 2, 'The Westminster Abbey dispute'.

church and the revenue authority, or a claim for professional negligence against a church architect.

This suggests that a church dispute may need to be categorised as a 'people' dispute or a 'problem' dispute, to see which model of mediation is more appropriate. Where relational issues are likely to be important, the community model is more appropriate than the commercial model; but where the issues are more problem-orientated, where factual issues need to be resolved rather than relationships healed, the commercial mediation model is better suited to the task.

vi The process

There are many differences between the community model and the commercial model process. From the parties' perspective, the main differences between commercial and community mediation are, first, the level of formality, and second, the level of personal emotional involvement. Commercial mediations are somewhat formal, almost stylised, especially for parties who have experienced the process already. Some insurers, for example, are very familiar with the mediation process, and know how to use it as part of the negotiation plan in a dispute. In contrast, community mediation is much more informal, and the parties are unlikely to have had much experience of the process before. Commercial mediations concentrate on the problem side of the conflict triangle; whereas community mediation – especially transformative mediation – concentrates on the relationships between the parties, and sees transforming these relationships as more important than resolving the particular problem which on the surface is the dispute between the parties.

This formality is partly related to the parties who are present at the mediation. Lawyers for one or more parties are frequently present in commercial mediations, but they are almost never present at a community mediation. If one party wanted to have a lawyer present, Camden Mediation Service would initially try to discourage them from this. If the party insisted on having a lawyer present, Camden Mediation Service would refuse to allow it, even if that meant that the mediation process came to an end, and the file had to be closed. Similarly, experts are often present at commercial mediations, but they will almost never be present at a community mediation. There are two reasons for this. First, the presence of lawyers and experts would be likely to detract from the transformative potential of the mediation process. Lawyers and experts would be likely to concentrate on the problem side of the mediation triangle, the facts of the dispute. The potential for the mediation to transform the relationships of the parties is thus reduced. Second, community mediation is intended to be informal and inexpensive. If one party has a lawyer or expert present, the other party is likely to be disempowered without similar support. The process will be more expensive, more formal, and almost indistinguishable from commercial mediation.

The practical arrangements for the mediation are different. In a commercial mediation, the parties usually do not meet the mediator until the mediation session. In community mediation, the home visits are an important element in the process, and take place before the face-to-face meeting. The result is that a commercial mediation can be much quicker than a community mediation: commercial mediations are frequently arranged and finished within a fortnight; community mediations frequently involve a visit to party A one week, a visit to party B a week or more later, and a face-to-face mediation a week or more later still. Commercial mediations take place in one long session, frequently lasting a whole day; face-to-face community mediations last from two to three hours. Commercial mediations take place during the working day; community mediations frequently take place during the evening or the weekend, because of the work commitments of the mediators or the parties. Commercial mediations frequently take place in expensive offices or hotel suites; community mediations take place in neutral territory, usually at the mediation service's own premises.

The stage in the dispute at which mediation takes place is also likely to be different. In commercial mediations it is common for the parties already to be enmeshed in legal proceedings; in community mediation this is unusual. The existence of proceedings is not a bar to the use of the community mediation model; it is just that in a relationship dispute, parties are likely to attempt mediation before they issue proceedings; whereas in a commercial dispute – especially a dispute essentially about money – it is often the case that mediation is only attempted after proceedings have been commenced. The result is that in commercial mediation much effort is frequently needed to negotiate the costs of the legal proceedings, whereas in community mediation this is not necessary.

In the case of church disputes, much dispute resolution takes place at an informal level, before positions become entrenched, and relationships broken.[112] The community mediation model can be seen as an extension of the informal process which already takes place within church life, and in which clergy and other church leaders already play a part. The commercial model is a more formal process, and one which seems less part of normal church life. It may however be appropriate for disputes between a church and outside bodies, or for other 'problem' disputes rather than 'people' disputes. The formality of commercial mediation is apparent in the need for a mediation agreement, the payment of fees, the need to deal with a professional organisation such as CEDR if the parties can not find a mediator directly, the presence of lawyers, and the possibility of legal proceedings if matters are not resolved. Settlements of commercial mediations are intended to have legal effect: settlement of community mediations are not. Community mediation centres on relationships rather than factual issues; and how a relationship works is not the subject of which most legal contracts are made.[113]

---

[112] See chapter 3, 'Church dispute resolution in the United Kingdom'.

[113] This may be a cultural matter. A cohabitation agreement is a document that spells out the terms of a relationship and often addresses fi-

vii The outcome

Commercial mediation thrives on statistics. Success rates are quoted, and the only outcome which is regarded as a success is a resolution of the dispute. The transformation model for mediation is suspicious of statistics, as it regards improved relationships as intangible and not susceptible of statistical analysis. However funders do require statistics, and mediation services therefore have to maintain them.

The statistics for Camden Mediation Service for the period April 1998 to March 1999 record success rates as good as any commercial mediation supplier, for the cases that actually go to a face-to-face mediation. The difficulty in both types of mediation is to persuade the parties to attempt to mediate at all. Of the 147 referrals in the 1998/99 year, 40 cases (27%) went to face-to-face mediations. Of these 40 face-to-face mediations, 38 (95%) resulted in an agreement at the mediation session. The outcome of the remaining cases is shown in figure 12.

---

nancial issues and how property will be divided if the relationship ends. It is said that some American cohabitation contracts even specify the frequency of matters such as love-making. For an example (which does not include this detail) see *www.neo-tech.com/love-contract/*.

Number of mediation sessions	40	27.2%
Cases resolved after visits by mediators	24	16.3%
Parties declined further involvement	33	22.4%
Clients moved away	3	2.1%
Inappropriate referrals	3	2.1%
No contact with second party	23	15.6%
Clients refused mediation	21	14.3%
Total	147	100.0%

Figure 12. Camden Mediation Service statistics[114]

The statistics for Bristol Mediation as at 1997 are similar.[115] Bristol Mediation had 128 referrals in the 1996/1997 year. 18 of these cases (14%) went to a face-to-face mediation, and of these 18, all but one face-to-face mediation resulted in an agreement. Shuttle mediations were 22%. 14% involved visits to both parties, but 50% did not get beyond first party visits. So there is a very good success rate where the parties go to face-to-face mediation, but only a small proportion of the cases proceed to this stage.

5. THE THEOLOGY OF THE COMMUNITY MEDIATION MODEL

In chapter 3, attention was drawn to an emerging pastoral theology of conflict resolution in the church. Both community and commercial mediation fit within this theology, but it will be

---

[114] The percentages have been slightly adjusted to make the total come to exactly 100%.

[115] Marian Liebmann, *Community and Neighbour Mediation*, pg. 99–100.

argued that the community model is more suitable theologically than the commercial model for most church disputes.

Where the community model really scores over the commercial model theologically is in the community model's potential to transform relationships. The gospel is about relationships: our relationship with God and our relationships with our fellow human beings. These are more important than our material possessions,[116] which are generally the stuff of commercial disputes. Jesus' summary of the law was to love God with all one's heart, soul and mind, and to love one's neighbour as oneself.[117] Where two Christians are in conflict, obedience to this commandment is difficult, if not impossible. Enabling the transformation of the relationship between the neighbours is itself being obedient to this commandment.

There is a recurrent theme in church disputes that the problem which presents itself to a mediator may only be the surface problem, and a mediator must be on the lookout for deeper issues, involving the relationships between the parties. If the dispute is an isolated event free from emotions and relationships, such as the *Goldberg* dispute over tax advice,[118] then the potential for transformed relationships which is the hallmark of the community model is irrelevant. Where the parties have always been at arm's length, and lawyers have become involved, the commercial model of mediation is appropriate. But where transformation of relationships is or may be relevant, and the parties are still prepared to speak to each other (in the presence of the mediator), the community model scores over the commercial model.

---

[116] Matthew 6:19.

[117] Matthew 22:37–39.

[118] *Liverpool RC Diocese v Goldberg* [2001] 1 All ER 172; *Liverpool RC Trustees Inc v Goldberg (No. 3) (Practice Note)* [2001] 1 WLR 2337.

It has already been argued[119] that the key tools of transformative mediation, empowerment and recognition, are thoroughly Christian concepts. But they are not the answer to every case of power imbalance. Bush and Folger point out the danger of mediation being used as a means of perpetuating oppression.[120] Mediation handles disputes without reference to other, similar cases, and without reference to the public interest, and thereby can be used to cover up a major social issue by dealing with each case privately and confidentially. Empowerment may not in practice be possible in cases of oppression, and mediation in such cases should only be used in conjunction with some other process to address the wider social concern. The Mennonites' training course encourages mediators to see beyond the parties to the larger issues that may be at stake. An example in the commercial context would be where party A has suffered injury from using a product manufactured by party B, and party B seeks a mediation of the dispute in order to avoid the risk of injury becoming public knowledge. Another example would be where a school sought to expel a black student, and the student threatened to take the school to court for racial discrimination. Mediation of the dispute between the student and the school would not in itself address the wider issue of racial prejudice and discrimination which may be present at the school. An example in a Church context would be using mediation to cover up instances of criminal conduct such as sexual abuse and some cases of racial discrimination.

Although the Church needs to be aware that mediation can be used for improper motives, this is no reason to reject its use for the many cases where it can properly help resolve disputes.

The need for empowerment is likely to arise in many church disputes. Any 'vertical' dispute (such as clergy vs. bishop, employer vs. employee) as opposed to 'horizontal' dispute (one

---

[119] Pg. 227.

[120] Robert Bush and Joseph Folger, *The Promise of Mediation*, pg. 22.

member of a team vs. another member of a team) will invariably have a power element; and community mediation addresses this power element far more than does commercial mediation.

The informality of community mediation has a theological significance. The incarnation involved Jesus humbling himself, and coming down from heaven to meet us where we are, as sinners.[121] Jesus entered into people's homes[122] to heal them or their families, and to transform their relationship to God.[123] In community mediation the process of empowerment and recognition begins in the home visits, not just when the parties meet at the face-to-face mediation. Here the community model is better suited to a church context than the mediation model taught by the Mennonites: the Mennonite model begins with the face-to-face meeting, and does not include home visits.[124]

The community model involves the mediator speaking directly to the parties, rather than to the parties through their lawyers or only to their lawyers. Jesus' question to the disciples was direct: 'But what about you? Who do you say I am?'[125] Jesus came to give us free access to God, without the need for an intermediary.[126] He spoke directly to people, as opposed to through inter-

---

[121] Philippians 2:5–9.

[122] Including the homes of outcasts such as Simon the leper: Matthew 26:6.

[123] See Matthew 8:14 and Mark 5:38 for examples of healings; Luke 19:1–10 tells the story of Zacchaeus, a man transformed by a home visit from Jesus.

[124] The director of the London Mennonite Centre disagrees with this criticism. It is his practice to visit or at least speak on the telephone to each party before a face-to-face mediation. Whatever his personal practice, the subject of home visits was not mentioned on the five-day training course attended by the author.

[125] Matthew 16:15.

[126] Romans 5:2; Ephesians 2:18.

mediaries such as the prophets.[127] Lawyers can greatly assist the mediation process by providing appropriate help to their client and to the mediator,[128] but they should not generally seek to prevent the mediator speaking directly to the parties.[129]

The Church is an institution, but it is more than an institution: it is a living body, seeking to follow its living Lord. Its theology needs to permeate every part of its activity. In seeking to resolve conflict the Church is healing its own body of the disease of disunity, and helping to restore peace. Mediation assists the Church in this task, and thereby assists it in its mission to the world.

The parallel between the geographical community and the Church as a community of believers has already been noted. Christians are described as a body, and 'as members of one body you were called to peace'.[130]

The concept of using mediators from within the Christian community to assist resolving Christian disputes corresponds also with the idea of using people's individual gifts for the benefit of the whole body.[131]

The Church can therefore embrace both forms of mediation with integrity, but the community mediation process is theologically more Christian – more like the ministry of Christ – than is commercial mediation.

---

[127] Hebrews 1:1-2.

[128] Brown and Marriott, *ADR Principles and Practice*, 2nd edn. chapter 19 covers the lawyer's role in detail.

[129] The author was assistant mediator in one commercial mediation where one party's lawyer took this course, and the whole day was wasted. Brown and Marriott, *ADR Principles and Practice*, 2nd edn. at pg. 433 states 'mediators are usually willing and sometimes keen to communicate as freely with the parties as with their lawyers'.

[130] Colossians 3:15.

[131] 1 Corinthians 12:12–27.

6. CONCLUSIONS

The first and most important conclusion is that the community model provides a very useful model for resolving many, if not most, church disputes. The community model has much in common with the mediation model which is used successfully by the Mennonite Church, and so the Church can be confident that the community model will work well. The key differences between the community model and the Mennonite model are (a) the community model use of home visits, and (b) the Mennonite emphasis on healing. The Church should have no difficulty theologically in applying the community model to church disputes. In short, in all cases where the issue between the parties may involve their relationship with each other, the community model has much to recommend it.

There are still some cases where the community model may not be appropriate. The commercial model is likely to be preferable where the relationship between the parties is purely professional, and should be considered in all cases where litigation has already begun. (Community mediation can still be used where litigation has begun, but if the parties want their lawyers to attend the mediation, then the commercial model is more apt for two reasons: first, the lawyers will be more familiar with the process; second, it is more suited to disputes which are the subject of litigation than is the community model.)

The advantages of the community model over the commercial model are many: the emphasis on transforming relationships; the low cost; the use of people within the community rather than outside professionals; the lack of need for lawyers; the informality of the process; and the length of the meetings (2-3 hours, rather than a whole day) are some that have been mentioned.

Conflict management is starting to be taught to clergy, and in particular to archdeacons. As the community mediation model is so appropriate for many church disputes, they should be taught about it, so that they can encourage its use in cases of conflict.

This teaching should include how to recognise those cases for which the commercial model may be more appropriate, and which cases may be appropriate for the consensus-building model described in chapter 6. The Mennonites caution about using mediation in every case, so clergy also need to learn to recognise where there are wider social issues in a dispute that cannot be addressed by mediation alone.

Churches need to encourage their members to train as community mediators (or to attend a course run by the Mennonite Church) to learn the skills of community mediation. Dioceses should start to maintain a list of names of Christians who have been taught these skills and who are willing to offer them to the Church as part of their Christian service, so that dioceses and archdeacons know upon whom to call in cases of need.

As has been shown, the community mediation model embodies much Christian theology, and yet does not recognise the fact. Many Christians have felt a call to work in this area, serving in local community mediation services, and in some cases founding, chairing or directing such services.[132] How much better it would be for the Church to offer mediation to the community, making express what is not recognised by community mediation, namely that this is a Christian ministry. Mediation is a practical expression of the Church's ministry of reconciliation. As the theological introduction to the Church of England's services of wholeness and healing states, 'healing, reconciliation and restoration are integral to the good news of Jesus Christ'.[133] Mending relationships is part of healing, a matter for Christian celebration,[134] and a

---

[132] Yvonne Craig, *Peacemaking for churches* (London, SPCK, 1999), pg. 74.

[133] *Common Worship: Pastoral Services* (London, Church House Publishing, 2000), pg. 10.

[134] See the intercessions in the service 'A Celebration of Wholeness and Healing', *Common Worship: Pastoral Services* (London, Church House Publishing, 2000), pg. 17: 'Mend broken relationships, and restore to those in distress soundness of mind and sincerity of spirit'. Similarly,

means for evangelism.[135] It is a work encouraged by both Christ[136] and the Apostles,[137] and of which we see examples in both the Old Testament[138] and the New.[139]

The Mennonites see their role as peacemakers for the world, not just for the Church.[140] 'Reconciliation is central to Christ's mission on earth. It is both our mission, and our distinguishing characteristic as followers of Christ.'[141] The Church of England should make a start in the same direction.

Most community mediation is provided free to the parties. But the cost of running a mediation service is significant. If the Church is to develop this kind of ministry in-house, a cost analysis needs to be carried out. The figures for Camden Mediation Service suggest that an administrative cost of approximately £500 per case may be about right. This figure is small in comparison

---

the Prayer of Penitence, 'We have not loved out neighbour as ourselves', and the Absolution, 'By the ministry of reconciliation entrusted by Christ to his Church, receive his pardon and peace', *ibid.*, pg. 18-19.

[135] Compare Mark 6:7-13, the commission to the disciples to preach and to heal.

[136] Matthew 5:9.

[137] Ephesians 4:3; James 3:18.

[138] Abraham: Genesis 13:8–9; Joab: 2 Samuel 14:1-23; Moses: Exodus 2:14 as explained in Acts 7:26. The parties in this instance refused to accept Moses as mediator.

[139] Philippians 4: 2–3. See pg. 7, fn. 28.

[140] Carolyn Schrock-Shenk and Lawrence Ressler, *Making Peace with Conflict* (Waterloo, Ontario, Herald Press, 1999), chapter 17, 'Global conflict'.

[141] Carolyn Schrock-Shenk (ed.), *Mediation and Facilitation Training Manual*, 4th edn., pg. 25. The following passages are referred to in support: 2 Corinthians 5:17–20; Ephesians 2:13–17; Colossians 1:19–22; and Colossians 3:10–11.

with the cost of any one dispute which escalates to legal proceedings.[142]

Although community mediation includes 'facilitation', the handling of large groups and building consensus amongst such groups, this is not the stuff of normal community mediation. For large congregational disputes, facilitators trained in these skills should be employed to assist. This is the subject of the next chapter.

---

[142] See the section 'Financial cost', pg. 478.

Chapter 6

CONSENSUS-BUILDING MEDIATION

Oure conseil was nat longe for to seche.
Us thoughte it was noght worth to make it wys
And graunted hym withouten moore avys,
And bad him seye his voirdit as hym leste.[1]

---

[1] Geoffrey Chaucer, *The Canterbury Tales*, 'The General Prologue' (lines 784–7) (London, Penguin Books, 1996).

In David Wright's translation:

> We were not long in making up our minds.
> It seemed not worth deliberating, so
> We gave our consent without more ado,
> Told him to give us what commands he wished.

Geoffrey Chaucer, *The Canterbury Tales*, translated by David Wright (Oxford University Press, 1985).

1. INTRODUCTION

Mediation as used in complex, multi-party, public disputes goes under a number of names: consensus-building is one of the more common. Others are *community participation, community problem-solving, public issue mediation,* or simply *large group mediation.* The key element which distinguishes this form of mediation from commercial and community mediation is the emphasis on the process side of the conflict triangle.

Different models of mediation tend to concentrate on different sides of the conflict triangle. Thus, commercial mediation tends to concentrate on resolving the problem side of the triangle, the factual dispute. Feelings are not ignored, but they play a lesser part. In many cases, the dispute is settled simply by a payment of money, and there is no continuing relationship between the parties. But in some cases the mediation has restored the personal relationship between the parties, and this leads to a settlement involving a new long-term commercial relationship.

Similarly, community mediation tends to concentrate on the people side of the triangle. One of the current debates among community mediators is whether the object of mediation is resolution of the dispute or transformation of the parties.[2] One of the seminars at the Mediation UK Annual Conference held in Sheffield in April 2001 was entitled 'Facts or Feelings', which puts the contrast well. In chapter 5, 'Community mediation', it has been argued that both facts and feelings are important, but that feelings come first. In many cases it is only when the relationship between the parties is transformed that they can begin to work construc-

---

[2] See Robert Bush and Joseph Folger, *The Promise of Mediation* (San Francisco, Jossey-Bass, 1994).

298

tively to resolve the particular problem which brought them to mediation. As has been shown, this perspective reflects Christian values, and this underlines its suitability in a Church context.

Consensus-building mediation concentrates on the third side of the conflict triangle, the process. This model is used for environmental disputes, health care issues, racial conflict, church congregations, industrial disputes, and voluntary organisations.[3] The mediator's task is to devise a process so that all the people involved, known as 'stakeholders', feel their interests are listened to, and can give their consent to the process and to the settlement which is reached. Much of the lead for this type of mediation has come from the USA.[4]

The three mediation models described in this and the last two chapters, and the different emphasis for each model is illustrated by a new triangle, the mediation model triangle, shown in figure 13.

---

[3] Henry Brown and Arthur Marriott, *ADR Principles and Practice*, 2nd edn. (London, Sweet & Maxwell, 1999), chapter 14; Lawrence Susskind, Sarah McKearnan and Jennifer Thomas-Larmer (ed.), *The Consensus Building Handbook*.

[4] Indeed, the USA has led the field also in commercial and community mediation; but these have now become well established in the UK. Consensus-building mediation in the UK is still in its infancy.

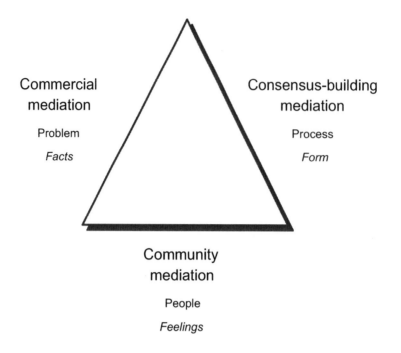

Commercial
mediation

Problem

Facts

Consensus-building
mediation

Process

Form

Community
mediation

People

Feelings

Figure 13. Mediation model triangle

The main elements of consensus-building mediation which distinguish it from commercial and community mediation are, first, its multi-party nature, and, second, its complexity. In environmental disputes, for example, even though the interested parties may be organised into representative groups, it is quite common for 50 or more groups to be interested at varying levels of involvement.[5] Similarly, a range of public policy issues are frequently in contention in environmental disputes, compounded by differences in national and local perspectives within each interest, together with related interests of power.

---

[5] Marian Liebmann, *Mediation in Context* (London, Jessica Kingsley Publishers, 2000), pg. 211.

In the USA, much of the training and leading work in this field is organised by the Consensus Building Institute.[6] In England, the Environment Council[7] pioneered the stakeholder dialogue approach to environmental decision-making, and conducts training in facilitation. Facilitation means a way of helping groups work together in meetings, while mediation means the intervention by an impartial person into a negotiation or dispute to help the people concerned resolve their differences in a voluntary and mutually acceptable manner. 'While most mediators are skilled facilitators, not all facilitators have been trained to mediate.'[8] In the context of church disputes affecting large numbers of people, a person is needed who is trained as a mediator, and who can handle large groups.

The following are some examples of recent consensus-building mediations:

i The decommissioning of the Brent Spar oil rig

When Shell's Brent Spar oil rig had completed its functions and needed to be decommissioned, a substantial dispute arose as to the method of disposal, led by Greenpeace. Shell commissioned the Environment Council to design a stakeholder dialogue process to ensure that Shell heard the concerns of and suggestions from a wide variety of stakeholders before taking its decision. Workshops were held in 1996 and 1997 attended by Greenpeace, Friends of the Earth, the Institute of Maritime Engineers, other

---

[6] The Consensus Building Institute Inc., 131 Mt. Auburn Street, Cambridge, MA 02138, USA. *www.cbi-web.org*.

[7] The Environment Council, 212 High Holborn, London WC1V 7VW. *www.the-environment-council.org.uk*. The Environment Council's training courses began in 1991. For the early history of consensus-building mediation in the UK, see Andrew Acland, *Resolving disputes without going to court* (London, Century Ltd, 1995), pg. 212–3.

[8] Lawrence Susskind, Sarah McKearnan and Jennifer Thomas-Larmer (ed.), *The Consensus Building Handbook*, pg. 8.

engineers, academics, trade unions, environmentalists, and consumer interests. Shell's final recommendation to the UK government in 1998 to reuse the Brent Spar and build a new quarry extension at Mekjarvik near Stavager in Norway, was one which 'would satisfy key stakeholders'.[9]

ii Amsterdam's Schiphol Airport

This was a development dispute triggered by ambitious plans to expand Amsterdam's Schiphol Airport in the 1980s. The case involved issues of airfield extension, configuration of the runways, noise abatement, and the regulation of night flights. Parties involved included municipal, provincial and national government agencies, and business interests.[10]

iii Northern Oxford County, Maine, Coalition

In 1991 a dispute arose between residents in Northern Oxford County, Maine, USA and a local paper mill over possible links between emissions from the mill, levels of air pollution, and cancer rates. The parties involved included local residents, health care providers, small businesses, the mill managers and government officials.[11]

iv A church dispute

Allegations of sexual and financial misconduct against the pastor of a church in the USA led to his resignation in 1990, and to the church being torn apart by the trauma of those who supported him and those who did not. The mediator developed with the

---

[9] Brown and Marriott, *ADR Principles and Practice*, 2nd edn. (London, Sweet & Maxwell, 1999), pg. 312; Liebmann, *Mediation in Context*, pg. 220.

[10] This is case study 1 in Lawrence Susskind, Sarah McKearnan and Jennifer Thomas-Larmer (ed.), *The Consensus Building Handbook*.

[11] This is case study 2 in Lawrence Susskind, Sarah McKearnan and Jennifer Thomas-Larmer (ed.), *The Consensus Building Handbook*.

church a reconciliation process which was held over two week-
ends in February 1993 and February 1994. This led to a healing of
the trauma, and to a church ready to move on to a new vision for
the future. The mediator describes the 'neutralising history' process, as 'an exercise designed to enable naming and letting go of
past painful events'. In chapter 5, the Mennonite mediation
model was described as combining problem solving with healing.
It is no surprise that the mediator of this case was formerly assistant director of the Mennonite Conciliation Service from 1986
to 1988.[12]

v HIV prevention

A consensus building process was used for HIV prevention
strategies in the state of Colorado in 1994.[13] The stakeholders included persons afflicted with AIDS, relatives of those infected,
gay rights activists, health care professionals and social workers,
and evangelical and fundamentalist Christians. There were
about 110 representatives of the various stakeholder groups present at the mediation.

vi Abortion

In 1996 a consensus-building process was used in 1996 and
concerned finding common ground between the pro-life and the
pro-choice abortion lobbies in the USA.[14] For those seeking com-

---

[12] This is case study 17 in Lawrence Susskind, Sarah McKearnan and
Jennifer Thomas-Larmer (ed.), *The Consensus Building Handbook*. It is
noteworthy that a church example is included as one of the 17 case
studies in this book.

[13] This is case study 15 in Lawrence Susskind, Sarah McKearnan and
Jennifer Thomas-Larmer (ed.), *The Consensus Building Handbook*.

[14] This is case study 16 in Lawrence Susskind, Sarah McKearnan and
Jennifer Thomas-Larmer (ed.), *The Consensus Building Handbook*. The
abortion issue has both religious and constitutional significance in the
USA, following the landmark decision of the Supreme Court in 1973 in
Roe v Wade (1973) 410 US 113.

plete reconciliation as the only acceptable outcome, the abortion mediation failed to produce consensus. But as a medium for mutual informing, evolving common ground, and building trust between the two lobby groups concerned, the process was 'overwhelmingly successful'.[15]

vii   Chichester

After serious flooding of Chichester from the River Lavant in 1996, the Environment Agency developed a scheme to prevent such flooding in the future. The scheme involved diverting water off the Lavant in times of flood and routing it through Pagham Rife into Pagham Harbour. Local residents were concerned as to the effect the scheme would have on Pagham village and the surrounding area. The mediation took place in May 2001 and involved the Pagham Parish Council representing local residents in Pagham, local landowners, the Environment Agency, and the West Sussex County Council.[16]

viii   Kenyan tribespeople and Alder Hey Hospital disputes

In 2002 a dispute between the Ministry of Defence and a group representing Kenyan tribespeople maimed or killed by British landmines in Kenya was resolved by mediation. Compensation of £4.5 million was agreed.[17] Also in 2002 a dispute between the NHS and a group representing the parents of children whose organs were retained without permission by Alder Hey Hospital was resolved by mediation. The settlement included financial

---

[15] Lawrence Susskind, Sarah McKearnan and Jennifer Thomas-Larmer (ed.), *The Consensus Building Handbook*, pg. 1046.

[16] The author is grateful to Christopher Napier, a former partner in Clifford Chance who was one of the mediators of the River Lavant mediation, for a copy of the report he wrote for CEDR of this mediation.

[17]: See *www.landmineaction.org/news139.asp*.

compensation, an apology to the parents, a memorial to the children at the hospital, and a donation to charity.[18]

These examples cover a large range of activities, mostly commercial; some international, some local; with several involving disputes over values deeply held by Christians and others.

The example of trauma recovery is perhaps not an obvious application of mediation for a church, but it is a documented example of mediation being used for a church dispute involving a whole congregation. More obvious applications for this type of mediation in the context of the Church are disputes over a proposed change, for example, an alteration to the church building, a decision to alter the services, or a decision to dispense with the choir. Consensus-building mediation can be used to shape church policy over controversial issues such as the church's attitude to homosexuals, or whether and how a church should welcome a convicted paedophile into the congregation. Consensus-building can be used to heal broken relationships, in particular a breakdown in the pastoral relationship between the parishioners and the priest.[19]

2. CONSENSUS-BUILDING DECISION-MAKING

Majority voting favours the greater number or the strongest grouping. A compromise suggests a midway position that satisfies nobody. In a debating or adversarial atmosphere, the result is likely to be a win for one party, and a loss for the other. A consensus decision is reached by open discussion, in which the parties collaborate to achieve a win-win solution. Decisions are reached by consent, with each party holding the power of veto. Everyone with an interest, and who is prepared to participate, is

---

[18] See *http://news.bbc.co.uk/1/hi/england/2410565.stm.*

[19] Mediation in the case of pastoral breakdown is expressly provided for in the Code of Practice promulgated by the House of Bishops under section 1 of the Incumbents (Vacation of Benefices) Measure 1997.

involved. The stakeholders are involved in the process of decision-making, as well as the decision itself. They develop and agree a procedure and ground rules which build trust and secure fairness and openness. Process is almost as important as outcome.

Consensus-building has a number of advantages over other methods of decision-making. Consensus-building enables an increased understanding of the issues involved. The procedures allow the parties to explore the problem and consider a range of possible solutions. It therefore produces more intelligent decisions, by incorporating the best thinking of everyone. It keeps people from getting into adversarial attitudes because ideas are treated as coming from the group as a whole, rather than from individuals in the group; so individual egos are not tied to particular proposals. The process of developing procedures itself increases trust between the participants, and this fosters a collaborative approach to resolving the substantive issues. The stakeholders feel they control the process, and that no solution is forced on them against their will. There are savings in time and money over the long term.[20]

However, consensus-building is subject to a number of limitations. First, it may not be possible to obtain consensus, especially where deeply held and non-negotiable beliefs are in issue. The very existence of a veto imports that no solution can be imposed on a party against its will. There is always a danger that the power of veto can be abused by persons seeking to further their own power in the group or to promote their personal advantage. Second, consensus-building can only partially redress major power imbalances. In a church context, for example, it may be difficult for the bishop or his representative to participate within a group as an equal, where the bishop has legal authority to decide

---

[20] Liebmann, *Mediation in Context,* pg. 213. Carolyn Schrock-Shenk (ed.), *Mediation and Facilitation Training Manual,* 4th edn. (Akron, Pennsylvania, Mennonite Conciliation Service, 2000), pg. 227.

the issue.[21] Similarly, a group may be dominated by outspoken or intimidating members. Third, some groups which should be represented in the mediation may lack sufficient organisation for representation to be effective. Fourth, reaching consensus is time-consuming and may be expensive, and the stakeholders may be unwilling to invest the time and money which is needed.[22]

A number of group conditions support consensus-building mediation. The first is a unity of purpose in the group. There should be a basic core of agreement, a common starting point. In a church congregation, there should be little difficulty with this, as all (or almost all) the members have a common Christian faith, even though they may differ as to how this works out in practice. The second condition is equal access to power for all members. This is a potential problem in a hierarchical church like the Church of England, if the dispute involves diocesan authorities as well as the congregation. The third is the willingness to spend the time to design the decision-making process, and to reach an agreement. A fourth requirement is a willingness to attend to attitudes. The building of trust between the members of the group is essential. 'This requires a commitment by individual members to examine their own attitudes and be open to change.'[23] In the

---

[21] But power is never absolute, and even limited power may be surrendered for good reason. Shell no doubt realised the commercial importance of participating in the Brent-Spar consensus-building mediation. Similarly, a bishop may decide (or may be prevailed upon by his brother bishops) to participate in a mediation process for the good of the Church as a whole. There is, after all, a good precedent for laying aside power: Philippians 2:5–9.

[22] Michel Avery et al., *Building United Judgment, a handbook for consensus decision making* (Maddison WI, Centre for Conflict Resolution, 1981, republished Routledge, MO, The Fellowship for Intentional Community, 1999), pg. 7.

[23] Michel Avery et al., *Building United Judgment*, pg. 8.

Mennonite congregational-mediation process,[24] healing of relationships and attitudes comes before problem-solving. Lastly,
there should be a willingness in the group to learn and practice
skills. Both the Mennonite and the Alban Institute[25] congregational-mediation processes include training for the members of
the congregation in conflict.

3. THE CONSENSUS-BUILDING MEDIATION PROCESS

The chapters on the commercial and community mediation
models set out in detail the process adopted for these types of
mediation. There is no one form of process for consensus-
building mediation; indeed one of the key features of consensus-
building mediation is the designing of a suitable process for the
particular dispute. In designing a tailor-made process for the
particular dispute, and getting that process agreed by all the
stakeholders involved in the dispute, every consensus-building
mediation is a 'one-off' process. Yet there are stages and features
which are common to most consensus-building processes, and
which distinguish consensus-building mediation from other mediation models.

i Preliminary

If consensus-building is to be effective, the interested parties
must be identified early, and all parties must have a say in the
terms of reference and the agenda. An analysis of the conflict
needs to be undertaken by the mediator, to consider whether the
mediation has any realistic prospects of reaching a consensual
outcome. The mediator will need to maintain demonstrable neutrality towards the various stakeholders, and seek to ensure that
the process is not abused by anyone for their personal advantage.
This initial assessment is usually undertaken through individual
interviews with likely stakeholders. The mediator will examine

---

[24] See pg. 314.

[25] See pg. 321.

some of the background to the dispute, and try to get a feel for the issues in the case.

The mediator will then make recommendations how to proceed, and may suggest a structure for the process, and whether or not mediation is likely to be appropriate. The mediator may need to approach several of the likely interest groups and stakeholders to make this assessment. 'Facilitators will need to guard against being over-optimistic.'[26]

The next task is to identify the stakeholders. These should include: anyone who will benefit from the proposals, or who may be adversely affected by them; anyone who may help or may delay and hinder the project; anyone who has skills, money or resources they can contribute; and anyone who ultimately is in a position to decide some or all of the issues if the parties cannot reach agreement. Stakeholders therefore are persons who will be affected by the outcome, or who may have some influence over it. In many cases, negotiations take place between groups rather than individuals, and so questions of representation have to be decided. People may need to be identified who can properly speak for the members of a group, and who will be accountable to that group.

Some groups may be well-organised, and properly able to argue their position. Other groups may be disorganised, or lack the resources to prepare their case to the same standard. Mediators may need to redress these power issues, without jeopardising their own neutrality. One way is to encourage the parties to find some representative to assist them. Being a representative for a group is a demanding task: as one becomes involved in the process, and begins to appreciate the other stakeholders' interests, the representative must report back to his group and carry it with him in the process. This includes explaining how particular proposals

---

[26] Brown and Marriott, *ADR Principles and Practice*, 2nd edn., pg. 320.

will affect other groups, and why it is in his group's interest to prefer, say, one option to another.[27]

The initial assessment may take considerable time, and itself require funding, even if the result of the assessment is that the mediation proceeds no further. In environmental disputes, the commercial company proposing to carry out the development may be able easily to fund the entire process, while the environmental groups may have very little funds in comparison. Some means of sharing the cost needs to be devised which is acceptable to all parties, and which does not compromise the mediator's neutrality, or public perception of their neutrality.[28]

ii Design the mediation process

Consensus-building mediations usually involve one or more facilitators, and a recorder. A recorder's function is to capture the group's discussion on flip-charts, and to produce draft meeting summaries. In general, written summaries of all group decisions, as well as points of agreement and disagreement in the dialogue, should be circulated after each meeting for group approval. If there are more than two categories of stakeholders involved in a consensus-building effort, it is useful to appoint an 'executive', 'process' or 'steering' committee, to make decisions between meetings, and to handle logistical decisions. Some consensus-building mediations are confidential, others are public. If members of the public are invited, ground rules for observers will need to be formulated.[29]

---

[27] Lawrence Susskind, Sarah McKearnan and Jennifer Thomas-Larmer (ed.), *The Consensus Building Handbook* chapter 6: 'Representation of stakeholding interests'.

[28] The issue of funding for congregational disputes is discussed at pg. 336.

[29] For example, stakeholders may agree to allow observers a brief comment period at the end of some sessions.

A list of the range of issues to be discussed needs to be agreed. A timetable needs to be arranged for each stage in the process. It is not a good idea to rush through procedural or preliminary matters in order to get to the 'important' issues sooner: for example, training in communication skills may be an important step before the parties can go further. Similarly, the process of discussing and agreeing procedural matters fosters trust between the parties, and leads to a more constructive approach to the substantive issues later in the mediation than if these 'preliminary' matters were rushed through.

Procedural ground rules need to be agreed. The parties may have raised procedural concerns during the initial assessment. The matters may include time-tabling – no meetings after 7 p.m., no meetings on Sundays, or whatever. They may include behavioural guidelines which participants will be expected to follow; rules governing what may or may not be said to the press; decision-making procedures (what matters may be left to a small committee to decide, rather than going to the whole group); strategies for handling disagreement; strategies for ensuring that any agreement which is reached is implemented. It is usual for all participants to sign a copy of the ground rules when they are agreed. Observers may be asked to sign a copy of the ground rules before being allowed to attend any meeting.

Fact-finding procedures may need to be agreed. If opposing parties each seek their own evidence or expert advice, the results are likely to be adversarial.[30] It is better if all participants can agree on a procedure to deal with fact-finding, including (a) what information is sought, (b) who should obtain the data, (c) what

---

[30] The situation is comparable to the use of expert evidence in civil litigation. In the Access to Justice Reports, expert evidence was identified as a major source of problems in the civil justice system. See Lord Woolf, *Interim Report on Access to Justice* (London, HMSO, June 1995), chapter 23, and Lord Woolf *Final Report on Access to Justice* (London, HMSO, July 1996), chapter 13.

method should be employed, and (d) how gaps or disagreements among technical sources will be handled. Appointing a joint fact-finding committee is a good way to build consensus, rather than having each party carry out its own investigation.

Group meetings need to be planned. To help a large group make a decision, it is sometimes useful to build consensus in small groups, and then expand from this to consensus in a large group.[31]

It may be appropriate to clarify the extent to which a precedent is being set. If everyone agrees that no precedent will be set it is usually easier to convince reluctant groups or organisations to participate.

iii   Collaborative problem-solving

Once trust has been established, procedures have been agreed, and any necessary training has been undertaken, the parties can move into the problem-solving stage of the process. As in commercial mediation, this involves generating options, evaluating them, negotiating, and then deciding. Ideas are listed, as many as possible, with the mediator discouraging evaluation until there is a diverse range of options available.

Evaluating involves examining thoughtfully the strengths and weaknesses of each option. To do this, the parties need to identify suitable criteria for evaluation: their respective interests. The parties/mediator will list the strengths and limits of each option, and the impact of each option on the parties. When each option has been evaluated in turn, the various options can be compared to see which best meets the needs of all the parties.

Negotiation should involve dialogue rather than debate. Parties must be encouraged to understand their own and each other's concerns, rather than to 'win'. Active listening should be

---

[31] For an example of this technique, see Carolyn Schrock-Shenk (ed.), *Mediation and Facilitation Training Manual*, 4th edn., pg. 231.

encouraged, listening to understand, rather than to answer. Conclusions should be tested by 'non-binding straw polls' before they are final.[32] The facilitator's job is to enable members to inform others of where their preferences are, and to get a sense of where the majority stands, before inviting consensus.[33]

iv Implementation

Procedures need to be adopted to ensure that a group's representative discusses with the group the penultimate draft before finalising any agreement. The agreement reached may or may not have contractual force, in the sense of creating a legally binding agreement, but with the goodwill built during the mediation process, and if all the options have been thoroughly considered at the mediation, the parties will want to implement it. For example, in the Chichester case, the parties agreed to a 'Memorandum of Understanding' which set out principles agreed between the parties regarding the flood alleviation scheme to be constructed by

---

[32] One way to test for the strength of agreement is to invite people to hold up 1–5 fingers to show their strength of support. Five fingers means unqualified support; four means general support; three means some concerns, but OK; two means lots of concerns, but choose not to block consensus; one means I cannot live with this decision and will block it. When the group responds with almost all 4s and 5s, there is near full approval. The people with 1s, 2s and 3s can be asked to help the group understand their concerns to see if the group as a whole can find ways of solving these concerns, so that they can be met in some way.

[33] A useful technique to prioritise items in a list is to give everyone the same number of coloured sticky dots, and invite them to stick a number of dots against the items which they see as most important. By counting the number of dots against each item, the meeting gets a clear sense of which items are seen as the most important by the group as a whole. This can be used as a way of evaluating between options, or choosing the issues the group sees as most important. It is important to stress however that this technique is not the same as voting, because it is provisional. It merely gives a sense of the meeting, not a final decision.

313

the Environment Agency. These included a monitoring group to monitor the implementation of the scheme, and further facilitation 'if there are any problems with progressing any of these principles'. The memorandum of understanding was not drafted in the form of a commercial contract,[34] but it contained provisions to ensure it would work.

In some cases the result of a mediation is merely an advisory document. The Brent Spa mediation was one such. In other cases, decisions reached must be ratified by some body or organisation – hence the need to have this body involved in the mediation process from an early stage. 'Successful implementation rests not only in having a well-crafted agreement but also in nurturing the passion and commitment of the stakeholders to "make the deal stick".'[35]

4. EXAMPLES FROM THE WIDER CHURCH

a) *The Mennonite congregational-mediation process*

The Mennonite model has six phases: preliminary, information-gathering, education, healing, problem-solving, and closure.

---

[34] The choice of title 'memorandum of understanding' is significant. The document was not described as an 'agreement' or a 'contract'. The document refers to 'principles which are agreed' rather than contractual obligations. The document contains no clause numbers, the language is simple and unlawyerly, and not all the parties provided consideration. Some of the principles are precise 'the Environment Agency agree to throttle flows at the Jarvis Hotel to 2 cumecs [i.e. cubic metres of water per second] next winter…', while others are phrased in very general terms: 'The maintenance of the Pagham Rife and the structures and channels associated with the scheme will be given high priority by the Environment Agency, to ensure that it is available to act as a flood relief channel, recognising its high environmental importance and that its ecological importance is not significantly compromised.'

[35] Lawrence Susskind, Sarah McKearnan and Jennifer Thomas-Larmer (ed.), *The Consensus Building Handbook* pg. 553.

i Preliminary

The preliminary phase clarifies for the church the purpose of the mediation and the mediator's role. The goals of the mediation and the steps in the process are explained to the church. Any contract between the church and the mediator (including any fee) is negotiated, and practical matters such as dates of availability are agreed.

The Mennonites see seven purposes of congregational mediation:

1. to discern accurately the exact nature of the disagreement;

2. to give all those involved in the conflict, or even all members of the congregation, a chance to voice their views on the disagreement;

3. to reduce tension in the congregation, and help healing of relationships;

4. to resolve the underlying interest behind people's differing positions, arriving at a solution everyone can at least live with, even if it is not their preferred choice;

5. to illustrate and teach conflict resolution techniques, to equip parties for the future;

6. to offer recommendations for improving the way the congregational system functions;

7. to do all this in a way that glorifies God and strengthens the church.[36]

The mediator would normally meet with the church leadership to explain these purposes to them, and seek their agreement or change the emphasis in any way they see as appropriate. If the leadership recommends proceeding, the mediator would seek an

---

[36] From materials given to the author in a Mennonite training course in 2001, copyright the Lombard Mennonite Peace Centre, 1991.

expression of the willingness of the congregation to proceed. This may involve both a congregational meeting, and some form of survey. As a guide, the London Mennonite Centre looks for a 2/3 majority in favour of proceeding with the mediation before continuing with the process.

ii Information-gathering, and education

The Mennonite training materials puts the education phase as coming before the information-gathering phase, but in fact the two phases are linked. Some information-gathering usually comes first, such as reviewing the church constitution (for non-Anglican churches), past minutes and other relevant documents, distributing a questionnaire to everyone in the church, and conducting telephone interviews with 8-12 key people in the church. But before starting any group-work, the mediator would normally run a workshop on handling conflict in the church, to educate people and empower them to make the best use of the mediation process.

During the interviewing stage, it is important that the people consulted by the mediator represent different interests in the congregation. It is usual to include new members, old members, and sometimes former ministers or members, so that the mediator sees as broad a picture as possible.

The training workshop for the congregation typically lasts for one day. It may involve some scriptural teaching,[37] People would be taught to use 'I' rather than 'you' statements, thus giving information about 'my' personal needs, the impact something has on 'me' personally, and 'my' preference, rather than describing what 'you' did, and blaming 'you' for everything.[38] The mediator

---

[37] The following passages contain teaching on this subject: Matthew 18:15-17; Ephesians 4:1-6, Ephesians 2:14-16; Acts 15.

[38] For further details, see Carolyn Schrock-Shenk (ed.), *Mediation and Facilitation Training Manual*, 4th edn., pg. 76.

would encourage the practice of direct communication rather than 'triangling', so that A speaks directly to B about the problem between them, rather than discussing the matter with C instead. If Fred is silent in the congregational meeting when people's views are sought, but never fails to talk to Sarah afterwards, that is triangling.[39] The mediator may teach the skills of active listening and summarising, so that members are enabled better to understand each other's points of view when dealing with the real issues in dispute.

These skills require practice. There may be on-going coaching of leaders or key members of the congregation throughout the mediation process.

The mediator will then facilitate small group meetings of up to 12 participants, to discuss key aspects of the congregational life. These sessions usually last for 1½ hours. The aim is to get a picture of the diversity of views on key areas of congregational life, and how strongly people hold particular views. One exercise which is sometimes used for this process is the 'conflict spectrum'.[40] The mediator identifies one end of the room for people strongly convinced about one viewpoint, and the other end is for people strongly convinced of the opposite viewpoint, with points between the two ends representing various in-between positions. People are asked to position themselves at an appropriate point in a room, and then to share why they have chosen the spot they are standing. Dialogue at these meetings is structured,[41] and the

---

[39] See Carolyn Schrock-Shenk (ed.), *Mediation and Facilitation Training Manual*, 4th edn., pg. 145 on how to resist getting 'triangled in' to another person's dispute.

[40] Sometimes referred to as a 'human rainbow'.

[41] For example, the facilitator may encourage the group to agree that everyone has a turn to speak before anyone speaks a second time. Similarly, the facilitator should ensure that no-one person or faction dominates the meeting. In his response to my survey, the bishop of New Westminster, Canada, said that he often used the 'native circle' model.

points which are raised are documented on flip-charts, and then summarised for future meetings.

The mediator may hold a church history evening for the whole congregation, gathering recollections from the past of important events in the life of that particular church. This provides an opportunity to participants to revisit both high and low points of the congregation's history. This is often a uniting and healing process, as all members take ownership of the church and its tradition, before moving on to the more overtly healing phase of the mediation process. The congregational history evening was a key feature of the trauma recovery case.[42]

At the end of the information-gathering phase, the mediator may prepare a written report summarising the information which has been gathered, using the recording sheets from the meetings to aid him in this task.

iii Healing

There is no one method or process to bring about healing. The method used in the church trauma recovery mediation[43] involved each participant writing down on 3" by 5" cards one or several memories from the recent trauma that were still difficult for them. They then each in turn came to the front, named what had been written on the card, and handed it to the mediator. In some cases, the members were not able to 'let go' of all they had written, and this was acknowledged by the mediator, who encouraged them to find some ritualised way of release, such as burning the card, when they were able to do so.

'People sit in a circle, my pectoral cross is handed round, and everyone can have their say while they are holding it. Resolutions tend to emerge slowly but effectively.'

[42] See pg. 302.

[43] See pg. 302, and compare the description in 'Working on the issues, or healing relationships' on pg. 255.

Another structure for these meetings is known as the Samoan circle.[44] Four to six chairs are placed in a semi-circle in the centre of the room, and the other chairs arranged on the outside. Anyone who wants to be part of the discussion must sit in one of the four chairs in the centre, and must talk loudly so that everyone can hear. Anyone who wants to become part of the discussion should stand behind a chair until that chair (or another one) becomes free, and similarly persons who are in the centre should not remain there indefinitely if there are people waiting to join the discussion. This is useful as it allows hurts to be addressed in a controlled manner, where others can identify with what is being said (because they can hear it), and thus can experience the same healing themselves.

Where the issues are particularly sensitive, the Mennonites advocate using in addition a 'listening chair'. One of the members of the semi-circle selects a person to sit in one of the chairs, and listen to the discussion. The listener's task is to paraphrase everything that the speaker says. This requires that the speaker pauses every few minutes to give the listener a chance to paraphrase. This is particularly effective if the person selecting the listener chooses someone whose views *disagree* with their own. The listener really does then have to try and understand the speaker's point of view, and if the listening is done well, the speaker realises that his concerns have been understood.

It is here that the lessons from the training workshop come into use. People are encouraged to use 'I' statements, and to accept shared responsibility for past hurts. The Mennonites typically will run two healing meetings for a congregation during the course of a Saturday morning, the first dealing with hurts from

---

[44] This goes under several different names. In his response to my survey, the bishop of Rupert's Land, Canada, refers to it as a 'healing circle'. It was used very effectively in the AIDS case, case 14 in Lawrence Susskind, Sarah McKearnan and Jennifer Thomas-Larmer (ed.), *The Consensus Building Handbook*.

the distant past, and the second dealing with more recent events. In some cases, several sessions are required for neutralising past hurts, and there may also be a need for interpersonal mediation between key parties, following the community mediation model. Past hurts may also help to reveal underlying tensions in the church, and these should be noted for use in the problem-solving stage of the process.

iv Problem-solving stage

The first stage here is to identify the key interests documented during the small and large group meetings. To make this manageable, the mediator needs to categorise these interests into seven to ten workable problem areas. One way is to write the interests up on a flip-chart, and invite people to assist in identifying ones which can be combined, or which say the same topic in different ways. When the list has been reduced this way, people can be invited to name the three interests on the list they see as the most important. The results are tallied, and the interests seen as most important to the group as a whole are thereby identified.

It is useful then for small groups to reflect on these interests, so that each person is satisfied they understand them, and how they relate to each other.

The Mennonites then suggest a brainstorming session, to generate ideas for a possible solution, followed by an evaluation of the ideas by small groups, with each small group working on one problem area. These small groups then report back to the large group, to develop proposals for the large group.

The mediator then seeks to build consensus or near consensus agreements within the large group, and where necessary seeks to obtain the agreement of those not present.

After the process is completed, the next Sunday morning service may include some formal reconciliation.[45]

v Closure

After the mediation, the mediator prepares a final written report to the congregation. This summarises the information gathered, sets out what has been agreed, outlines any findings, and recommends what work the congregation might do in the future to implement the agreements, and to address any structural concerns raised in the intervention. There will be a long-term implementation by the congregation of agreements reached during the mediation process, over a one-to-three year period. For the first six-to-twelve months of this process, the mediator will contact the congregation from time to time, to check on the progress of the implementation, and to offer further help if this is needed.

b) The Alban Institute congregational-mediation model

The mediation model used by the Alban Institute is similar to the Mennonite model. A major contribution by the Alban Institute to the thinking in this area is the concept of levels of conflict. The preliminary and information-gathering stages are geared to assessing the level of the conflict on a scale of 1 to 5. This determines the mediation process which the mediator then recommends.[46] This is shown in figure 14.

---

[45] For example, one of the Church of England's services of wholeness and healing: see *Common Worship: Pastoral Services* (London, Church House Publishing, 2000).

[46] See generally, Speed B. Leas, *Moving your church through conflict* (Washington DC, Alban Institute, 1985); Carolyn Schrock-Shenk and Lawrence Ressler, *Making Peace with Conflict* (Waterloo, Ontario, Herald Press, 1999) pg. 173.

Level	Name	Parties' concern	Mediation process
1	problem to solve	solving the problem	• problem-solving collaboration
2	disagreement	self-protection	• restore trust • then as level 1
3	contest	winning	• training in communication skills • restore trust • structured dialogue • structure process
4	fight/flight	hurt or get rid of the other	• outside professional help • establish and monitor ground rules • work with Church hierarchy
5	intractable situations	destroy the other	• mediation not possible • Church hierarchy to intervene and take control

Figure 14. Levels of conflict

Level 1 is described as a 'problem to solve'. At level 1 there is a conflict of goals, values, needs or plans, but the participants are problem-orientated rather than person-orientated. They are willing to collaborate in seeking a solution. The parties are willing to listen to each other, and trust each other. At level 1, most churches can deal with this on their own without the need for a mediator, though they or the leaders may need some basic training in handling conflict.

Level 2 conflict, 'disagreement', is characterised by a tendency to personalise problems. The parties would like to solve the problem, but they are each concerned not to get hurt or have their reputation diminished in the process. Self-protection is therefore an important feature. People are more shrewd, calling on friends to discuss the problem and asking for advice, planning strategies to deal with the conflict when it is next expressed in a meeting or relationship. There may be hostile humour, a barbed comment to put down the other person or their point of view.

The strategy at level 2 is to work to reduce fear, and increase trust. A skilled mediator may be needed for this, but often the skills can be found in the congregation among pastors or trained lay members. A broad participation of persons involved should be encouraged. Good communication skills should be taught ('I' messages, no triangling, active listening, being open about feelings, sharing freely, making no threats, identifying sources of information). Once trust is re-established, the parties can collaborate more easily to resolve the underlying issues.

At level 3 conflict, 'contest', the objectives of the parties have shifted from self-protection to winning the dispute. Factions develop in the church, people take sides, but attitudes are not so serious that the parties want to hurt or get rid of their opponent. Language shifts and perceptions become distorted with generalisations: 'You always', 'He never', 'Everybody'. People make threats about leaving. At level 3, conflict is serious, and difficult. An outside mediator is very helpful in these situations, if not indispensable. The strategies here include training in communication skills, in conflict management, and in human interaction. Activities to increase trust, such as a church history evening are valuable. Structured dialogue in groups is needed, with ground rules established to help people join in the process with a sense of safety.[47] A clear decision-making process needs to be formulated, with the church leaders getting the commitment of the congregation to the process.

At level 4, 'fight/flight', conflict has moved from wanting to win to wanting to hurt or get rid of the other. The parties want to break the relationship. Parties either leave the church or try to force others to leave. At this level, people seek to punish or humiliate others, factions become solidified, the integrity of others is challenged, and stereotypes become rigid. 'An intensive intervention process, facilitated by outside persons who are skilled professionals in consulting with church systems' is typically needed to address conflict at this level.' The denomination hierarchy will almost certainly be involved at this stage, and the mediator will need to report regularly to the bishop or whoever is appointed to oversee the situation.[48] Careful ground rules will need

---

[47] The following ground rules are recommended in Speed B. Leas, *Moving your church through conflict*, pg. 49.
- all parties acknowledge there is a problem;
- everyone affected is invited to participate in data gathering, analysis and decision-making;
- all parties are encouraged to clarify their own wants;
- each party is encouraged to share its wants with the others;
- all relevant data is gathered and shared by all parties involved;
- problem definitions are agreed on;
- a mutual search for solutions to each problem is engaged in and all the alternatives are listed before the problem-solving group;
- one solution for each problem is chosen by the total group, by consensus.

[48] The bishop is of course a stakeholder in all churches in his diocese, but it is especially important in level 4 conflicts that he be involved and kept informed of the progress of the mediation, so that if his formal assistance is required at any stage he is not presented with a *fait accompli*.

to be established, and the church will need to monitor them to ensure they are honoured.[49]

Level 5 conflicts, 'intractable situations', are too late for resolution by mediation. The opposition is seen not just as harmful to the particular church, but harmful to the whole church or even to the whole society. Parties become fanatics about their position, seeking to destroy each other. An example would be where members of a church which has dismissed a pastor try to prevent the pastor ever getting another church position. At level 5, parties see themselves as fighting an eternal cause, fighting for eternal principles, and see it as wrong to stop fighting. At this level, decision-making cannot remain in the hands of the people who are the leaders of the conflict. Outside intervention is required, by the diocesan authorities or whoever is appropriate, to take control, determine the issues, and take whatever steps are necessary to restore peace. Removal of certain members of the congregation (where this can be achieved) may be required.[50] If the priest-in-charge or vicar is removed or resigns, an interim pastor may be appointed for a couple of years while trust is rebuilt, before seeking a permanent replacement.[51]

---

[49] Speed Leas recommends that if the monitoring committee discovers that an individual has been breaking the ground rules, for example by makes allegations behind someone's back, a member of the monitoring committee should speak directly to that person and inform them that this is not acceptable.

[50] 'In law parishioners have the right to enter into their parish church for attendance at divine service and to remain there for its duration. This is the only right of access conferred by the general law upon the laity at large as opposed to the minister and churchwardens, to whom different principles apply', per Briden Ch in *In re St Michael's, Orchard Portman* [2001] 2 WLR 1687, 1689.

[51] According to Carolyn Schrock-Shenk, Associate Professor of Peace, Justice and Conflict Studies at Goshen College, Indiana, USA, it is becoming quite common in the USA to appoint an interim pastor in these

The usefulness of the Alban Institute 5-level classification is in determining the appropriate expertise required to resolve the dispute. Levels 1 and 2 can be resolved 'in-house' with little outside assistance; level 3 requires a person with more experience than is likely to be found within the congregation; level 4 disputes require considerable expertise, and also active participation by diocesan authorities during the mediation process. At level 5, the diocesan authorities need to take control of the situation, and not spend time on mediation.

c) The Quaker model of consensus

Quakers are often described as Nonconformist Christians, but they differ greatly from Baptists and Methodists. They have no creed, no priests, no formal prayers, and no hymns. They believe that a person's relationship with God is a matter of direct communication between God and that person, and that God is in everyone. Some Quakers see themselves as Christians; others are universalist, with a broad range of spiritual beliefs.[52]

The Quaker meetings for worship are characterised by silence. People at the meeting continue to sit in silence unless someone is moved to speak. 'Silence is one of the best preparations for communion [with God] and for the reception of inspiration and guid-

---

circumstances. This is borne out by the responses of the bishops of Michigan, Kansas and Milwaukee to the survey in chapter 7. England seems to be starting to follow suit: on the one-week mediation training course run by the London Mennonites in 2000, one of the participants was an interim vicar in Norfolk appointed following a major conflict.

[52] See Anthony Bradney and Fiona Cownie, *Living without law; an ethnography of Quaker decision-making, dispute avoidance and dispute resolution* (Aldershot, Ashgate, 2000), pg. 49–52. See also Frank Cranmer, 'Regulation within the Religious Society of Friends', 7 Ecc LJ 176.

ance.'[53] Silence involves concentration, commitment, and self-discipline. When someone speaks, all those present will use the silence to think deeply about what is said, before anyone else speaks.

Silence is also one of the key features of Quaker decision-making. The basis of Quaker decision-making is that it involves decisions taken with the agreement of all present, in the light of God's guidance. This does not mean that everyone has to agree completely with every aspect of the decision, but everyone must feel it right to let the decision go ahead. Quakers seek to achieve a special form of consensus. It is not enough, they say, to seek a consensus of the membership. Rather, the meeting must seek the will of God in a particular matter. Therefore Quaker meetings for business are always preceded by worship, that is, by silence.[54] And when anyone speaks at a meeting for business, everyone present exercises the self-discipline to listen, without interrupting, and to consider deeply in silence what is said before replying.[55] Silence prevents any form of arguing, and is useful 'at any sticky points'.[56]

Quaker meetings are led by a person known as the clerk. The clerk draws up the agenda, takes the meeting through the agenda, and draws up the minute which concludes each item. The clerk's role is very similar to a facilitator: the clerk needs to be neutral, a

---

[53] *Quaker Faith and Practice* (London, The Religious Society of Friends (Quakers), 1995), par. 2.16, quoted in Anthony Bradney and Fiona Cownie, *Living without law*, pg. 59.

[54] Anthony Bradney and Fiona Cownie found that some committee meetings which deal with uncontroversial items may have only a very short period of silence; but silence is key to important meetings. Bradney and Cownie, *Living without law*, pg. 147.

[55] Anthony Bradney and Fiona Cownie, *Living without law*, pg. 74; Frank Cranmer, 'Regulation within the Religious Society of Friends', 7 Ecc LJ 176.

[56] Anthony Bradney and Fiona Cownie, *Living without law*, pg. 144.

good listener, and to discern and sum up the meeting's feelings. The clerk is familiar with the Quaker business method, and is trusted and respected by the membership.

Other features of the Quaker business method echo the secular consensus-building model. These are: the use of minutes, the time taken to reach consensus, the trust between the members, the use of ground rules, and the true consensus which emerges.

i minutes

The writing of minutes immediately after each item, and agreeing the minute before moving on to the next item, bring to mind the secular mediation practice of using flip-charts to record people's contributions to secular consensus-building meetings at the time they are spoken, and then using these flip-charts to prepare a group note for the stakeholders.

ii full deliberation

The consensus reached at a Quaker business meeting is not just a spur of the moment agreement, which may be regretted later. Instead, decisions come only after full deliberation. Quakers anticipate difficulties in implementation or changes of circumstances, and find ways of addressing them. Quakers make an intensive effort to reach the 'correct' decision which will still be correct even in the light of future developments.[57]

iii trust

The Quaker business meeting is an integral part of a worshipping community, composed of individuals who know each other well and trust one another on a spiritual level.[58] Trust is an important part of consensus-building mediation, and where trust has

---

[57] Anthony Bradney and Fiona Cownie, *Living without law*, pg. 146.
[58] Anthony Bradney and Fiona Cownie, *Living without law*, pg. 79.

been broken, it needs to be restored within the group before collaborative consensus-building can continue.

iv ground rules

Ground rules, or norms of behaviour, are intrinsic to the
Quaker business method. These include sitting in a circle or
square, speaking briefly unless the subject really demands otherwise, addressing the meeting as a whole rather than one individual, drafting the minutes in the meeting, not holding private
conversations, and not reading the agenda or other papers while
others are talking.[59]

The consensus which emerges from the Quaker business
method is described by Bradney and Cownie in glowing terms;[60]
but there is a down-side. Quaker business meetings progress
sometimes at a glacial speed.[61] If it is impossible to reach a consensus or discern the will of God at a meeting, matters are left to a
later meeting, delaying the decision still further. The drafting of
minutes at the meeting itself adds to the time these meetings take.
The Quaker business method values quality of outcome and

---

[59] Anthony Bradney and Fiona Cownie, *Living without law*, pg. 79.

[60] Anthony Bradney and Fiona Cownie, *Living without law*, pg. 80:
  In a Quaker decision, there are in the end no deep divisions, no
  winners and losers in the conventional sense. This is not because
  people have compromised, but because the group has reached
  'unity'. It is a method which assumes ownership of the decision by
  all who are present. Everyone's view is taken into account, everyone who has something to say is listened to, and their ideas are
  considered seriously. Even someone who disagrees, but says they
  are willing to put that aside because they believe the decision is
  right for the group remains part of the group.

[61] Anthony Bradney and Fiona Cownie, *Living without law*, pg. 147.

group commitment at the expense of efficiency, and is therefore unsuitable in cases where a decision needs to be taken quickly.[62]

5. THE THEOLOGY OF CONSENSUS-BUILDING MEDIATION

A conflict which affected the whole church is described in the New Testament in Acts 15. The issue was whether Gentiles who became Christians needed to be circumcised and to obey the Jewish laws. One sees in the account of this dispute several elements of good decision-making practice.[63] The dispute was referred to a group, the apostles and elders, for decision.[64] They recognised the issue which needed to be decided.[65] Plenty of time was allowed for discussion.[66] Both sides were heard.[67] There was active listening.[68] The apostles and elders reached unanimous agreement,[69]

---

[62] For another study of the Quaker method, see Glen Bartoo, *Decisions by Consensus: a study of the Quaker Method* (Chicago, Progressive Publisher, 1978), referred to in Michel Avery et al., *Building United Judgment* .

[63] Some of the material in this paragraph is based on a Bible Study on Acts 15 contained in Doug Baker, *Handling Disagreements in the Church* (Belfast, Conciliation Committee of the Presbyterian Church in Ireland, available from the General Secretary's Office, Church House, Belfast BT1 6DW, 1996).

[64] Acts 15:2.

[65] Acts 15:1–3, 5–6.

[66] Acts 15:6–7.

[67] Acts 15:5–11.

[68] Acts 15:12.

[69] Acts 15:25. The New American Standard Version has 'having become of one mind'; the Revised Standard Version has 'having come to one accord'. The Greek word used in this verse, ὁμοθυμαδὸν (*homothumadon*), means 'unanimously'. Similarly, in Acts 15:28 the decision 'seemed good to the Holy Spirit *and to us*'.

and the conclusion was approved by all the others present.[70] As in the Quaker practice, the apostles and elders sought God's will in the situation.[71] When the decision was made, it was communicated to those affected by it, and the reasons for it were clearly explained.[72]

Not all the elements of consensus-building mediation can be found in this one story,[73] and there is a note of realism in the account later in the same chapter of a dispute between Paul and Barnabas which was so sharp that they parted company.[74] But the Church can be satisfied that there is a New Testament precedent for seeking to resolve church disputes by the use of consensus.

Consensus-building has a very American feel to it. English people may be unused to flip-charts and other visual aids, being organised in groups, and all the other tools of the facilitator's trade.[75] 'I'-centred communication, and especially expressing one's feelings openly, are also foreign to the English phlegm.[76] One may ask, would Jesus have used flip-charts? I answer, why not? If the Church has embraced worship songs on screens instead of hymnbooks,[77] what is wrong with flip-charts? I suggest

---

[70] Acts 15:22 refers to the decision of the 'whole church' to send persons with Paul and Barnabas to Antioch with the letter.

[71] Acts 15:28.

[72] Acts 15:22–29.

[73] A similar passage is the resolution of the conflict in Acts 6:1–5. In Acts 6:5 it is recorded that the apostles' proposal 'pleased the whole group'.

[74] Acts 15:36–40.

[75] Though these American processes are increasingly being used in business decision-making in the UK.

[76] They are used in commercial and community mediation as well as in consensus-building mediation.

[77] Sunrise Software, PO Box 19, Carlisle CA3 0HP sells a computer program Presentation Manager for £275 to display songs, Bible passages

that He who wrote on the ground with his finger,[78] would have had no objection. And as for expressing one's emotions, our Lord said that it is only when we open our hearts that we can truly hear and understand what others are saying.[79]

So one must distinguish between cultural and theological concerns. A mediator working in an English church may need to be somewhat gentler and more subtle than a mediator working in the USA. But the principle is theologically sound, even though the practice may need to be tempered to the English culture.

For example, bringing in a person described as a professional church-dispute mediator may raise hackles in some English churches, whereas such a person would be readily accepted in the USA. In contrast, a member of the diocesan staff, a member of the clergy, a trained lay person, or someone recommended by the diocese or a nearby diocese 'to help resolve the dispute' would not encounter the same resistance. Dioceses should therefore encourage individuals to be trained in the consensus-building process. They can then be a resource, to be sent in as mediators rather than as 'professional dispute-resolvers'.

6. APPLICATION

a) Choosing the most appropriate mediation model

We can now look at each of the 15 main types of church dispute, and see which model of mediation is best suited to it. In some cases more than one model may be appropriate. Some cases may involve several issues, and may not fit conveniently into one category. But figure 15 provides a starting point.

---

and notices on a screen in church. Two churches using this software are Holy Trinity, Brompton, London SW7 1JA and St Andrew's Church, Linton Rd, Oxford OX2 6UG.

[78] John 8:6. This is the only recorded occasion of Jesus writing.

[79] Matthew 13:15.

332

Type of dispute	Issue	Mediation Model
church buildings	people/ process	Community/ Consensus-building
church governance	problem	Commercial
personality conflict	people	Community
pastoral breakdown	people/ process	Community/ Consensus-building
worship/ doctrine	people/ process	Community/ Consensus-building
gay and gender issue	people/ process	Community/ Consensus-building
racial discrimination	people	Community
employment/ work	people/ problem	Community/ Commercial
minor discipline	people	Community
property ownership	problem	Commercial
financial (non-criminal)	problem	Commercial
defamation	people	Community
personal injury	people/ problem	Community/ Commercial
contractual	problem	Commercial
taxation	problem	Commercial

Figure 15. Matching mediation model to church dispute type

In all the cases where consensus-building mediation is mentioned, community mediation is put as an alternative. There are three reasons for this. First, some disputes in these categories involve only a small number of people, say up to six, while others involve a large number, possibly the whole congregation. Second, even if potentially the whole congregation is involved, there may be a central core of people most affected. In such a case, a mediator may prefer to do inter-personal mediation according to the community mediation model with this central core, in the expectation that if this resolves the dispute it may not be necessary to do consensus-building mediation with the whole congregation. Third, mediators involved in consensus-building mediation in a church congregation frequently have to combine this with inter-personal mediation between key individuals as part of the process.[80]

Take, for example, the church buildings category. A dispute over a proposed reordering of the church which has split the congregation lends itself to a consensus-building mediation. But a dispute between a grieving family and the vicar over what wording is or is not allowed on a gravestone[81] is suitable for the community mediation model.

The survey in chapter 7 of mediation in the Anglican Communion will identify the four types of dispute most suitable for mediation as personality conflict, employment, pastoral breakdown, and church governance. Of these, pastoral breakdown is the one most suitable for consensus-building mediation. Diocesan authorities can therefore recommend with some confidence a consensus-building mediation to a church facing a pastoral breakdown.

---

[80] In the Mennonite model, this inter-personal mediation takes place during the healing stage of the process: Carolyn Schrock-Shenk (ed.), *Mediation and Facilitation Training Manual*, 4th edn., pg. 258.

b) Church decision-making and leadership

Leadership at the parish level in the Church of England is shared between the parish priest, the churchwardens and the PCC.[82] But this simple concept allows a great diversity in practice. Becker categorises churches into five principal models, described as House of Worship, Family, Community, Leader, and Mixed.[83] She found that different models tend to have conflicts over different issues,[84] and tend also to have different leadership styles.[85] For example, she found leadership in House of Worship churches tends to be very formal, following denominational guidelines; but in Family churches it is very informal, with lay leaders making

---

[81] For an example, see *In re Holy Trinity Churchyard, Freckleton* [1994] 1 WLR 1588, (1994) 3 Ecc LJ 350.

[82] For the constitutional position of the PCC, see the Parochial Church Councils (Powers) Measure 1956 section 2. See generally, James Behrens, *Practical Church Management* (Leominster, Gracewing, 1998) chapters 2 and 3.

[83] Penny Edgell Becker, *Congregations in Conflict: Cultural Models of Local Religious Life* (Cambridge University Press 1999), pg. 12–14. A congregation which is primarily the provider of religious goods and services to individuals – worship, religious education, and rituals like weddings and funerals – is a House of Worship model. A congregation where worship, religious education, and providing close-knit and supportive relationships for members are the core tasks is the Family model. A church which is primarily a community of intimate ties and shared values, where the policies and programs of the congregation express the values and commitments of the members regarding social issues, is a Community model. In Leader churches, intimacy is less valued than in other models; what is important is standing for the denomination or tradition of the church, and witnessing to its truth to outsiders. Her study was of 23 congregations in an urban suburb nine miles from the centre of Chicago, of a number of Christian denominations, and two Jewish synagogues.

[84] Penny Edgell Becker, *Congregations in Conflict*, pg. 175–7.

[85] Penny Edgell Becker, *Congregations in Conflict*, pg. 184–5.

many decisions outside formal structures. It is not difficult to recognise Becker's different models within the Church of England, or to appreciate that different Church of England congregations have different leadership models.

For some churches, where leadership is informal, consensus-building may be seen as a natural process, perhaps not too different from the decision-making which takes place regularly in the church. For other churches, where the priest and PCC exercise a rigid control over everything, or where the PCC merely rubber-stamps the priest's decisions, the leadership may be unwilling to consider sharing issues with the congregation at large. Where leadership style is an issue in the conflict, the mediator may need to work separately within the leadership, using inter-personal mediation to build up trust within the leadership team, before encouraging the use of consensus-building mediation for the whole congregation.

c) Resources

There are four linked resource implications: cost, time, personnel, and training. As to cost, one consensus-building mediation by the London Mennonite Centre in 2000 lasted seven months, and cost the church £7,000.[86] The London Mennonite's experience is that where fees reach this level, a large proportion is borne by the church hierarchy rather than the congregation. This makes sense in the Church of England, where it is the diocese rather than the parish which is likely to bear the (much more expensive) cost of proceedings under the Incumbent (Vacation of Benefices) Measure 1977, if the pastoral relationship can not be restored.[87]

---

[86] The London Mennonite Centre hourly rates for mediations are £35 for work on site, £20 for office work, and £10 for travelling.

[87] The seven-months mediation run by the London Mennonites in 2000 involved a Baptist Congregation.

336

There is a difference in culture between American and English churches over the question of fees. In the USA professional mediators are well-known in commercial, community and church contexts. American congregations are accustomed to paying professional mediators, and the money to do so is provided either from within the congregation or from the denomination.[88] In England there are few organisations and individuals involved in this work. Some dioceses may have members of the clergy who can undertake this task at no additional cost to the diocese; but the time commitment on the part of the mediator or mediators may be several hundred hours, and not many persons can spare this time.

Practical experience has shown that it is far better not to have one individual taking on the role of mediator, but to have two.[89] It is very difficult for just one person to oversee the process, help the parties recognise the issues, handle emotional outbursts, act as recorder, observe people's non-verbal communication, and carry out all the other tasks a mediator needs to undertake. If there are two mediators, one can lead while the other observes, the person observing can intervene if the one leading is struggling, or comment on the process rather than the issues. The tasks can be divided, with one mediator perhaps handling interpersonal mediation between two parties, while the other mediator handles discussions by a large group. Perhaps most importantly, where mediators work in pairs, they are less vulnerable to accusations of bias. One mediator may be from within the denomination, the other from outside. One may be female, the other male; one ordained, the other lay; one black, the other white. This is consonant with many examples in the New Testament of teams of two: the 12 disciples,[90] the 72 others,[91] Paul and Barnabas,[92] Barnabas

---

[88]Speed B. Leas, *Moving your church through conflict*, pg. 59.

[89] Martin Eggleton and David Trafford, *At Cross Purposes: Handling Conflict in the Church* (Peterborough, Foundery Press, 2000), pg. 21.

[90] Matthew 21:1; Mark 6:7; Mark 11:1; Mark 14:13.

and Mark,[93] Paul and Silas,[94] Timothy and Erastus,[95] and un-named disciples.[96]

The difference in culture between the USA and England has already been noted. There is training, both secular[97] and church-based[98] in the UK. On the London Mennonite course in 2000, there were 20 participants, mostly English, including three Roman Catholic priests, four Church of England vicars, and one United Reformed Church minister. The Methodists are also involved in this work.[99] There are therefore mediators trained in this work who are familiar with English church culture.

---

[91] Luke 10:1.

[92] Acts 13:1.

[93] Acts 15:39.

[94] Acts 15:40.

[95] Acts 19:22.

[96] Acts 9:38.

[97] The Environment Council.

[98] The Mennonites.

[99] See Martin Eggleton and David Trafford, *At Cross Purposes*. Martin Eggleton is a Methodist minister. David Trafford is a minister working as a pastoral consultant in the Thames North Province of the United Reformed Church. The book was commissioned by the Methodist Church Pastoral Care Committee. The book aims to be non-denominational. For example, it refers to 'leadership groups like elders, deacons, church councils or PCCs' (pg. 34).

7. CONCLUSION

Acland identifies seven appropriate situations for consensus-building.[100]

(1) Where there are many parties and many issues, 'consensus-building really comes into its own'. This is typically the case in large congregational disputes.

(2) Where there are varying moral and political values, 'people need a process which enables everybody to appreciate, if not always understand or accept, the range of feelings, beliefs and perceptions involved'. In the church context, politics is not relevant; but moral values certainly are, and Acland's comment is apt.

(3) Where there is an absence of agreed information, consensus-building encourages participants to identify areas of uncertainty and jointly agree how the information necessary for good decisions can be acquired. This may well be an issue for a church considering a project, whether to do with building, outreach or social concern.

(4) Where there are differing organisational structures, this can lead to misunderstandings and accusations of bad faith. Consensus-building gives people time to understand how others are operating. Misunderstandings are certainly a cause of conflict in the church, often caused by failures in communication. Consensus-building restores the trust by building proper communication between the parties.

(5) Where the only alternative appears to be some adversarial procedure, consensus-building can provide a means of avoiding the damage this can cause. Consensus-building processes are always designed to fit the problem they are intended to address, and this includes training the parties how to participate in them.

---

[100] Andrew Acland, *Resolving disputes without going to court*, pg. 214.

(6) Where there is no investment in future relationships, consensus-building is directed towards the future and the need for sustainable solutions, and therefore invests time and effort in building relationships as well as agreements. Consensus-building treats the church as a body, rather than as a collection of individuals.[101]

(7) Where there is a need to prevent future disputes, consensus-building enables the parties to learn how to work together to anticipate and defuse disputes before they can escalate and cause real problems. Consensus-building therefore has an educative role for the church, as well as dealing with the instant problem.

It is clear from this survey that consensus-building mediation is already used for church disputes. It is also clear that it has a considerable potential in the area of pastoral breakdown, and for some other types of congregational dispute. The procedure is relatively unknown in the UK, and there may be some practical difficulty in persuading congregations of its likely benefit. There is also likely to be some cultural resistance to adopting some of the consensus-building methods. But the process is theologically sound, and is well-tried in the USA, both for church and for secular disputes.

Consensus-building mediation is not a panacea for all congregational conflicts. In some cases the conflict may have reached the level 5 stage,[102] where it is impossible to resolve without outside authoritative intervention. In some cases the parties may be unwilling even to attempt the process. But in those cases where the congregation is willing to work with a mediator, the process can bring healing and reconciliation to the parties, and help them

---

[101] See 1 Corinthians 12:12–27.

[102] See pg. 325.

reach not only a resolution of the issues between them, but one which can be discerned to be God's will for the congregation.

Chapter 7

MEDIATION IN THE ANGLICAN COMMUNION

1. THE NEED FOR AN INTERNATIONAL SURVEY

i Questions arising from the research in the UK

The research within the British Isles was hampered by the fact that mediation is a somewhat new and untried method for resolving church disputes. The archdeacons provided much valuable information on the extent to which mediation is used in the Church of England. But a number of questions arise from their responses.

First, they provided evidence as to the types of disputes which arise. But it would be useful to know what types of dispute are most suitable for mediation, and what types of dispute are less suitable.

343

Second, the archdeacons pointed to the wide field of human resources available in many dioceses to act as mediators. In some cases professional mediators act in this role, in other cases the bishop, archdeacons or other members of the clergy. This leads to a number of questions. As so much depends on the skill of the mediators, how does the diocese choose mediators for a particular dispute? How often do they use clergy and other church leaders, and how often do they bring in professional mediators? Do they find each type effective? The survey of the archdeacons pointed to the financial cost of conflict resolution, but there is no statistical evidence as to the cost-effectiveness of employing professional mediators. Does the diocese maintain a list of suitable persons to act as mediators when the need arises? How often does the bishop act as a mediator? A number of archdeacons said it was difficult for them to act as mediator because of their role as the bishop's officer. If it is difficult for the archdeacon, it may be even more difficult for the bishop to act as mediator, because of his disciplinary and judicial role. It is difficult to judge whether this is in practice a major difficulty.

Third, a number of archdeacons referred to the need for training in conflict management, and said that conflict resolution was beginning to be taught in theological college. Because this training was in its infancy, it is difficult to judge how useful it is, and whether other dioceses should be offering the same training.

Fourth, a number of archdeacons referred to pastoral breakdown disputes affecting a whole congregation. There did not seem to be any uniform way of handling these disputes, nor any evidence to determine whether any one way was better than another.

ii Mediation in other countries

To answer these questions, the experience of other churches in the Anglican Communion would be useful. As well as covering the above subjects the models of mediation used elsewhere in the

Anglican Communion would assist in recommending an appropriate model for the Church of England.

The Anglican Communion is a fellowship of churches in communion with the See of Canterbury. It comprises 39 self-governing churches, each organised as a national, regional, or provincial church, and includes extra-provincial dioceses, and united churches.[1] The Anglican Communion developed in the seventeenth century, when Anglicanism was established by colo-

---

[1] As at 2001 the list of member Churches or provinces, and of councils, is: The Anglican Church in Aotearoa, New Zealand and Polynesia; The Anglican Church of Australia; The Church of Bangladesh; The Episcopal Anglican Church of Brazil; The Episcopal Church of Burundi; The Anglican Church of Canada; The Church of the Province of Central Africa; The Anglican Church of the Central American Region; The Anglican Church of the Congo; The Church of England; The Ethiopian Episcopal Church; Hong Kong Sheng Kung Hui; The Church of the Province of the Indian Ocean; The Church of Ireland; The Anglican Communion in Japan (Nippon Sei Ko Kai); The Episcopal Church in Jerusalem and the Middle East; The Anglican Church of Kenya; The Anglican Church of Korea; The Church of the Province of Melanesia; The Anglican Church of Mexico; The Church of the Province of Myanmar; The Church of Nigeria (Anglican Communion); The Church of North India; The Church of Pakistan; The Anglican Church of Papua New Guinea; The Episcopal Church in the Philippines; The Episcopal Church of Rwanda; The Scottish Episcopal Church; The Church of the Province of South East Asia; The Church of South India; The Church of the Province of Southern Africa; The Anglican Church of the Southern Cone of America; The Episcopal Church of the Sudan; The Anglican Church of Tanzania; The Church of the Province of Uganda; The Episcopal Church in the United States of America; The Church in Wales; The Church of the Province of West Africa; The Church in the Province of the West Indies. There are also the following Extra-Provincial Dioceses and other Churches: The Anglican Church of Bermuda; The Anglican Church in Ceylon; The Episcopal Church of Cuba; The Lusitanian Church of Portugal; The Reformed Episcopal Church of Spain; The Anglican Church in Venezuela; The Episcopal Church of Puerto Rico; Falkland Islands.

nisation in countries such as Australia, Canada, New Zealand, Southern Africa and the USA.[2] As a result of missionary work at the end of the nineteenth century, the churches in Japan, Melanesia, the Philippines, the West Indies and other countries joined the Anglican Communion. The province of Hong Kong was formed in 1998.[3]

Australia, Canada, Hong Kong,[4] New Zealand, South Africa and the USA all have considerably more experience of using mediation for secular disputes than does the United Kingdom. As has been described in chapter 4, governments in these countries are expressing great interest in mediation, and wide consultation is taking place with providers of mediation services, mediation training organisations, the public, court users, lawyers, and statutory bodies providing dispute resolution procedures.[5] Legislation concerning mediation either already exists or is being drafted in several of these countries.[6] Community mediation is

---

[2] The Anglican Church came to Virginia, USA in 1607. The Anglican Church came to Australia in 1788. The first Anglican bishop for South Africa was appointed in 1847.

[3] For a useful summary, see the Church of England Year Book 2001 (London, Church House Publishing, 2001), pg. 315, and Norman Doe, *Canon Law in the Anglican Communion* (Oxford, Clarendon Press, 1998).

[4] Hong Kong is considered as a country for the purpose of this chapter, although as Hong Kong is governed by China this is incorrect as a matter of international law.

[5] For government interest see pg. 158; for Australia, pg. 158; for the USA, pg. 161; and for South Africa, pg. 161.

[6] Arbitration and Conciliation Act 2000, Act No 7 of 2000 (Uganda); Hong Kong Arbitration Ordinance 1989; Hong Kong Arbitration Amendment Ordinance of 1996; Hong Kong Arbitration Amendment Ordinance 2000; Labour Relations Act 1965 (No 66 of 1995) (South Africa); Labour Relations Amendment Act 1966 (No 42 of 1996) (South Africa); Labour Relations Amendment Act 1968 (No 127 of 1998) (South Africa); Short Process Courts and Mediation in Certain Civil Cases Act

well established in parts of Australia (particularly New South Wales), Canada, South Africa and the USA.[7]

AUSTRALIA

In Australia, the National Alternative Dispute Resolution Advisory Council (NADRAC) was established in October 1995 to provide independent advice to the Commonwealth Attorney-General. Its publications have already been mentioned.[8]

CANADA

In Canada, there have been a number of court-annexed ADR schemes since the early 1990s. In Toronto and Ottawa Carletons, all civil non-family cases must go to mediation before proceedings may be commenced, unless a judge gives permission otherwise. There are plans to introduce mediation systems outside the court in Ontario. A pilot project for mandatory mediation in Saskatchewan is being extended over time throughout the whole province. In Quebec mediation is already used in family matters and the provincial Government is considering the application of mandatory mediation to other High Court cases.[9]

No 103 of 1991 (South Africa); Uniform Mediation Act 2001 (USA), awaiting adoption by each state.

[7] Brown and Marriott, *ADR Principles and Practice,* 2nd edn. (London, Sweet & Maxwell, 1999), pg. 281 for Australia, Canada, and the USA. For South Africa, see chapter 4, 'Commercial mediation'.

[8] See pg. 158. They include: *Issues of fairness and justice in alternative dispute resolution* (Australia, National Alternative Dispute Resolution Advisory Council (NADRAC), November 1997); *Primary dispute resolution in family law* (Australia, National Alternative Dispute Resolution Advisory Council (NADRAC), March 1997); *The Development of Standards for ADR Discussion Paper* (Australia, National Alternative Dispute Resolution Advisory Council (NADRAC), March 2000).

[9] Brown and Marriott, *ADR Principles and Practice*, 2nd edn., pg. 95–6.

The Anglican Church in Canada is using mediation for some of the cases arising out of its involvement with the Indian Residential Schools system that used to exist in Canada.[10]

HONG KONG

The Hong Kong Arbitration Ordinance[11] provides the legislative support to mediation and arbitration in Hong Kong. Sect. 2(B) of the Ordinance deals with mediation during the course of arbitration proceedings and the continuation of those proceedings if the mediation fails. This provision was much influenced by the Chinese practice of combining mediation with arbitration.[12]

---

[10] The dioceses of Cariboo, Qu'Appelle and Huron are facing possible bankruptcy from the litigation arising from the abuse committed at these schools. See *www.anglican.ca/ministry/rs*, and for details of the litigation and alternative dispute resolution processes, see *www.anglican.ca/ministry/rs/litigation/*. The Government of Canada is being sued by an estimated 7,000 survivors of residential schools, and the Anglican Church is named as a co-defendant in approximately 1,200 of those cases. Some cases involve a single individual; some involve many. Only one (at December 1999) had come to trial. Some cases may be withdrawn if it is possible to address the concerns of the plaintiffs through alternative dispute resolution.

[11] The Hong Kong Arbitration Ordinance 1989, as amended by the Hong Kong Arbitration Amendment Ordinance of 1996 and the Hong Kong Arbitration Amendment Ordinance 2000.

[12] A feature of Chinese arbitration is the combination of arbitration with mediation. Subject to the agreement of the parties, the arbitration tribunal may mediate cases in arbitration proceedings. In other words, the arbitration tribunal may conduct an arbitration procedure and a mediation procedure at the same time, combing the two procedures together: see Brown and Marriott, *ADR Principles and Practice,* 2nd edn., pg. 80. In England, unless the parties had agreed in advance to allow a mediator to act as arbitrator if the mediation fails, an award made by a mediator

NEW ZEALAND

In January 1997, the Courts Consultative Committee published a report, *Court Referral to Alternative Dispute Resolution*.[13] This describes the work done in the Disputes Tribunal where referees are required to settle small claims without formal process. The report refers to mediation having a long tradition in industrial disputes, with 80% of cases going to mediation, and 90% of those cases settling.

SOUTH AFRICA

The development of community, commercial and workplace mediation in South Africa has already been described.[14]

THE USA

The project to produce a Uniform Mediation Act has been described.[15] So far as church mediations are concerned, the Canons of the Episcopal Church of the USA provide for mediation and conciliation.[16]

It has been seen how slow England has been to take up commercial mediation in comparison with other countries, in particular Australia, Canada, Hong Kong, New Zealand, South Africa,

---

who did so would be invalid: *Glencot Development and Design Co Ltd v Ben Barrett & Son (Contractors) Ltd* [2001] B.L.R. 207; (2001) 3 T.C.L.R. 11.

[13] *Courts Referral to Alternative Dispute Resolution* (New Zealand Courts Consultative Committee, January 1997)

[14] pg. 161.

[15] pg. 161.

[16] Disagreements affecting the pastoral relation – Canons of the Episcopal Church of the USA Title III, Canon 20; dissolution of the pastoral relationship – Title III, Canon 21, section 3; the duties of bishops (where a Diocesan Bishop declines to visit a Parish or Congregation for three years) – Title III, Canons 24.4(c); and non-serious disciplinary matters – Title IV, Canon 16.

and the USA.[17] The slow take-up of mediation by the Church of England seems to mirror the slow take-up of mediation by the secular and commercial world.

In 2000, the Lord Chancellor's Department conducted a survey to see whether mediation should be given a 'kick-start' by being made compulsory for certain types of case, as it is in, for example, the USA, Australia and Canada. Following the survey, the Lord Chancellor's Department decided against this course.[18] It would be useful to know whether the Church in these countries considers mediation should be compulsory for certain types of dispute.

Chapters 4, 5 and 6 identify three very different models for mediation. It would be useful to know from the experience of other countries, which model of mediation other churches in the Anglican Communion have found most useful. It would be useful to know the views of the Anglican Church generally on the need for training in mediation, and any other lessons they have learned about the mediation of church disputes.

2. THE SURVEY

These factors indicated the need to conduct an international survey. The experience of the Churches in other countries would provide very useful guidance for the Church of England. A survey was therefore addressed to all diocesan bishops in these six

---

[17] See chapter 4, 'Commercial mediation'.

[18] *Legal Week*, 31 August 2000, pg. 1, 'Govt drops compulsory mediation'. The subject was mooted in *Alternative Dispute Resolution – a Discussion Paper* (London, Lord Chancellor's Department, 1999), but there was overwhelming opposition to compulsory mediation from judges, law firms and mediation companies. Several respondents pointed out that compulsory mediation could amount to a breach of Article Six of the Human Rights Act 1998: the right to a fair trial. (The contrary argument is that mediation does not prevent a fair trial: mediation tries to promote settlement, but the parties' rights to a trial remain if the mediation is unsuccessful.)

countries.[19] The survey was divided into the following main sections:

A   aims to identify which types of church dispute are suitable for mediation, and which are not.

B   aims to identify who are the best people to use as mediators.

C   aims to determine whether mediation should remain entirely voluntary, or whether it should ever be compulsory.

D   aims to find out what training is, or should be, provided in conflict resolution.

E   aims to find out how the church handles disputes involving large numbers of people.

F   aims to find out what type of mediation model works best for church disputes.

G   aims to find out what lessons they have drawn from their experience in this area.

H   aims to identify possible other contacts.

I   asks for any general comments.

188 questionnaires were sent out and 98 responses were received, which represents a response rate of 52%.[20] It is significant

---

[19] The text of the letter sent to diocesan bishops and the questionnaire enclosed with the letter is set out in appendix 2. In many dioceses there are also one or more assistant bishops. The communication offices for ECUSA (the Episcopal Church in the USA) recommended the author to write only to the one diocesan bishop in each diocese. The same principle was adopted for all the countries in the survey.

[20] Arranged by country and diocese, the following responses were received:

and encouraging that the overall response rate was over 50%.[21] It indicates, first, that the Anglican Churches in these countries con-

---

Australia: Adelaide, Bendigo, Brisbane, Bunbury, Canberra and Goulburn, Gippsland, Melbourne, Newcastle, North Queensland, Northern Territory, Sydney, Tasmania, The Murray, Wangaratta, Willochra.

Canada: Algoma, Arctic, Central Newfoundland, Eastern Newfoundland and Labrador, Edmonton, Huron, Montreal, Moosonee, New Westminster, Nova Scotia and Prince Edward Island, Ontario, Qu'Appelle, Quebec, Rupert's Land, Saskatoon, Toronto.

Hong Kong: Hong Kong Island.

New Zealand: Christchurch, Waikato, Wellington.

South Africa: Bloemfontein, Cape Town, Christ the King, Highveld, Johannesburg, Klerksdorp, Namibia, Port Elizabeth, Pretoria, St Mark the Evangelist Northern Province, Swaziland.

The USA: Alaska, Arkansas, Atlanta, Bethlehem, Central Florida, Central Pennsylvania, Chicago, Delaware, Delaware, East Michigan, East Tennessee, Eau Claire, Florida, Fond du Lac, Georgia, Indeanapolis, Kansas, Kansas City, Long Island, Los Angeles, Louisiana, Maine, Michigan, Milwaukee, Mississippi, Missouri, Nebraska, Nevada, New Hampshire, New York, Newark, Northern California, Northern Michigan, North-West Texas, Ohio, Olympia, Oregon, Pennsylvania, Pittsburgh, Quincy, Rio Grande, San Diego, South Carolina, SouthWest Virginia, SW Florida, Utah, Virginia, Washington, West Missouri, West Tennessee, Western Louisiana, Western North Carolina.

[21] Of the 98 responses, 87 responded using the survey questionnaire, and 11 responded by letter giving general comments. These 11 were

Australia: Canberra and Goulburn.

Canada: Algoma, Arctic, Montreal, Quebec.

The USA: East Tennessee, Georgia, Long Island, Pittsburgh, Rio Grande, South Carolina.

The bishop of the Arctic in Canada said that his diocese is not familiar with mediation, and so any comments by him would be purely hypothetical. His letter was positive in tone, and he said that he 'would be very interested in learning of your conclusions'. The author has no qualms about including his response in the overall total. He has some

sider the topic as important. Secondly it indicates that some confidence can be placed in the picture which emerges. Only in the case of Hong Kong should the results be looked at with any caution, as only one response was received from that country.[22] The responses from the USA make up the largest individual group, but the proportion from outside the USA is 47%, which gives a useful balance.[23] Of the 98 responses, 88 were from bishops, and 10 from archbishops.[24] The response rate for each country is shown in figure 16.[25]

---

misgivings about including the response from the Rio Grande (USA), as the bishop's personal assistant wrote 'This letter is to let you know that we will not be participating in the survey'. This was the only 'negative' response to the questionnaire. If the response from the bishop of the Rio Grande is not counted, the number of effective responses is reduced to 97, or 52% of the 188 questionnaires sent out. If (contrary to my personal view) the response from the bishop of the Arctic should not be counted, the number of effective responses is reduced to 96, or 51%.

[22] Though the response from Hong Kong was from the Archbishop.

[23] This is illustrated by the results for section A of the questionnaire. In the USA, employment was considered the most suitable type of dispute for mediation; but the overall most suitable type of dispute was personality conflict.

[24] The archbishops were from the following dioceses:

Australia: Adelaide, Brisbane, Melbourne, Sydney.

Canada: Huron, Nova Scotia and Prince Edward Island, Ontario, Saskatoon.

Hong Kong: Hong Kong Island.

South Africa: Cape Town.

[25] The questionnaires were sent out at the beginning of July 2000. The questionnaire asked for responses by the end of August 2000 if possible, but said that responses received later would still be welcome. 23 responses were received in July, 23 in August, 8 in September, and 12 in October. A further copy of the survey together with a reminder letter was sent out in October to all those who had not responded. (Some of the responses in October followed the reminder letter). 25 responses

Country	Sent	Responses	Response rate	Proportion
Australia	23	15	65%	15%
Canada	32	16	50%	17%
Hong Kong	4	1	25%	1%
New Zealand	7	3	43%	3%
South Africa	22	11	50%	11%
The USA	100	52	52%	53%
Total	188	98	52%	100%

Figure 16. Responses to international survey[26]

3. SUITABILITY OF DIFFERENT TYPES OF DISPUTE

The first section of the questionnaire read as follows:

A. Types of church dispute

I want to find out what sorts of church disputes you consider most suitable for mediation, and what sorts you consider are not suitable.

Please mark with an X the appropriate box number for each type of dispute according to the following guide. 1 = unsuitable you would not use mediation for this type of dispute. 5 = completely suitable you would encourage mediation for this type of dispute.

---

were then received in November, 3 in December, 3 in January 2001, and 1 in March 2001. 87 responses were sent by post, five by fax, and six by email.

[26] When showing percentages as round numbers, it is sometimes necessary to adjust one or more of the figures to make the total come to 100 per cent.

Type of dispute	How suitable?
	1 2 3 4 5
1. alterations to church buildings and grave-yards	☐ ☐ ☐ ☐ ☐
2. church governance: disputes between a church and the diocesan authorities or the Bishop	☐ ☐ ☐ ☐ ☐
3. personality conflicts: e.g. disputes between clergy working in a team, usually involving six people or less	☐ ☐ ☐ ☐ ☐
4. pastoral breakdown	☐ ☐ ☐ ☐ ☐
5. disputes over forms of worship/doctrine	☐ ☐ ☐ ☐ ☐
6. gay or gender issues	☐ ☐ ☐ ☐ ☐
7. racial discrimination	☐ ☐ ☐ ☐ ☐
8. employment disputes	☐ ☐ ☐ ☐ ☐
9. minor discipline matters, not involving sexual allegations	☐ ☐ ☐ ☐ ☐
10. property disputes	☐ ☐ ☐ ☐ ☐
11. financial disputes	☐ ☐ ☐ ☐ ☐
12. defamation	☐ ☐ ☐ ☐ ☐
13. personal injury	☐ ☐ ☐ ☐ ☐
14. commercial contract disputes	☐ ☐ ☐ ☐ ☐
15. tax disputes	☐ ☐ ☐ ☐ ☐

What other types of church dispute are particularly suitable for mediation?	

What other types of church dispute are particularly unsuitable for mediation?	

Any comments?	

The overall result for each type of dispute mentioned in the questionnaire is shown in figure 17.

These have been shown in descending order of suitability. The four types of dispute seen as most suitable for mediation are personality conflicts, employment disputes, pastoral breakdowns, and disputes about church governance. The four types of dispute seen as least suitable for mediation are defamation, tax disputes, gay or gender issues, and disputes over forms of worship and doctrine.

Only two types of dispute was considered overall to be unsuitable, i.e. below 3 on the scale of 1 to 5: disputes about gay or gender issues, which scored 2.99 (only just below 3), and disputes about forms or worship or doctrine, which scored 2.90. The overall average was 3.40, i.e. suitable rather than unsuitable.

Property ownership, financial (non-criminal), and contractual disputes also scored quite highly.

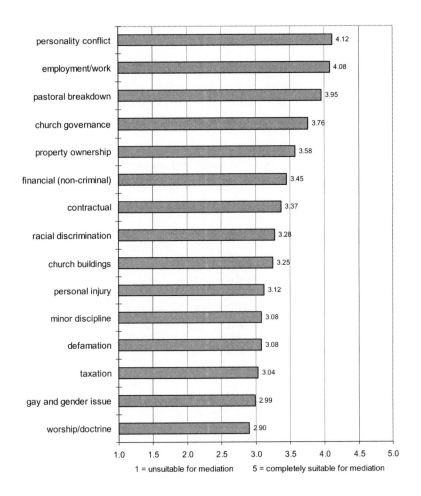

Figure 17. Dispute ratings (Summary)

A number of comments can be made about the groupings for the top end, the bottom end, and the middle of this set of results. It is interesting that in the three highest scoring types of dispute, human relationships are very important. A personality conflict is almost by definition concerned with relationships. Some em-

357

ployment disputes are concerned with factual matters such as disciplinary practices, hours and salary, and holiday arrangements; but many also contain a human element, the personal relationship between, say, the vicar and the person employed by the church. The third most suitable dispute type, pastoral breakdown, is by definition concerned with the relationship between the vicar and the members of the parish.

Among the middle scorers, property ownership, financial and contractual disputes, relationships are less important. These are the types of dispute most suited to commercial mediation.

In both the low scorers, disputes about gay or gender issues, and disputes about forms of worship or doctrine, often some deep principle is at issue, theological or moral, and this may make mediation difficult. There is however evidence in the UK of mediation being successfully used for these types of disputes.[27]

The ratings given by each country show a consistent trend at the top and the bottom of the table. The top three scorers for each individual country are shown in figure 18, the bottom three scorers in figure 19.

---

[27] Yvonne Craig, *Peacemaking for churches* (SPCK, 1999), pg. 22 gives an example of a gender conflict which was resolved by mediation. The survey in chapter 3, 'Church dispute resolution in the United Kingdom', indicates that archdeacons frequently mediate disputes about forms of worship and church buildings.

Rate	1	2	3
Australia	personality conflict	employment	pastoral breakdown
Canada	personality conflict	pastoral breakdown	employment
Hong Kong	pastoral breakdown	personality conflict	church buildings
New Zealand	employment	pastoral breakdown	personality conflict
South Africa	personality conflict	employment	church governance
The USA	employment	personality conflict	pastoral breakdown

Figure 18. Best dispute types for mediation

Employment disputes and personality conflicts thus score top in the USA, Australia and South Africa. Personality conflicts and pastoral breakdown score top in Canada, Hong Kong and New Zealand. The only additional types which reach the top three are church buildings (Hong Kong), and church governance (South Africa).

Rate	13	14	15
Australia	taxation	minor discipline	personal injury
Canada	worship doctrine	gay gender	taxation
Hong Kong	taxation	gay gender	racial discriminat ion
New Zealand	minor discipline	worship doctrine	taxation
South Africa	worship doctrine	minor discipline	gay gender
The USA	defamation	worship doctrine	gay gender

Figure 19. Worst dispute types for mediation

Amongst the disputes considered most unsuitable there was more variety. In all countries except for New Zealand, gay or gender issues was either rated 14 or 15 out of the 15 choices.[28] Worship and doctrine was rated 14 or 15 in the USA and New Zealand.

Figure 20 shows the ratings given by each country for each type of dispute.

---

[28] Gay and gender issues in fact rated 10 out of 15 in New Zealand, scoring 3.00.

	Australia	Canada	HongKong	New Zealand	South Africa	The USA	Average
church buildings	3.29	2.90	5.00	3.67	3.27	3.25	3.25
church governance	3.38	3.73	5.00	3.00	4.36	3.76	3.76
contractual	3.08	2.82	3.00	3.67	4.18	3.38	3.37
defamation	2.92	2.92	3.00	3.33	4.18	2.89	3.08
employment/ work	4.08	4.00	3.00	4.00	4.55	4.02	4.08
financial (non-criminal)	3.23	3.18	4.00	2.67	4.00	3.49	3.45
gay and gender issue	3.38	2.75	3.00	3.00	3.00	2.93	2.99
minor discipline	2.69	2.83	4.00	2.00	3.09	3.31	3.08
pastoral breakdown	3.77	4.08	5.00	4.00	4.09	3.91	3.95
personal injury	2.82	3.00	3.00	3.33	4.09	2.98	3.12
personality conflict	4.15	4.17	5.00	3.67	4.55	4.00	4.12
property ownership	3.75	3.36	4.00	2.67	4.18	3.49	3.58
racial discrimination	3.50	3.08	3.00	3.00	3.27	3.30	3.28
taxation	2.54	2.82	3.00	2.67	3.55	3.14	3.04
worship/ doctrine	2.92	2.58	5.00	2.33	3.10	2.93	2.90
Average	3.30	3.22	3.87	3.13	3.83	3.39	3.40

Figure 20. Dispute ratings (Figures)

75 of the 87 bishops (86%) who answered section A of the questionnaire gave a rating for all 15 types of dispute.[29] Figure 21 shows the number of responses for each type of dispute (arranged in descending order).

---

[29] Five bishops gave ratings for 14 types of dispute, two bishops for 13 types, one bishop for 9 types, two bishops for 6 types, and one bishop gave ratings for only 2 types of dispute.

pastoral breakdown	86		gay or gender issues	84
minor discipline	85		worship/doctrine	84
employment disputes	85		church buildings alterations	83
defamation	85		property disputes	83
personality conflicts	85		racial discrimination	83
church governance	84		personal injury	82
contract disputes	84		tax disputes	81
financial disputes	84			

Figure 21. Response rates for dispute types

Minor discipline and defamation rank equal second in this table, even though they rank respectively 11th and 12th out of 15 in the suitability table. In some cases the bishops said that they did not have experience of disputes in some of the areas for which they gave a figure.[30] These points indicate that bishops were not simply giving high marks to dispute types with which they were familiar, and low marks to those of which they had no experience. The ratings therefore combine both actual experience and perceived wisdom; and they are arguably all the more reliable for this.

i Individual countries

AUSTRALIA

The dispute ratings for Australia are shown in figure 22.

---

[30] An example is Highveld (South Africa).

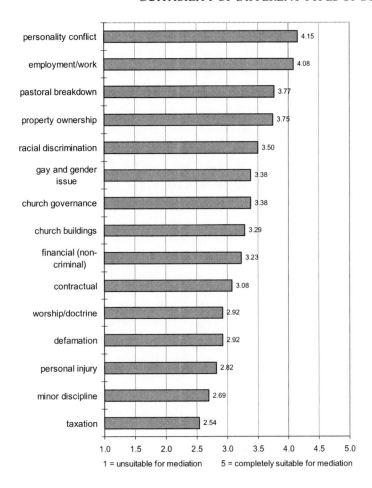

Figure 22. Dispute ratings (Australia)

The average score was 3.30, slightly under the overall average of 3.40 for the whole survey. The four types of dispute seen as most suitable for mediation are personality conflict, employment/work, pastoral breakdown, and property ownership. The four types of dispute seen as least suitable for mediation are defamation, personal injury, minor discipline, and taxation. The

363

rating for gay or gender issue disputes and its position in the overall table was higher in Australia than in any other country, but the comments from the bishops do not suggest any reason for this.[31]

Disputes between congregations, disputes about ministry style, social issues such as drugs, prostitution and AIDS/HIV care, disputes between parish leaders, and church closures were all considered suitable for mediation.[32] Financial and sexual misconduct,[33] matters governed by canon law, and cases where there is a significant power imbalance were all considered unsuitable.[34] Yet

---

[31] Gay and gender issues rated 13th in the USA, 6th in Australia, 14th in Canada, 14th in Hong Kong, 10th in New Zealand, 15th in South Africa, and 14th overall. The only bishop to comment specifically on gay and gender issues was the bishop of Bunbury: 'Not clear what Q means as to gay issues. Does the Q refer to ordination or same-sex marriage? If so, the tradition of the Church is clear'.

[32] Australian bishops identified the following additional topics as suitable for mediation:

'Pastoral breakdown is particularly suited to mediation. Stress caused by pastoral breakdown often occasions further exacerbation. Church discipline is related to ordinances.' (The Murray).

'Governance issues and personality conflicts.' (Wangaratta).

'Disputes between congregations in multi-centred parishes.' (Willochra).

'Disputes about ministry "style" and "direction".' (Sydney).

'Social issues of a controversial nature, such as drugs, prostitution, AIDS/HIV care.' (Newcastle).

'Disputes between parish leaders.' (Adelaide).

'Parish closures/amalgamations; disbursement of proceeds of sale.' (Melbourne).

[33] Willochra and Sydney.

[34] The following topics were identified as being unsuitable for mediation:

'Matters related to doctrine and church order.' (Wangaratta)

there were some differences between dioceses: in one diocese, for example, mediation *does* take place in sexual misconduct cases.[35] Amongst the general comments one bishop said that mediation requires goodwill, and this is likely to have disappeared once legal processes have begun. The moral is clear: mediation should be begun sooner rather than later.[36]

'Legal issues e.g. financial misconduct and sexual misconduct.' (Willochra)

'Allegations of sexual misconduct or criminal or immoral behaviour.' (Sydney)

'Those that are governed specifically by canon law or legislation which are not easily alterable.' (Newcastle).

'Disputes where there is significant power imbalance between parties.' (Melbourne)

[35] 'Our sexual harassment protocol provides for mediation; also in our Ecclesiastical Offences Act; 5 years ago there was an incident of improper touching which we dealt [with?] by convening an ad hoc panel.' In the bishop's covering letter he stated that this incident 'was resolved by our setting up an ad hoc panel which interviewed both parties.' (Bendigo).

[36] Australian bishops made the following general comments:

'All that I have not marked could all benefit from an encouraged mediation.' (Gippsland).

'On racial discrimination: racism is alive and well, discrimination is illegal.' (North Queensland).

'The church in Bunbury has a history of breakdown connected to baptisms, marriages etc. A number of clergy have adopted a "rigorist" policy. I have made it clear that we come in the business of opening doors and not closing them. I will [...] churchwardens and clergy to [...] about these issues. Not clear what Q means as to gay issues. Does the Q refer to ordination or same-sex marriage? If so, the tradition of the Church is clear.' (Bunbury).

'See our Synod Select Committee Report and Parish Disputes Ordinance 1999 sent as attachment to e mail recently.' (Sydney).

365

CANADA

The dispute ratings for Canada are shown in figure 23. The average score was 3.22, the second lowest score in the survey. The four types of dispute seen as most suitable for mediation were personality conflict, pastoral breakdown, employment/work, and church governance. The four types of dispute seen as least suitable for mediation are contractual, taxation, gay or gender issue, and worship/doctrine. The average score was 3.22.

One bishop commented that where the balance of power is equal, mediation is appropriate; where most of the power is held by one party, it is not.[37] Sexual abuse was only mentioned by one bishop, who considered it unsuitable for mediation.[38] Among the general comments,[39] the same point was made as in the USA, that mediation is best if begun early.[40]

'Mediation works best when there is a common good outcome anticipated by the parties – and where mature compromise is possible.' (Newcastle).

'Goodwill is required. This is likely to have disappeared if legal processes have begun.' (Adelaide).

[37] Moosonee.

[38] Central Newfoundland.

[39] Canada bishops identified the following additional topics as suitable for mediation:

'Rector vs. congregation; rector vs. wardens and other lay officials; new building – congregation.' (Toronto).

'In situations of roughly equal power, and where there is some respect for other viewpoints, and a *desire* to resolve a difficulty and move forward.' (Moosonee).

'The listing, as it would involve this diocese, is quite inclusive.' (Eastern Newfoundland and Labrador).

'Non adherence to constitutional issues by parish or congregation.' (Central Newfoundland).

One bishop categorised some disputes by reference to the people involved: rector vs. congregation,[41] rector vs. wardens and other lay officials, saying these were all suitable for mediation.[42]

The following were unsuitable for mediation:

'Clergy incompetence leading to pastoral breakdown and conflict. Marital conflict. Best approach is through pastoral intervention by the archdeacon and/or bishop.' (Nova Scotia and Prince Edward Island).

'Where all or most of the power is seen to be held in one party, and there is an unwillingness to surrender this to a mediation process.' (Moosonee).

'Sexual abuse; criminal behaviour.' (Central Newfoundland).

General comments made by the bishops on this topic were:

'The first box represents the Christian ideal.' (Moosonee)

'Items marked with low priority are generally so because of already existing procedures, or, litigation usually has begun.' (Qu'Appelle). The bishop gave a 1 to church building alterations, gay and gender issues, racial discrimination, property, financial, contract, and tax disputes. He gave a 2 to worship/doctrine, defamation, and personal injury.

'The question of appropriateness depends on the specific nature and circumstances of the dispute.' (Rupert's Land).

'Most situations are open to mediation in the beginning.' (Ontario).

'Preventative measures, then spelling out of initial expectations, then … establishing shared responsibilities nearly always minimises conflict.' (Saskatoon)

[40] Ontario.

[41] Toronto.

[42] Toronto.

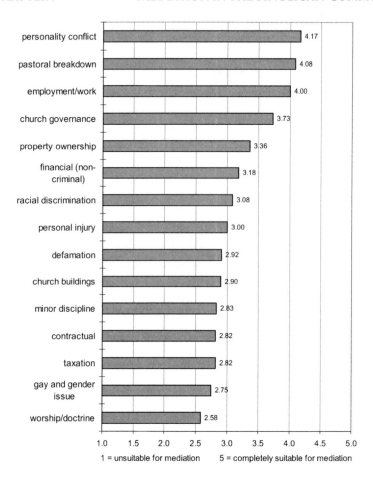

Figure 23. Dispute ratings (Canada)

HONG KONG

The dispute ratings for Hong Kong are shown in figure 24. As only one response was received from Hong Kong, these results should be treated with some caution, but the average score was 3.87, the highest in the survey. It is encouraging that the Archbishop of Hong Kong considered that pastoral breakdown, personality conflict, church buildings, church governance and worship/doctrine disputes are all completely suitable for mediation; and that no topic was unsuitable.

The Archbishop mentioned only one additional area of dispute as suitable for mediation: disputes about deployment of clergy.

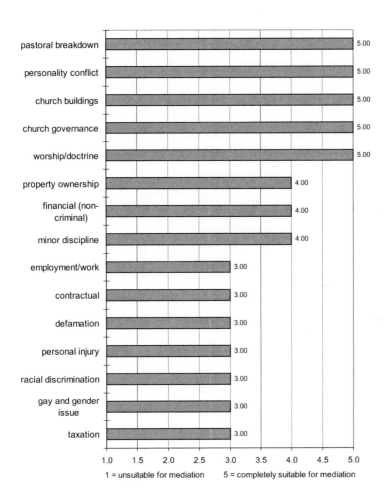

Figure 24. Dispute ratings (Hong Kong)

369

NEW ZEALAND

The dispute ratings for New Zealand are shown in figure 25.

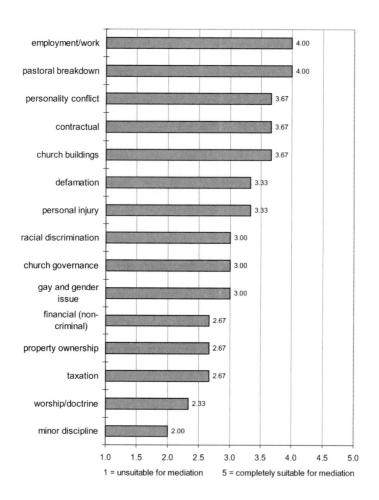

Figure 25. Dispute ratings (New Zealand)

The average was 3.13, the lowest in the survey. The four types of dispute seen as most suitable for mediation are employment/work, pastoral breakdown, personality conflict, and contractual. The four types of dispute seen as least suitable are property ownership, taxation, worship/doctrine, and minor discipline. Gay and gender issues came 10th in the list, and defamation 6th, both significantly better than the overall rating in the survey.

Two of the New Zealand bishops mentioned that disputes about sexual misconduct[43] are unsuitable for mediation.[44] One of these two linked this with abuse of power:[45]

> In cases involving abuse of power or sexual misconduct, we have found that mediation is completely inappropriate.[46]

One bishop recommended as follows:

> 'There needs to be a sequential approach to resolving disputes: (1) try 1-1; (2) try mediators; (3) try authorities; (4) try rules.' [47]

SOUTH AFRICA

The dispute ratings for South Africa are shown in figure 26. The average was 3.83, the second highest in the survey. The four most suitable types of dispute for mediation are personality conflict, employment/work, church governance, and defamation.

---

[43] Sexual misconduct covers a whole range of matters, some criminal, some not. It is not clear whether the bishops had in mind all types.

[44] Wellington and Christchurch.

[45] Abuse of power is not always a bar to mediation. The key factor is whether the abuse will prevent the innocent party taking a proper part in the mediation. In family mediation, for example, the mediators interview the parties separately before the mediation, to decide whether instances of domestic violence will so prevent the abused party from being able to take a proper part in the mediation. In many cases, mediation can proceed provided ground rules are put in place to protect the abused party from possible further violence.

[46] 'In cases involving abuse of power or sexual misconduct, we have found that mediation is completely inappropriate.' (Christchurch).

[47] Waikato.

The four types of dispute seen as least suitable for mediation are racial discrimination, worship/doctrine, minor discipline, and gay or gender issues. The lowest score, for gay or gender issue disputes, was exactly 3.[48] The average score was 3.83, the highest score in the survey.

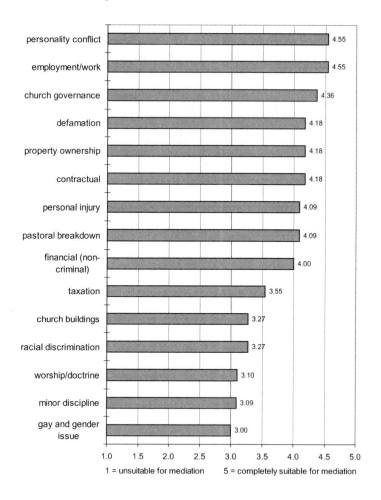

personality conflict — 4.55
employment/work — 4.55
church governance — 4.36
defamation — 4.18
property ownership — 4.18
contractual — 4.18
personal injury — 4.09
pastoral breakdown — 4.09
financial (non-criminal) — 4.00
taxation — 3.55
church buildings — 3.27
racial discrimination — 3.27
worship/doctrine — 3.10
minor discipline — 3.09
gay and gender issue — 3.00

1.0   1.5   2.0   2.5   3.0   3.5   4.0   4.5   5.0

1 = unsuitable for mediation   5 = completely suitable for mediation

---

[48] This is probably connected with the fact that the South African bishops have a very conservative attitude to homosexuality.

Figure 26. Dispute ratings (South Africa)

The comments from South Africa are perhaps the most interesting of all the comments received, as they identify a number of important themes.[49]

---

[49] South African bishops identified the following topics as suitable for mediation:

'Particularly suitable are power struggles (1) between clergy and lay leaders, and (2) between stipendiary and non-stipendiary clergy.' (St Mark the Evangelist, Northern Province).

'None.' (Cape Town).

'Conflicts between rector/vicar and parishioners over parish leadership.' (Port Elizabeth).

'Disputes between clergy and lay leaders and/or congregation.' (Johannesburg)

'All issues involving interpersonal differences of opinion.' (Klerksdorp).

'Clergy/organist; traditional/charismatic parishioners'. (Pretoria).

South African bishops considered the following topics unsuitable:

'Not suitable are those where there is not an obvious "right" and "wrong" – where people may need help in opening up to God's grace, or seeing each others' points of view.' (St Mark the Evangelist, Northern Province).

'Interfaith disputes.' (Cape Town).

'On issues of principle, for example, in the case of the bishop's right to act canonically in the dismissal of a priest/cleric.' (Port Elizabeth).

'Marriage problems of clergy.' (Bloemfontein).

'Any issues involving key theological issues over which the issues are fundamental and non-negotiable.' (Johannesburg).

The bishops in South Africa made the following comments:

Alterations to church buildings and property disputes: needs trustees. Gay or gender issues: depends! Racial discrimination sometimes requires a firm hand. I understand mediation as a person/persons facilitating a process of mutual understanding and reconciliation, so that the dispute can be resolved in the best way possible. We experience very

First, a number of bishops see disputes not in terms of some factual or legal categorisation, but by reference to the parties. So, disputes between clergy and lay leaders,[50] between stipendiary and non-stipendiary clergy,[51] between rector/vicar and parishioners over parish leadership,[52] between clergy and lay leaders and/or congregation,[53] between clergy and organist,[54] between traditional and charismatic parishioners,[55] and between church and state,[56] were all suitable for mediation.

Second, the bishops commented that key issues of principle,[57] or key non-negotiable theological issues[58] are not suitable for mediation.

---

little litigation in South Africa. We encourage people to work through their problems, and try to facilitate the process.' (St Mark the Evangelist, Northern Province),

'Our practice in this diocese is to resolve issues ourselves within the diocesan family using our own people and not calling on outside mediators.' (Port Elizabeth)

'I am not happy with these answers. I can foresee examples where in one case mediation is the way forward, in another disastrous, both in the same category.' (Pretoria).

'Most of my answers on pg. 1 are of a theoretical nature: we – as a diocese– have been wonderfully free of dispute for a good number of years.' (Highveld).

[50] St Mark the Evangelist, Northern Province.

[51] St Mark the Evangelist, Northern Province.

[52] Port Elizabeth.

[53] Johannesburg.

[54] Pretoria.

[55] Pretoria.

[56] Swaziland.

[57] Port Elizabeth.

[58] Johannesburg.

Third, one bishop sees the diocese as a family, and attempts to resolve a dispute internally without calling on outside mediators. This brings to mind Community mediation and the theological application of this to the church community.[59]

THE USA

The dispute ratings for the USA are shown in figure 27.

The average was 3.39, a fraction below the overall average of 3.40 for the survey. The figures for the USA are very similar to those for Canada. In the USA the four types of dispute seen as most suitable for mediation are employment, personality conflict, pastoral breakdown, and church governance. The four types of dispute seen as least suitable for mediation are personal injury, gay or gender issues, worship/doctrine, and defamation. The average score was 3.39, just below the overall average for all countries, 3.40.

_____

[59] See chapter 5, 'Community mediation'.

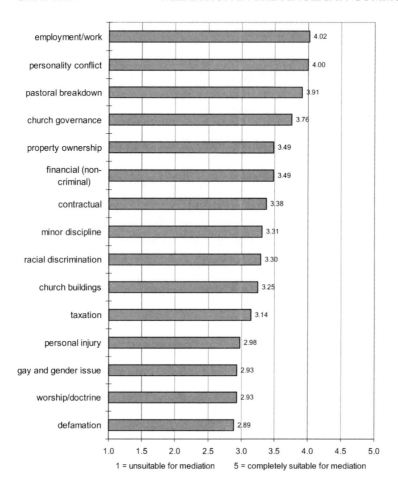

Figure 27. Dispute ratings (The USA)

The American bishops suggested a range of other dispute types suitable for mediation[60] and a range of unsuitable dispute

---

[60] The following were considered suitable:

'An impasse in the calling process for a new rector or vicar.' (San Diego).

'Violation of sexual boundaries, i.e. poor judgment, harassment, abuse, exploitation. We have a detailed process that involves trained fact-finders and a support person for both victim and perpetrator. The whole process is spelled out in published step by step format. The victim and the perpetrator get a copy at the outset and know that the diocesan authorities will follow the format. The bishop plays a key pastoral role. Early on the bishop tries to learn from the victim what justice might look like. In ±30 such cases [we] have not had to resort to canonical disciplinary procedures.' (Washington).

'Shared use of buildings.' (Olympia).

'Seeking to avoid a dissolution of the pastoral relationship (Canon III.21).' (Michigan).

'Disputes over pastoral style, and what the "mandate" is for a new priest.' (Bethlehem).

'Use of memorial funds.' (Maine).

'Any dispute over style, presentation, vision and/or goals.' (Chicago).

'Generally those disputes that involve specific remedies and so allow a win-win approach. Also where there is a BATNA which helps move parties to agreement rather than continuing conflict.' (Delaware). This response indicates familiarity with mediation jargon. BATNA stands for the 'best alternative to a negotiated agreement', i.e. what is the best course of action for a party if settlement is not reached.

'Disputes which deal with temporal or material matters.' (New Hampshire).

'Disputes with high potential for abuse of the process.' (Utah). An example would be where a party's motive in attending a mediation is to obtain information to assist with a court case rather than genuinely to seek to resolve the dispute.

'Disputes between rector and vestry (the ECUSA equivalent of the Church of England parochial church council).' (Virginia).

'Property in parish vs. diocese; diocese vs. "national church".' (Quincy).

'Removal of a priest from a parish – mediate separation agreement.' (Florida).

'Proposed dissolution of the pastoral relationship.' (Central Pennsylvania).

'Between priest and people; between "yoked" parishes.' (Milwaukee).

types.[61] They do not seem to fit any particular factual categories. Sexual misconduct is considered suitable for mediation in one

---

'Goal definition and implementation; personality conflict leaning towards serious inability to perform as expected; cultural conflict i.e. racism etc.' (Western Louisiana).

'Clergy vs. congregation disputes.' (New York).

[61] The following were considered unsuitable:

'Issues with external advocacy groups i.e. environmentalists, those opposed to any new church construction, homophobic, and far right conservative church groups.' (Washington).

'Liturgical and theological disputes.' (Olympia). This is covered by forms of worship and doctrine, but is worth emphasis.

'Most disciplinary actions have emotional levels that make informal resolutions very difficult.' (Michigan).

'Probably whether a particular person should be ordained, though forms of mediation could be helpful here.' (Los Angeles).

'Where there is a clear violation of church canon; where there is a great difference between parties and one or both parties are uncooperative.' (Maine).

'Issues which have a specific interpretation in church constitution and canons.' (Fond du Lac).

'Disputes over objective acts of injustice.' (Chicago).

'Where it is just a fight with deep positions and little or no BATNA. Where the motive to fight is to remove the other party or do significant personal damage.' (Delaware). Notice the use of mediation jargon.

'Pastoral concerns between parishioners.' (Missouri).

'Authority questions that can be handled by reference to canons.' (Missouri).

'Things which deal with primarily spiritual matters should be dealt with in a pastoral way by church professionals.' (New Hampshire).

'Disputes in which the power imbalance cannot be overcome by the mediator.' (Utah).

'Allegations of sexual misconduct.' (Virginia).

diocese[62] but unsuitable in others,[63] except where it takes place *after* discipline.[64] There were different views on the suitability of mediation for dissolution of the pastoral relationship.[65] Power imbalance was recognised as a factor against mediation.[66] Amongst the general comments,[67] motivation by all parties to mediate was recognised as a key factor for success.[68]

'Sexual misconduct – except to mediate consequences.' (Florida).

'[Where] lawsuits filed.' (Milwaukee).

'Dissolution of pastoral relationship.' (Arkansas).

'Monetary or misconduct occasions.' (Western Louisiana).

'Sexual boundary violations.' (New York).

[62] Washington.

[63] Virginia, Florida and New York. The bishop of Washington seems to be referring to more minor cases than New York and Florida. In Florida, mediation is considered suitable for the 'consequences' of sexual misconduct.

[64] Maine.

[65] Dissolution of the pastoral relationship is considered suitable for mediation in Michigan and Central Pennsylvania, but unsuitable in Arkansas.

[66] Utah.

[67] The following comments were made by the bishops in the USA:

'On gay and gender issues, we have a clear and consistent policy of truth telling re orientation that begins in pre-ordination process and continues through clergy deployment. The result has been no confrontations that required 3rd party intervention. If gay clergy have a partner it is known. There is one standard for all clergy – chastity or fidelity and monogamy.' The same bishop reported: 'In my 3 years as suffragan and 10 as diocesan we have not had an issue in areas 1–15 except item 4 [pastoral breakdown] and 8 [employment].' (Washington).

'The more a dispute is cognizable by the civil court, the more non-judicial resolution takes on the role of seeking to avoid one or both parties going to court. Therefore it becomes more difficult to gain mutual

379

A number of bishops identified disputes by reference to the parties involved, rather than by the factual or legal category of dispute: rector vs. vestry (the American equivalent of the PCC),[69] diocese vs. 'national church',[70] between priest and people,[71] be-

---

'acceptance of alternative process because, in the American litigious culture, one or all want their day in court.' (Michigan).

'The key to the success of mediation is (1) a skilled mediator who is objective, and (2) motivation by all parties to mediate.' (Maine).

'We are a small diocese and can usually depend on primary relationships to deal with matters which arise. I am in favour of mediation, though, when that fails.' (Northern Michigan).

'Church disputes tend to be more difficult than civil matters. This seems to be due in part to the strongly held positions that get personalised in religious communities.' (Delaware).

'Any circumstance in which professional (financial, sexual etc.) misconduct has occurred needs to be dealt with by discipline *before* mediation can occur. Mediation cannot replace discipline or else the substance of clergy discipline will be eroded.' (Maine).

'I think nearly all types of dispute can be helped with mediation.' (Eau Claire).

'The answers may depend on which parties are in dispute. So e.g. alterations to church buildings – between church members or between church and local government; similarly tax disputes. Minor discipline may have canonical or rubrics requirements.' (Indeanapolis).

'We don't have established procedures for reaction to various kinds of problems. We are lucky in the diocese to have an Alban Institute trained Crisis Counsellor or Mediation Counsellor, who does most of her work for the Federal Judiciary System in Georgia. She is an active communicant and has always been helpful with congregations in trouble in the diocese. We also have Fr. Liam Collins who has a Master's Degree in Family Systems Counselling.' (Georgia).

[68] Maine.

[69] Virginia.

[70] Quincy.

tween 'yoked' parishes,[72] all these were considered suitable for mediation. Pastoral concerns between parishioners were considered unsuitable.[73]

ii Conclusions

One of the conclusions which emerges from the survey figures and the bishops' comments is that there is more than one way to analyse many church disputes. The questionnaire concentrated on the substantive issues between the parties, and analysed disputes in terms of well-known legal categories: defamation, personal injury etc. The bishops' responses point also to procedural and psychological concerns which need to be taken into account in deciding whether or not a dispute is suitable for mediation.

We see here once again the three elements of the conflict triangle. The survey indicates that the conflict triangle is useful before mediation begins, to see whether a particular dispute is suitable for mediation. There are three tests, one for each side of the triangle:

- The *problem* test. What is the substantive issue? What is the legal and factual background to the dispute?

- The *people* test. What are the psychological and emotional issues? What is the relationship between the parties to the dispute?

- The *process* test. Is there a procedural reason to use some other dispute resolution process in preference to mediation?

iii The 'problem' test.

The first analysis is to see a dispute in terms of legal or factual categories. Some examples of the legal categories into which a

---

[71] Milwaukee. Similarly 'clergy vs. congregation' (New York).

[72] Milwaukee.

[73] Missouri.

dispute might fall are: a contractual dispute, a personal injury dispute, an employment dispute, or a case of defamation. These are categories well known to lawyers, and it is clear that categorising a dispute in such terms may enable one to see whether it is appropriate for mediation. From the results of the survey one may say that employment, contract and property disputes are very suitable for mediation, and that defamation, racial discrimination, personal injury and taxation are less so. It is noteworthy that these four categories where mediation is less suitable may involve criminal conduct.[74] Where criminal conduct is in issue, as has been pointed out,[75] mediation is not appropriate.

Some church disputes do not fit into any obvious legal categories, and can best be seen in terms of the area of church life to which they relate. Disputes in the following areas of church life were recognised as very suitable for mediation:

- church governance

- disagreements over goals and vision for church[76]

- shared use of church buildings[77]

- memorial funds[78]

- deployment of clergy[79]

- clergy appointments[80]

---

[74] For defamation, see *St James, Hockwold*, pg. 114; for racial discrimination, see pg. 107; personal injury may arise from careless driving, or a breach of health and safety regulations; tax evasion, as opposed to tax avoidance, is a criminal offence.

[75] See pg. 114 and 193.

[76] Chicago (USA); Western Louisiana (USA).

[77] Olympia (USA).

[78] Maine (USA).

[79] Hong Kong.

- pastoral style[81]

- removal of a priest from a parish[82]

- social issues such as drugs[83]

- parish closures and amalgamations.[84]

Disputes in the following areas were considered less suitable for mediation:

- worship/doctrine disputes

- gay or gender issues

- clergy incompetence[85]

- liturgical and theological disputes[86]

- disciplinary action[87]

- whether a particular person should be ordained[88]

- sexual misconduct[89]

---

[80] San Diego (USA).

[81] Bethlehem (USA).

[82] Florida (USA); Central Pennsylvania (USA); but dissolution of pastoral relationship was considered unsuitable for mediation in Arkansas (USA).

[83] Newcastle (Australia).

[84] Melbourne (Australia).

[85] Nova Scotia and Prince Edward Island (Canada).

[86] Olympia (USA).

[87] Michigan (USA).

[88] Los Angeles (USA).

[89] Wellington (New Zealand); Christchurch (New Zealand); Virginia (USA); Florida (USA); Sydney (Australia); New York (USA) Central Newfoundland (Canada).

- interfaith disputes[90]

- issues of principal/ theological issues.[91]

iv The 'people' test

The second analysis is to consider the parties to the dispute and their relationship. Mediation is more appropriate for disputes between certain categories of persons than certain other categories. A personality conflict between clergy working together in a team may arise from any number of causes, and these are amongst the most suitable disputes for mediation. The following 'people' circumstances were identified as being suitable for mediation:

- personality conflict within a team[92]

- disputes between parish leaders[93]

- situations of roughly equal power[94]

- pastoral breakdown[95]

- disputes between congregations in multi-centred parishes[96]

- disputes between rector, wardens, other lay officials and the congregation, or any combination of these[97]

---

[90] Cape Town (South Africa).

[91] Port Elizabeth (South Africa); Johannesburg (South Africa)

[92] 'All issues involving interpersonal differences of opinion'. Johannesburg (South Africa).

[93] Adelaide (Australia).

[94] Moosonee (Canada).

[95] The Murray (Australia).

[96] Willochra (Australia).

[97] Toronto (Canada); Port Elizabeth (South Africa); Virginia (USA); Christ the King (South Africa).

- disputes between the diocese and the 'national church'[98]
- disputes between clergy and the organist[99]
- disputes between traditional and charismatic parishioners[100]
- disputes between church and state.[101]

Only three 'people' circumstances were seen as making a dispute unsuitable for mediation: where an external lobbying group is involved,[102] where one party's motive is to remove the other party or do significant personal damage,[103] and situations of significant power imbalance.[104]

One bishop[105] pointed out that a number of the dispute categories can be seen as primarily relational. He identified personality conflicts, gay or gender issues, racial discrimination and employment disputes as falling into this category. He considered that mediation should be compulsory for any relational disputes.

v The 'process' test

The third analysis is to consider mediation as an alternative to other forms of legal process, and consider which is best for the situation. Mediation is inappropriate, for example, where the matters in dispute should be made public, and where it might be

---

[98] Quincy (USA).

[99] Pretoria (South Africa).

[100] Pretoria (South Africa).

[101] Swaziland (South Africa).

[102] Washington (USA). The bishop gave the following examples: environmentalists, those opposed to any new church construction, homophobic, and far right conservative church groups.

[103] Delaware (USA). This can be seen as a level 4 or level 5 conflict: see figure 14 'Levels of conflict', pg. 322.

[104] Adelaide (Australia), Moosonee (Canada), Utah (USA).

[105] Olympia, USA.

thought that the Church was trying to hide a problem by using mediation. Typical examples would be cases of serious racial or sexual harassment, sexual misconduct, or criminal activity.

Some bishops considered mediation inappropriate in cases where their authority as bishop is called into question. Although these bishops did not give a reason for this view, they presumably considered that their authority and power as bishop is non-negotiable.[106]

Mediation is inappropriate where the process is likely to be abused. This would include a party which uses the mediation simply to escalate the dispute (e.g. by threatening the other party), or to gather information to strengthen its case in court, rather than to try to seek a solution.

Two bishops said that mediation is inappropriate if some other legal process has already begun.[107] This view is not accepted, for two reasons. First, there is always uncertainty and expense involved in legal proceedings which can make it an advantage to attempt mediation. Second, statistics for the four court mediation schemes described in chapter 4 indicate high settlement rates for cases which were referred to mediation by the court.[108]

The following were the main areas where some other process was considered preferable to mediation:

---

[106] Compare the Kidderminster dispute in the UK, see pg. 110. The bishop considered mediation inappropriate because he regarded the key issue as being one of discipline, whereas Mr Raven was willing to work within the terms of his licence. By 'discipline' the bishop meant canonical obedience. He was not at that stage referring to disciplinary proceedings.

[107] Milwaukee (USA). Adelaide (Australia): 'Goodwill is required. This is likely to have disappeared if legal processes have begun.'

[108] These range from 89.6% in the case sent to mediation by the Commercial Court, to 61.9% for cases sent to mediation by the Central London County Court.

- sexual wrongs: these should usually be dealt with by church discipline or a criminal court;[109]

- monetary or misconduct occasions;[110] criminal conduct;[111]

- where some objective act of injustice has taken place;[112]

- where church discipline is more appropriate;[113]

- where church order is involved, as in a refusal to submit to the bishop;[114]

- where the canonical law is clear;[115]

- where there are clear 'legal' issues;[116]

- where pastoral help is required instead, such as marital conflict;[117]

- where the parties are uncooperative;[118]

---

[109] Wellington (New Zealand); Christchurch (New Zealand). In some states, adultery is a crime. For example it is a Class B misdemeanour under Section 13A, 13–2 of the Criminal Code of Alabama.

[110] Western Louisiana (USA).

[111] Central Newfoundland (Canada).

[112] Chicago (USA).

[113] Michigan (USA).

[114] Wangaratta (Australia); or 'in the case of the bishop's right to act canonically in the dismissal of a priest/cleric.' Port Elizabeth (South Africa)

[115] 'Those that are governed specifically by canon law or legislation which are not easily alterable.' Newcastle (Australia).

[116] 'Legal issues e.g. financial misconduct and sexual misconduct'. Willochra (Australia).

[117] Nova Scotia and Prince Edward Island (Canada); Bloemfontein (South Africa).

[118] Maine (USA).

- where there is high potential for abuse of the process;[119]

- where a theological issue of principle is involved.[120]

The process test is essentially a negative test: one looks to see if there are factors which point against the use of mediation. Such factors are pointers rather than hard and fast rules, and there may be other factors pointing in favour of using mediation for a particular dispute. Thus, for example, the Church in Canada is using alternative dispute resolution in the disputes arising from its involvement with the Indian Residential Schools system, even though some of these cases involve allegations of sexual misconduct against children.

In conclusion, the questionnaire analysed disputes only in terms of the first of these tests, the 'problem' test. The survey indicates that while this is helpful, and that certain 'problems' are more suitable for mediation than others, this is not the whole story. One needs also to look at the relationship between the people involved in the dispute, and at the appropriateness of mediation in comparison to other means of resolving the dispute, and conduct a balancing exercise. One bishop described the process as follows:

> 'One has to determine whether a matter is pastoral, canonical, personality conflict, procedural etc. and then determine how best to handle each.' [121]

---

[119] Utah (USA).

[120] Port Elizabeth (South Africa): 'on issues of principle, for example, in the case of the bishop's right to act canonically in the dismissal of a priest/cleric'. Johannesburg (South Africa): 'Any issues involving key theological issues over which the issues are fundamental and non-negotiable.'

[121] Missouri, USA.

4. CHOICE OF MEDIATOR

The next section of the questionnaire addressed the issue of the choice of mediator.

B.   Who do you use as mediators?

I want to find out how often you use external professional mediators, or whether you prefer to use clergy and other church leaders as mediators. I want to find out how effective each has been, and also how cost-effective.

Please mark with an X the appropriate box number according to the scale 1–5.

Who are the mediators you use?	1 2 3 4 5
1. Do you often use external professional mediators to help resolve church disputes? [1 = never; 5 = almost always]	☐☐☐☐☐
2. How effective have external professional mediators been in helping to resolve church disputes? [1 = not effective; 5 = very effective]	☐☐☐☐☐
3. How cost-effective has using external professional mediators been? [1 = not cost-effective; 5 = very cost-effective]	☐☐☐☐☐
4. Do you often use clergy and other church leaders as mediators?	☐☐☐☐☐
5. How effective have they been?	☐☐☐☐☐
6. How cost-effective?	☐☐☐☐☐

7. How do you find suitable mediators when you need them? [1 = personal recommendation; 2 = maintain a diocesan list of suitable mediators; 3 = use one of your clergy; 4 = use a mediation agency; 5 = encourage the church to find a mediator itself. Mark as many as appropriate.]	☐☐☐☐☐
8. How often do you act as mediator yourself? [1 = never; 5 = very often]	☐☐☐☐☐

Any comments?	

Figure 28 shows the result of the survey. It is clear that dioceses use both clergy and professionals to mediate disputes, with clergy being used about twice as often as professionals.[122] The bishops considered that clergy were very effective in this role, and professionals only slightly less effective. It was fairly cost-effective to use clergy as mediators, but only just cost-effective to use professionals.[123]

---

[122] 66% clergy: **34%** professionals.

[123] Details of the mathematics are as follows. To ascertain what proportion of the time the church uses professional mediators as opposed to clergy, the answer to question 1 was compared with the answer to question 4. If the answer to question 1 is p and the answer to question 4 is c, the proportion of disputes handled by clergy is $\frac{c-1}{c+p-2}$, and the proportion handled by professionals is $\frac{p-1}{c+p-2}$.

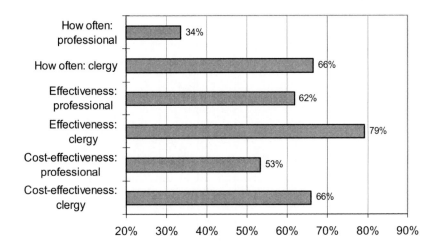

Figure 28. Professional mediator or clergy

If one combines the figures for clergy and professional mediators, there is an overall effectiveness of 73%, and an overall cost-effectiveness of 62%. If one is looking for evidence that mediation works, these figures are certainly encouraging.

Figure 29 shows the results from individual countries. All countries use clergy more than professional mediators. Only Hong Kong used only clergy. All countries found clergy very effective, apart from Hong Kong where their effectiveness was only 50%. The cost-effectiveness of using professionals varied: it was

---

As the scale goes from 1 to 5, with 1 representing 'never', 1 must be subtracted from the nominator and 2 from the denominator (1 for c, plus 1 for p) to get a correct proportion.

In calculating effectiveness and cost-effectiveness, the average score was calculated and then expressed as a percentage, with 1 being shown as 0% and 5 as 100%.

70% in Canada, but around 50% in all other countries. The cost-effectiveness of using clergy varied, but was never less than 50%.

	Australia	Canada	Hong Kong	New Zealand	South Africa	The USA
How often: professional	29%	31%	0%	50%	29%	36%
How often: clergy	71%	69%	100%	50%	71%	64%
Effectiveness: professional	48%	73%		67%	68%	62%
Effectiveness: clergy	79%	80%	50%	75%	88%	78%
Cost-effectiveness: professional	48%	70%		50%	46%	52%
Cost-effectiveness: clergy	56%	61%	50%	67%	78%	68%

Figure 29. Professional mediator or clergy (individual countries)

Figure 30 shows that the three most used methods for finding a mediator were, first, using one of the diocese's own clergy, and equal second, personal recommendation and using a person on a diocesan list of mediators. Churches were quite frequently encouraged to find a mediator themselves (sometimes with a pointer in the right direction).[124] Using a mediation agency was the least used choice.[125]

---

[124] 'I encourage church to find mediator itself from the Alban Institute.' Michigan (USA).

[125] No rating was asked for each different item, so it may be argued that comparisons between the various categories is not statistically valid. There is some force in this, but the overall picture is still useful. If it were necessary to establish the percentages accurately, rather than sim-

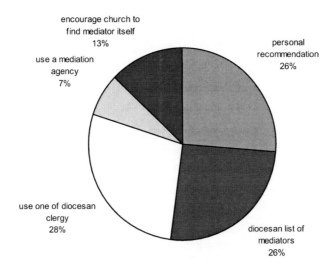

Figure 30. How mediators are found

ply obtain an overall picture, a further survey seeking ratings for each item would be needed.

Figure 31 shows how the individual countries found media-tors. There was much variety. For example, in Hong Kong a di-ocesan list of mediators is used for all cases, and in New Zealand for 75% of cases. This can be contrasted with Australia, Canada and the USA, where a diocesan list is used in about 25% of cases, and in South Africa where it is used in only 14% of cases.

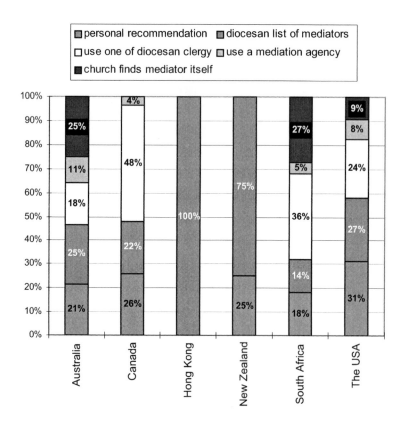

Figure 31. How mediators are found (individual countries)

The bishops varied in their willingness to act as mediators. This is shown in figure 32. The average score was 3.14, i.e. sometimes.

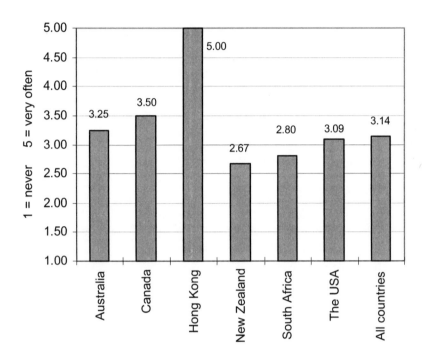

Figure 32. Bishop as mediator

i Individual countries

AUSTRALIA

In Brisbane, independent outside professional mediators are brought in to help in sexual abuse cases, but in pastoral cases an archdeacon or regional bishop is usually used. The bishop of Willochra said that the episcopal role is not seen as neutral, and therefore is not very useful in difficult mediation. The bishops act

395

as mediator in all dioceses, though one bishop said he seldom used formal mediation.[126]

CANADA

Three dioceses reported using external mediators, two with good results, the other not.[127] External professional services are usually given free of charge.[128] One diocese reported using trained volunteers.[129]

All the bishops act as mediators on occasions, though not where discipline is in issue.[130] One seemed to be resigned to the role.[131]

\

---

[126] 'I seldom use formal mediation. More informal mechanisms of consulting with parties and fostering agreed ways forward.' (Adelaide).

[127] Good results in Nova Scotia and Prince Edward Island; good results in Saskatoon; poor results in Qu'Appelle. 'External mediators are engaged through the office of the diocesan chancellor.' (Nova Scotia and Prince Edward Island). 'Generally, I find using clergy who have reputation for fairness, insight and competence is far more effective than an "outside" "professional".' (Qu'Appelle). 'In the last 15 years I have had to resort to mediation twice, that is to external mediation. Personal involvement nearly always leads to agreed conclusions.' (Saskatoon).

[128] 'External professional mediator services are given free of charge. Cost-effectiveness is therefore excellent!' (Saskatoon). '1. often use my archdeacon; 2. often use my permanent lay program staff consultant; 3. we maintain, recruit and train volunteers as mediators.' (Toronto).

[129] Toronto.

[130] 'Depends on situation. My role as bishop having to deal with discipline rules me out of participating as mediators. Nevertheless there are frequently situations where discipline is not involved and I can be involved as mediator.' (Ontario).

[131] 'I tend to get involved when other avenues have failed.' (Central Newfoundland).

HONG KONG

The archbishop of Hong Kong never uses professional mediators. He finds clergy mediators fairly effective, and fairly cost-effective. He uses a diocesan list of mediators, and also very often acts as mediator himself.

NEW ZEALAND

All three bishops said they act as mediator sometimes. A note of caution was expressed by the bishop of Waikato: 'The bishop is usually the last point of reference, as the judge.'

SOUTH AFRICA

Two of the bishops said they never act as mediator.[132] The reason expressed by one was concern as to the bishop's judicial role.[133] Three of the dioceses use both professional and volunteer mediators. In all cases these persons give their service freely to the church.[134] One bishop commented that he uses clergy as mediators as they are the readily available resource, and no thought of costs enters into the decision.[135]

---

[132] Cape Town and Klerksdorp.

[133] 'It is not advisable for diocesan bishop to be involved in mediation on church matters since in the end he must make the final judgment on any matter. The bishop would appoint a commission to look into such matters to seek to mediate and advise diocesan.' (Klerksdorp).

[134] 'I have never used a professional mediator. But we have professional people who serve the church in a voluntary capacity. We certainly use them from time to time.' (St Mark the Evangelist, Northern Province). 'Professionals often offer to act *pro Deo* as members of the church'. (Christ the King). 'We have always used clergy and – if necessary – leading laity. No cost has ever been involved. As a member of Chapter, I have been involved in advice, rather than in detail.' (Pretoria).

[135] Swaziland.

THE USA

Several dioceses reported having a group of trained lay leaders or clergy for use as mediators.[136] Professional mediators are brought in when needed,[137] but they are not always considered effective.[138] In one diocese clergy are only brought in to mediate outside their own venue.[139] Similarly, another diocese said that

---

[136] The responses for these diocese were:

'Several of our lay leaders have been trained for congregational conflict resolution. I also use legal and financial mediators where their expertise is required.' (San Diego).

'We have cadre of trained consultants available. Bishop frequently helps avoid necessity of mediation by ability to engage people and systems. Bishop does not enter mediation in any situation he will eventually need to adjudicate.' (Olympia).

'We have a congregational development team consisting of some professional mediators.' (West Tennessee). The bishop enclosed a brochure covering the team's 'conflict management' roles, and the fees payable.

'We try to train some clergy and lay persons as conflict management consultants and mediators.' (Virginia).

'Our diocesan chancellor often assists the bishop as a mediator. As well, members of a pastoral response team (clergy and laity)' (Florida).

'I use people within the diocese or sometimes employ outside mediators. We have been very pleased with our two mediators and sometimes they have referred a congregation to some other person here in Georgia to handle a particular problem.' (Georgia).

[137] San Diego.

[138] 'External professional mediators not effective because the clergy who is part of the problem does not accept the professional comments and decisions of the mediator.' (Fond du Lac).

[139] 'Only use clergy outside their own venue; they are very effective when objective.' (Maine).

independent third parties should be from outside the diocese or portion of the system in dispute.[140]

The role of bishops as mediator varies greatly from diocese to diocese. In five dioceses, the bishops said they act 'very often' as mediator,[141] in four dioceses 'never'.[142] In most cases the response was somewhere between these extremes. One bishop said he is 'often the principal mediator';[143] one felt constrained by law about acting as mediator.[144] Two bishops said they are unwilling to mediate in any situation they would eventually need to adjudicate;[145] and one bishop would only mediate in the initial stages of a dispute.[146] One bishop describes being a mediator as 'problematic';[147] one said that parties are not frank with him when

---

[140] 'Mediation requires a neutral and it almost always needs to be a 3rd party outside the diocese or portion of the system in dispute.' (Delaware). The bishop of Washington reported: 'Having clear and consistent policies that are part of our diocesan culture encourages pro-active rather than re-active response. Our clergy association formulated specific guidelines re sexuality – self-care – discretionary funds – confidentiality. The guidelines are part of our orientation for new clergy in the diocese'. It is not clear why this response relates to this question in the survey.

[141] i.e. a response of 5.

[142] i.e. a response of 1.

[143] Bethlehem.

[144] 'Re #8, the role of the episcopate is defined and limited canonically.' (Western Louisiana).

[145] 'Bishop does not enter mediation in any situation he will eventually need to adjudicate.' (Olympia). 'When the Bishop will make the final decision as in a PECUSA pastoral dissolution he/she cannot be an effective mediator even when the canons make that a duty.' (Delaware). (PECUSA stands for the Protestant Episcopal Church in the USA.)

[146] 'Bishop only acts as preliminary resource.' (Maine).

[147] 'It is problematic for a number of reasons for the bishop to serve as a mediator, not the least of which is the time needed to set up and perform

he acts as mediator;[148] and one said he is assisted in mediation by his chancellor.[149]

ii Conclusions

There is evidently a varied practice both between one country and another and between one diocese and another within the same country. Many dioceses use volunteer mediators, and have trained them up as mediators; others have brought in professional mediators where needed, with mixed results. There is a feeling that mediators are more likely to be accepted as independent if they come from outside the area of the dispute. Some bishops are comfortable with being a mediator, and are often involved in the early stages of a dispute. Others see their judicial role as preventing them from acting as mediator in many cases.

5. CANON LAW

The next section of the questionnaire dealt with Canon Law.

C   Should Canon law encourage mediation?

In England, mediation will be one of the procedures under the new Clergy Discipline Measure when this becomes law.

---

a mediation. I think the bishop's role is to facilitate the decision to mediate.' (Maine).

[148] 'I usually find when I am acting as mediator that parties are not always as open as they could be about issues.' (Kansas City).

[149] 'Our diocesan chancellor often assists the bishop as a mediator.' (Florida). It is not clear whether this means that the chancellor co-mediates with the bishop, or whether they each do mediations on their own.

Canon Law	1 2 3 4 5
Are you in favour of Canon law encouraging parties to attempt mediation for church disputes before they resort to litigation or other formal process? [1 = very much against; 5 = very much in favour]	☐ ☐ ☐ ☐ ☐
Are you in favour of Canon law ever making mediation compulsory before litigation or other formal process is commenced? [1 = very much against; 5 = very much in favour]	☐ ☐ ☐ ☐ ☐

If you are in favour of compulsory mediation, what types of church dispute should be subject to this requirement? (The list of types of dispute on page 1 may be helpful.)	

Any comments?	

Figure 33 shows that the bishops were very much in favour of Canon Law encouraging mediation, and slightly in favour of Canon Law making mediation compulsory. However the comments made by the bishops indicate that the Church should be hesitant to make mediation compulsory in many areas.

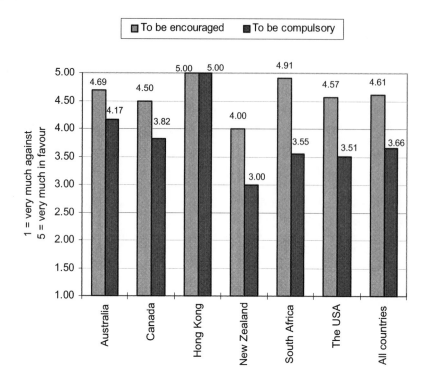

Figure 33. Canon law and mediation

i Individual countries

AUSTRALIA

The Australian bishops said that mediation should be compulsory for the following categories of dispute: church buildings,[150] church governance,[151] personality conflicts,[152] pastoral break-

---

[150] Adelaide, Brisbane.

[151] Adelaide, Brisbane, Wangaratta.

[152] Adelaide, Brisbane, Bunbury, Newcastle ('parish relationships'), Tasmania ('conflicted congregations'), Wangaratta ('personnel disputes' – perhaps a reference to employment disputes).

down,[153] employment disputes,[154] minor discipline,[155] property disputes,[156] financial disputes,[157] and commercial contract disputes.[158]

One bishop expressed concern that mediation would not be effective if it was compulsory.[159] One said there needs to be education on the theology of mediation.[160]

CANADA

Canadian bishops identified 13 of the 15 categories of dispute as suitable for compulsory mediation: church governance,[161] clergy discipline,[162] defamation,[163] employment,[164] employment disputes,[165] financial disputes,[166] forms of worship/doctrine,[167]

---

[153] Adelaide ('possibly pastoral breakdown'), Brisbane, Bunbury, Melbourne, Newcastle, Tasmania.

[154] Adelaide, Brisbane, Wangaratta ('personnel disputes').

[155] Adelaide, Brisbane, Newcastle, The Murray ('Mediation should be compulsory when there are allegations of neglect of pastoral care').

[156] Adelaide, Bunbury, Newcastle.

[157] Adelaide, Bunbury ('diocesan assessments').

[158] Adelaide.

[159] 'Not sure that mediation can be effective if compulsory.' (North Queensland).

[160] 'There needs to be an educative process that sees mediation as a theological concept that is in harmony with the divine mediation, where wholeness & redemption is the outcome.' (Newcastle).

[161] Eastern Newfoundland and Labrador, Huron, Nova Scotia and Prince Edward Island.

[162] Edmonton.

[163] Nova Scotia and Prince Edward Island.

[164] Edmonton, Moosonee ('employment/appointment issues').

[165] Eastern Newfoundland and Labrador, Huron, Nova Scotia and Prince Edward Island.

gay/gender,[168] pastoral breakdown,[169] personal injury,[170] personality conflicts,[171] property,[172] and racial disputes.[173] The two omissions are commercial contract and tax disputes. The highest scorers were church governance and employment disputes, both mentioned by four bishops.

One bishop said that worship and doctrine disputes and minor discipline matters are best dealt with through intervention by the archdeacon and/or bishop.[174] One bishop was against compulsory mediation completely.[175] One bishop said that it is scriptural to try mediation at the beginning of any dispute, though he did not identify the scripture he had in mind.[176]

HONG KONG

The archbishop was very much in favour of compulsory mediation for disputes over church governance, pastoral breakdown,

---

[166] Nova Scotia and Prince Edward Island, Central Newfoundland.

[167] Eastern Newfoundland and Labrador, Huron.

[168] Huron.

[169] Huron, Nova Scotia and Prince Edward Island, Edmonton ('pastoral matters').

[170] Nova Scotia and Prince Edward Island.

[171] Nova Scotia and Prince Edward Island.

[172] Moosonee, Nova Scotia and Prince Edward Island.

[173] Huron.

[174] Nova Scotia and Prince Edward Island.

[175] 'Compulsory mediation seems like a contradiction in terms. Mediation assumes willingness of parties to participate.' (Rupert's Land).

[176] 'The scriptures direct us to mediation at the beginning of any dispute.' (Ontario). The bishop probably had in mind 1 Corinthians 6:1–8 and Matthew 18:15–17.

financial disputes, commercial contract disputes, and property disputes.

NEW ZEALAND

The bishop of Waikato said mediation should be compulsory for 'everything except sexual harassment or emotional harassment'. The bishop of Wellington said that mediation should be compulsory for church governance, personality conflicts, pastoral breakdown, employment, defamation, personal injury and commercial contract disputes.

SOUTH AFRICA

Two bishops said that mediation should be compulsory for most types of dispute.[177] One bishop said mediation should be compulsory for all disputes except those classified as criminal offences.[178] One bishop said mediation should be compulsory for inter-personal problems, provided that the bishop's rights are not infringed.[179]

THE USA

The method used by most of the American bishops to identify suitable disputes for compulsory mediation is by reference to the type of parties involved in the dispute. They suggested disputes between particular groups of people such as rector–vestry, bishop–parish, diocese–parish, clergy–bishop, or rector–parish.[180]

---

[177] 'The majority of types on page 1.' (Capetown). 'Most of page 1.' (Christ the King).

[178] Namibia.

[179] St Mark the Evangelist, Northern Province.

[180] rector–vestry conflict (Florida, Virginia), bishop–parish conflict (Florida), clergy–bishop conflict (Fond du Lac), rector–parish (Kansas), diocese–parish (Michigan).

They also identified relational disputes,[181] property disputes,[182] employment disputes,[183] gay and gender disputes,[184] and minor discipline[185] as appropriate for compulsory mediation. One bishop said that 'all disputes should be open to mediation for the good of the whole'.[186] One said mediation should be compulsory for most disputes.[187] One referred to the canon requiring mediation in cases of pastoral breakdown.[188]

ii Conclusions

A number of bishops were in favour of mediation but did not think it necessary to legislate about it.[189] They said that mediation

---

[181] 'Personal disputes' (Fond du Lac); 'compulsory should be any that are relational at basis of dispute: i.e. personality conflicts, gay or gender issues, racial discrimination, employment disputes.' (Olympia); pastoral breakdown (Western North Carolina).

[182] Arkansas, Western North Carolina, Indeanapolis.

[183] Fond du Lac, Indeanapolis, Olympia.

[184] 'Gay or gender; racial, pastoral breakdown.' (Kansas City).

[185] Mississippi.

[186] Western Louisiana.

[187] 'Most of those on page 1' [i.e. the types of dispute listed in section A of the survey questionnaire]. (Los Angeles).

[188] 'The Canons of ECUSA [i.e. Title III, Canon 20 Of the Reconciliation of Disagreements Affecting the Pastoral Relation] require the Bishop to supply such counselling and mediation in the case that a parish asks for termination of their pastor's relationship with them. I have not yet, in my six years as Bishop, had it come to that final issue. But, a number of times the use of mediation has brought some healing to both the congregation and the priest even though, in some cases, the priest has found a way to a new cure. My experience (four pastoral breakdowns) in several cases the mediators were able to surface for the attention of the community a number of issues that were unspoken and that have brought about some real healing in the congregations.' (Georgia).

[189] Thus:

should be encouraged but not made compulsory.[190] Several commented that mediation is essentially a voluntary process, and therefore should not be made compulsory.[191] These bishops preferred to deal with situations on a case by case basis.[192] In some

---

'Generally in favour, but my 14 years as diocesan bishop have not made this a pressing issue.' Washington (USA).

'As a Church, we are moving in this direction, albeit slowly.' Bethlehem (USA).

'[The bishops] typically manage disputes, occasionally calling in others. We have not had occasion to use professional for-fee mediators nor would we want to mandate or require it by canonical requirement.' South Carolina (USA).

[190] 'Encouraging mediation would work better here than anything compulsory.' Gippsland (Australia).

'Mostly those that are between two or more entities, such as diocese and parish. Internal disputes mediation could be encouraged, but our diocese is reluctant to be directive and authoritarian. The 1st amendment of US Constitution prevents many civil actions where issues involve or touch on doctrine, discipline or governance. Therefore, required mediation prior to formal internal process is focus of answers.' Michigan (USA).

[191] 'Mediation should not be compulsory. For mediation to be effective those involved must want to enter into the discussion.' Northern California (USA).

'Not in favour of compulsory mediation.' Delaware (USA).

'Not sure that mediation can be effective if compulsory.' North Queensland (Australia).

'Compulsory mediation seems like a contradiction in terms. Mediation assumes willingness of parties to participate.' Rupert's Land (Canada).

[192] 'The case would determine whether mediation was appropriate.' Wellington (New Zealand).

'We would tend to respond to situations on a case by case basis rather than to legislate.' Northern Michigan (USA).

cases, mediation was inappropriate and counterproductive.[193] In particular, mediation cannot replace discipline,[194] and is therefore generally inappropriate for cases of sexual or racial harassment, or where criminal conduct is in issue.

Two bishops in the USA pointed out that ECUSA has compulsory mediation for cases of pastoral breakdown, and is making it compulsory for cases of dissolution of the pastoral relationship.[195] There is a similar provision in Canada.[196]

The survey gave an overall score of 4.61 for canon law encouraging mediation and a score of 3.66 for making it compulsory.

'Canonical additions are unnecessary. They only deal with maintenance issues – like restaking claims on the Titanic. Allowing bishops to make choices about canonical interference is the best model.' Louisiana (USA).

[193] 'Mediation in some circumstances may be inappropriate and counterproductive, would prefer, as we have in our canon law – the right of appeal.' Johannesburg (South Africa).

[194] 'Any circumstance in which professional (financial, sexual etc.) misconduct has occurred needs to be dealt with by discipline *before* mediation can occur. Mediation cannot replace discipline or else the substance of clergy discipline will be eroded.' Maine (USA).

[195] The letter to ECUSA bishops referred to disagreements affecting the pastoral relation – Title III, Canon 20; dissolution of the pastoral relationship – Title III, Canon 21, section 3; the duties of bishops (where a Diocesan Bishop declines to visit a Parish or Congregation for three years) – Title III, Canons 24.4(c); and non-serious disciplinary matters – Title IV, Canon 16.

'The Canons of the American Church mandate mediation in some cases as you have noted. Title IV is being revised and will include more.' West Tennessee (USA).

'ECUSA has soon in the case of the dissolution of the pastoral relationship.' New Hampshire (USA).

[196] 'By canon, if cleric is given severance, she/he can appeal [...] through mediation.' Toronto (Canada). The bishop's hand-writing was difficult to read.

But the comments indicate considerable unease over making mediation compulsory. It is already built into the procedures for pastoral breakdown in the USA and Canada. There is some support for it being compulsory for almost all the types of dispute mentioned in the survey. But there is no clear agreement that it should be compulsory for any particular type of dispute, despite the overall score. Encouragement for mediation is most strong for relational disputes, and for disputes between particular types of parties such as priest against lay leaders, priest against congregation, and priest or parish against diocese.

Two theological comments from Canada support these conclusions. The archbishop of Ontario pointed out that 'the scriptures direct us to mediation at the beginning of any dispute.'[197] There is thus the clearest encouragement for mediation, and Canon law should therefore make provision for it and encourage its use.

But a warning is sounded by the bishop of New Westminster.

'This whole line of thought moves the church toward a secular and legalistic model and away from a Biblical, covenanting model of community.' [198]

The bishop's argument is that even thinking in terms of compulsory mediation is a secular approach. A Biblical, covenanting community is dependent on God, not on man-made laws. In so far as Canon law touches the subject at all, it should therefore encourage rather than command mediation.

---

[197] See pg. 404, fn. 176.

[198] The bishop gave a 2 to each of the questions.

6. TRAINING AND EDUCATION

Section D of the questionnaire read as follows:

D.   Training and education

Training and education	Yes No
1. Is handling conflict a subject which is taught to clergy and other church leaders in your diocese?	☐ ☐
2. If no, do you feel it should be?	☐ ☐

What form might such training take?	

Any comments	

Figure 34 indicates that handling conflict is taught in 53% of dioceses. There was 100% concurrence that the subject should be taught.[199]

There was much common ground in the responses from all the countries in the survey, and it is unnecessary to set out each country's responses in detail. The responses from the USA are summarised first as they were the most comprehensive, followed by some points mentioned by other countries.

---

[199] Seven bishops ticked both boxes: Atlanta (USA), Delaware (USA), Los Angeles (USA), Ohio (USA), Washington (USA), The Murray (Australia), and Central Newfoundland (Canada).

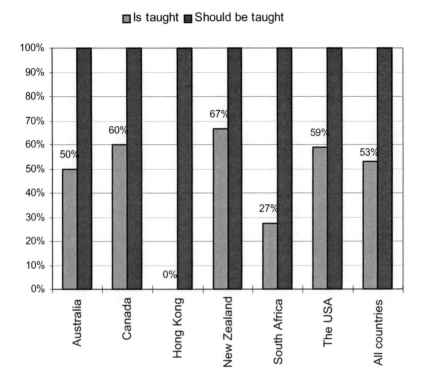

Figure 34. Training and education

(Handling conflict is not currently taught in Hong Kong, so the figure for 'is taught' in Hong Kong is 0%.)

i Individual countries

THE USA

A number of suggestions were made as to the form training might take, and who should undertake it. Many of the terms used overlap, but the suggestions included both pre- and post-ordination training for clergy, and training sessions for lay lead-

411

ers.[200] Pre-ordination training included theological[201] and seminary[202] education. Post-ordination training included both formal and informal training in the subject. Formal training included workshops,[203] seminars,[204] short term courses,[205] clergy conferences,[206] and other forms of continuing education.[207] In some cases this training is provided 'in-house' by the diocese. In other cases, external consultants[208] or lay mediators[209] are brought in to train, or clergy are sent on training courses with external organisations such as the Alban Institute.[210] Informal training for clergy[211] is provided by one-to-one coaching or mentoring.[212]

---

[200] Western North Carolina.

[201] Los Angeles.

[202] Michigan, Florida ('should be part of seminary training').

[203] Maine, West Tennessee, New Hampshire, Virginia, Atlanta ('intensive workshops'), Indeanapolis.

[204] Nebraska, SouthWest Virginia, Utah, Quincy.

[205] Washington, Delaware ('There are conflict training courses available. For the most part clergy take them for continuing education. Now and again a particular cleric or lay person might be encouraged and enabled to go because of their ability in negotiation'.)

[206] Washington, Michigan, Los Angeles, Missouri, Central Pennsylvania, Georgia.

[207] Michigan, Northern Michigan, Central Pennsylvania, Florida. 'Learning leadership skills' (Olympia).
'Classes' (Nevada).
'Part of the ministry development curriculum' (Northern Michigan).
'Clergy training sessions' (Kansas City, and Western North Carolina).
'Family systems training' (New York).

[208] Northern California.

[209] 'A secular mediator could easily outline the steps and issues and outline ways to deal along the mediation path.' (Western Louisiana).

[210] 'Alban Institute among other conduct training sessions.' (Mississippi).

There is general agreement that 'book-learning' is not the way to learn handling conflict.[213] The subject needs demonstrating or coaching, with role plays[214] or hands-on training of some sort.[215] One bishop said that clergy are hesitant to face this issue and actually resist pre-training.[216] This may be linked with a misunderstanding about the nature of conflict.

> We have had at our annual conference for presbyters presentation on conflict resolution or handling conflict. Most of the clergy were surprised to discover that conflict can be an opportunity for real growth and not just something to try to cover over.[217]

It is useful to highlight that conflict management should be taught to clergy both before and after ordination, and also to lay leaders.

CANADA

Canadian bishops mentioned the Alban Institute,[218] the Toronto School of Theology,[219] the Mennonite Centre for Peace and

---

'Alban Institute (Speed Lees) has done a lot of work in this area and are quite good as facilitators'. (NorthWest Texas).

'The Alban Institute offers excellent basic training for conflict resolution for clergy and laity.' (San Diego)

'Train by those trained and very experienced.' (Milwaukee).

[211] Chicago.

[212] 'One-to-one coaching or mentoring of the clergy.' (Maine).

[213] '"Book-learning" is not the way to learn this.' (Maine).

[214] Los Angeles, Maine.

[215] Maine.

[216] Western Louisiana.

[217] Georgia.

[218] Nova Scotia and Prince Edward Island.

[219] Toronto (Canada).

Reconciliation,[220] and particular individuals[221] as sources of training. In one diocese ADR is routinely taught to archdeacons and regional deans.[222] In another diocese conflict management is a very popular subject in seminary.[223]

HONG KONG

The archbishop of Hong Kong mentioned the importance of training lay leaders as well as clergy.[224]

NEW ZEALAND

Two dioceses mentioned that their clergy had done courses with the Alban Institute.[225]

SOUTH AFRICA

One bishop set out the elements of the training he considers necessary, using the headings theological, attitudes, and skills training. He pointed to the recent history of South Africa as giv-

---

[220] Ontario (Canada).

[221] 'We value the work of Peter Steinke and John Savidge (lead consultants), both USA based.' (Toronto). Query whether this John Savidge (*sic*) is the same as the Australian John Savage, mentioned in fn. 292 pg. 441.

[222] 'ADR is routinely taught to our archdeacons and regional deans, who do most our intervention work.' (New Westminster).

[223] '"Conflict management" is a very popular subject in Seminary. Currently it is the "in thing".' Eastern Newfoundland and Labrador.

[224] '1. add units to the current theological training curriculum for candidates for ordination and lay leaders. 2. case study for regular clergy meetings.' (Hong Kong).

[225] 'Ministry school subject; special seminars. The Revd Speed Leas from the Alban Institute is very helpful.' (Waikato).

'Not necessarily, it is a choice. Some of our clergy have done one-day or longer courses, particularly with Speed Leas.' (Christchurch).

ing him experience in the area.[226] Two bishops said they need professional help in conflict resolution training.[227] One commented that conflict resolution is a growth industry in South Africa.[228]

ii Conclusions

The survey shows that all dioceses recognise the importance of conflict training, but that only just over half actually do any. The bishops recommend both formal training courses and informal training in the subject, and that both clergy and laity should be trained. It is apparent that there is no uniformity of approach between dioceses even within each country. If the Church of England decides to implement training in conflict resolution, one of the issues it will need to address is whether this should be left to each diocese, or should be organised centrally.

---

[226] 'Theological: repentance, forgiveness, acceptance. Attitudes: respect, honesty, openness. Skills training: listening, I-messages, i.e. communication. We are still in early days, but the clergy and parish leaders have identified it as a priority. We have some experience with our recent history in South Africa – and tend to deal with conflict in an honest, transparent and often quite courageous way.' (St Mark the Evangelist, Northern Province).

[227] 'I feel that some of our clergy lack conflict resolution skills and this is an area in which we need professional help to better equip our clergy.' (Port Elizabeth).

'We need professional training in conflict resolution.' (Bloemfontein).

[228] 'Conflict resolution is a growth industry in S Africa – training courses are at many levels and costs, and readily available. But I need to do my own homework on this.' (Christ the King).

7. LARGE CONGREGATIONAL DISPUTES

The next section of the questionnaire was the first not to contain any check boxes for mathematical analysis.

E.   Disputes involving a large number of people

How do you handle disputes involving a large number of people, such as a congregational dispute, or a breakdown in the pastoral relationship?	

Any comments	

76 bishops (78% of the responses) answered these questions. They referred to a number of methods of handling large congregational disputes, and several bishops used more than one method. Some of the responses concentrated on the people whom the diocese use in such situations, others concentrated on the process to be used. In some cases there is an overlap: thus personal intervention by the bishop often takes the form of being present at group meetings, so these come under both categories.

i Individual countries

AUSTRALIA

13 bishops (87% of the responses from Australia) answered this question. The responses indicate a much more low-key approach than in the USA, described below. Bringing in consultants was mentioned by only 2 dioceses, and in each case they were consult-

ants from within the diocese.[229] None of the bishops referred to team interventions, but 5 referred to meetings with a senior cleric or a personal intervention by the bishop.[230] The most low-key approach was that of the Bishop of Bendigo: 'Sit and talk', adding the comment, 'effective so far'.

---

[229] 'Consultants from diocese would act in such situations. Archdeacons might also have a role. Recommendations would be made to the Bishop. Bishop called in as person of last resort.' (Adelaide).

'We make use of an independent consultancy process drawing in outside trained consultants in conflict resolution who work with the conflicted parties. The diocese has 3 consultants in training who are part of an ecumenical network. This provides the capacity to make use of people outside the Anglican Church if and where appropriate.' (Tasmania).

[230] '(a) The parties are brought separately to be heard by someone in authority e.g. the regional bishop. (b) They are then brought together by him. (c) The regional bishop makes a recommendation to the Archbishop, or Archbishop-in-Council, who determines the matter.' (Brisbane).

'A senior cleric (occasionally a skilled lay person) to meet with the congregation initially (or Parish Council), then with the priest, then (if possible) together. Congregations are usually more forgiving and cooperative than the clergy.' (Bunbury).

'Personally, at the suggestion of the people and their archdeacon. This is a small diocese that lends itself to such personal intervention.' (Gippsland).

'Input and mediation (archdeacon – first level; regional bishop – second level).' (Melbourne).

'A) Archdeacon or senior cleric will meet with clergy and parish council to determine key areas of conflict, B) seek to establish best outcome – redemptive motif as central to life of community, C) prayerful discernment by the Bishop and senior staff as to most appropriate mediation process, D) Congregational meeting as catharsis with Bishop or designated mediator, E) enable open discussion, ascertain facts, encourage mutually-agreed to solutions.' (Newcastle).

417

The Bishop of Sydney referred to the Parish Disputes Ordinance 1999 which is used in that diocese.[231] This is a low-key, non-litigious, non-adversarial system for dispute resolution within a parish, especially between the minister and the parish. Parishioners are encouraged to bring concerns first to the minister and the parish council with a view to resolution of disputes within the parish. Only if this fails may the dispute be notified to the bishop, who may then refer the dispute to a reconciliation panel consisting of two people selected from a 'synod pool' of trained persons, the minister choosing one and the lay persons choosing the other. The panel then meets the parties first individually and then together, informally, for mediation.[232] Like the

---

[231] *www.sydney.anglican.asn.au/synod/ords/1999/39parishdisputes.o99.html*. The ordinance was passed by the synod of the Diocese of Sydney on 13 October 1999. The archbishop of Sydney described the background to the ordinance: 'Our Synod set up a Select Committee on the issue, of which I was Chair, in the mid 90's. It arose from a fairly difficult parochial dispute which caused much controversy in the Diocese. The Select Committee recommended, and the Synod eventually adopted, a non-litigious and non-adversarial system for dispute resolution within a parish, especially between the Minister and the parish. It is entitled *Parish Disputes Ordinance 1999* and the text is attached.'

[232] Section 11 sets out the objectives of the reconciliation panel, and section 13 sets out the procedure, as follows:
'11. To achieve reconciliation in a way which expresses biblical values including –
(a) prayerfully working together so that we glorify the God and Father of our Lord Jesus Christ;
(b) appealing to all to look not only to their own interests but to the interests of others; and
(c) finding a way forward whereby the parties may agree to differ but will work together in love being one in spirit and purpose.
13. Meetings between the Reconciliation Panel and each party will be confidential between the Reconciliation Panel and the parties and be conducted in the following manner–
(a) informal, in that formal evidence will not be taken;

community mediation model, no legal representation is allowed. The reconciliation panel has no power to decide between the parties, but if the mediation fails to produce a settlement either party can then call for a separate 'advisory panel', where the hearing is more formal.[233] This advisory panel at the end makes a recommendation to the parties or to the archbishop on how to resolve the dispute.

The Sydney ordinance does not distinguish disputes involving a large group of parishioners from disputes involving only a small number of parties; though from his answer the bishop clearly envisaged that the ordinance would be used for large congregational disputes. The system has only been in use for a year, so it is early days to see how well it works. The regional bishops and archdeacons will no doubt need to steer disputes towards the process, and members of the synod pool will need to be trained so that the mediation part of the procedure stands a good prospect of success.

A similar procedure is used in Tasmania, under the Ministry and Tribunal Ordinance 1998. This includes a number of informal procedures to resolve issues such as conflict and breakdown in pastoral relationship. If the parties cannot themselves resolve the issue, it is referred to the archdeacon. The archdeacon will at-

---

(b) free of legal representation;
(c) held with each party individually, with the parties only joining when, and if, the Reconciliation Panel believes it is appropriate;
(d) not subject to minutes but the Reconciliation Panel may keep a record of meetings held and agreed outcomes;
(e) except where the Reconciliation Panel consists of 1 person under subclause 9(4), a quorum will be the full Reconciliation Panel, that is, the clergy member and the lay member; and
(f) open and close with prayer.'

[233] Legal representation is not allowed, but the parties may call witnesses, and the rules of procedural fairness must be observed: Section 22.

tempt to resolve the matter by counselling and discussion. If he is unable to do so, he may refer the parties for mediation. If this is unsuccessful or inappropriate, the archdeacon refers the matter to the bishop. The bishop gives all affected parties an opportunity to be heard. Parties may be represented before the bishop by anyone they may choose. The bishop then determines the matter, though there is a right of appeal to an appeals board whose decision is binding on all parties including the bishop.

CANADA

11 bishops (69% of the responses from Canada) answered this question. One diocese uses a trained diocesan consultant, and has a 'trauma team'.[234] Several responses identified that there might be different levels of intervention. Two bishops use a low-key approach, such as sending in a husband and wife team to make a report.[235] Two start low-key at the regional deanery level, with a view to escalating to the archdeacon and then to the bishop where necessary.[236] Two bishops use lay people to assist.[237] The remain-

---

[234] Toronto.

[235] 'A husband and wife team move Into a parish, both qualified in theology, sociology and mediation techniques. They interview the leadership, lay and clergy, parishioners, local clergy and others in the community. From these a confidential report on the priest is written for the diocesan bishop (confidential until he has seen it). If the priest's leadership is in question, the report is also sent to the diocesan bishop. This has been done in ten situations in the last seven years.' (Huron).

[236] 'At progressive stages, starting rather low keyed, and if unsuccessful escalating to Regional Deanery intervention, then Territorial Archdeacon – finally, and by then it has attained serious proportions, on to me and my Council of Advice. It tends to work in most cases.' (Eastern Newfoundland and Labrador).

'Negotiation by the archdeacon and regional dean with the bishop's office as the "court of last appeal". Intervention engaged early in the dising five bishops all intervene personally, first holding meetings with the main protagonists or groups, and only then holding large congregational meetings.[238] One described the 'native circle' model he uses at large congregational meetings.[239] One bishop spoke of the need to keep the congregation well informed as early as possible.[240]

---

pute and striking of compromise have proven a meaningful path to follow.' (Nova Scotia and Prince Edward Island).

[237] 'Choose a committee mostly competent but very ordinary lay folk who are known for their balanced approach to life and problems and good listeners, perceptive, positive, not easily disturbed persons.' (Central Newfoundland).

'By having trained lay people available to be of service in a particular situation.' (Ontario).

[238] '1. Try to work with proper authorities e.g. churchwardens, parish councils etc. 2. Use of a mentor if priest involved. 3. Use of mediator if counsellor, usually a priest. 4. Congregational meetings with clear, agreed agenda and purpose. Success here is mixed, but mostly positive. The ever constant threat of litigation hangs like a dark cloud.' (Qu'Appelle).

'Work with leadership to identify nature of conflict, issues, personalities, and appropriate process of intervention with various options; congregation meetings, interview process, healing circle, outside intervention.' (Rupert's Land).

'1. If possible, bring together only the main protagonists – Keep it small. 2. Meet with vestry and parties. 3. Meet with congregation only as last resort. 4. Seek mutually agreed reverence.' The bishop commented: 'Small dioceses such as mine provide early [illegible] ... Seldom do conflicts reach the full blown congregational stage.' (Saskatoon).

[239] 'This is usually the bishop's responsibility. I often use the "native circle" model: people sit in a circle, my pectoral cross is handed round, and everyone can have their say while they are holding it. Resolutions tend to emerge slowly but effectively'. (New Westminster).

[240] 'Deal with congregation at arms' length, but keep them well informed, as early as possible. Deal with leaders, those responsible to/for

HONG KONG

The archbishop of Hong Kong (the only response from Hong Kong) sets up a pastoral and mediation team to look into the matter. The members of the team comprise both clergy and lay leaders.

NEW ZEALAND

Three bishops (100% of the responses from New Zealand) answered this question. One uses a 'response team'.[241] One uses a mediator from within the diocese 'using pre-agreed procedures'.[242] One uses either a professionally trained mediator or a suitably trained person.[243]

SOUTH AFRICA

10 bishops (91% of the responses from South Africa) answered this question. They use a variety of methods, including sending in mediators, and holding both large and small group meetings. Large group meetings have met with mixed success. The problem of apartheid has inclined people to violence, leading to meetings being disrupted.[244] One bishop holds public meetings using mediators, and then small groups with facilitators to address the is-

---

others. Identify problems, not persons; work out plans for resolving disputes, and elicit support of leadership to convey this through.' (Moosonee).

[241] 'Response Team approach.' (Christchurch).

[242] 'Mediator from within the diocese using pre-agreed procedures.' (Waikato).

[243] 'Professional mediator or a suitably trained person.' (Wellington).

[244] 'With difficulty. Apartheid has inclined people to solve problems by violence. It is not uncommon to have disruption of public worship, "demos", threats etc. In this context, very time consuming and nasty to resolve.' (Christ the King).

422

sues raised in the public meetings.[245] In contrast, one bishop said that open meetings do not work well, but he did not indicate whether he used mediators to assist running them.[246]

Three bishops referred to 'conflict resolution', mediation and negotiation.[247] One bishop appoints a commission of enquiry.[248] One delegates using clergy and lay leaders to intervene and me-

---

[245] 'Through public meetings using mediators. Often we use small groups and facilitators to surface and process issues raised in public plenary.' (Johannesburg).

[246] 'Experience has shown that efforts to negotiate with a crowd of people is not successful. Open meetings become over-emotional and create greater divisions.' (Bloemfontein).

[247] 'Through conflict resolution and mediation' (Highveld).

'Negotiation with the leadership of the groups in the dispute.' (Namibia).

'Using a sort of conflict resolution technique combined with exercises to encourage the seeing of the other party's point of view. Often it is difficult to change people's views where they see a benefit in their chosen / given side of the dispute.' (Swaziland).

[248] 'Appoint a commission of enquiry to hear all points of view, and proceed from there. We have had a number of such situations where the parties involved have not been prepared to discuss the issues in the commission, and have been unwilling to resolve the issue amongst themselves. In such cases, reluctantly, the church has been closed to allow a "cooling off" period. In most cases, this church has sought reconciliation with diocesan bishop and diocese after 6 months to 1 year.' (Klerksdorp).

diate.[249] One delegates to his archdeacon, bringing in resource people as needed.[250] One bishop exorcises the parish![251]

THE USA

38 bishops (73% of the responses from the USA) answered this question. 17 bishops bring in outside consultants[252] or media-

---

[249] 'I've tried to delegate and used clergy and lay leaders to intervene and mediate. Only as a last resort getting involved myself as bishop. It seems that in some cases people expect to be "heard" by the bishop, and so if I had become involved earlier it would have helped to speed up the process of reconciliation.' (Port Elizabeth).

[250] 'The Archdeacon takes charge of the process, in consultation with the Bishop and Chapter. Resource people may be drawn in. The Bishop serves as a 'court of appeal' for any final ruling that may be required. Although it may take time, we usually manage to resolve these disputes in the end.' (St Mark the Evangelist, Northern Province).

[251] 'Recently we had a problem in a parish: some 6–8 members were dominating the parish. The Bishop called upon surrounding clergy to be with him to exorcise the parish. It seems to have worked – but a number of people have no idea of the influence of evil in this manner.' (Pretoria).

[252] Comments referring to consultants were as follows:

'We usually employ the services of a consultant/mediator from Alban Institute or similar organisation'. (Nebraska).

'1. Use a consultant/mediator to identify the issues 2. Urge annual ministry reviews 3. Try to address issues as soon as possible, and with the smallest reasonable group, i.e. bishop and vestry.' (Washington).

'Provide consultants who offer skills in listening working through issues – gather data from whole group – communicate clear responsibility regarding where and how decisions are made – help people learn how to articulate shared values and work based on values. Reference: Leadership without easy answers by Ronald Heifitz, Harvard University.' (Olympia).

tors[253] to handle these disputes. 8 bishops send in a team from within the diocese, under various names: a 'mediation team',[254] a

---

'Have a process of group meetings and small group work, generally followed by work with either an interim rector (where cure is vacant or vacated) or consultant.' (Michigan).

'Generally I meet with the leadership of the congregation and urge them to enter into consultation with a skilled consultant/mediator. I may also have a few fact-finding conversations. Once again, I believe the bishop's role is to educate people about the usefulness of consultation/mediation – and help them gain access to a qualified resource person.' (Maine)

'We use parish consultants, tools such as mutual ministry review or re-visioning, or conflict resolution firms.' (Chicago).

'Use consultants/mediators to help parish design team structure and parish conference.' (Virginia).

'We have used consultants to help involved parties identify issues, clar-ify expectations, and sort through what is realistic. On occasion we have "negotiated" a leave-taking. Our canons specify I can mandate the terms, but I have to continue an effective relationship with the parish.' (Indeanapolis).

'When we have conflict between a pastor and a congregation or when we have conflict within a congregation I try to get them to agree, the congregation and pastor to employ an outside consultant to lead them in discerning issues causing the conflict. Most of the time they do.' (Georgia).

[253] Nebraska, Washington, Maine (quoted above) use the word consult-ant and mediator as interchangeable.

Outside mediators are brought in to handle these disputes in Nebraska, Washington, Virginia (all quoted above).

'I use a mediator if the pastor is unwilling to resign voluntarily. I have met frequently with a congregation when the pastor has agreed to resign and the congregation needs to get on with their mission and ministry. Often an Interim Pastor will then serve such situations.' (Kansas City).

'Canon Missioner or other professional serves as facilitator/mediator with Bishop as ultimate resource. If the Bishop is involved too early, the

425

'crisis response team' (indicating perhaps a panic reaction), [255] a more positively named 'congregational development team',[256] or the neutral 'pastoral response team'[257] or 'team of conflict managers'.[258]

26 bishops refer to the use of 'intervention'. In most cases this involves the bishop chairing group meetings or meeting leaders of the congregation or other parties,[259] sometimes with the assistance

---

process is more likely to be manipulated by the parties with a negative outcome.' (Utah).

'In a breakdown with pastoral relationship I use a mediator. I also meet with congregation to define mediation process, to listen to observations and failings, and to outline immediate needs for ordained ministry.' (West Missouri).

'Professional mediators or interim clergy for a period of 1 to 2 years.' (Milwaukee).

'Diocesan mediator or mediation team.' (Atlanta).

'Often I go in, then mediators if this is necessary.' (Kansas).

[254] 'Diocesan mediator or mediation team.' (Atlanta).

[255] Northern Michigan.

[256] West Tennessee.

[257] 'Use a pastoral response team trained to engage congregational conflict. Clergy misconduct has a wide-spread affect on parish, family, and clergy colleagues in the diocese.' (Florida).

[258] 'Use a team of 2–3 conflict managers.' (Bethlehem).

'We usually send in a team to assist.' (Los Angeles).

'We have a crisis response team trained to deal with this sort of matter.' (Northern Michigan).

'We use our congregational development team.' (West Tennessee).

[259] San Diego, Washington, Maine, Delaware, Kansas City, West Missouri, Kansas, Arkansas, Georgia (already quoted). Also the following:

'Historically in this diocese the bishop has intervened directly.' (SouthWest Virginia).

'With congregational meeting and bishop present.' (Mississippi).

of a co-mediator,[260] but it can sound almost like a hit squad.[261] In one diocese, the bishop intervenes 'in a somewhat authoritative

---

'We have no standard procedure. Often the Bishop is called upon to mediate.' (Eau Claire).

'Call a parish meeting, and gather complaints. Then and/or someone else mediates.' (Quincy).

'Meet with parties involved: vestry, congregational meetings; shape a process with evaluation and decision benchmarks.' (Central Pennsylvania).

'1st. work with the rector; 2nd. work with the vestry; 3rd. work with the congregation.' (Western North Carolina).

'Canonically and personal involvement when appropriate and to the extent allowed canonically. The bishop never knows soon enough – situation usually out of hand when the bishop is called in.' (Western Louisiana).

'The bishop meets with parish leaders and/or a public meeting.' (New York).

'Personal intervention – i.e. calling an all-parish meeting. but I take along trained lay leaders to help me.' (San Diego).

'As a bishop, intervene and get them into a process that will allow movement toward resolution. As a mediator, assess the situation by interviews with the parties, use a co-mediator and design a process that will involve all the necessary parties. Bishop's role is best to push the parties to the need for agreement that meets their deeper needs rather than upholds the stated position. The sooner the intervention the better. Long held and acted upon positions do not easily soften in church disputes.' (Delaware).

See also Arkansas (already quoted).

[260] Co-mediator with the bishop:

'As a bishop, intervene and get them into a process that will allow movement toward resolution. As a mediator, assess the situation by interviews with the parties, use a co-mediator and design a process that will involve all the necessary parties. Bishop's role is best to push the parties to the need for agreement that meets their deeper needs rather than upholds the stated position. The sooner the intervention the better.

427

manner, as the bishop'.[262] In some cases the bishop prefers to stand back and let other clergy deal with the problem, stepping in only after their efforts have failed.[263] Some bishops act together with other members of the diocesan staff,[264] or with trained lay leaders.[265] In many cases, the bishop sees mediation as part of the intervention process,[266] or as a first stage to formal legal process.[267]

Two bishops referred to the use of an interim rector if a parish is vacant, or vacated.[268] Only 3 bishops mentioned canon law.[269] One of these said that when the bishop was called in the situation was usually 'out of hand'.[270] However, the mediation procedures adopted, including employing a consultant or a conciliator, are provided for by canon; so the bishops were in fact following canon law procedures.[271]

Long held and acted upon positions do not easily soften in church disputes.' (Delaware).

'Bishop intervention; same time co-mediator also present.' (Arkansas).

[261] 'Use pastoral intervention team.' (SW Florida).

[262] 'I now handle these disputes in a somewhat authoritative manner, as the Bishop.' (Fond du Lac).

[263] 'We send our regional vicar (an archdeacon in most dioceses) in to take care of the matter. Bishop need to stand in (*sic*) back of the person he or she sends in.' (Nevada). See also Utah (already quoted).

[264] 'Bishop and staff act in their roles appropriately.' (Louisiana).

[265] San Diego (quoted above).

[266] Kansas City.

[267] 'Mediation first, then canonically.' (New Hampshire).

[268] Michigan, Milwaukee.

[269] Indeanapolis, New Hampshire, Western Louisiana.

[270] Western Louisiana.

[271] Title III, Canon 20: Of the Reconciliation of Disagreements Affecting the Pastoral Relation states:
> When the pastoral relationship in a parish between a Rector
> and the Vestry or Congregation is imperilled by disagreement

or dissension, and the issues are deemed serious by a majority vote of the Vestry or the Rector, either party may petition the Ecclesiastical Authority, in writing, to intervene and assist the parties in their efforts to resolve the disagreement. The Ecclesiastical Authority shall initiate such proceedings as are deemed appropriate under the circumstances for that purpose by the Ecclesiastical Authority, which may include the appointment of a consultant. The parties to the disagreement, following the recommendations of the Ecclesiastical Authority, shall labour in good faith that the parties may be reconciled. Whenever the Standing Committee is the Ecclesiastical Authority, it shall request the Bishop of a neighbouring Diocese to perform the duties of the Ecclesiastical Authority under this Canon.

Title IV, Canon 16: Of Conciliation of Disciplinary Matters, states:

Section 1. If the Ecclesiastical Authority or the Standing Committee, as the case may be, shall receive a complaint or Charge against a Priest or Deacon, or if the Presiding Bishop shall receive a complaint or Charge against a Bishop, which complaint or Charge on its face, if true, would constitute an Offence and the Ecclesiastical Authority or Standing Committee or Presiding Bishop, as the case may be, considers the complaint or Charge not to be a serious Offence against the Church and its good order and Discipline, but an interpersonal conflict not involving immorality or serious personal misconduct, or one that may be a technical commission of another Offence, the Ecclesiastical Authority or Standing Committee or Presiding Bishop may offer the persons involved the opportunity for conciliation in lieu of canonical proceedings seeking a Presentment.
Interpersonal conflict.

Section 2. If all persons involved in the matter agree that conciliation is desirable and are willing for the matter to be conciliated, the Ecclesiastical Authority or the Standing Committee or the Presiding Bishop receiving the complaint or Charge shall appoint a Conciliator, who shall labour with those involved in the conflict that they may be reconciled.
Conciliation.

Section 3. If the Conciliator is unable to achieve conciliation within a period of thirty (30) days, which may be extended by consent of all the participants to the conciliation for additional periods not to exceed a total of ninety (90) days from the date of the appointment of the Conciliator, the Conciliator shall refer the matter back to the ap-

What is apparent from the responses is the wide variety of approaches used in different dioceses to these types of disputes, whether mediation or intervention.

ii Conclusions

Although there is a wide variety of approaches to congregational disputes, there are indications that each country has its own preferred method or methods. Thus, in the USA a more heavy-handed approach is adopted than, for example, in Australia. In the USA, there is much use of 'intervention', and sending in teams to resolve the dispute; whereas in Australia, a low-key approach of meetings with the various groups concerned is usually adopted. The Sydney ordinance is indicative of this low-key approach, where informal mediation by two members of a diocesan team is the preferred method for resolving congregational disputes. In Canada, the approach starts low-key at the local level, and then escalates if this does not work. The bishops there seem comfortable with holding both small and large group meetings. In Hong Kong and New Zealand, mediators or mediation teams are the norm. In South Africa there is considerable variety of methods, from informal mediation and group meetings, to a commission of enquiry and exorcism!

---

pointing authority without recommendation for further proceedings under this Title.

Time periods.

Section 4. If conciliation is achieved, the Conciliator shall report back to the appointing authority with the results of the conciliation. The Conciliator's report shall be in writing, concisely state the allegations of the original complaint or Charge, state the terms, if any, and the results of the conciliation, which shall be agreed to, signed and Acknowledged by and between the participants in the conciliation.

See *www.ecusa.anglican.org/governance/canons/FrameSet.html*.

8. MEDIATION MODEL

Section F of the questionnaire read as follows:

F.   Mediation model

Mediation model	1 2 3 4 5
1. How long do most conflicts take to resolve by mediation? [1 = a week or less; 2 = less than one month; 3 = less than 3 months; 4 = less than 6 months; 5 = no clear picture]	☐☐☐☐☐
2. Do most mediations involve meeting on just one day, or are several meetings needed over a period of time? [1 = 1 meeting, 2 = 2 meetings, 3 = 3 meetings, 4 = 4 meetings, 5 = 5 or more meetings]	☐☐☐☐☐
3. How long do most mediation meetings last? [1 = 1–2 hours, 2 = 2–4 hours, 3 = 4–6 hours, 4 = 6–8 hours, 5 = 8 or more hours]	☐☐☐☐☐

Is there any particular format which you have found generally works best?	

Any comments?	

i Average length of dispute

34% of responses said that there was no clear picture for the average length of a dispute. 32% of responses considered the average length of a dispute is one-to-three months.[272] 20% considered the average length of a dispute is three-to-six months. 13% considered the average length of a dispute is one month. This is shown in figure 35.

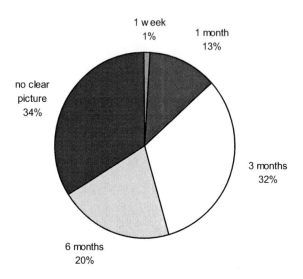

Figure 35. Average length of dispute

The individual countries show a fairly consistent picture. This is shown in figure 36. Only one diocese said that disputes are

---

[272] A number of bishops ticked more than one box. In such cases the higher number is taken.

usually resolved in one week.[273] Only in South Africa was the score for six months higher than the score for three months.

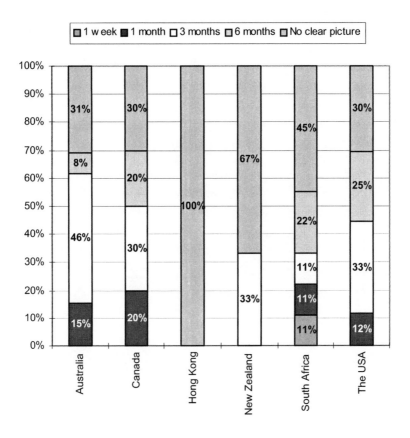

Figure 36. Average length of dispute (individual countries)

---

[273] Johannesburg (South Africa).

ii Number of meetings

All countries found that disputes usually require several meetings to resolve by mediation, the highest scores being equally divided between three meetings and five or more meetings. This is shown in figure 37.

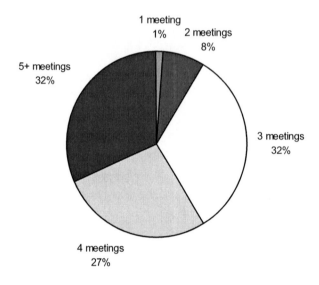

Figure 37. How many meetings

The results for individual countries is shown in figure 38.

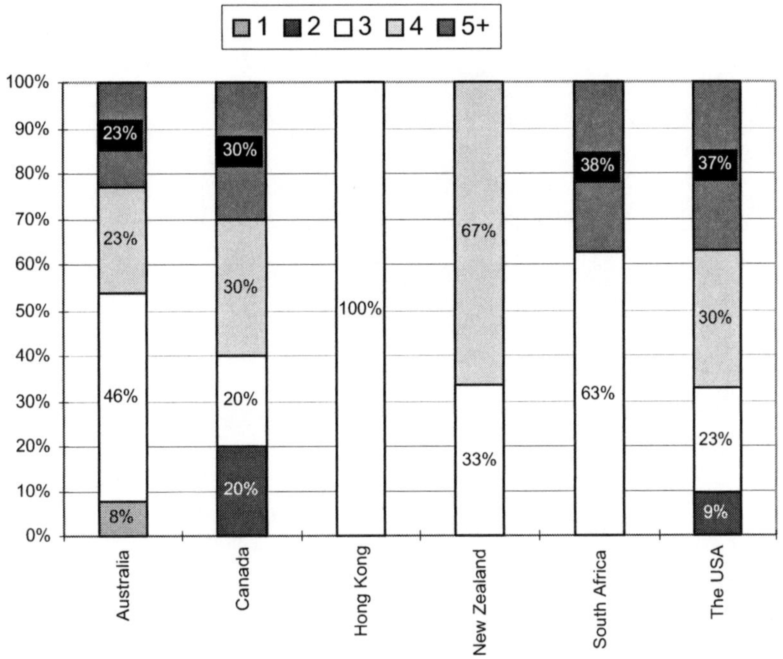

Figure 38. How many meetings (individual countries)

iii Length of meetings

The average length of meetings is shown in figure 39 (the overall picture) and figure 40 (individual countries). Most mediation meetings are 2–4 hours in duration, but quite a large number are 1–2 hours. However in Hong Kong, New Zealand and South Africa it was not uncommon to hold meetings more than 4 hours long, and one bishop in South Africa reported meetings of 8 hours or more.

435

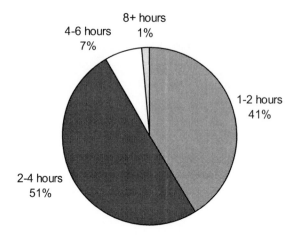

Figure 39. Average length of meeting

The message is clear: in general a number of meetings of up to half a day is preferred to one long meeting. This is interesting in comparison to the commercial mediation approach described in chapter 5, where mediations generally take place at one sitting, lasting up to a full day (in some cases longer). In the community model, the mediator meets the parties individually, and then there is usually only one face-to-face meeting of 2–3 hours.

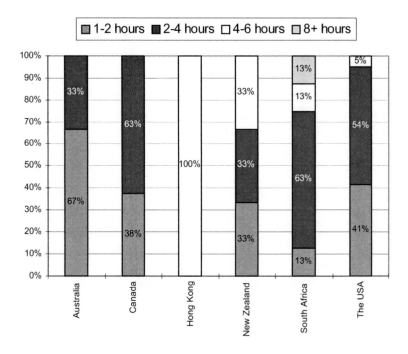

Figure 40. Average length of meeting (individual countries)

iv   Average mediation time per dispute

Multiplying the average number of meetings by the average length of meetings indicates that an overall average of 13 hours' mediation time is spent per dispute.[274] This is longer than the average mediation time for both the commercial and the community model. Similarly, church mediations take on average longer than both community and commercial mediations to resolve: church disputes typically take three months to resolve, whereas com-

---

[274] The overall average length of a meeting was 3.4 hours; the overall average number of meetings was 3.81.

munity mediations take two months, and commercial mediations are frequently resolved within one month.[275]

v Formats

The formats generally used have much in common with the community model, but some emphasise the specifically Christian element involved.

AUSTRALIA

Two bishops said that every case is different.[276] One bishop referred to meeting with the parties separately, then together.[277] One bishop prefers holding a number of short meetings, rather than one 'long slog'.[278] One bishop referred to the Alban Institute model for mediation.[279] Three stressed the low-key approach: going alone without diocesan officials,[280] holding the mediation on neutral territory,[281] but keeping some structure to the process.[282]

---

[275] Camden Mediation Service aims to complete each case within two months from the case being referred to it. Commercial mediations are frequently arranged and finished within a month.

[276] 'No. Depends on circumstances.' (Adelaide).

'No two situations are ever the same ' (North Queensland).

'We make use of a range of formats according to the situation. There are some base line principles we adhere to: e.g. we ensure that the conflicted parties agree on the process to be used and sign up for it.' (Tasmania).

[277] 'Mediator meeting with parties separately in the first instance then with groups together.' (Wangaratta).

[278] 'Frequent short meetings, rather than "long slog" meetings'. (Willochra).

[279] 'Speed Leas – Conflict Resolution Alban Institute – mediation process.' (Newcastle).

[280] 'Going alone without diocesan officials.' (Gippsland).

[281] '"neutral territory" discussion in "professional" setting.' (Melbourne).

438

One said he had not enough experience to comment.[283] One bishop's approach seemed to be judicial: he referred to moving the priest where necessary.[284]

CANADA

There was very little agreement on the best method in Canada. Four bishops said that every case is different.[285] One described a Christian model, involving interaction before the meeting starts, worship, listening, summarising, and using a mediation committee.[286] One bishop recommends a series of 1–1½ hour meetings

---

[282] 'Enabling each party to agree first on the goals of the mediation exercise and then ensuring some ground rules about how the discussion ensues.' (Northern Territory).

[283] Bendigo.

[284] 'Stating the problem, hearing both sides, recourse to ordinances for guidance, relieving the priest of his charge by moving him.' (The Murray).

[285] 'No. Each needs to be tailored to the specific situation.' (Eastern Newfoundland and Labrador).

'Depends on the situation.' (Rupert's Land).

'We try to tailor each one to fit circumstances.' (Toronto).

'Different mediations have different time patterns. Ideally this should take place as expeditiously as possible, but some require a step-by-step approach openness and honesty, with a trusted and competent facilitator'. (Moosonee).

[286] Unfortunately, this now retired bishop's hand-writing was difficult to read. 'Lots of interaction with people present before meeting starts to [stabil...] some degree of [fr...] and using eye contact with as much affirmation as possible. Worship – lead by unbiased persons. Listen to problem; reverberate it back to see if presentation accurate. Then ask those spoken to make no response until opposition has been heard and echoed back to them. Not have groups interacting with each other but with the mediation committee (usually 4–5 people). Tends to clarify

over a whole weekend.[287] One bishop used the 'native circle' format.[288] One bishop stressed the need to ensure that all parties feel they have been heard, and that they understand the Christian dimension to the dispute.[289] One described how to build consensus in groups.[290] One recommends intervention by the archdeacon.[291]

HONG KONG

The archbishop of Hong Kong did not recommend any particular format.

---

misunderstandings and prepares mutually acceptable terminology.' (Central Newfoundland).

[287] 'Usually six months – 1 year. Individual meetings take 1 – 1½ hours. The series of meetings may begin on Friday evening 7 p.m., and run until Sunday 4 p.m., during daylight hours and outside of worship times.' (Huron).

[288] New Westminster.

[289] 'People must feel that they have been allowed to have their say. Those involved need to be constantly reminded of the larger picture and purpose for being, but without hitting them with the Bible, or, "let's pray!"' (Qu'Appelle).

[290] 'We have too few case histories to provide guidelines. Work on degrees of consensus. Spell out best-case worse-case. Seek to know the "will" of those gathered. Seek resolution which saves the greatest dignity for all concerned. Work early with inside groups – vestry, individuals.' (Saskatoon).

[291] 'Early intervention by the archdeacon with the Incumbent and elected parish officials.' (Nova Scotia and Prince Edward Island).

NEW ZEALAND

One bishop from New Zealand recommended two formats: the Salvation Army method from Australia,[292] and the Alban Institute method.[293]

SOUTH AFRICA

Five bishops said that each situation is different.[294] A number said that it was necessary in Africa to spend time building up relationships in order to heal conflict.[295] One referred to using a small 'review team'.[296]

---

[292] A Salvation Army resource person in Australia, John Savage, offers seminars in Australia and New Zealand on a number of human dynamics including conflict resolution. He is well-known for training people in new listening skills. The contact for John Savage in New Zealand is through the Anglican Resource Centre, Wellington.

[293] 'The "Savage" Method: (Salvation Army Australia). The Revd Speed Leas method from the Alban Institute.' (Waikato).

[294] 'Each situation is different.' (Highveld).

'Difficult to answer question. Mediations differ dramatically in terms of complexity and intensity of feelings involved. The duration of the problem also affects length of mediation. Attempt to focus on perceptions and feelings rather than a simple litany of "facts". Focus is always "win-win".' (Johannesburg).

'Each situation is different and needs to be handled differently.' (Port Elizabeth).

'In all these cases it depends on the nature and complexity of the problem.' (St Mark the Evangelist, Northern Province).

'I am not sure. The question of how many meeting depends on the issues involved in the conflict, and the type of persons involved.' (Swaziland).

[295] '"less haste – more speed". In this rural African context, the mediation process can *never* be hurried. In the event of no successful conclu-

THE USA

Several bishops said that every case is different.[297] Two said they did not use mediation enough to have established a pattern.[298] Those who gave a preferred format usually referred to

---

sion to the mediation process, the "cooling off" period invariably brings parish church back into life of diocese.' (Klerksdorp).

'In Africa, a great deal of time is devoted to building relationships and trust as part of the process of reconciliation.' (St Mark the Evangelist, Northern Province).

[296] 'We have a small "review team" on standby for instant intervention should the situation warrant it.' (Bloemfontein).

[297] 'Depends on the context.' (Delaware).

'Each situation will require its tailored response.' (Florida).

'My experience with mediation, having to do with the length, depends on the seriousness of the issue and how much energy the parties of the issue have to bring about a healing resolution. Some of them take a considerable amount of time. Others seem to have solved most of the issues so that people can live comfortably together and get on with ministry in as short a time as three months.' (Georgia).

'Lengths of meetings vary. Format depends on situation and skills of mediators.' (Los Angeles).

'No. We treat each situation appropriately.' (Louisiana).

'Depends on who is in conflict.' (Michigan).

'No.' (Milwaukee).

'No.' (New Hampshire).

'I leave the format up to the mediator.' (West Missouri).

'Each situation is different and there is not certain model or pattern.' (West Tennessee).

'No, varies from incident to incident.' (Western Louisiana).

'No.' (Washington).

[298] 'We do not use formal mediation enough to have established a pattern.' (SouthWest Virginia).

'Not much experience.' (Fond du Lac).

three stages: the first involved setting ground rules, listening, and making sure each party feels heard; the second involved clarification of the issues; the third involved working on the issues, prioritising them, and discussing options for resolution.[299] Several others referred to one or more of these stages – especially the first stage of listening to all parties;[300] a number referred to the use of prayer;[301] one bishop referred to the models used by the Quakers

---

[299] 'Format clearly developed related to issue and people involved but begins with each individual having opportunity to be heard.' (Olympia).

'Good listening. "I" statements. Get issues on paper and mutually agreed to. Prioritise.' (Washington).

'1. prayer, scripture, and overview. 2. statements by both parties. 3. clarification of the issues. 4. list of workable options. 5. attempt at mediation. 6. prayer and closure.' (Missouri).

'Setting ground rules for discussion; making sure everyone feels heard; providing objective expression as reflection of what's offered; clarification of expectations; re-negotiation.' (Indeanapolis).

'This particular model is geared for reconciliation. However if reconciliation appears impossible it is still very useful for all the information and discoveries that are forthcoming. My usual format is as follows: Phase 1: interviewing staff and congregants; formulating issues raised in interviews. Phase 2: conflict resolution based on issues and gleanings from interviews.' (Kansas City).

[300] 'Both sides listening to one another.' (Arkansas).

'A good deal of listening and "depersonalising", where possible, is helpful.' (Los Angeles).

'Listening before defining or speaking; be a "non-anxious" presence.' (New York).

'Building the bridge of a common language between disputants, and labour to get all issues to the surface.' (Bethlehem).

'Involve people representative of all sides of a dispute to form a design team with the consultants.' (Virginia).

[301] Missouri (see above).

'Lots of prayer before, during and after.' (Quincy).

and Mennonites;[302] and one to a specifically Christian model of 'prayer, truth telling, questions; conclude with prayer and/or renewal of baptismal vows'.[303]

vi Bishops' comments

The bishops' comments can be divided into three main categories: the first category describes the format of meetings (which is what the question asked); the second focused on establishing the issues in the dispute; the third described the pastoral approach required to resolve disputes. In some cases the bishops' comments covered two or all three of these categories. There is a parallel here with the conflict triangle discussed earlier.[304] Establishing the issues focuses on the *problem*; the format of the meetings describes the *process*; and the pastoral approach concentrates on the *people* involved.

vii A Christian element

It is clear that several bishops succeed in adapting the secular mediation process for Christian disputes. This is not just a question of adding some liturgical element, though several bishops use prayer, worship and scripture readings as part of the mediation process. Where these are used, it is clear that the bishops believe they are not just a formality, but have an effect on the process. In particular, they enable the parties to see the dispute in a new, Christian, light, and to seek to resolve it according to Christian principles and in a Christian manner. Making Christ central to the process emphasises that the parties and the mediator are all

---

[302] 'These traditions set mediation within a theological framework which is important to our congregations. This promotes mediation as an educational process I have been most impressed with (and have found greatest success with) the formats and principles used by the Mennonite and Quaker traditions.' (Maine).

[303] Western North Carolina.

[304] See pg. 16.

on the same level, and that the mediator's role is not a judicial role. It emphasises that the mediator is not exercising authority over the parties to the dispute, but is ministering to the parties to help the parties resolve their own disagreement. The mediator and the parties are there together, at the same level, all seeking to follow Christ, and seeking His guidance.

Several comments refer to dispute resolution teaching from other organisations which the bishops found useful. Three in particular were mentioned several times: the Mennonites, the Quakers, and the Alban Institute of the USA. The Quakers have been much involved in setting up community mediation in the UK, and the Mennonite model is very similar to the community mediation model. But the Mennonite model adds a specifically Christian element to the secular model. Mennonites see conflict resolution as a calling for all Christians, and believe that Jesus is present when Christians are attempting to resolve their own or other people's disputes.[305]

The effect of prayer is not something which can be proved in a court of law.[306] The same may no doubt be said about many other tenets of the Christian faith. But the survey shows that there is a perceived Christian dimension to resolving conflicts. This is es-

---

[305] At a Mennonite training course the author attended in September 2000, it was pointed out that the well-known verse 'For where two or three come together in my name, there am I with them', comes at the end of a passage dealing with how Christians should handle conflicts: Matthew 18:15–20. On the same Mennonite course attention was drawn to Mark 12:28–34. It was explained that this is an excellent example of the skill used by mediators called 'active listening'. The teacher of the law listened to Jesus' answer to his question, and then summarised it back to Jesus showing that he had understood what Jesus had said. He also added a gloss at the end to show he appreciated the significance of Jesus' answer.

[306] *Gilmour v Coates* [1949] AC 426, 426 per Lord Simonds. Lord Simonds was referring only to intercessory prayer; but the point is more general.

pecially the case in Church disputes, where either all or at least some of the parties are Christians.[307] In chapter 3, attention was drawn to an emerging pastoral theology of conflict management.[308]

Indeed, the survey indicates that Christ is seen to be *central* to the resolution process.[309] Christian mediation is not an additional element tacked on to an existing secular model, but is something which permeates the whole of the model, and is *central* to it. For this reason, the church dispute triangle shown below illustrates a better approach to resolving Church disputes than the standard conflict triangle.

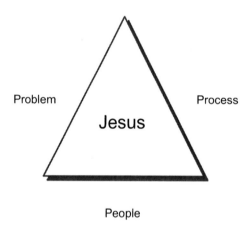

Figure 41. The church dispute triangle

---

[307] Some church disputes involve outside persons or bodies, who may or may not be Christian.

[308] See pg. 138.

[309] This is dealt with more fully in section 9, 'Lessons', below.

Making Christ central to the process therefore has a spiritual function, not one which can be explained just in human psychological terms. The bishops see mediation of church disputes in essentially theological rather than legal terms. To take a trite analogy, when a machine is badly damaged it may need to go back to the maker for repair: when the Christian body is damaged by a dispute, it is the creator and redeemer of that body who knows best how to put it right.

9. LESSONS

Section G of the questionnaire asked:

Are there any lessons from your own experience in this area which you consider would be useful to pass on to others?	

55 bishops replied to this question. The majority of the comments concerned at least one of the four elements in the church dispute triangle. A number of comments also mentioned the need for church members and leaders to be trained in conflict resolution.

i Individual countries

AUSTRALIA

A number of Australian bishops see mediation in theological rather than legal terms. Conflict can be 'a sign of real health',[310] and the outcome 'redemption and new beginnings'.[311] In contrast, unresolved conflict leads to 'unhealthy congregations'.[312] Two bishops said that mediation is best if used early in a dispute.[313] One said that archdeacons need to be encouraged to use mediation.[314] One bishop recommended three-yearly parish consulta-

---

[310] 'It is difficult and time consuming, but absolutely essential. We need to acknowledge we have conflict in the church, sometimes it is a sign of real health and needs to be dealt with carefully.' (North Queensland).

[311] 'If the outcome expected is justice and redress in legal terms, mediation offers no winners. If the outcome is motivated as a gospel community seeking redemption and new beginnings (Sin, Repentance, Sanctification) healing comes as a gift to be received with thanksgiving.' (Newcastle).

[312] 'The main lesson is that unresolved conflict will produce unhealthy congregations. Failure to resolve conflicts leads churches into 5 year cycles of conflict. If conflicts are faced and resolved congregations can return to a "normal" life within 12 month.' (Tasmania).

[313] 'Use of mediation processes are best engaged early in a suitable dispute, well in advance of signs of intractability; "last resort" usage is generally too late.' (Melbourne).

'Engage the mediation programme early rather than as a last resort.' (Wangaratta).

[314] 'It is very important to get on side and keep on side the "gatekeepers" i.e. those who get to hear of the disputes – Bishops, Archdeacons, Area/Rural Deans etc. so that they consider using dispute resolution procedures rather than more formal procedures or worse, doing nothing. Our Synod set up a Select Committee on the issue, of which I was Chair, in the mid 90's. It arose from a fairly difficult parochial dispute which caused much controversy in the Diocese. The Select Committee recommended, and the Synod eventually adopted, a non-litigious

tions as a preventative measure.[315] One bishop referred to the need for training for bishops.[316] One bishop commented that a senior priest and competent lay person is a good combination as a mediation team.[317]

Four bishops referred to legal provisions: bishops need powers to intervene in case of pastoral breakdown,[318] and where the parties refuse to mediate.[319] One bishop referred to draft legislation modelled on the English canon.[320] The archbishop of Sydney and the bishop of Tasmania referred to the legislation in use in these dioceses, both of which provide for mediation.[321] Sydney uses a model similar to community mediation, but with an explicit Christian emphasis.[322] Thus, legal representation is not allowed,

---

and non-adversarial system for dispute resolution within a parish, especially between the Minister and the parish. It is entitled *Parish Disputes Ordinance 1999* and the text is attached.' (Sydney).

[315] 'Parish consultations should be held every 3 years.' (Bunbury).

[316] 'I wish I had been taught such skills earlier.' (Bendigo).

[317] 'A senior priest and competent lay person are a good combination as a mediation team. After the mediators have been with people and priest separately, it is important they meet together. If this does not happen the outlook is not good.' (Bunbury).

[318] 'Bishops need some powers to act in situations of pastoral breakdown. At present lay people expect the Bishop to intervene but his powers to do so are limited.' (Adelaide).

[319] 'There are some people who will not engage in a mediation process under any circumstances. After endless effort, sometimes it is necessary to take a "heavy handed" approach.' (Willochra).

[320] 'An ordinance is being prepared which will, if adopted by Synod, be able to address all issues including financial loss to the incumbent. We have used the English Canon as a model and adopted it to local conditions.' (The Murray).

[321] The Parish Disputes Ordinance 1999 for Sydney; the Ministry and Tribunal Ordinance 1998 for Tasmania.

[322] See pg. 418, fn. 231, pg. 418, fn. 232, and pg. 419, fn. 233.

as in community mediation; and the objective is stated to be 'reconciliation in a way which expresses biblical values', including 'prayerfully working together'.[323] The Tasmanian legislation does not specify any format for the mediation process.

CANADA

A number of comments show a positive approach to conflict in New Zealand, for example, using conflict to enable people's concerns to be heard.[324] Mediation is a flexible process,[325] but is not an excuse to avoid tough decisions over incompetent or ineffective leadership.[326] One bishop said that using independent mediators enables the bishop to remain as pastor once people begin to come

---

[323] The Parish Disputes Ordinance 1999 for Sydney, sections 11 and 12.

[324] 'Don't avoid conflicts. Don't be rushed into mediation. People need to feel their concerns are being heard, and they have ownership in the final outcome. Clear communication is vital. Follow up must be done at as early a date as pos. Then move on.' (Moosonee).

'Basic knowledge of group dynamics is very essential. All must be encouraged to speak etc. Making certain that communication is clear and understood.' (Central Newfoundland).

[325] 'The process tends to work better under a flexible format which can be adapted to local situations. Care has to be taken not to give the incident more importance than it deserves.' (Eastern Newfoundland and Labrador).

[326] 'Mediation can often be a way to avoid dealing with clear issues, such as incompetent or ineffective leadership.' (New Westminster).

together again.[327] Four bishops referred to the need to be ready to handle conflict in its early stages.[328]

HONG KONG

The archbishop of Hong Kong referred to mediation skills of listening, sincerity, honesty, fairness, openness, and wisdom.[329]

NEW ZEALAND

One bishop commented that the process never goes smoothly.[330] Another commented on the need for both suitably

---

[327] 'As bishop there is always a difficult line to draw between "employer of clergy", "Father in God" to priest and people, and "pastor of the pastors". In serious "church conflicts" the use of qualified mediators allows the bishop to exercise his or her talents as pastor once people begin to come together.' (Huron).

[328] 'Have found tremendous value in having trained archdeacons to engage in intervention when conflict situations seem to be ready to develop.' (Nova Scotia and Prince Edward Island).

'When the possibility of first signs of conflict appear, get on to it quickly – subtly if possible.' (Qu'Appelle).

'We need to spend a great deal more energy than we do in preparing clergy and congregations to deal with conflict.' (Rupert's Land).

'Be proactive, enter early, speak clearly, listen well, don't be afraid to make tough decisions, seek the dignity of all involved as much as possible; when not possible, excise!' (Saskatoon).

[329] 'Being a mediator one needs to be willing to listen in sincerity and honesty. One has to [be] fair and open; and one needs to be wise to be able to discern the guile [?] involved.' (Hong Kong).

[330] 'No process ever goes as predicted or smoothly for all. The process is always challenged.' (Waikato).

qualified mediators and a lawyer to whom the bishop can turn to for advice.[331]

South Africa

Two bishops stated they were having conflict resolution training.[332] Two referred to theological principles of reconciliation, and the power of God to heal and resolve the most difficult situations.[333] One bishop referred to scripture.[334] One referred to using a process with which everyone involved was comfortable.[335]

---

[331] '1. need for suitably qualified mediators. 2. need for appropriate "friends at court" – not necessarily lawyers. 3. a lawyer with knowledge in area a Bishop can turn to for advice.' (Wellington).

[332] 'I am about to embark upon formal conflict resolution training, and I should have done so before.' (Christ the King).

'Only my practical experience. Currently involved in Masters degree in Peace Studies and Conflict Resolution.' (Highveld).

[333] 'Encourage people to sit down together and solve their own problems. We worship a living God, and Jesus rose from the dead. We must believe in the power of God to heal and resolve the most difficult situations. Lots of prayer with intercessors backing up.' (Port Elizabeth).

'We cannot afford to fight one another in court. Mediation / reconciliation is a process that requires a long-term commitment from all involved. Jesus Christ is our mediator, example, and source of wisdom and strength. If we hold on to him, any dispute can be resolved. We can expect and demand that from people in the Church' (St Mark the Evangelist, Northern Province).

[334] 'Apply the principle of 1 Corinthians 6. Don't follow the herd and rush to litigation.' (Pretoria).

[335] 'It is good to have a strategy in place which is familiar to all stakeholders.' (Bloemfontein).

THE USA

Lessons on the process included not seeing one party alone after the process had begun,[336] not acting alone,[337] helping the parties come to mediation with the right approach,[338] and find their own solution,[339] being business-like, and yet keeping Christ central.[340]

Building trust in the mediator was behind many of the comments made about the need for patience,[341] listening skills,[342] honesty,[343] and proceeding slowly.[344]

---

[336] 'Never meet with one party alone after the process has begun.' (Bethlehem).

[337] 'Don't do it alone.' (Florida).

[338] 'One of the hardest points of this area of concern is helping the parties come to an acceptance that there is a conflict, rather than just "he's wrong, I'm right". Both (all) sides need to come to mediation with equal resolve to reach an agreement, and in a state of mind which prepares them to "give" a little to reach agreement.' (Maine).

[339] 'Mediators rarely resolve the disputes. At best, they help the participants frame the disputed issues and work out resolution for themselves.' (Virginia).

[340] '1. be clear about agreements, policies, canons, assigned duties and lines of authority. 2. keep clear concise notes of all meetings. 3. do lots of hands on training. 4. Keep Christ central.' (Missouri).

[341] 'Patience is very necessary.' (Kansas City).

'Be patient; be willing to receive criticism; be willing to listen. PRAY.' (Western North Carolina).

[342] 'Earning trust for fairness; listening are of course important.' (Los Angeles).

'Learn to listen; do not get caught up in anger or the feeling. "non-anxious" presence.' (New York).

[343] 'Being honest and upfront helps and shortens time to reconciliation.' (Milwaukee).

453

Several bishops see mediation in terms of Christian reconciliation and healing, rather than in legal terms.[345] They commented that Christian disputes are frequently not addressed in a Christian way.[346] Parties can be intransigent,[347] and the outcome is not al-

---

[344] 'Dealing with conflict is like bomb disposal: take all the time it takes, move slowly; do nothing that you do not have both a well reasoned purpose for doing and a pretty fair idea of what the result will be; have a plan and do not be driven off it by panic (either own or others) or getting "hooked" by emotional position of others in anxious system that is in conflict. i.e. cutting wires on the bomb is complex and serious business – take your time and cut carefully. Generally there are no second chances or do overs.' (Michigan).

'The most important thing is building long term, trusting relationships.' (Northern Michigan).

[345] 'Mediation usually involves dealing with a conflict that leads to a decision about a matter. More common here is a reconciliation process which does not lead to a decision but to healing, and it is far more difficult to achieve.' (Central Pennsylvania).

'Reconciliation is one of the most important faith-in-action lessons we can help our members learn. It begins in granting respect and proceeds in growing in love – even in the midst of disagreement.' (Indeanapolis).

'Being honest and upfront helps and shortens time to reconciliation.' (Milwaukee).

[346] 'Church conflicts never actually resolve themselves so long as the antagonists remain in place. Church conflict is seldom addressed in a "Christian" manner – hurt refuses to heal, forgiveness not given etc.' (Western Louisiana).

[347] 'No one model works everywhere. If participants are not interested in greater well-being then attempts are often futile.' (Olympia).

ways success,[348] but opinions were generally positive about church mediation.[349]

A number referred to conflict resolution theories and training they use: family systems theory,[350] and other methods.[351] One recommends the use of trained conflict managers,[352] others recommend training leaders in mediation,[353] and hands-on training for themselves.[354]

ii Conclusions

The lessons were positive, with advice on the process, the skills needed, and on the need for training. The comments from South Africa were particularly open about the reality of the Christian element in church mediations.

> Encourage people to sit down together and solve their own problems. We worship a living God, and Jesus rose from the dead. We must believe in the power of God to heal and

---

[348] 'It is always a mixed bag. But I favour the mediation process, especially when clergy relationships with congregation break down.' (West Missouri).

[349] 'Court mediation has not helped me (property); parish mediation (priest vs. people) has.' (Quincy).

[350] 'A mediator who does not know family systems theory as it applies to congregations is pretty useless.' (Chicago).

[351] 'I generally use the approach I learned at Harvard from Frank Sander et al.' (Delaware).

[352] 'We in the Church need trained conflict managers available to help deal with inevitable disputes.' (Eau Claire).

[353] 'Encourage all church leaders to educate themselves in mediation techniques.' (SouthWest Virginia).

'More church leaders need to be trained in the mediation process.' (Utah).

[354] '1. be clear about agreements, policies, canons, assigned duties and lines of authority. 2. keep clear concise notes of all meetings. 3. do lots of hands on training. 4. Keep Christ central.' (Missouri).

resolve the most difficult situations. Lots of prayer with intercessors backing up.[355]

We cannot afford to fight one another in court. Mediation/reconciliation is a process that requires a long-term commitment from all involved. Jesus Christ is our mediator, example, and source of wisdom and strength. If we hold on to him, any dispute can be resolved. We can expect and demand that from people in the Church.[356]

Similarly, one bishop from the USA referred to the need to 'keep Christ central',[357] two referred to the need for prayer,[358] and bishops from the USA and Australia considered the whole process as a part of the Christian ministry of reconciliation.

10. OTHER CONTACTS

In section H, the questionnaire asked

Is there anyone else you would recommend me to get in touch with who may be able to help me with my research?	

---

[355] Port Elizabeth.

[356] St Mark the Evangelist, Northern Province. In Christian theology, Christ is the mediator between God and man, rather than between men (1 Timothy 2:5). Yet if Christ can mediate between God and man in eternal matters, so too He can assist in man's mundane disputes. No one could ask for a better mediator for these. Christ became man and is able 'to sympathise with our weaknesses' (Hebrews 4:15), which is similar to the key mediation skill of empathy.

[357] Missouri (USA).

[358] Western North Carolina (USA); Port Elizabeth (South Africa).

Several bishops from Australia, Canada, New Zealand and the USA[359] recommended the Alban Institute.[360] The Alban Institute publishes a number of books dealing with church conflict, and offers both training and a consultancy service. Particular mention was made of the Revd Speed B. Leas, author and senior consultant at the Alban Institute.[361]

Two American bishops[362] mentioned the Mennonite Conciliation Service.[363]

Three bishops mentioned other bishops with particular experience in this area, two in the USA,[364] one in South Africa.[365] Indi-

---

[359] The Alban Institute was recommended by eight American bishops: Florida, Georgia, Milwaukee, Mississippi, Nebraska, NorthWest Texas, Olympia and San Diego; by the bishop of Newcastle (Australia); by the bishop of Nova Scotia and Prince Edward Island (Canada); and by the bishop of Waikato (New Zealand). The bishops of Mississippi and San Diego (USA), the bishop of Nova Scotia and Prince Edward Island, and the bishop of Waikato (New Zealand) praised the Alban Institute's training programme. The bishop of Michigan (USA) encourages churches to approach the Alban Institute for a mediator.

[360] The Alban Institute, Suite 1250 West, 7315 Wisconsin Avenue, Bethesda, MD 20814, USA. See *www.alban.org*.

[361] The Revd Leas was recommended by the bishop of Olympia (USA), Waikato (New Zealand), Florida (USA), NorthWest Texas (USA), Newcastle (Australia). The bishops of Wellington (New Zealand) and Christchurch (New Zealand) said they had used Mr Leas for training programmes.

[362] Maine and Milwaukee (USA).

[363] The Mennonite Conciliation Service, 21 South 12th Street, P.O. Box 500, Akron, PA 17501–0500, USA.

[364] The Bishop of New Pennsylvania, The Rt Revd Robert Rowley, was recommended by the bishop of Bethlehem (USA). The retired bishop of Delaware, The Rt Revd Cabell Tennis, was recommended by the bishop

457

vidual clergy were mentioned in the USA,[366] Canada,[367] and South
Africa.[368] A married couple who practice as church consultants
were mentioned in Canada.[369] Two other individuals in Australia,[370] and one in the USA[371] were mentioned. Two Australian

---

of the Central Gulf Coast, USA. The author wrote to Bishop Tennis, and
his response is included in the survey.

[365] The Bishop of Grahamstown, The Rt Revd David Russell, was recommended by the bishop of Swaziland (South Africa).

[366] The Revd John A Coil, 7917 Lamar, Overland Park, KS 66208, recommended by the bishop of Kansas City (USA).

The Rev Marie Fortune, 'Centre for the Prevention of Sexual and Domestic Abuse', Seattle, USA was recommended by the bishop of Christchurch (New Zealand). The author questions the criterion for this recommendation, as he suspects mediation plays only a small part of her
work.

[367] Walter Deller, the Ven. Colin Jackson, The Revd Dawn Davis, all
at 135 Adelaide Street, 135 Toronto Ont. MSC IL8, recommended by the
bishop of Toronto (Canada).

[368] Canon Michael McCoy, 30 Capt. Proctor Street, Brandwag, 9301
Bloemfontein, South Africa, recommended by the bishop of Bloemfontein (South Africa).

[369] Joan and John Steer, Church Consultants, 389 Rankin Blvd, Windsor,
Ontario, recommended by the bishop of Huron (Canada).

[370] Les Scarborough, John Mask Ministries, 3 Hill Street, Glenbrook,
N.S.W. Australia. 02 4739 5038, recommended by the bishop of Tasmania.

Meredith Edger, former director of Lifeworks, Melbourne, recommended by the bishop of Wangaratta.

[371] Jack W Burtch, PO Box 1463, Richmond VA 23212 USA, 'an attorney
& frequent mediator', recommended by the bishop of Virginia.

458

bishops referred to their chancellors,[372] as did one American bishop.[373]

11. GENERAL COMMENTS

Section I of the questionnaire asked

Are there any other comments you would like to make?	

A number of responses were personal. Bishops considered the subject important,[374] wished the author well with the research,[375] and expressed interest in the results.[376] A number offered to corre-

---

[372] The bishops of Bendigo and Adelaide. The author met the chancellor of Bendigo in September 2000.

[373] 'I have forwarded your letter and questionnaire to the chancellor of this diocese, Edwin G. Hebb, Esq. As out diocesan attorney, Mr Hebb is the person best qualified to answer these questions, and to comment on our experience and practice.' (Connecticut, USA). In the event, the author heard nothing from Mr Hebb.

[374] 'This is an important area of research.' (Virginia, USA).

[375] Gippsland, Australia; Chicago, USA; St Mark the Evangelist, Northern Province, South Africa; Bendigo, Australia.

'Your letter indicates that the situation in England is quite different from here in Canada. I hope this response is helpful to you.' (Moosonee, Canada).

[376] 'Thank you for your work – it could be very helpful for the American Church!' (Florida, USA).

'I thank you for undertaking this survey, and am interested in your findings and recommendations.' (San Diego, USA).

spond further.[377] Only one expressed any negative criticism of the survey form.[378]

Conflict was recognised as being inevitable.[379] A number of comments were directed to the legal vs. theological approach to dispute resolution, which this survey has highlighted.[380] Thus, on

---

'Would very much like to see a copy of your findings.' (Johannesburg, South Africa).

'I wish you every success in your research and would be very interested in learning of your conclusions.' (The Arctic, Canada).

[377] 'I would be pleased to elaborate on any of these rather sparse answers via email. dharvey@anglicanenl.nf.net.' (Eastern Newfoundland and Labrador, Canada). This is one of several such comments.

[378] 'In attempting to fill out this questionnaire it would have been helpful to have a statement of your understanding of mediation and your assumptions. There are too many variables in each situation for precise responses to your questions.' (Rupert's Land, Canada).

[379] 'Conflicts are bound to occur from time to time and people (clergy and parishioners) are no longer willing to simply accept decisions imposed on them by the hierarchy.' (Bloemfontein, South Africa).

[380] 'The Church should consider designing a dispute resolution system that is in place and tested. We tend to use discipline processes for disagreements over doctrine, style, point of view, and so increase the personal element making it difficult to resolve.' (Delaware, USA).

'In general terms, I would prefer mediation to a court case, and I would prefer some form of church mediation to a secular model. My first preference, however, is a pastoral model involving the Bishop and the particular people affected. There are a great variety of means to deal with church disputes. Such is the case even within a diocese, and it must be so across diocesan and national church borders.' (East Tennessee, USA).

'Mediation has long been a biblical way of proceeding but is now in legal circles and in ecumenical law arenas. Much needs to be learnt by church members at all levels. Synod procedures have encouraged adversarial approaches based upon parliamentary procedure.' (Adelaide, Australia).

the one hand, synods in several dioceses have brought or are bringing in legislation to handle conflict,[381] and in some cases this legislation itself provides for mediation;[382] on the other hand, many bishops prefer to handle disputes pastorally. Two examples demonstrate this:

> 'The key is building good enough relationships that a dispute can be caught early and managed before it escalates.' [383]

> In general terms, I would prefer mediation to a court case, and I would prefer some form of church mediation to a secular model. My first preference, however, is a pastoral model involving the Bishop and the particular people affected.[384]

'Most issues of mediation are taken within a framework of Canons, Guidelines, Synod Resolutions and ethical documents. It would seem to me that this learning environment that is prevalent in a diocese is as important to understanding the process. The theological ground of the ecclesial community needs to be constantly referred to if we are serious for mediation to be seen as within the ongoing redemptive act of Christ.' (Newcastle, Australia).

[381] For example, the Ministry and Tribunal Ordinance 1998 for the diocese of Tasmania (Australia), the Parish Disputes Ordinance 1999 for the diocese of Sydney, the Anglican New Zealand Title D 'Process'.

[382] 'Our sexual harassment protocol provides for mediation; also in our Ecclesiastical Offences Act; 5 years ago there was an incident of improper touching which we dealt by convening an ad hoc panel.' (Bendigo, Australia). This suggests that on that occasion the diocese used a judicial procedure rather than mediation.

[383] South Carolina, USA. This response was in a letter, but the comments have been included in this section of the survey.

[384] East Tennessee (USA).

461

Comments about church lawyers were generally positive;[385] but one diocese said that it was the lawyers who were against mediation, because they are so used to the adversarial system.[386]

Two Canadian bishops said that they did not use mediation in their diocese.[387]

Many dioceses saw the value of resolving disputes 'in-house', by training up people within the diocese to help when necessary.[388] Some pointed to the difficulty of encouraging churches to

---

[385] 'My experience with the lawyers who are chancellors and vice-chancellors as well as others on diocesan committees is positive – so no need to apologise for the legal profession.' (Olympia, USA).

[386] 'There were and are three main issues: 1. To make the dispute resolution process truly effective, in that parties are prepared to participate, it is probably necessary to take out any heavy sanctions. This has both advantages and disadvantages. 2. The Lawyers (of which I am one) are the most resistant to alternative dispute resolution processes as they are so used to the adversarial system. 3. The 'gate-keepers' of the Diocese, in our case the regional Bishops and Archdeacons, must be trained and encouraged to steer disputes towards the process. They are sometimes resistant which is hard to understand as they are the ones who otherwise have to sort out the disputes! Our process includes many compromises as it had to negotiate our Synod which is heavily populated by Judges, Barristers and Solicitors, not to mention the innumerable "bush lawyers".' (Sydney, Australia).

[387] 'Our diocese does not use mediation, so we have no experience on which to respond to your questionnaire.' (Algoma, Canada).

'I regret that mediation is not a process with which we are familiar in the Diocese of the Arctic, and not one which we have used.' (Arctic, Canada).

[388] 'We try to be pro-active and not just reactive. We have our own training program for consultants. We use them for training lay leaders as well as in mediation. We believe early entrance into situations is important.' (New York, USA).

462

use mediation, especially where the church would have to contribute to the cost of professional mediation.[389]

One Canadian bishop emphasised the importance of maintaining confidentiality.[390] One American bishop gave advice on the choice of mediators:

'In our diocese, the canon, director of administration and myself (the bishop) are the primary mediation team. We do have a few internal task forces that deal with various issues, but the three of us, together, handle a majority of the issues. Fortunately, we have not had the need for outside mediation and have been able to resolve the conflicts "in house".' (Pittsburgh, USA).

'We've not used outside mediators, but used our own resources, God's people, from within the diocese. As a Christian family, we must have the resources within the Body to heal our own conflict.' (Port Elizabeth, South Africa).

'We are basically a harmonious group – black and white, some materially rich, many poor. Thankfully (on the whole) we manage to sort out our differences at local levels, and we have never had to employ any outside mediators. Thankfully, we seem to be free of dispute, at least at a major or diocesan level. That's not to say we are all "yes, men", but we discuss amicably.' (Pretoria, South Africa).

[389] 'Another difficult issue in this area of concern is how hard it is to propose/foster mediation when the conflict has "ripened" to a severe stage. Early intervention yields higher likelihood of success. Yet many congregations strenuously resist entering into mediation (often because they do not want to spend the money) and wait until the situation is quite severe before seeking mediation.' (Maine, USA).

'We certainly try to go to mediation if litigation is possible or threatened. There is generally a death of qualified mediators who will act in an honorary or near-honorary capacity, and insufficient funds to pay for much in the way of professional mediation.' (Brisbane, Australia).

[390] 'Be very careful to respect confidentiality. Keep the possibility of litigation in mind. Dispute resolution should be as open as possible. People need to be assured "this is my church, and I too have responsibility". Have sound legal advice.' (Qu'Appelle, Canada).

It is important to use mediators who are conversant with church life and sensitive to it. They need not be Anglicans.[391]

12. GENERAL CONCLUSIONS

A number of general conclusions can be drawn from the survey. The first, and perhaps the most important, conclusion is that in all the six countries of the survey, the Church has had considerable experience of church disputes, and of using mediation to resolve them, and that mediation has generally been very effective for this purpose. The evidence that mediation is effective in 73% of cases overall is significant.[392]

The survey points very clearly towards relational types of dispute being suitable for mediation. Of the types of dispute listed in the questionnaire, personality conflict and employment disputes are shown to be very suitable for mediation. In contrast, the results indicate that disputes about gay or gender issues, and about worship and doctrine, are marginally unsuitable for mediation.

The research points to new ways of categorising disputes. The questionnaire listed disputes by the type of problem, but many responses also drew attention to the identity of the parties in dispute, and the appropriateness of mediation as a process. For example, almost any dispute between members of a team, such as parish leaders, or between leaders and congregation, is in principle suitable for mediation. In contrast, where sexual misconduct is alleged, discipline is usually a more appropriate process than mediation.

Clergy and trained lay leaders act as mediators of church disputes twice as often as professional mediators, and with more success. Bishops also act as mediators, though sometimes their judicial role inhibits them from being as effective as mediators as

---

[391] New Hampshire, USA.

[392] See pg. 391.

they would otherwise be. There is a reluctance to use external professionals (cost being a major disincentive), except for cases of pastoral breakdown affecting whole congregations. In large congregational disputes, professional mediators' facilitation skills – in particular, their knowledge of group process and consensus building – is valued by bishops.

There was unanimous agreement that Canon law should encourage mediation, though disagreement as to whether or not mediation should ever be made compulsory. There is a general acceptance of mediation being built into diocesan legal structures as an option available in cases of parish disputes. Senior clergy encourage the parties to make use of this process where appropriate.

The survey shows that training in conflict management is becoming a very popular option in theological colleges and seminaries. Senior clergy too are starting to study it, both academically and with hands-on training. There is general agreement that practical hands-on training is needed, and that this should be provided both before ordination, and as part of clergy continuing education. The need to train leading lay members of the church is also recognised, in particular because a lay person working together with a clergyman is a very good mediation team for many church disputes.

There is general agreement that no one mediation model is appropriate for all disputes. But there is a clear trend towards holding a number of 2–4 hour meetings rather than trying to do everything at one go. An average of 13 hours mediation time per dispute is significantly longer than for either the commercial or community mediation models, and shows the need to take time to build trust and confidence in the process. It is perhaps discouraging that in general church disputes take three months to resolve.

A number of bishops point to a clear Christian element in church mediations, and see mediation in theological rather than legal terms. The emphasis is much closer to the community

465

model of reconciling parties than the commercial model of resolving the problem; but there are key differences from the community model. In particular, church mediations go further than the community model by seeing the process as part of the on-going reconciliation work of Christ. Indeed, bishops prefer to see resolving disputes as a pastoral rather than a legal matter, and the emphasis on legal processes as foreign to what should be a gospel, covenant community. The need for Christ's presence is seen as central to the resolution of church disputes, and all parties need to understand this. Bishops spoke also of the theological understanding of the Church as Christ's body, and said that as Christ's body, the Church should have the resources within itself to heal itself.

Bishops drew attention to the need for a number of mediation skills: good listening skills, integrity, fairness and openness, to name but a few. They recommend generally that parties should be encouraged towards mediation at an early stage in a conflict. But they also recommend that legal procedures should be available to resolve the conflict if mediation should fail, or if the parties be unwilling to try it.

Lastly, the survey confirms the work of the Mennonites and Quakers as leaders in this field, and identifies the Alban Institute as one of the other major contributors to work in this area.

Chapter 8

CONCLUSIONS

Upon this word we han assented soone,
For, as it seemed, it was for to doone[1]

---

[1] Geoffrey Chaucer, *The Canterbury Tales*, 'The Parson's Prologue' (lines 61–62). (London, Penguin Books, 1996). In David Wright's translation:

   These words we very soon assented to,
   It was the right thing, so we thought, to do.

Geoffrey Chaucer, *The Canterbury Tales*, translated by David Wright (Oxford University Press, 1985). This passage could have been used also at the start of chapter 6, 'Consensus-building mediation'.

1. A REVIEW

I n chapter 1 the study began with an examination of the Scriptural foundations for dispute resolution. It was found that Scripture encourages the informal resolution of disputes, that mediation is consistent with Scripture, that the mediation of Christ is an important doctrine of the Christian faith, and that peacemakers (which term includes mediators) are blessed by Christ, being called sons of God. Next, Church tradition was examined, and it was found that from the early Church fathers up to the 1850s, bishops and ecclesiastical judges have seen their duty as being first and foremost to reconcile disputing parties if possible, and that they successfully combined the role of mediator with that of judge. It was seen that the inquisitorial procedure used in the English Church courts up to the 1850s was a feature which assisted the ecclesiastical judges to combine these two roles. It was noted that Canon law codes for both the Western and the Eastern Roman Catholic Church provide expressly for mediation as a means for resolving church disputes. The conclusion was reached that there was good reason to believe that mediation might have a role, or more of a role, in dispute resolution within the Church of England; and that there were grounds for suspecting that the modern adversarial procedure may not be the best way to resolve church disputes.

In chapter 2 the Westminster Abbey dispute was examined in detail. It was found that when the dispute first arose, the process followed by the Dean did not accord with Scriptural principles,[2] and that this had disastrous consequences. In particular the fact that he allowed the dispute to become public when it first arose inflamed relations, and caused the dispute to become adversarial. Even if trust had been broken, both Scripture and a historical precedent within Westminster Abbey itself suggested that trust could have been restored, and the contest thus avoided. Money became no object in the dispute: the financial sum in dispute was

---

[2] Specifically, Matthew 18:15–17.

468

£13,900, yet the dispute led to a twelve-day hearing, with total legal costs estimated at £600,000. The dispute attracted much adverse publicity. The whole episode can only be described as a disaster, the wounds of which are still painful.

In chapter 3 a survey of the archdeacons and diocesan secretaries in England resulted in the identification of fifteen main categories of church dispute, namely:

- alterations to church buildings and graveyards

- church governance: disputes between a church and the diocesan authorities or the Bishop

- personality conflicts: e.g. disputes between clergy working in a team, usually involving six people or less

- pastoral breakdown

- disputes over forms of worship/doctrine

- gay or gender issues

- racial discrimination

- employment disputes

- minor discipline matters, not involving sexual allegations

- property disputes

- financial disputes

- defamation

- personal injury

- commercial contract disputes, and

- tax disputes.

In Chapters 4, 5 and 6 respectively, three models of mediation were examined: the commercial model, the community model,

469

and the consensus-building model. Each of these models are recent developments in England, and it was seen that Australia, Canada, Hong Kong, New Zealand, South Africa and the USA all have considerably more experience of using mediation for secular disputes than does England. We saw that the various pilot schemes for commercial mediation in England all had good settlement rates, but in each case the take-up was extremely small. But the tide is starting to turn. Government interest in mediation and the Civil Procedure Rules 1998 have led to an increase in commercial mediation.

In chapter 5 we saw that the main emphasis in community mediation is transformation of the parties, and that this makes the community model particularly appropriate for those church disputes where the relationship between the parties is important (which in practice is likely to be most disputes). We saw however that community mediation, despite its Quaker origins, is secular; whereas the Mennonite model, whilst in many respects similar to the community mediation model, incorporates a clear Christian element.

In chapter 6 we saw that the consensus-building model is used for complex, multi-party, public disputes; and it is suitable for church disputes involving a whole congregation or some other large group within the Church. We saw how the consensus-building model is used by the Mennonites, the Quakers, and the Alban Institute.

Chapter 7 contained the results of a survey carried out in the year 2000 of the Anglican Churches in Australia, Canada, Hong Kong, New Zealand, South Africa and the USA. It is clear from the results of this survey that these Churches have wide experience of using mediation, and their experience provides useful guidance for the Church of England.

In summary, the mediation of church disputes has been examined from a number of different aspects, theological, historical, legal, empirical, and practical. Theology and church tradition have already been considered. Both formal and informal means of resolving church disputes have been examined, together with both church and secular legislation. Empirical evidence of current mediation practice was obtained from 72 per cent of the dioceses in England, and 52 per cent of the dioceses in Australia, Canada, Hong Kong, New Zealand, South Africa and the USA, from contact with Christians from other denominations, and from a study of one local community mediation service in London. Practical matters considered include financial cost, human resources, mediation training, and the use of the internet.

The main focus of this book has been on the Church of England, but the experience of other Churches in handling disputes has also been examined, in particular the Anglican Church in several countries, the Quakers, the Roman Catholic Church, the Mennonites, the Baptist Union, the United Reformed Church, the Methodists, the Episcopal Church of Scotland, the Church of Scotland, the Church in Wales, and the Episcopal Church in Ireland. The examination of other Churches indicates that they have a broadly similar range of church disputes to those of the Church of England, and a similar approach in how to handle such disputes. However the mediation training provided by the Mennonites and the United Reformed Church goes well beyond any which is currently available for the Church of England.

2. MAIN FINDINGS

The first, and most important, finding is a resounding endorsement in favour of mediation. Mediation is more suitable scripturally and theologically than adversarial methods of resolving church disputes. Mediation accords with the tradition of the Church for almost the whole of its history. Mediation is well-tried and well-endorsed by Anglican Churches in other countries, and is effective. The Church of England is behind other Anglican Churches in its experience of mediation, but it is clear that there is a willingness in many dioceses to use it, albeit many clergy have little knowledge of it.

A number of themes which occur in several chapters need now to be drawn together.

a) The church dispute triangle

The conflict triangle, it will be recalled, involves three elements: the problem, the parties and the process. Church conflicts typically involve two and sometimes all three elements of this triangle; and any attempt to see a particular dispute as 'just' a problem issue, a people issue, or a process issue will probably fail to resolve the dispute properly. The way the parties first present the dispute may not fully reflect the underlying issues between them. Many disputes have a history, so the current issue may only be the 'final straw'. A person seeking to resolve the conflict needs to do more than find a 'quick fix' for the current issue. Church disputes typically involve more than just the factual problem presented by the parties. The history needs to be drawn out, and where the history is painful, its effects may need to be neutralised. This 'neutralising' process can be seen as a specifically Christian part of the mediation process.

We have seen that disputes frequently involve the relationships of the people concerned. A formal legal process, such as that used to resolve the Westminster Abbey dispute, is blinkered, in that it looks at facts and not relationships. Resolution of a dispute involves not just the problem, but the people; not just facts, but also feelings; and feelings come first. As was said in chapter 1, transformed relationships can lead to the resolution of even commercial disputes.[3]

It is also clear that many church disputes involve a number of parties, each of whom may have a different perception of the underlying problem. Resolving a dispute which divides a whole congregation requires a very different approach to resolving a dispute between just two or three people. Where large numbers

---

[3] See pg. 12.

are involved, a mediator needs to devise a process which enables all parties to feel heard and understood.

Commercial mediation, community mediation and consensus-building mediation each concentrate on one side of the mediation triangle. It is more than just a question of emphasis, but affects the whole philosophy of the mediation model. Commercial mediation's aim is a resolution of the problem, community mediation's aim is the transformation of the parties, and consensus-building mediation's aim is a fair and suitable process to enable the parties to reach agreement.

Church disputes, like trust disputes,[4] frequently involve all three sides of the mediation triangle. Facts, feelings and form are all important. But even this is not the complete picture. The resolution of church disputes is perceived to involve also a specifically Christian element. The three secular models are insufficient, both individually and in combination. A Christian format, involving Christ's presence, is perceived as the extra element which is required. This can be provided for in legislation, as in the Parish Disputes Ordinance 1999 in use in Sydney,[5] or it can be left to the skill and spiritual perception of a mediator who understands this additional element.

This Christian element is not just part of the process side of the triangle. The Church is centred on Christ;[6] and resolving church disputes needs Christ at the centre, not just of the process, but also of the problem and of the people involved in the conflict.

b) *Combining the role of mediator with that of judge*

The archdeacons expressed concern over combining the role of mediator, which they see as a pastoral role, with their disciplinary

---

[4] See James Behrens, 'The Mediation of Trust Disputes', (2001) 151 New Law Journal 1183.

[5] See pg. 418 fn. 232.

[6] Ephesians 5:23; Colossians 1:18.

functions. The same difficulties were expressed in the responses by bishops in the Anglican Communion. Yet historically, from the time of the bishops' courts of Constantine in the fourth century, up to at least the sixteenth century, bishops and other church judges felt able to combine their role as mediator and judge with no difficulty, and, certainly in the early Church, used to swap between the roles of mediator, judge and arbitrator as they thought fit throughout their handling of a dispute. The modern reluctance for those with a judicial role to combine this with a mediator's role may be the result of the modern distinction between the two functions.[7] The modern view is to see the mediator's lack of authority as one of mediation's virtues: yet this appears to be a post-1600 development, at variance with Church tradition prior to this date. Some judges, both in secular disputes and in church disputes, manage to combine the role of mediator and judge; and this is very much in accordance with tradition.[8]

c) Training

Both the English archdeacons and the Anglican bishops drew attention to the importance of practical training, for clergy and lay office holders in the church, and for those most called upon to manage church conflict. There is excellent training in England provided by the London Mennonite Centre, and similar high quality, though secular, training provided by local community mediation services. There is also training in consensus-building

---

[7] This may be compared to the position in modern China, which of course is not a common law country, and where mediators become arbitrators with power to determine the issue if the mediation does not result in a settlement.

[8] For an account of one judge who blurs the distinction between adjudication and mediation in her secular work, see the profile of Juju Atkinson in chapter 9 of Deborah Kolb, *When Talk Works* (San Francisco, California, Jossey-Bass, 1994). For a modern example in a case of a church dispute, see James Behrens, *Practical Church Management* (Leominster, Gracewing, 1998), pg. 322–3.

mediation provided by the Environment Council, and training in commercial mediation provided by CEDR and other commercial mediation service providers. In the USA, there is training provided by the Mennonites and the Alban Institute. Despite this, only half the dioceses in the Anglican Communion actually offer any training in dispute resolution to their members.

This training needs to be rooted in Scripture. Conflict training includes a theological understanding of one's own role when faced with a conflict. For that, the starting point is to seek to resolve the dispute informally and privately.[9] Only if this fails should any other party become involved, whether as mediator or otherwise.

The Westminster Abbey dispute highlights the importance of training. The Cameron Report's suggested new standing commission for the royal peculiars provides only part of the solution.[10] Mediation can resolve many disputes, but the full answer includes, in addition to the new procedures to assist when things go wrong, training to ensure a proper Scriptural understanding of how to handle conflict when it first arises.

d) Theological basis for mediation models

The community mediation model is theologically the most attractive of the three mediation models. Community mediation's emphasis on transforming relationships, its use of home visits, its informality, the directness of speaking to the parties without the need for an intermediary such as a lawyer,[11] its use of co-mediation (two mediators), and the fact that the mediators come from within the community, all have theological significance, and place it head and shoulders above the commercial model.

---

[9] Matthew 18:15–17, quoted on pg. 70.

[10] See pg. 79.

[11] Indeed the need for an intermediary between a party and the mediator is incongruous, almost a contradiction in terms.

Yet community mediation is not the complete answer. First, despite its Christian roots, it is avowedly secular, and has no recognition of the spiritual nature of the reconciliation process. Second, there are church disputes for which it is not best suited. Where the parties are strangers or have only a professional relationship the commercial model may be more appropriate, because there is no personal relationship to transform; and where there are numerous parties the consensus-building model is better, because process issues assume much more significance. The internet mediation model is a non-starter for church disputes.[12]

e) Length of meetings

The survey of the Anglican Churches found that most Churches prefer the community and consensus-building mediation format of a number of 2–4 hour meetings, rather than the commercial mediation format of trying to resolve the whole dispute in one session lasting up to a full day (or even longer). The survey found that the average time to mediate a church dispute is 13 hours, significantly longer than the 8–10 hours average time to mediate a commercial dispute. A weakness of the survey is that the questionnaire did not cater properly for the number of meetings sometimes required for consensus-building mediation. The 13 hour average is almost certainly an underestimate for dealing with a consensus-building mediation.

f) Types of dispute suitable for mediation

The survey of the Anglican Churches has identified that the four types of dispute seen as most suitable for mediation are personality conflicts, employment disputes, pastoral breakdowns, and disputes about church governance. What is perhaps most helpful is to combine the dispute ratings table from this survey[13]

---

[12] See appendix 1, pg. 495.

[13] See figure 20, pg. 361.

with the mediation model table from chapter 6,[14] and to show the dispute types in order of suitability for mediation.

Dispute type	Suitability rating	Mediation Model
personality conflict	4.12	Community
employment/work	4.08	Community Commercial
pastoral breakdown	3.95	Community Consensus-building
church governance	3.76	Commercial
property ownership	3.58	Commercial
financial (non-criminal)	3.45	Commercial
contractual	3.37	Commercial
racial discrimination	3.28	Community
church buildings	3.25	Community Consensus-building
personal injury	3.12	Community Commercial
defamation	3.08	Community
minor discipline	3.08	Community
taxation	3.04	Commercial
gay or gender issue	2.99	Community Consensus-building
worship/doctrine	2.90	Community Consensus-building

Figure 42. Dispute ratings and mediation model

---

[14] See figure 15, pg. 333.

The ratings were from 1 to 5. 1 represents unsuitable, and 5 completely suitable for mediation. The Anglican Churches survey indicates that all but two of the 15 types of dispute were considered suitable for mediation. These two, disputes about gay or gender issues, and disputes about forms or worship or doctrine, were both considered marginally unsuitable for mediation. This study has found examples of cases where both gay and gender disputes have been successfully resolved by mediation,[15] though not disputes about forms of worship or doctrine.[16]

Linking together dispute ratings and mediation model in this way highlights the importance of the community mediation model, and the perception, based on Scripture, that church dispute resolution is mostly to be seen in terms of reconciliation and transformation of the parties.

g) Financial cost

A common theme running through the survey is the cost of mediation, and how this compares to the cost of other forms of dispute resolution. The costs of the Westminster Abbey dispute were exceptional at £600,000, but the three contested proceedings under the Ecclesiastical Jurisdiction Measure 1963 cost the Church of England a total of £425,000.

A conservative estimate of the costs of the average disputed court case is likely to be £5,000 to £10,000. In the analysis of High

---

[15] See, for example, the HIV prevention dispute, pg. 303, and the case of cathedral clergy referred to in Yvonne Craig, *Peacemaking for churches* (London, SPCK, 1999), pg. 22.

[16] A dispute which is presented as one about forms of worship and doctrine may underneath reflect different concerns. A typical example would be where a new incumbent brings about changes to the forms of service in his or her church. The underlying issues here may be about personal relationships and pastoral breakdown, which are eminently suitable for mediation, rather than strictly a worship/doctrine issue.

478

Court costs by Lord Woolf,[17] 'the average costs among the most straightforward cases are relatively stable at around £6,000 irrespective of case type'.[18] The overall statistics for all cases in Lord Woolf's sample was as follows:

Costs allowed on taxation	Percentage of cases
£10,000 or less	42%
£10,000 to £20,000	28%
£20,000 to £30,000	10%
Over £30,000	20%
Total	100%

Figure 43. Average costs of litigation

Three comments can be made: first, these figures are for cases in the period 1990–1995, which pre-date the new provisions for costs in the Civil Procedure Rules 1998;[19] second, this analysis is across the broad range of civil claims, and is therefore not repre-

---

[17] Lord Woolf, *Final Report on Access to Justice* (London, HMSO, July 1996) Annex III gives a statistical analysis of 2184 cases sampled from those submitted to the Supreme Court Taxing Office during the period 1990–1995.

[18] Lord Woolf, *Final Report on Access to Justice*, Annex III paragraph 11.

[19] Specifically, CPR Parts 43 to 48. But case management, and the different case tracks also affect the amount of legal costs. See pg. 182. At the time of writing no statistical evidence has been published as to average costs under the new CPR regime, but there is a general perception that costs have gone up rather than down: *Civil Procedure News*, Issue 02/02, pg. 7 (London, Sweet & Maxwell, February 2002); Michael Cooke, 'A simple solution to the ludicrous lottery of litigation costs', *The Times*, 26 February 2002, Law, pg. 2.

sentative of the types of church disputes which may become the subject of litigation; and third, the survey is limited to the High Court. It is felt none-the-less that the overall estimate of £5,000 to £10,000 is unlikely to be too high, and may be on the low side.[20]

In contrast, the average cost per case for the Camden Mediation Service is £500; and even a seven-month consensus-building mediation run by the London Mennonite Centre costs only £7,000.

The conclusion is obvious. Mediation will save the Church of England thousands of pound each year in comparison to the legal fees it is currently paying. This may be an underestimate. The saving may be hundreds of thousands of pounds.[21]

h) Legislation

Several of the chapters consider the use of legislation to promote or compel the use of mediation. The Anglican Churches survey was very much in favour of Canon Law encouraging mediation, and there was some support for making mediation compulsory, though many bishops expressed concerns about the latter. Mediation is already built into the procedures for pastoral breakdown in the USA and Canada. The warning by the bishop of New Westminster in Canada[22] expressed a theological concern, which shows again how theology needs to underpin any proposals in this area.

-----

[20] Lord Woolf, *Final Report on Access to Justice,* Annex III does not state an overall average cost for all disputes. Based on the median costs given in table 3 of the Annex, the present author calculates an overall average cost of £19,800 for all cases in the sample. The weighted average of the costs set out in figure 43 (taking the bottom band as £5,000, the top band as £35,000, and adopting mid-way point for the remaining bands) is £15,800.

[21] It is possible that the savings may be less if more disputes come forward when a cheaper method of resolution is available. If so, the cost is well-spent in resolving such disputes.

[22] See pg. 409.

480

It is here that we can learn from the Roman Catholic Church experience, described below. It will be seen that legislation in itself is not enough.

3. A LESSON FROM THE ROMAN CATHOLIC CHURCH

We have seen that the Canon law of the Roman Catholic Church supports the use of mediation.[23] Yet the experience of the last 30 years in the Roman Catholic Church indicates that there is very little resolve within the Roman Catholic Church to use mediation. In England there is not even a trickle of cases. In the USA there is a trickle, albeit not yet a stream.

a) 'Due Process' in the USA

In 1969 the National Conference of Catholic Bishops in America adopted and recommended to its members the procedures proposed in the *Due Process Report*.[24] The report contained suggested procedures for conciliation and arbitration, among other recommendations, and the bishops were urged to experiment with them and adapt them to their local circumstances.

In the intervening years many dioceses have adopted some form of grievance procedure, and most were based on the NCCB Due Process Report. However, the level of success and satisfaction reported by these dioceses is very modest. Coriden, writing in 1986,[25] gives a number of reasons for this: the lack of public knowledge that the procedures exist; the bishops' unwillingness to submit to the procedures; the fact that the procedures are too

---

[23] See pg. 22.

[24] *On Due Process* (Washington, National Council of Catholic Bishops, 1969). These procedures received a *Nihil obstat* from the Holy See on Oct. 27, 1971. (A *Nihil obstat* is the approval by the Roman Catholic authority for the publication of a book or writing: canons 823–832.)

[25] James Coriden, 'Alternative dispute resolution in the church', Canon Law Society of America Proceedings 48 (1986), pg. 73.

cumbersome and time-consuming, too elaborate and too unfamiliar; and a lack of training for those charged with the administration of the programs. Twelve years later (1998) McKenna writes

> In the United States diocesan mediation boards have been available since the early 1970s, but for a variety of reason they seem to have been generally ineffective; in some dioceses they have never even been utilised.[26]

McKenna gives the same reasons as Coriden for this failure, and adds one more: the refusal of respondents who are cited to participate in a conciliation process. If mediation is to remain a voluntary process, there seems to be no answer to the problem that people may simply choose not to use it.

Coriden's article sets out in an appendix the Due Process Program established for the Catholic diocese of Seattle in the USA. Although the Seattle program refers to conciliation, mediation, and other forms of dispute resolution such as arbitration, the program does not describe in any detail what actually takes place at a mediation session. It is noteworthy that the program emphasises employment disputes as being suitable for mediation. This supports the findings of the survey of the Anglican Churches that employment disputes are the type of church dispute most suitable for mediation.

> The fact is that employment disputes can and do arise. There are disputes about disciplinary practices, about staff morale, about hours and salary, about discrimination, or unreasonable work load, about termination, about almost any term or condition of employment. These kinds of disputes are as common in the workplace as disputes about parked cars and barking dogs are among neighbours. The Archdiocese as an employer recognises that conflict will occur in any employment setting and that this is not a reflec-

---

[26] Kevin McKenna, *The Ministry of Law in the Church Today* (Notre Dame, Indiana, University of Notre Dame Press, 1998) pg. 67.

482

tion on either the quality of the employee or the quality of the working environment.[27]

The Seattle Due Process Program involved a Due Process Office within the diocese, and any employment dispute can be referred to it by either the employer or the employee. The first step is described as conciliation:

> Conciliation is always the first step in any dispute resolution process because it involves bringing the parties together to talk to each other. Any manager, supervisor, or employee of the Archdiocese may contact the Due Process Administrator at any time to begin the conciliation process. The role of the Due Process office at this stage is to help the parties think through their concerns, determine what they want, and negotiate effectively with the other party. …There is never any charge for the use of the conciliation service of the Office for Due Process.

The next step is mediation:

> Mediation is a process in which the parties to a dispute sit down to negotiate their differences with a neutral third party, the mediator… The Archdeacon is aware of the great value of co-operative problem-solving and therefore offers all employees the right to mediate an employment dispute with very few exceptions. Mediation is not appropriate when the subject matter involved is not open to negotiation (e.g. when a criminal charge or a matter of Church teaching is in issue) or when the parties for some reason are not able to participate in a mediation process…
> The Due Process Administrator will work with the parties to set up the mediation session and help them understand the details of the process. Once again, there is no charge for the time of the Due Process Administrator, but the parties are usually expected to contribute to the cost of the mediation. The parties will generally agree in advance to split the mediator's fees. Sometimes the parish or agency involved in the dispute will pay the entire cost of the mediation. On

---

[27] From the Due Process Program for the Archdiocese of Seattle.

some occasions, volunteer mediators from the community
will be available to the parties. The Due Process Administrator will discuss all these possibilities with the disputants
at the beginning of the process and arrangements will be
made that are fair to all parties.

The take-up of 'due process' mediation is increasing. The latest
statistics are that 76 dioceses in the USA reported experience with
cases submitted for 'due process' consideration, amounting to
slightly over 40% of the 185 dioceses in the USA. Where they
have been established, 'these diocesan offices have proven to be
somewhat effective in resolving administrative conflicts'.[28] However, the number of dioceses with substantial experience is very
small. Five dioceses (3% of the 185), account for 69% of the cases
decided.[29]

b) *Recent developments in England*

In England in the 1970s the Canon Law Society of Great Britain
and Ireland 'laboured'[30] to produce a conciliation procedure. The
process is described by Walsh:

> The English version took much longer to prepare [than the
> American model]. A working party was set up by the
> Canon Law Society of Great Britain and Ireland ... in 1971.
> Two years and three drafts later the working party, now
> expanded to include six canonists and one civil lawyer,
> presented their report on conciliation procedure, which was
> then submitted to the episcopal conference. It was quietly
> accepted by the hierarchy of England and Wales.[31]

---

[28] Beal, Coriden, and Green, *New Commentary on the Code of Canon Law*
(New York, Paulist Press, 2000) pg. 1827.

[29] Beal, Coriden, and Green, *New Commentary on the Code of Canon Law*,
pg. 1828.

[30] The word used by Robert Ombres OP, 'Justice and Equity in the 1983
Code', *Priests & People* (1987) 143 at pg. 147.

[31] Michael Walsh, 'Protecting Rights in the Church', *The Month*
(1978) 131–134.

The word 'quietly' was deliberate.

> To date we know of no diocese where this procedure has been promulgated or the requisite preliminary provisions for the procedure put into operation.[32]

Writing three years later (1978), Walsh continued:

> That was three years and more ago. It still does not seem that the 'preliminary provisions' have been undertaken, or the conciliation machinery resorted to.
>
> The main 'preliminary provision' is the appointment of two conciliators in each diocese, and a list of chairmen drawn up at provincial level, consisting of two people from each diocese. The appointment of conciliators and chairmen is entirely in the hands of the bishop, although it is expected that he consult his clergy.

Walsh describes the procedure as a two-stage process.

> A complainant had first to approach a diocesan conciliator, who would put down in writing the substance of the complaint. He would then attempt to reconcile the parties at odds. Should this fail, however, each party draws up a list of five mediators from amongst whom they agree on two names. The two mediators chosen in this way then select a chairman from the provincial list. Once a chairman is agreed upon, it is he who conducts all meetings of the conciliation panel, the proceedings of which are strictly confidential. After the hearings the chairman and mediators issue the two parties with a brief outline of the facts, and any recommendations they can make to resolve the dispute. The panel, of course, has no means of enforcing its decisions, but since both parties willingly undertook this form of conciliation it is believed that they will consider themselves 'bound in honour' to observe the terms of the recommendations.

---

[32] Canon Law Society Newsletter, March 1975, cited in Michael Walsh, 'Protecting Rights in the Church', *The Month* (1978) 131–134.

485

The English procedure specifically excludes disputes concerning doctrine. The procedure suggests instead referring them to Rome. This ties in with the Anglican Churches survey suggesting that disputes about doctrine are unsuitable for mediation. However, referring a doctrine dispute to Rome is not an ideal alternative, first because of the distance and language difficulties, and secondly there is likely to be the feeling that as the Roman authorities have appointed the bishops, it would be very odd if they failed to back their decisions. The American model does not exclude doctrinal disputes. It suggests that bishops submit their decisions on doctrinal matters to their episcopal peers on a regional basis, or better still, to a national theological commission.

The Polish Archbishop Zenon Grocholewski,[33] writing in 1986 in Italian, describes the English conciliation procedure as follows:[34]

> In 1973 the Canon Law Association of Great Britain and Ireland introduced a project called *A Conciliation Procedure*, which is much simpler than the *Due Process* procedure, and leads more easily to the dispute being resolved. The project is aimed and directed at conciliation between the parties, in a spirit of love, and without either side being able to claim victory; aiming to restore the relationship which had been lost. The procedure is in two phases: the first can be called informal conciliation, the second formal conciliation. The second phase only takes place if the first phase fails to achieve a result. Each stage ends with the giving of recommendations and warnings, which the parties have a duty and feel obliged to follow. This procedure just pro-

---

[33] Archbishop Grocholewski is currently (2001) prefect of the Congregation for Catholic Education. He has worked in the Vatican since 1972, and has been prefect of the Holy See's supreme tribunal, the Apostolic Signatura, since October 1998. Grocholewski has a doctorate in canon law from the Gregorian University.

[34] Z. Grocholewski, 'Giustizia Amministrativa nel nuovo Codice di Diritto Canonico', *Angelicum* (1986) 333–355; at pg. 343.

posed is an alternative to that found in administrative tribunals.[35]

The fact is that despite all the effort to get it written, the model
conciliation procedure was still-born. Indeed, in the year 2000 the
Canon Law Society of Great Britain and Ireland was unable to lo-
cate a copy of the procedure, or even suggest where one might be
found.[36]

c) Summary

Alternative dispute resolution has been under active consideration by the Roman Catholic Church for over thirty years, and
follows a tradition dating back to the early Church, and even the
New Testament. The *Due Process* report in the USA dates
from 1969; Walsh was writing in the 1970s; Coriden, Archbishop
Grocholewski and Ombres were writing in the 1980s, the Code of
Canon Law itself dates from 1983; and McKenna was writing in
the 1990s. Sterling efforts have been made by canon lawyers in

---

[35] The present author's translation. The original reads as follows:
L'Associazione Canonistica della Gran Bretagna ed Irlanda ha
presentato nel 1973 un progetto sotto il titolo A Conciliation
Procedure, che è molto più semplice e più facilmente conduce alla
conclusione della controversia che il Due Process. Il progetto è
orientato e diretto, alla conciliazione fra le parti, con spirito di carità
e senza pretesa di vittoria da nessuna parte; tende alla restaurazione
dell'amicizia venuta meno. La procedura si svolge in due fasi: la
prima si potrebbe chiamare della conciliazione informale, la seconda
della conciliazione formale. A questa è possibile ricorrere soltanto
dopo esito negativo della precedente. Tutto il processo si conclude
praticamente con la consegna di ammonimenti e consigli, e le parti
dovrebbero sentirsi obbligate ad eseguirli. Questa procedura viene
proposta come alternativa al processo presso i tribunali
amministrativi.

[36] Letter from the Secretary of the Canon Law Society of Great Britain, 1
July 2000. The secretary even arranged for someone to ask at the annual
general meeting if anyone knew where a copy of the model mediation
procedure could be located. Unfortunately no-one amongst that august
body had any idea.

both the USA and England to develop model procedures at the diocesan level for both these countries. In the USA, progress is very slow, but these efforts are just beginning to bear fruit. In England, as yet, the tree is still bare.

As McKenna writes

> A broad range and large number of conflicts arise within the local church on a regular basis – disputes between pastors and parish councils, questions about the inadmission of persons to sacraments, issues between pastors and parish staffs – many of which could be resolved with the assistance of alternative dispute resolution. Dioceses should consider establishing offices that could offer such services and assist in such problematic situations.[37]

Again, comparing this with the categories of disputes identified earlier, we see issues of church governance, worship and doctrine (or discipline), employment issues, and possibly personality disputes, being recommended for mediation.

Both Coriden and McKenna suggest that alternative dispute resolution might even be established as mandatory in the sense that the parties would be prevented from access to a diocesan tribunal, hierarchical recourse, or other more formal due process or grievance procedures until alternative dispute resolution had been attempted in good faith and had failed to resolve the dispute. This is not a suggestion which accords with the general view within the Anglican Communion or in England. But McKenna correctly identifies saving in cost, speedy resolution and the avoidance of delay, recognition of each others' viewpoints,[38] and restoring relationships as the major benefits of using conciliation procedures.[39]

---

[37] Kevin McKenna, *The Ministry of Law in the Church Today*, at pg. 68.

[38] A major theme in community mediation, see the section 'The object of mediation: resolution or transformation?', pg. 223.

[39] McKenna writes:

But at the moment, in England, this is a lost opportunity.[40]

The experience of the Roman Catholic Church, particularly in England, shows that legislation in itself is not enough. There needs to be a general determination to use mediation in the Church, or else laws will simply be ignored. What is needed is a vision of where this could lead. The final section seeks to capture this vision.

4. A WITNESS TO CHRIST

The current adversarial method of dispute resolution is a witness, not to the glories of Christ's new creation,[41] but to the failure of His Church to live up to His calling.[42] It is not overstating matters to say that dispute resolution in the Church of England is a

---

For many people, the cost of obtaining justice through the civil court system is high. In most cases, mediation services are free or at least very reasonable. Often, disputes to be resolved in courts are backlogged for long periods. Mediation cases are usually heard shortly after the disputes arise. Perhaps most important, free from the usual rules of civil court procedures and processes, disputants in conciliation, with the assistance of trained mediators, can get to the root causes of a dispute. Once given the opportunity to state their own case fully, they are usually better able to hear the other party's point of view. Such an airing of grievances can positively mend relationship among families, friends, parishioners, pastoral staffs, and others who make up our Church communities.

Kevin McKenna, *The Ministry of Law in the Church Today*, at pg. 69.

[40] It would be misleading to state that the Roman Catholic Church in England *never* uses mediation. In 2002 the author was retained as an expert witness in a case involving the Roman Catholic Church where the parties had previously gone to mediation. Although some progress had been made at the mediation, no settlement was reached.

[41] 2 Corinthians 3:18, 5:17; Romans 8:18.

[42] Ephesians 4:1.

matter of both embarrassment and ridicule.[43] Comparisons with Trollope[44] over the Westminster Abbey dispute are apt.[45]

The Westminster Abbey case was exceptional: in the publicity it achieved, in the financial cost of the dispute, in the parties and institutions involved, and in the formality of the process. What is perhaps not so exceptional was the increasing intransigence of the two main participants as the dispute progressed, and the seeming inevitability of the final court battle.

It is this personal element which formal Church procedures cannot touch, but which mediation can and does. The gospel is about transforming people into Christ's likeness.[46] St Paul writes:

---

[43] For example, the picture in the *Mail on Sunday*, 19 April 1998, pg. 3 describing the Westminster Abbey dispute as a 'Holy war'.

[44] Anthony Trollope (1815-1882) wrote a number of books dealing with fictional ecclesiastical disputes. *Barchester Towers* (Oxford University Press, 1989), for example, is a hilarious story of the struggle between the bishop's chaplain, the oily Mr Slope, and the bishop's wife Mrs Proudie, for control of the diocese of Barchester.

[45] *Sunday Times*, 5 April 1998, Sunday, Home news; *Daily Telegraph*, 11 December 1998, Friday, pg. 28.

[46] 2 Corinthians 3:18.

> Do not conform any longer to the pattern of this world, but be transformed by the renewing of your mind. Then you will be able to test and approve what God's will is – his good, pleasing and perfect will.[47]

Dispute resolution within the Church of England needs to be transformed. Mediation provides the key to this process, although it is not the whole story. The Church of England needs also to rediscover the Scriptural principles of conflict resolution. When the Church starts to resolve its own disputes in this way, it will be a witness to the world of the transforming power of Christ.

---

[47] Romans 12:2.

Appendices

Appendix 1

MEDIATION USING THE INTERNET

1. THE NEED FOR ON-LINE DISPUTE SETTLEMENT SYSTEMS[1]

'The rapid level of on-line dispute settlement systems and codes of conduct for e-commerce in the EU and at global level is a matter of urgency to increase consumer confidence and business predictability.'[2]

The growth of e-commerce has led to concern how best to resolve the disputes which inevitably arise between users of this new means of conducting business. In particular, there has been great interest in on-line arbitration and mediation, which has become known by the acronym ODR, to contrast it

---

[1] See pg. 215 for the reference to this appendix.

[2] *eEurope Impact and Priorities*, a communication by the Commission of the European Communities to the Spring European Council in Stockholm, 23–24 March 2001, paragraph 3.4. *europa.eu.int/comm/information_society/eeurope/pdf/impact_en.pdf.*

with normal arbitration and mediation collectively known as ADR.[3]

2. ENGLISH ODR SERVICES

a) On-line arbitration

In October 2000 the Chartered Institute of Arbitrators and Ford Motor Company launched what is claimed to be Europe's first independent on-line consumer arbitration scheme. Cases are submitted through email, but customers have the opportunity to present cases through normal post or through a mixture of post and email. Thus, if copies of documents are being referred to, they can be sent by post or scanned and sent by email if this is preferred. In practice, the guidance notes and rules envisage that parties will send to each other copies of contracts, correspondence and other documents relied upon. There is not much ODR about the scheme, except that you fill in the application form for the appointment of an arbitrator on-line, and can communicate with the arbitrator using email.[4]

b) On-line mediation

The first mediation on-line scheme is Consensus Mediation of Norwich *www.consensus.uk.com*. Consensus recommend its use for disputes that arise out of an on-line relationship, or where the amount at stake is less than £10,000. They point to some advantages of electronic mediation: where a deal needs to be done but a party can't justify a whole day out of the office to mediate; where a party feels it may be uncomfortable or disadvantaged at a face-

---

[3] Mediators tend to think of the expression ADR (alternative dispute resolution) as referring principally to mediation; arbitrators tend to include both arbitration and mediation within the expression. ODR is generally taken as including both mediation and arbitration.

[4] For details, click the FordJourney logo at *www.arbitrators.org*.

to-face meeting; and where the parties are geographically too far apart to make a face-to-face mediation practical.

There is a six-step procedure

1. The party asking for mediation completes a simple, confidential form on-line giving details about the dispute, the people involved, and what has happened so far in the dispute.

2. Consensus contacts the other party to see if they are interested in resolving the dispute by electronic mediation. If they agree they will also complete a confidential form. (If they do not agree or there is no response within a reasonable time the mediation cannot proceed.)

3. A mediator is appointed from Consensus' mediator panel.

4. Each party pays their mediation fee.

5. An Agreement to Mediate will be sent to everyone, setting out the rules and the timetable for the checking and exchange of e-mail messages.

6. The mediator will exchange e-mail messages with each party until the mediation is concluded. Consensus' fee structure allows for 6 hours of the mediators' time, on and off-line, 'which is usually enough to resolve most disputes'.

7. If terms of agreement are reached the mediator will prepare a draft Settlement Agreement for approval. The agreement will be binding when all parties have approved the Settlement Agreement

Consensus' normal fee for a face-to-face mediation ranges from £150 per party (plus VAT) for a junior mediator handling a claim up to £5,000, to £2,000 per party for a 'consultant mediator' on a claim between £1m and £5m. Consensus' fee for an electronic mediation is one-half the fee for a face-to-face mediation.

3. FEATURES OF ON-LINE INTERACTION AT MEDIATION

The following are the main differences between on-line mediation and normal face-to-face mediation.

i No physical presence

The main difference between ordinary mediation and on-line mediation is the absence of physical presence, either of the parties with each other, or of the parties with the mediator. On-line disputes are frequently between two people who have never met and probably never will meet. Why then, so it is said, should it be necessary for the mediator to meet the parties face-to-face? Buyers and sellers may well be separated by great distances, they have no prior relationship, and they will probably never meet face-to-face. The key issue for a mediator is whether he can build up empathy and trust with each party without meeting them face-to-face.

ii Geographical distance, different time zones

On-line mediation has an advantage where the parties are in different countries, in saving the costs of travel to the mediation. This advantage is more significant where the amount in dispute is relatively small. In a business-to-business dispute over many thousands of pounds, the cost of travel will assume less significance than for a dispute over, say, non-delivery of a few groceries ordered from *www.tesco.com*.

iii Less immediacy or spontaneity

Most commercial face-to-face mediations take place at one long session. On-line mediation can take place over a period of time – over several days even – with the parties logging on, communicating with the mediator or with each other, without the pressure that a long mediation day brings. This can be a benefit. It can also be a disadvantage, because a face-to-face meeting builds up an impetus to settle, which may not be the case if a mediation is conducted on-line.

iv Text predominates, not yet image or spoken word

This means that matters such as eye contact, reading body language, and the other tools of the mediator's trade find either no place at all, or much less of a place, in on-line mediation. Emotions, especially anger, are sometimes expressed in emails in a more forthright manner than in formal correspondence, but the lack of visual contact may make it difficult for the mediator to assess how a party feels about what has happened in the dispute, or how the party feels about a particular possible solution.

v Different languages and cultures

This applies especially to e-commerce transactions between different countries. As more people become familiar with using the internet for international transactions – an example would be an English person purchasing a car abroad via the internet – so there will be an inevitable increase of disputes between parties of different language. There will be a need for bilingual mediators or interpreters to assist communication.

vi Different legal and regulatory systems

There may be uncertainty as to the proper law of the contract. Even if both parties agree that one particular law applies, one or other party may not appreciate the finer points of, say, the measure of damages under Italian contract law. The parties' expectations may therefore be different, even if the legal position is clear.

vii Uncertainty as to identity

The need for private and public key cryptography indicates the difficulty of establishing that a person who sends a message on the internet is in fact who he claims to be. The parties and the mediator need to consider what degree of checking needs to be carried out by the mediator and the parties as to each other's identities before sending confidential communications to each other.

viii Vulnerable to interception

Linked with this is the risk that confidential communications by the mediator to one party may be intercepted by the other party or some third party. The information which is being exchanged may be commercially sensitive. Again, the parties need to consider what degree of protection they should take to ensure that this confidential information does not pass into the wrong hands.

ix Confidentiality benefits

There are incidental benefits of on-line mediation over a face-to-face mediation. In a face-to-face mediation, if the mediator is not with one party, that party knows that the mediator is spending time with the other party. If a mediator needs to spend more time with party A than with party B, party B will know that fact, and may draw certain conclusions. In the case of on-line mediation on-line caucuses can take place without the other side being aware that they are happening. This places the parties on an even footing, and avoids either party knowing how the mediator is handling the process, and from this drawing any conclusions as to the way the negotiations are progressing.

4. DIFFICULTIES INHERENT IN ON-LINE MEDIATION

Even if a dispute is primarily commercial, there are likely to be underlying relational difficulties between the parties which need to be addressed. It is difficult for the mediator to recognise, acknowledge and handle these on-line, as there is no 'non-verbal' communication for the mediator to see.

If these relational issues are not addressed, the parties may be unwilling to settle the dispute. And even where they have been expressed openly by the parties, it may be more difficult to address them adequately on-line, without the benefit of a face-to-face meeting. For example, an apology may be seen as more sincere if given face-to-face.

Enforcement of a settlement agreement is usually less of an issue than enforcement of an arbitration award. Yet the mediator and the parties do need to take care, especially where some jurisdictional issue arises, that the settlement agreement will be adhered to, and will be enforceable if it is not. Potentially a mediator may owe a duty of care to the disputing parties to take reasonable care to ensure that any settlement reached is valid and enforceable.

5. ODR MEDIATION SETTLEMENT RATES.

CEDR and other mediation service providers claim high success rate for commercial mediations, a success being seen as the parties reaching a settlement agreement on the day. CEDR's statistics indicate that 85% of cases which go to mediation settle. Many parties and mediators would not limit success to this definition, but would include an improved relationship between the parties as a success, even if no settlement is reached.[5]

In contrast, ODR does not involve 'getting everyone around the table in a relaxed atmosphere'.[6] Relationships are neither addressed nor transformed by ODR. The statistics for on-line mediation are anecdotal, but are much lower than for face-to-face mediations. Settlement rates are typically only 40%.[7] It seems that

---

[5] See the discussion of success rates in chapter 4, 'Commercial mediation', and chapter 5, 'Community mediation'.

[6] *Mediation in the Planning System* (London, Department of the Environment, Transport and the Regions, June 2000), paragraph 5.2.1. The report is also available at *www.planning.detr.gov.uk/mediation/index.htm*.

[7] See, e.g. the 40 per cent success rate claimed for Web Mediate *http://www.masslaw.com/adr2002story.cfm*. The author is grateful to Margaret Doyle for this information. Margaret Doyle is the ADR policy and development officer at Advice Services Alliance, and the author of *Advising on ADR: the essential guide to appropriate dispute resolution* (London, Advice Services Alliance, 2000). In her article 'Getting on stream with

modern technology cannot replace the advantage of human inter-action and empathy developed by a face-to-face meeting.

6. CONCLUSIONS: ON-LINE MEDIATION

On-line mediation is a nice idea. Mediation is a buzz word, and so why not have on-line mediation for on-line disputes? But the bottom line is that it does not work. On-line mediation fails to address the human elements of many disputes. Mediators are taught that most communication is non-verbal, and to recognise and handle this non-verbal side in helping the parties reach a settlement. While on-line mediation remains almost exclusively text-based, this non-verbal communication is effectively ignored; and this probably explains the low settlement rates which are achieved for on-line mediation. When video-conferencing becomes more widespread, mediators will be able to see the parties on screen, and to read non-verbal communication. When this happens, settlement rates for on-line mediations will no doubt improve.

7. APPLICATION FOR CHURCH DISPUTES

ODR is aimed principally at commercial disputes. It may have advantages where the parties are geographically far apart, and where the commercial sum involved does not justify the time spent in travelling to the mediation. But it has precious little if any relevance to church disputes. It is of no use in transforming relationships, which is the key element in community mediation, and which has a sound Christian basis to it. It might have a limited use in financial disputes between a church and some commercial supplier over goods ordered over the internet; but even in such cases, the settlement rates are not encouraging. Geographical distance is not usually an issue in church disputes. There are no advantages to be seen from this form of mediation.

---

on-line mediation', Mediation Magazine, February 2001, pg. 8 (Bristol, Mediation UK, 2001), she describes her own involvement with ODR.

That is not to say the internet is of no use in church mediation. The parties may well use emails to correspond with each other and with the mediator before the face-to-face mediation takes place. But that is as far as it goes.

Appendix 2

SURVEYS

1. LETTER TO ARCHDEACONS[1]

25th February 1999

Dear Archdeacon,

I am a barrister, and the author of the book 'Practical Church Management' (Gracewing, 1998).

When I was writing my book, the then archdeacon of Berkshire, The Ven. Michael Hill, suggested to me that I should include a chapter on resolving local church conflicts and disputes. I enclose a copy of the chapter from my book, in case it would interest you, and you will see that it covers matters ranging from serious pastoral breakdown to small incidents which have blown up.

I am now doing further research with the intention of writing in much greater depth about resolving church disputes. I am trying to build up a picture of (a) how conflicts can be avoided before they start, (b) how they can best be resolved in practice, and (c) what lessons can be learned from those disputes which could not be resolved. I hope in due course to be able to provide a guide which will be of use to the Church of England generally, and possibly to other Churches as well.

---

[1] See chapter 3 for the survey of archdeacons and diocesan secretaries.

505

I mention in my chapter the very important role which archdeacons play in giving help to parishes when a dispute arises. I am writing to ask if you would be able to share with me any of your personal experience in this area. (I am writing this same letter to all current archdeacons.) I fully appreciate that the names of parishes and individuals should remain confidential and not be identifiable, and of course I agree to this. But any advice or comments you may be able to give me on the subject would be of great value.

I am particularly interested in the role mediation can play in helping to resolve church disputes. I have myself been trained as a mediator, and have seen both commercial and non-commercial disputes resolved by mediation. Do you have any personal experience of acting as a mediator in church disputes? Do you know whether the diocese of … has any people trained or experienced in mediation available to assist in resolving such disputes? Are there any plans to have such people available in the future? Is there anyone you know who I can get in touch with, and who may be able to give me more information?

Do please telephone me if anything is unclear, or if you are hesitant about mentioning any details. But subject to that, I would be very grateful for any information you can give me on the subject, and hope very much to hear from you.

Perhaps I should add that I will probably be back in touch at a later date to ascertain your reactions to proposed models which I may devise.

Yours sincerely,

2. LETTER TO DIOCESAN SECRETARIES[2]

26th February 1999

Dear ...

I am a barrister, and the author of the book 'Practical Church Management' (Gracewing, 1998).

When I was writing my book, the then archdeacon of Berkshire, The Ven. Michael Hill, suggested to me that I should include a chapter on resolving local church conflicts and disputes. I enclose a copy of the chapter from my book, in case it would interest you, and you will see that it covers matters ranging from serious pastoral breakdown to small incidents which have blown up.

I am now doing further research with the intention of writing in much greater depth about resolving church disputes. I am trying to build up a picture of (a) how conflicts can be avoided before they start, (b) how they can best be resolved in practice, and (c) what lessons can be learned from those disputes which could not be resolved. I hope in due course to be able to provide a guide which will be of use to the Church of England generally, and possibly to other Churches as well.

I am therefore writing to ask if you would be able to share with me any of the diocese of ...'s experience in this area. (I am writing this same letter to all the diocesan secretaries.) I fully appreciate that the names of parishes and individuals should remain confidential and not be identifiable, and of course I agree to this. But any information or comments you may be able to give me on the subject would be of great value.

I am particularly interested in the role mediation can play in helping to resolve church disputes. I have myself been trained as

---

[2] See chapter 3 for the survey of archdeacons and diocesan secretaries.

a mediator, and have seen both commercial and non-commercial disputes resolved by mediation. Do you know whether the diocese of ... has any people trained or experienced in mediation available to assist in resolving such disputes? Are there any plans to have such people available in the future? Is there anyone you know who I can get in touch with, and who may be able to give me more information?

Do please telephone me if anything is unclear, or if you are hesitant about mentioning any details. But subject to that, I would be very grateful for any information you can give me on the subject, and hope very much to hear from you.

Perhaps I should add that I will probably be back in touch at a later date to ascertain your reactions to proposed models which I may devise.

Yours sincerely,

3. LETTER TO BISHOPS[3]

14th July 2000

Dear Bishop ...

I am a barrister, and the author of two books on church law: 'Confirmation, Sacrament of Grace' (Gracewing, 1995), and 'Practical Church Management' (Gracewing, 1998). I am also on the editorial board of the Ecclesiastical Law Journal. I am currently researching the use of mediation as a possible means for resolving church disputes. I hope in due course to be able to provide a guide which will be of use to the Anglican Church generally, and possibly to other Churches as well. I am in the second year of my research, and hope to complete it next year.

So far I have examined the kinds of internal Church disputes which may be appropriate for mediation. I have studied the mediation model which the commercial and legal world uses for resolving disputes, and have reached a number of conclusions on how appropriate such a model is for church disputes, and how it needs to be adapted. I have carried out a survey of the use of mediation within all dioceses of the Church of England; and I have examined the mediation training which is available in England through the United Reformed Church and through the Mennonite Church. I am also in contact with the Roman Catholic Church.

I would now like to look at the position in the Anglican Church outside England. In particular I would like to get a feel for the use of mediation to resolve church disputes in South Africa. I suspect that mediation is used much more widely in South Africa for resolving church disputes than in England, and that we in this country have much to learn from you about the subject.

---

[3] See chapter 7 for the survey of bishops in the Anglican Communion.

I have set out the above in some depth so that you may be assured of my positive and well-meaning intentions. I fully appreciate that the Church in many countries is somewhat apprehensive of lawyers; and even our Lord was not complimentary about them.

I am therefore sending the enclosed questionnaire to all diocesan bishops in South Africa to ask your views on this subject. I have sent a similar questionnaire to diocesan bishops in America, Australia, Canada, Hong Kong and New Zealand.

My research so far suggests that no one model of mediation is suitable for all types of church dispute. So it may be that you cannot give a simple answer to some of these questions. Do feel free to expand any answers which you think would be helpful.

Thank you very much for taking the time to consider these points. I look forward to hearing from you in due course. I enclose an envelope for your reply. I apologise that I do not have a supply of South Africa postage stamps to send you one. As I mention on the questionnaire, if you would prefer to reply by email, copies of the questionnaire are available in Word format. My email address is jbehrens@serlecourt.co.uk. If you wish to fax your answers, please be sure to mark the fax for my personal attention.

Yours sincerely,

4. ANGLICAN COMMUNION QUESTIONNAIRE[4]

Dear Bishop,

Please would you send your answers by 31 August 2000 if possible, but answers received later will still be welcome. If you would like to reply by email, copies of this document are available in Word format. My email address is jbehrens@serlecourt.co.uk. If you wish to fax your answers, please be sure to mark the fax for the attention of James Behrens. My fax number is 0944 20 7405 4004 from South Africa.

Do feel free to expand any answers which you think would be helpful. There is space at the end, or use a separate sheet of paper.

A.   Types of church dispute

I want to find out what sorts of church disputes you consider most suitable for mediation, and what sorts you consider are not suitable.

Please mark with an X the appropriate box number for each type of dispute according to the following guide. 1 = unsuitable – you would not use mediation for this type of dispute. 5 = completely suitable – you would encourage mediation for this type of dispute.

---

[4] See chapter 7 for the survey of bishops in the Anglican Communion.

Type of dispute		How suitable?
		1 2 3 4 5
1.	alterations to church buildings and graveyards	☐ ☐ ☐ ☐ ☐
2.	church governance: disputes between a church and the diocesan authorities or the Bishop	☐ ☐ ☐ ☐ ☐
3.	personality conflicts: e.g. disputes between clergy working in a team, usually involving six people or less	☐ ☐ ☐ ☐ ☐
4.	pastoral breakdown	☐ ☐ ☐ ☐ ☐
5.	disputes over forms of worship/doctrine	☐ ☐ ☐ ☐ ☐
6.	gay or gender issues	☐ ☐ ☐ ☐ ☐
7.	racial discrimination	☐ ☐ ☐ ☐ ☐
8.	employment disputes	☐ ☐ ☐ ☐ ☐
9.	minor discipline matters, not involving sexual allegations	☐ ☐ ☐ ☐ ☐
10.	property disputes	☐ ☐ ☐ ☐ ☐
11.	financial disputes	☐ ☐ ☐ ☐ ☐
12.	defamation	☐ ☐ ☐ ☐ ☐
13.	personal injury	☐ ☐ ☐ ☐ ☐
14.	commercial contract disputes	☐ ☐ ☐ ☐ ☐
15.	tax disputes	☐ ☐ ☐ ☐ ☐

What other types of church dispute are particularly suitable for mediation?	

What other types of church dispute are particularly unsuitable for mediation?	

Any comments?	

B. **Who do you use as mediators?**

I want to find out how often you use external professional mediators, or whether you prefer to use clergy and other church leaders as mediators. I want to find out how effective each has been, and also how cost-effective.

Please mark with an X the appropriate box number according to the scale 1-5.

	Who are the mediators you use?	1 2 3 4 5
1.	Do you often use external professional mediators to help resolve church disputes? [1 = never; 5 = almost always]	☐☐☐☐☐
2.	How effective have external professional mediators been in helping to resolve church disputes? [1 = not effective; 5 = very effective]	☐☐☐☐☐
3.	How cost-effective has using external professional mediators been? [1 = not cost-effective; 5 = very cost-effective]	☐☐☐☐☐
4.	Do you often use clergy and other church leaders as mediators?	☐☐☐☐☐
5.	How effective have they been?	☐☐☐☐☐
6.	How cost-effective?	☐☐☐☐☐

7. How do you find suitable mediators when you need them? [1 = personal recommendation; 2 = maintain a diocesan list of suitable mediators; 3 = use one of your clergy; 4 = use a mediation agency; 5 = encourage the church to find a mediator itself. Mark as many as appropriate.]	☐ ☐ ☐ ☐ ☐
8. How often do you act as mediator yourself? [1 = never; 5 = very often]	☐ ☐ ☐ ☐ ☐

Any comments?	

C   Should Canon law encourage mediation?

In England, mediation will be one of the procedures under the new Clergy Discipline Measure when this becomes law.

Canon Law	1 2 3 4 5
Are you in favour of Canon law encouraging parties to attempt mediation for church disputes before they resort to litigation or other formal process? [1 = very much against; 5 = very much in favour]	☐ ☐ ☐ ☐ ☐
Are you in favour of Canon law ever making mediation compulsory before litigation or other formal process is commenced? [1 = very much against; 5 = very much in favour]	☐ ☐ ☐ ☐ ☐

If you are in favour of compulsory mediation, what types of church dispute should be subject to this requirement? (The list of types of dispute on page 1 may be helpful.)	

Any comments?	

D. Training and education

Training and education	Yes No
1. Is handling conflict a subject which is taught to clergy and other church leaders in your diocese?	☐ ☐
2. If no, do you feel it should be?	☐ ☐

What form might such training take?	

Any comments	

515

E.   Disputes involving a large number of people

How do you handle disputes involving a large number of people, such as a congregational dispute, or a breakdown in the pastoral relationship?	

Any comments	

F.   Mediation model

Mediation model	1 2 3 4 5
1. How long do most conflicts take to resolve by mediation? [1 = a week or less; 2 = less than one month; 3 = less than 3 months; 4 = less than 6 months; 5 = no clear picture]	☐☐☐☐☐
2. Do most mediations involve meeting on just one day, or are several meetings needed over a period of time? [1 = 1 meeting, 2 = 2 meetings, 3 = 3 meetings, 4 = 4 meetings, 5 = 5 or more meetings]	☐☐☐☐☐
3. How long do most mediation meetings last? [1 = 1–2 hours, 2 = 2–4 hours, 3 = 4–6 hours, 4 = 6–8 hours, 5 = 8 or more hours]	☐☐☐☐☐

Is there any particular format which you have found generally works best?	

Any comments?	

G.   Lessons

Are there any lessons from your own experience in this area which you consider would be useful to pass on to others?	

H.   Other contacts

Is there anyone else you would recommend me to get in touch with who may be able to help me with my research?	

I. **General comments**

Are there any other comments you would like to make?	

J. **Your diocese**

It would assist me if you would also give me the following information.

Your name	
Your address	
Your country	
Your diocese	
Your email address	

Thank you very much for your time.

Yours sincerely,

APPENDIX 3

BIBLIOGRAPHY AND TABLES

1.   BIBLIOGRAPHY

Abbey Story, The, BBC Radio 4, 10 and 17 June 1999 ....71, 74

Aberdeen Press..99

Acland, Andrew. *Resolving disputes without going to court* (London, Century Business Books, 1995) 175, 301

Alternative Dispute Resolution – a Discussion Paper (London, Lord Chancellor's Department, 1999)..............150, 151, 154, 158, 195, 210, 212, 350

Alternative Dispute Resolution (South Africa, South African Law Commission, Issue Paper 8, Project 94, 1997), ISBN 0–621–27319–8 .162, 163

Alternative Dispute Resolution Definitions (Australia, National Alternative Dispute Resolution Advisory Council (NADRAC), March 1997) 195

Annual report on the Commercial Court [1999] 2 Lloyds 802 178

Atkin's Court Forms 2nd edn. (London, Butterworths, 1961–2002) 143, 175, 177, 178

Avery, Michel et al. *Building United Judgment, a handbook for consensus decision making* (Maddison WI, Centre for Conflict Resolution, 1981, republished Routledge, MO, The Fellowship for Intentional Community, 1999) 307, 330

Baker, Doug. *Handling Disagreements in the Church* (Belfast, Conciliation Committee of the Presbyterian Church in Ireland, available from the General Secretary's Office, Church House, Belfast BT1 6DW, 1996) 330

Baker, J.H. *Monuments of Endlesse Labours* (London, Hambledon Press, 1998) 21

Barber, Paul. 'The Fall and Rise of Doctors' Commons?', 4 Ecc LJ 462 ...21

Bartoo, Glen. *Decisions by Consensus: a study of the Quaker Method* (Chicago, Progressive Publisher, 1978) 330

Bath Chronicle 81

Beal, J., Coriden, J., and Green, T. *New Commentary on the Code of Canon Law* (New York, Paulist Press, 2000)..29, 484

Becker, Penny Edgell. *Congregations in conflict* (Cambridge University Press, 1999) 275, 335

Beer, Jennifer and Steif, Eileen. *The Mediator's Handbook*, 3rd edn. (Gabriola Island, BC, Canada, New Society Publishers, 1997) 77, 221, 230, 246, 247, 249, 261, 262, 264, 266

Behrens, James. 'The Churchwardens Measure 2001', 6 Ecc LJ 97...35, 211

Behrens, James. 'The Mediation of Trust Disputes', (2001) 151 New Law Journal 1183..473

Behrens, James. *Confirmation, Sacrament of Grace* (Leominster, Gracewing, 1995) 48, 88, 509

Behrens, James. *Practical Church Management* (Leominster, Gracewing, 1998) 48, 49, 57, 94, 98, 107, 108, 115, 116, 121, 125, 132, 137, 335, 474, 505, 507, 509

Belfast News Letter 81

Berkhof, Louis. *Systematic Theology* (Edinburgh, Banner of Truth Trust, 1958) 9

Bernstein, R., Tackaberry, J., Marriott, A., and Wood, D. *Handbook of Arbitration Practice* (London, Sweet & Maxwell, 1998) 144, 154

Bible, The........................6, 7, 8, 9, 71, 74, 89, 103, 133, 227, 228, 245, 289, 291, 292, 295, 307, 316, 330, 331, 332, 337, 338, 340, 404, 440, 445, 452, 456, 468, 473, 489, 490, 491

Birmingham Evening Mail 102

Birmingham Post 62, 81

Bloor, R.H. 'Clocks, bells and cockerels', (1995) 3 Ecc LJ 393 88

Book of Common Prayer (Oxford University Press) 7, 205

Borkowski, Andrew. *Textbook on Roman Law*, 2nd edn. (London, Black-
stone Press, 1997)..166

Bradney, Anthony and Cownie, Fiona. *Living without law; an ethnography
of Quaker decision-making, dispute avoidance and dispute resolution*
(Aldershot, Ashgate, 2000) 221, 233, 327, 328, 329

Briden, Timothy, and Hanson, Brian. *Moore's Introduction to English
Canon Law*, 3rd edn. (London, Mowbray, 1992) 42

Bridging the Gap, the Bridge Builders Newsletter, Issue no. 1 (London,
Bridge Builders (The London Mennonites) September 2001) 214

Bristol Evening Post 81, 112

Brown, Henry and Marriott, Arthur. *ADR Principles and Practice*, 2nd
edn. (London, Sweet & Maxwell, 1999)................................150, 163, 179,
218, 228, 249, 257, 258, 268, 273, 278, 292, 299, 302, 347, 348

Brundage, James. *Medieval Canon Law* (London,
Longman, 1995) 13, 14, 15

Buckland, W.W. *A Text-Book of Roman Law from Augustus to Justinian*, 3rd
edn. (rev. Peter Stein) (Cambridge University Press 1968)................166

Bursell, Rupert. *Liturgy, Order and the Law* (Oxford, Clarendon Press,
1996) 47

Bush, Robert and Folger, Joseph. *The Promise of Mediation* (San Francisco,
Jossey-Bass, 1994) 224, 225, 227, 229, 230,
232, 253, 254, 261, 265, 290, 298

Butterworths Tax Journal 1998 118

Caller, Russell. *ADR and Commercial Disputes* (London, Sweet & Max-
well, 2001)..179

Calvo, J. *Codigo de Derecho Canonico* (Pamplona: EUNSA, 1983) 870 13

Canon Law Society Newsletter, March 1975, cited in Michael Walsh,
'Protecting Rights in the Church', *The Month* (1978) 131–134. 485

Caparros, E., Thériault, M. and Thorn, J. *Code of Canon Law Annotated*
(Montreal, Wilson & Lafleur Limitée, 1993) 13, 24

CEDR Civil Justice Audit (London, CEDR, April 2000)............................156

Chambers & Partners Guide to the Legal Profession 2002–2003 (London,
Chambers & Partners Publishing, 2002)..48

Chaucer, Geoffrey. *The Canterbury Tales* (London, Penguin Books,
1996) 1, 14, 141, 217, 297, 467

Chaucer, Geoffrey. *The Canterbury Tales*, translated by David Wright (Oxford University Press, 1985)...........................1, 15, 141, 217, 297, 467

Church of England Year Book (London, Church House Publishing, 2001)128

Church Times..................................67, 68, 69, 75, 79, 81, 86, 95, 96, 97, 99, 102, 106, 107, 108, 109, 110, 112, 114, 118, 127, 191, 197, 282

Churchyards Handbook, The (London, Church House Publishing, 2001) 115

Civil Court Practice 2001 (London, Butterworths, 2001) 148

Civil Procedure (The White Book Service 2001) (London, Sweet & Maxwell, 2001) 147

Civil Procedure (The White Book Service 2003) (London, Sweet & Maxwell, 2003) 145, 147, 209

Civil Procedure News, Issue 02/02, pg. 7 (London, Sweet & Maxwell, February 2002)...479

Code of Canon Law Annotated, ed. Ernest Caparros, Michel Thériault and Jean Thorn (Montreal, Wilson and Lafleur Limitée, 1993) 22

Code of Conduct for the Bar (London, The General Council of the Bar of England and Wales, 1998) 231

Common Worship: Pastoral Services (London, Church House Publishing, 2000) 294, 321

Compston, Christopher. 'Fighting for Justice', Relational Justice bulletin, issue 2, April 1999, pg. 3 (The Relationships Foundation, Cambridge, 1999) 63, 66, 73

Consultation paper on the recommendations of the Review Group on the Royal Peculiars (London, Lord Chancellor's Department, 2001)....................80

Cooke, Michael. 'A simple solution to the ludicrous lottery of litigation costs', *The Times*, 26 February 2002, Law, pg. 2 479

Coriden, J., Green, T. and Heintschel, D. *The Code of Canon Law, a text and commentary* (New York, Paulist Press, 1985)....................................22, 27

Coriden, James. 'Alternative dispute resolution in the church', Canon Law Society of America Proceedings 48 (1986), pg. 64–77 ....13, 23, 28, 481

Coriden, James. *An Introduction to Canon Law* (New York, Paulist Press, 1991) 24, 25

Courts Referral to Alternative Dispute Resolution (New Zealand Courts Consultative Committee, January 1997)...349

Craig, Yvonne. *Peacemaking for Churches* (London, SPCK, 1999) 106, 205, 208, 294, 358, 478

Cranmer, Frank. 'Church-State Relations in the United Kingdom: A Westminster View', 6 Ecc LJ 111 87

Cranmer, Frank. 'Regulation within the Religious Society of Friends', 7
Ecc LJ 176 ....326, 327

Culver, T.S. *Canon B 16: excommunication in the Church of England*',
(University of Wales unpublished LLM Dissertation, Cardiff Law
School, 1996)..111

Cutting the Cost of Conflict: Highlights 1997–1998 (London,
CEDR, 1999) 179, 189, 196

Daily Express..65, 81

Daily Mail...57, 81, 93, 99, 100, 103, 107, 109, 112

Daily Mirror 57, 91, 99

Daily Telegraph..60, 61, 64, 81, 91, 93, 94, 95, 98,
99, 102, 103, 106, 108, 109, 110, 112, 114, 115, 490

Development of Standards for ADR Discussion Paper, The (Australia, National Alternative Dispute Resolution Advisory Council (NADRAC),
March 2000) 159, 211, 347

Didache, The (New York, Paulist Press, 1948)..10

Didascalia Apostolorum, cited in Jill Harries, *Law and Empire in Late Antiquity* (Cambridge University Press, 1998)...10

Doe, Norman. *Canon Law in the Anglican Communion* (Oxford, Clarendon
Press, 1998) 346

Doe, Norman. *Legal Framework of the Church of England* (Oxford, Claren-
don Press, 1996) 44

Doyle, Margaret. 'Getting on stream with online mediation', Mediation
Magazine, February 2001, pg. 8 (Bristol, Mediation UK, 2001) 502

Doyle, Margaret. *Advising on ADR: the essential guide to appropriate dispute
resolution* (London, Advice Services Alliance, 2000)............................501

Edinburgh Evening News..108, 109

eEurope Impact and Priorities, (Brussels, Commission of the European
Communities, March 2001) 495

Eggleton, Martin and Trafford, David. *At Cross Purposes: Handling Conflict in the Church* (Peterborough, Foundery Press, 2000) 337, 338

Ely Ensign 97

Evans, G. R. *Discipline & Justice in the Church of England* (Leominster,
Gracewing, 1998) 46

Evening Chronicle (Newcastle, UK)..81

Evening Herald (Plymouth) 82

Evening News (Edinburgh) 82

Evening Standard 64, 69, 74, 82, 91

Exeter Express & Echo..62

Hill, Mark. *Ecclesiastical Law*, 2nd edn. (Oxford University Press, 2001) 95, 96, 105, 126, 192

Hill, Mark. *The Resolution of Conflict in English Canon Law* (University of Wales unpublished LLM Dissertation, Cardiff Law School, 1994) 3

Hite, J. and Ward, D. *Readings, cases, materials in Canon Law* (Collegeville, Minnesota, Liturgical Press, 1990) 22, 25

Holdsworth, William. *A History of English Law* (London, Sweet & Maxwell, 1922–66) 20, 21

Hostiensis, *Lectura in quinque libros Decretalium* (Venice, 1581) 19

Houlbrooke, Ralph. *Church Courts and the People during the English Reformation* (Oxford University Press, 1979) 17, 18

In Tune With Heaven, the Report of the Archbishops Commission on Church Music (London, Church House Publishing and Hodder & Stoughton, 1992) 99

Incumbents (Vacation of Benefices) Measure 1997 Code of Practice (London, Church House Publishing, 1997)...305

Independent, The.......................................56, 63, 82, 94, 95, 105, 109

Issues of fairness and justice in alternative dispute resolution (Australia, National Alternative Dispute Resolution Advisory Council (NADRAC), November 1997)..158, 159, 347

Jolowicz, H.F. and Nicholas, B. *Historical Introduction to the study of Roman Law*, 3rd edn. (Cambridge University Press 1972) 166

Journal (Newcastle, UK)...82

Kemp, Eric. 'The spirit of the canon law and its application in England' (1987–1988) 1 Ecc LJ (1,2) 5 16

Kemp, Eric. *Review of the Report of the Archbishops' Commission on Cathedrals*, 3 Ecc LJ 343 79

Kolb, Deborah. *When Talk Works* (San Francisco, California, Jossey-Bass, 1994) 474

Lawyers Christian Fellowship Newsletter (The Lawyers, Christian Fellowship, 33 St James' Square, Bath BA1 2TT)...157

Leas, Speed. *Moving your church through conflict* (Washington DC, Alban Institute, 1985)..321, 324, 337

Legal Week, 31 August 2000, pg. 1, 'Govt drops compulsory mediation'350

Liebmann, Marian. *Community and Neighbour Mediation*, (London, Cavendish Publishing, 1998)..218, 219, 236

Liebmann, Marian. *Mediation in Context* (London, Jessica Kingsley Publishers, 2000) 114, 218, 219, 300

Lott, David B. (ed.) *Conflict Management in Congregations* (Bethesda, Maryland, USA, Alban Institute, 2001) 119

Lyndwood's *Provinciale*, the text of the canons therein contained, reprinted from the translation made in 1534, edited by J.V. Bullard and H. Chalmer Bell (London, Faith Press, 1929) (copy in the Inner Temple library)...19

Mackie, K., Miles, D., and Marsh, W. *Commercial Dispute Resolution: an ADR practice guide* (London, Butterworths, 2nd edn. 1999)................144

Mail on Sunday 59, 82, 490

Marshall, T. and Walpole, M. *Bringing People Together: Mediation and Reparation Projects in Great Britain*, (London, Home Office Research and Planning Unit, Paper 33, HMSO, 1985) 219

Marshall, T. *Reparation, Conciliation and Mediation*, (London, Home Office Research and Planning Unit, Paper 27, 1984).............................218

McKenna, Kevin. *The Ministry of Law in the Church Today* (Notre Dame, Indiana, University of Notre Dame Press, 1998)..................482, 488, 489

Mediation in the Planning System (London, Department of the Environment, Transport and the Regions, June 2000)...............................152, 501

Mediation Magazine (Bristol, Mediation UK, 2001) issue 67 (September 2001), pg. 1...114

Mediation UK *Annual Report 2000* (Bristol, Mediation UK, 2000)..222, 223

Mediation UK *Annual Reports 1991–2000* (Bristol, Mediation UK, 1991–2000) 219

Mediation UK, Annual Report 2001 (Bristol, Mediation UK, 2001)..........213

Mediation UK, *Training Manual in Community Mediation Skills* (Bristol, Mediation UK, 1995, reprinted 1999)....................221, 223, 226, 230, 238, 240, 245, 247, 249, 252, 262, 264, 271

Mediation Visits – Purpose (London, Camden Mediation Service training materials, 2000) 237

Mediator Training Course Handbook (London, CEDR, 1997) 120, 144, 165, 256

Mennonite training course materials (Akron, Pennsylvannia, Lombard Mennonite Peace Centre, 1991)..315

Mulcahy, Linda. *Mediating medical negligence claims* (London, HMSO, 1999) 151

Munro, C.R. 'Does Scotland have an established Church?', 4 Ecc LJ 639...87

New Bible Dictionary (London, Inter-Varsity Press, 1962) 8

Newcastle Evening Chronicle 96, 191

Newcastle Journal 96, 106, 191

Newsom, G.H. and G.L. *Faculty Jurisdiction of the Church of England*, 2nd
    edn. (Sweet & Maxwell, 1993) 92

Northern Echo..100, 112

Observer, The..82

Ombres, Robert. 'Justice and Equity in the 1983 Code', *Priests & People*
    (1987) 143 ....25, 484

On Due Process (Washington, National Council of Catholic Bishops,
    1969) 481, 482, 483, 486, 487

Oxford Bible Commentary (Oxford University Press, 2001)........................10

Oxford Dictionary of the Christian Church, 3rd. edn. (Oxford University
    Press, 1997) 6, 29, 47

Pix, Stephen. 'Archdeacon of Cheltenham v Bland: A sledgehammer to
    crack a nut', 6 Ecc LJ 135..35

Primary dispute resolution in family law (Australia, National Alternative
    Dispute Resolution Advisory Council (NADRAC),
    March 1997) 159, 347

Quaker Faith and Practice (London, The Religious Society of Friends
    (Quakers), 1995) 327

Report of the Archbishops' Commission on Cathedrals (London, Church
    House Publishing, 1994) 79

Report of the Review Group on the Royal Peculiars (London, Church House
    Publishing, 2001) 80

Resolutions, Issue 24 (London, CEDR, 1999) 196

Resourcing Bishops (London, Church House Publishing, 2001)...................2

Response by the General Council of the Bar to the Lord Chancellor's Depart-
    ment's discussion paper on ADR (London, General Council of the Bar,
    2000) 154, 156, 195

Scholes, Percy. *Oxford Companion to Music* (Oxford University Press,
    1970) 74

Schrock-Shenk, Carolyn (ed.) *Mediation and Facilitation Training Manual*,
    4th edn. (Akron, Pennsylvania, Mennonite Conciliation Service,
    2000) 306, 312, 316, 317, 334

Schrock-Shenk, Carolyn and Ressler, Lawrence. *Making Peace with Con-*
    flict (Waterloo, Ontario, Herald Press, 1999) 295, 321

Scotland on Sunday 99

Scotsman, The..82, 99, 108, 109, 111, 112

Shillito, Richard. 'Mediation in libel actions' New Law Journal 2000,
    150(6921), 122–123 178

Smith, P. 'The Advowson: The history and development of a most peculiar property' (2000) 5 Ecc LJ 320 17

Solicitor's Gazette (London, the Law Society) 157, 199

Stein, Peter. *Roman Law in European History* (Cambridge University Press, 1999) 12

Sunday Telegraph 82, 94, 97

Sunday Times 54, 57, 58, 59, 63, 83, 91, 93, 94, 99, 106, 109, 111, 114, 490

Supreme Court Costs Office Guide to the summary assessment of costs, revised by senior costs judge Peter Hurst, February 2001 (London, Crown Copyright, 2001) 187

Susskind, Lawrence; McKearnan, Sarah; and Thomas-Larmer, Jennifer (ed.) *The Consensus Building Handbook* (London, Sage Publications, 1999) 299, 301, 302, 303, 304, 310, 314, 319

Thomas, Sarah; and Watkin, Thomas. 'Oh Noisy Bells Be Dumb' (1995) Journal of Planning and Environmental Law 1097 88

Times, The.....................56, 57, 59, 60, 61, 62, 64, 68, 72, 76, 83, 91, 93, 94, 96, 98, 99, 100, 102, 103, 104, 105, 107, 108, 109, 114, 191

Tractatus de legibus et consuetudinibus regni Anglie qui Glanvilla vocatur, (The treatise on the laws and customs of the realm of England commonly called Glanvill) (Oxford, Clarendon Press, 1993) 17

Trollope, Anthony. *Barchester Towers* (Oxford University Press, 1989) .490

Trott, Stephen. 'Dignity at Work', 6 Ecc LJ 51 42

Under Authority, Report on Clergy Discipline (London, Church House Publishing, 1996) 109, 111, 194

Vine, W. E. *Expository Dictionary of Biblical Words* (Nashville, TN, Thomas Nelson Publishers, 1985) 7

Walsh, Michael. 'Protecting Rights in the Church', *The Month* (1978) 131–134. (The Month, 114 Mount Street, London W1Y 6AH) 484

Watkin, Thomas. 'A happy noise to hear? Church bells and the law of nuisance' 4 Ecc LJ 545 88

Watkin, Thomas. *A Historical Introduction to Modern Civil Law* (Aldershot, Ashgate, 1999) 12

Western Daily Press 83

Wharton's *Dictionary of Jurisprudence* (London, Stevens & Sons, 1876) .166

Woolf, Lord. *Final Report on Access to Justice* (London, HMSO, July 1996) 209, 311, 479, 480

Woolf, Lord. *Interim Report on Access to Justice* (London, HMSO, June 1995) 209, 311

2.   Cases

3.   STATUTES

4.   MEASURES

7.   Canons (Roman Catholic)

8.   Canons (Episcopal Church of the USA)

9.   Non-UK legislation

10. NON-UK CHURCH LEGISLATION

11. SCRIPTURAL REFERENCES

12. Disputes

13.   ORGANISATIONS

INDEX

For the many organisations referred to in this book, see also the table of organisations on page 540.